영단기 TOEFL
ACTUAL TEST
LISTENING

직접 시험 보고 연구한 저자의 REAL 콘텐츠

해설집

커넥츠 영단기

영단기 TOEFL
ACTUAL TEST LISTENING

저자	크리스틴 한
기획 총괄	고영관 공정아
기획·편집	정유상
마케팅·영업	양광열 이진홍 손지한 김정현 양윤화 김보경 김은지
표지 디자인	김보라
내지 디자인	장용주
펴낸날	2판 1쇄 2019년 11월 15일
펴낸이	윤성혁
펴낸곳	㈜에스티유니타스
등록번호	제2015-000186호
홈페이지	eng.conects.com
고객센터	카카오톡 플러스 친구 [영단기] / 커넥츠 영단기 1:1 게시판
주소	서울시 강남구 영동대로 417 오토웨이타워 2층
ISBN	979-11-6371-655-6 13740

잘못 만들어진 책은 구입처에서 바꿔 드립니다.
가격은 뒤표지에 있습니다.
이 책에 실린 모든 글과 사진, 일러스트를 포함한 디자인 및 편집 형태, 배포에 대한 권리는
㈜에스티유니타스에 있으므로 무단으로 전재하거나 복제, 배포할 수 없습니다.

저자의 한마디

토플은 여러분 인생의 아주 작은 부분입니다. 하지만 토플에서부터 여러분의 인생은 크게 달라질 것입니다. 외국의 대학이나 대학원에 입학하거나 교환 학생 프로그램에 참여하는 것은 쉬운 일이 아니고 누구에게나 주어지는 기회도 아닙니다. 저 역시 10년의 유학 생활을 하며 힘들 때가 많았습니다. 하지만 그 시간은 저에게 많은 선택지를 보장해 주었습니다. 외국에서의 학위가 부귀영화를 보장하는 것은 아니지만, 적어도 남과 다른 길을 걸었다는 자부심과 용기는 여러분의 큰 자산이 될 것입니다.

그 여정의 시작이 바로 토플입니다. 그 중 한국인이 가장 어렵게 느끼는 것이 리스닝입니다. 다른 분야에 비해 평균 점수가 낮은 만큼, 많은 학생이 리스닝을 부담스러워합니다. 그래서 저는 이 분야를 집중적으로 연구하면서 얻은 다년 간의 노하우를 공유하려 합니다. 접근 방법만 바꿀 수 있다면, 누구나 고득점을 받을 수 있는 분야가 바로 리스닝입니다. 내용을 다 듣지 않더라도 출제자의 의도를 이해하면 점수를 얻는다는 기본 원칙, 시험이기에 패턴화된 문제 유형과 정답, 오답 유형. 이 시험은 청취력 테스트가 아닌 영어로 된 논리력 시험이라는 것을 함께 이해했으면 합니다. 그러한 토대 위에서 실제 시험에 적용할 수 있는 방법들을 이 책에 모두 담았습니다.

이 책의 도움으로 원하는 토플 점수를 얻은 뒤에 교환 학생 프로그램이나 대학, 대학원으로 떠나게 될 여러분에게 드리고 싶은 말씀은, 언젠가 학교를 졸업하고 사회인이 되어 책임져야 할 일들이 많아질 때가 올 것입니다. 그때부터는 다람쥐가 쳇바퀴 돌 듯 반복되는 일상을 보내게 될 수도 있습니다. 그러니 유학 또는 교환 학생이라는 그 시간을 즐기길 바랍니다. 어쩌면 인생에 다시 없을 기회입니다. 바쁜 일상에서 벗어나 학업과 타국에 대한 경험에 전념하여 나를 충전할 수 있는 기회 말입니다. 그러니 그 시간 동안 고민하지 말고, 밖으로 나가 경험하고, 실수도 하며 자신을 알아가는 계기로 삼았으면 합니다. 자신을 위한 삶을 살아가시기를 바랍니다.

그런 시간의 시작에 제가 함께할 수 있어 영광입니다.
여러분의 건승을 기원합니다.

크리스틴 한

부족한 저를 도와주신 분들께 감사드립니다.
(제 강의를 열심히 들어 주시고 좋은 결과로 저를 늘 행복하게 해 주는 여러분들, I sincerely respect "YOU", 윤성혁 대표님을 비롯한 ST Unitas, 영단기 토플 여러 관계자분들, 사랑하는 가족 incl. 노루 & 나의 우주)

목차

저자의 한마디	001	TOEFL iBT Listening 소개	008
이 책의 구성 및 특징	004	**LISTENING STRATEGIES**	010
TOEFL iBT 소개	006		

해설집

Actual Test 01   027
Set 1 Conversation
Set 1 Lecture 1
Set 2 Conversation
Set 2 Lecture 1
Set 2 Lecture 2

Actual Test 02   051
Set 1 Conversation
Set 1 Lecture 1
Set 1 Lecture 2
Set 2 Conversation
Set 2 Lecture 1

Actual Test 03   074
Set 1 Conversation
Set 1 Lecture 1
Set 2 Conversation
Set 2 Lecture 1
Set 2 Lecture 2

Actual Test 04   099
Set 1 Conversation
Set 1 Lecture 1
Set 1 Lecture 2
Set 2 Conversation
Set 2 Lecture 1

Actual Test 05   123
Set 1 Conversation

Set 1 Lecture 1
Set 2 Conversation
Set 2 Lecture 1
Set 2 Lecture 2

Actual Test 06   149

Set 1 Conversation
Set 1 Lecture 1
Set 1 Lecture 2
Set 2 Conversation
Set 2 Lecture 1

Actual Test 07   173

Set 1 Conversation
Set 1 Lecture 1
Set 2 Conversation
Set 2 Lecture 1
Set 2 Lecture 2

Actual Test 08   197

Set 1 Conversation
Set 1 Lecture 1
Set 1 Lecture 2
Set 2 Conversation
Set 2 Lecture 1

Actual Test 09   221

Set 1 Conversation
Set 1 Lecture 1
Set 2 Conversation
Set 2 Lecture 1
Set 2 Lecture 2

문제집 (책속의 책)

Actual Test 01~09

이 책의 구성 및 특징

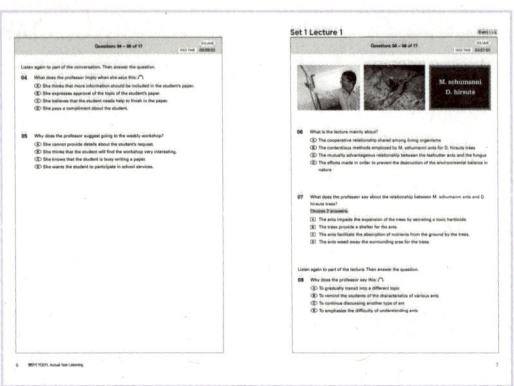

최신 경향 반영 9회분의 문제

최신 TOEFL iBT 출제 경향을 반영한 문제를 실제 iBT 시험 화면과 가장 유사한 형태로 제시하였으며, 학생들이 실전에 앞서 충분히 준비할 수 있도록 총 9회분의 모의고사를 수록하였습니다.

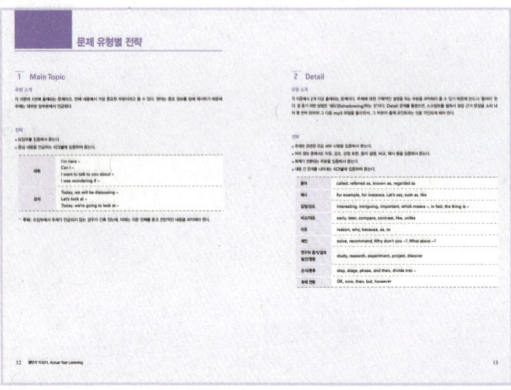

고득점을 위한 LISTENING STRATEGIES

TOEFL iBT LISTENING에 출제되는 문제 유형을 분석하고, 고득점을 얻기 위한 유형별 전략을 단계적으로 제시하였습니다.

출제 예상 부분을 짚는 TIP

실전을 대비하기 위해 훈련하는 학생들이 LISTENING 영역에서 고득점을 받는 데 도움이 될 문제 출제 예상 부분을 Tip으로 제시하였습니다.

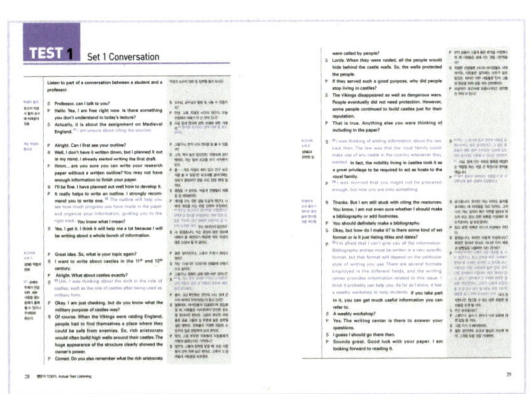

지문 구조 분석

듣기 스크립트의 내용을 분석하고 요약하여 내용을 이해하기 쉽게 표시하였습니다.

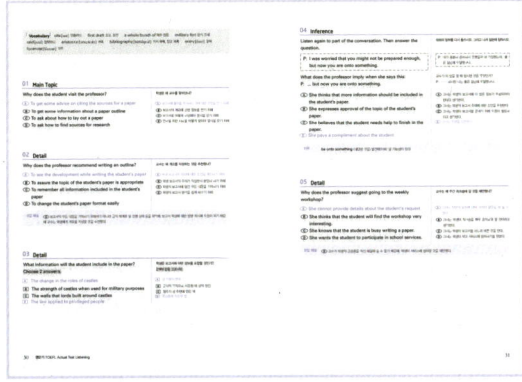

정답 및 오답 해설

정답의 근거가 되는 부분을 지문에 표시하였고, 정답 해설 및 오답 해설을 상세히 제시하였습니다.

TOEFL iBT 소개

TOEFL iBT란?

TOEFL(Test of English as a Foreign Language) iBT(Internet-Based Test)는 인터넷을 기반으로 하는 시험으로, 영어가 모국어가 아닌 학생들이 대학 수업에서 읽고, 쓰고, 듣고, 말할 때 영어를 사용하고 이해하는 능력을 평가합니다. TOEFL 시험은 Reading, Listening, Speaking, Writing 총 4개의 영역으로 이루어져 있으며, 4개의 영역 모두 note-taking이 허용됩니다.

TOEFL iBT의 구성

영역	문항 수	시험 소요시간	배점 점수 범위	배점 수준
Reading	3~4개의 지문 지문당 10문항	54~72분	0~30	상 22~30 중 15~21 하 0~14
Listening	Lecture: 3~4개의 강의 　　　　　강의당 6문항 Conversation: 2~3개의 대화 　　　　　대화당 5문항	41~57분	0~30	상 22~30 중 15~21 하 0~14
휴식: 10분					
Speaking	Independent: 1문항 Integrated: 3문항	17분	0~30	우수 26~30 양호 18~25 부족 10~17 취약 0~9
Writing	Integrated: 1문항 Independent: 1문항	50분	0~30	우수 24~30 양호 17~23 부족 1~16
		총 소요 시간: 약 3시간 30분	총점: 0~120점	

TOEFL iBT 응시 정보

STEP 1 시험 전! – 시험 접수

접수 방법	www.ets.org 또는 www.ets.org/ko/toefl에서 온라인 등록
시험 응시료	US $200 (2019년 11월 기준)
정규 등록 마감일	시험 응시일 7일 전 (시험 응시일이 8월 13일이면 8월 6일까지 등록)
추가 등록 마감일	• 시험 응시일 4일 전 (시험 응시일이 8월 13일이면 마지막 등록 기회는 8월 9일까지) • 수수료 US $40 발생
시험 일정 조정 마감일	• 시험 응시일 4일 전 • 수수료 US $60 발생
응시료 지불 방식	• 신용/직불카드 • 미국 또는 미국령 내에 본인의 은행 계좌가 있으면, PayPal 계좌 또는 전자수표 (e-check) 가능

STEP 2 시험 당일! – 시험 응시

준비물	• 공인된 신분증 (여권, 주민등록증, 운전면허증) • 등록 번호
입실	시험 시작 30분 전까지 시험장에 도착 (늦으면 시험에 응시할 수 없음)
입실 절차	• 체크인: 신분 확인 후 기밀 서약서 작성, 해당 고사실 입실 전 사진 촬영 및 신분 확인 • 노트 필기를 위한 용지와 필기구 제공 (시험 종료 후 반환) • 시험 관리자가 지정해 주는 자리에 착석
반입물	• 신분증만 가지고 들어갈 수 있음 • 휴대 전화와 기타 전자 기기는 허용되지 않음 • 따로 물품 보관 장소가 없는 시험장의 경우는 각 수험생의 의자 아래에 준비된 비닐 가방에 개인 용품을 보관할 수 있음

STEP 3 시험 이후! – 시험 결과 확인

성적 확인	시험 응시일로부터 대략 10일 후에 온라인상에서 확인 가능
성적표 수령	• 우편 수령: 등록 시에 성적표 수령지를 선택하면 우편으로 성적표를 받아 볼 수 있으며, 시험 응시일 전에 선택한 최대 4개 기관으로 무료로 발송 • 성적표 다운로드: 시험 응시일로부터 대략 13일 후에 수험생의 계정에서 PDF 성적표를 다운로드할 수 있음
성적 유효 기간	시험 응시일로부터 2년간 유효 * 2019년 8월부로, 최근 2년간의 시험 성적 중 영역별 최고 점수를 합산한 성적을 인정하는 MyBest Scores 제도 시행

TOEFL iBT Listening 소개

TOEFL iBT Listening 영역은 크게 Conversation(대화)과 Lecture(강의)로 이루어져 있습니다. Conversation은 주로 학교 내에서 흔히 발생하는 상황에 대해 학생이 교수나 담당 직원과 이야기하는 내용을 다룹니다. Lecture에서는 주로 대학에서 다루는 여러 학문에 관한 내용을 다룹니다. 교수 혼자 진행하는 형식과 교수와 한두 명의 학생이 토론하는 형식이 있습니다.

TOEFL iBT Listening 구성

세트 수	구성	문항 수	소요 시간	점수 범위
2세트	**Conversation 2개** **Lecture 3개** *시험은 기본 2세트로 구성되며 더미가 있을 경우 총 3세트로 구성됨.	총 **28문항** Conversation: 각 5문항 Lecture: 각 6문항	총 41분	0~30
3세트	**Conversation 3개** **Lecture 4개**	총 **39문항** Conversation: 각 5문항 Lecture: 각 6문항	총 57분	

* 더미는 ETS에서 문제 수준을 테스트하기 위해 만든 세트이며, 응시자가 어떤 문제인지 알 수는 없으나 대개 마지막 세트에 나오는 경우가 많습니다. 더미 세트의 문제는 점수에 포함되지 않습니다.

TOEFL iBT Listening 문제 유형

유형 구분	유형 설명
Main Topic	방문 목적, 대화 및 강의의 주제를 묻는 문제
Detail	세부 정보를 묻는 문제
Inference	추론하는 문제
Organization	내용의 구조를 묻는 문제

TOEFL iBT Listening 화면 구성

대화 / 강의 들을 때 화면

지문을 들려주는 동안은 화면에 교수와 학생 사진이나 교수의 사진만 나옵니다. 강의에서는 중간에 이해를 돕기 위한 주제 관련 이미지나 용어를 화면에 보여주기도 합니다. 지문이 끝나면 곧바로 문제 화면으로 넘어갑니다.

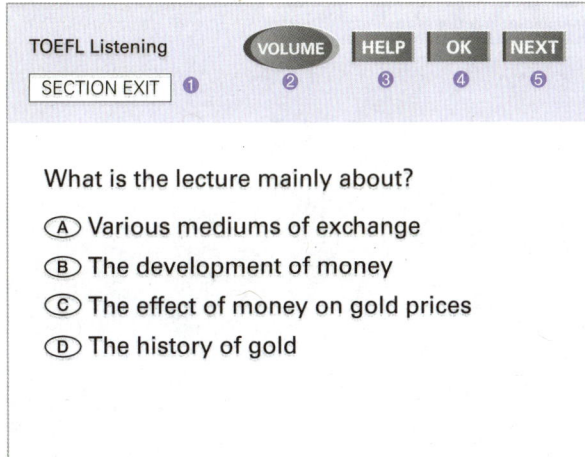

문제 화면

문제는 화면에 한 문제씩 음성과 함께 제시되고, 이어서 보기가 나옵니다. 반드시 A~D 중 한 가지를 답으로 선택하고 NEXT 버튼을 눌러야 합니다(답 2개 선택하는 문제의 경우 2개 선택). 그 후, OK 버튼을 최종적으로 누르면 다음 문제로 넘어갈 수 있습니다. OK 버튼을 누른 후에는 이전 문제로 다시 돌아갈 수 없으니 유의하도록 합니다.

화면 상단 버튼 안내

❶ **Listening Section**에서 나갈 수 있습니다.
❷ 버튼을 누르면 밑에 나타나는 바를 좌우로 조정해 음량을 조절할 수 있습니다.
❸ 시험 진행에 대한 정보를 알 수 있습니다.
❹ 다음 문제로 넘어갈 수 있습니다.
❺ 정답을 선택한 후 버튼을 누릅니다.

TOEFL iBT
LISTENING

LISTENING STRATEGIES

문제 유형별 전략

1 Main Topic

유형 소개

각 지문의 1번에 출제되는 문제이고, 전체 내용에서 가장 중요한 부분이라고 볼 수 있다. 영어는 중요 정보를 앞에 제시하기 때문에 주제는 대부분 앞부분에서 언급된다.

전략

- 도입부를 집중해서 듣는다.
- 중심 내용을 언급하는 **시그널**에 집중하며 듣는다.

대화	I'm here ~ Can I ~ I want to talk to you about ~ I was wondering if ~
강의	Today, we will be discussing ~ Let's look at ~ Today, we're going to look at ~

** **주의**: 도입부에서 주제가 언급되지 않는 경우가 간혹 있는데, 이때는 지문 전체를 듣고 전반적인 내용을 파악해야 한다.

2 Detail

유형 소개

각 지문에서 2개 이상 출제되는 문제이다. 주제에 대한 구체적인 설명을 하는 부분을 파악해야 풀 수 있기 때문에 반드시 '들어야' 한다. 잘 듣기 위한 방법은 '쉐도잉(shadowing)하는 것'이다. Detail 문제를 틀렸으면, 스크립트를 펼쳐서 정답 근거 문장을 소리 내어 몇 번씩 읽어라! 그 다음 mp3 파일을 들으면서, 그 부분이 출제 포인트라는 것을 각인되게 해야 한다.

전략

- 주제와 관련된 주요 세부 사항을 집중해서 듣는다.
- 여러 정보 중에서도 이유, 강조, 감정 표현, 용어 설명, 비교, 예시 등을 집중해서 듣는다.
- 화제가 전환되는 부분을 집중해서 듣는다.
- 내용 간 관계를 나타내는 **시그널**에 집중하며 듣는다.

용어	called, referred as, known as, regarded as
예시	for example, for instance, Let's say, such as, like
감정/강조	interesting, intriguing, important, which means ~, in fact, the thing is ~
비교/대조	early, later, compare, contrast, like, unlike
이유	reason, why, because, as, to
제안	solve, recommend, Why don't you ~?, What about ~?
연구의 증거/결과 발견/영향	study, research, experiment, project, discover
순서/분류	step, stage, phase, and then, divide into ~
화제 전환	OK, now, then, but, however

3 Inference

유형 소개

추론 문제는 내용에 대한 일반적인 추론과 일부분을 다시 들려 주는 의도 추론으로 나눌 수 있다. 의도 추론은 들을 수 있는 기회가 두 번 주어지기 때문에, 듣는 것 자체에 대한 부담감은 덜하지만 다른 문제에 비해 보기가 더 많이 꼬아서 출제되는 편이다.
예를 들어, "잘 했어."라는 부분을 다시 들려 준 뒤 "이 말을 왜 했는가?"라는 추론 문제의 경우 "잘 했어."의 사전적 의미인 "칭찬하기 위해서"를 오답으로 출제하는 것이다. **추론 문제는 들은 내용의 사전적 의미를 물어 보는 것이 아니라, 궁극적인 의도를 물어 보는 것**이라는 점을 명심해야 한다. 따라서 이 말이 나온 앞뒤 상황을 세심히 들어야 한다.

전략

- 다시 들려 주는 부분에 대한 사전적 의미 해석보다는 들려 부분의 앞뒤 상황 파악이 중요하다.
- 보기를 까다롭게 내는 경우가 많아서, 보기를 꼼꼼히 분석해서 오답을 패턴화해 놓는 것이 좋다.

4 Organization

유형 소개

설명을 돕기 위해 예시를 추가하는 부분에서 출제되는 문제이다.
예) 나는 예뻐 마치 사과처럼.
사과를 언급한 이유를 묻는 문제에 대한 답은 사과의 아름다움을 강조하기 위해서가 아니라 나의 아름다움을 강조하기 위해서이다.

전략

- 주제에서 중요 정보에 대한 설명을 돕기 위한 예를 든 부분을 집중해서 듣는다.
- 강의에 나온 예시나 설명은 궁극적으로 주제를 설명하려는 목적을 가지고 있다. 따라서 **보기 중 주제와 가장 가까운 것이 정답**이 될 가능성이 높다.

전략 적용

1 대화

(1) 대화 듣기 Tip

Tip 1.

대화의 목적은 상황을 전달하는 것이다. 따라서 '이유'를 중심으로 전체적인 흐름을 잡아야 한다. 예를 들어, 기숙사 방을 바꿔 달라고 요청하기 위해 왔다면 왜 방을 바꾸려고 하는지, 제안을 거절하면 왜 거절했는지를 파악해야 한다. 즉, 조각을 가지고 퍼즐을 맞추는 것이 아니라, 전체적인 그림을 대략적으로 파악해 빠진 조각을 맞춰가야 하는 것이다. 그렇게 그림이 완성되면 다행이고, 설령 퍼즐이 완성되지 않더라도 전체 그림에는 흔들림이 없도록 연습해야 한다.

Tip 2.

세부 내용에서 '이유'를 찾는 것이 중요하다. 특히, 이유가 열거되거나 요청한 사항이 거절되면 그것이 안 되는 이유가 제시되는 부분이 문제로 출제된다고 봐도 된다. 예를 들어, "방을 지금 바꿔줄 수는 없어. 학기 중이라 방이 남은 게 없거든."이라고 그 이유가 제시되면 '방을 바꿔 줄 수 없는 이유는 무엇인가?'라는 문제가 출제된다.

Tip 3.

이유를 말할 때 설득하기 위해 구체적인 예시를 드는 부분을 잡아내도록 한다. 예를 들어, "내 친구 Tommy가 그러는데, 방이 남는 게 있다던데."라는 말이 나오면, '학생은 왜 Tommy를 언급했나?'라는 문제가 출제된다.

(2) 대화 듣기

Listen to part of a conversation between a student and a professor.

S   Hi. Professor Smith, you wanted to see me?
P   Oh, hi. Chris, come on in. **01 So, how is your presentation going? I asked you to visit my office because I'd like to see which topic you are preparing for your class presentation.** I've actually been talking to each student on the topics they have chosen. From the outline which you handed in weeks ago, you were planning to do research on the genetic trait, right? Can you tell me more details about your topic?
S   Oh, sure. But, can I ask you something if you don't mind?
P   Sure, go ahead.
S   Do you like carrots?
P   Carrots? You mean the orange vegetable?
S   Yea, the vegetable. How about broccoli?
P   Well, frankly speaking, I don't like vegetables.
S   Actually, I don't like vegetables either and I guess I am not the only one. There are many people who don't like vegetables.
P   Umm... Hold on a second. Does this have something to do with your presentation?
S   Yes. I thought people didn't like vegetables because of traumatic events they experienced during their childhood. However, I found interesting research explaining why some people don't like vegetables, and their bitter taste. **02 A biologist once said that it is a gene that decides whether or not a person likes vegetables. Specifically, a certain gene in our DNA makes some people more sensitive to the bitterness of vegetables.** This argument requires more research, but I think this is a very intriguing claim.
P   **03 So, you mean a genetic predisposition prevents some people from enjoying the taste of vegetables? Isn't that just a made up story?**
S   But, even if it turns out to be wrong, isn't it still a good excuse? If my mom forces me to eat vegetables, I can say I don't have the vegetable gene in my DNA.
P   That's true. The topic sounds fun to me. I can't wait to see your presentation.

학생과 교수의 대화 중 일부를 들어 보시오.

S   안녕하세요. Smith 교수님, 저 찾으셨죠?
P   안녕. Chris, 들어오렴. 01 그래서 프레젠테이션은 어떻게 되고 있니? 네가 준비하는 수업 프레젠테이션 주제가 무엇인지 궁금해서 내 사무실에 방문하라고 했단다. 각각 학생들과 선택한 주제가 무엇인지에 대해 이야기하고 있거든. 지난 주에 제출했던 개요에 따르면, 유전 특질에 대해 조사할 계획인 거지? 주제에 대해 자세하게 얘기해 줄 수 있니?
S   오, 물론이죠. 그런데 혹시 괜찮으시면 제가 뭘 좀 여쭤 볼 수 있을까요?
P   물론, 물어 봐.
S   당근 좋아하시나요?
P   당근? 주황색 채소 말이니?
S   네, 채소요. 브로콜리는 어떤가요?
P   음, 솔직하게 말해서 나는 채소는 좋아하지 않아.
S   사실 저도 채소를 좋아하지 않아요. 제가 생각하기에 저만 그런 거 같지는 않아요. 채소를 좋아하지 않는 많은 사람들이 있거든요.
P   음…… 잠깐만. 이게 너의 프레젠테이션과 관련이 있니?
S   맞아요. 저는 사람들이 어린 시절에 겪었던 정신적 외상을 초래한 정도의 사건 때문에 채소를 좋아하지 않는다고 생각했어요. 그런데 저는 왜 사람들이 채소와 채소의 쓴 맛을 좋아하지 않는지를 설명하는 흥미로운 연구를 발견했어요. 02 어떤 생물학자에 따르면 특별하게 우리 DNA에 있는 특정한 유전자가 어떤 사람들을 채소의 쓴맛에 더 민감하게 만든데요. 이 주장은 더 많은 조사가 필요하지만, 저는 매우 흥미로운 주장이라고 생각하거든요.
P   03 그래서 네가 의미하는 게 유전적인 성향이 어떤 사람들이 채소의 맛을 즐기지 못하게 한다는 거야? 그냥 만들어진 이야기가 아닐까?
S   그러나 만약 이게 아니라고 밝혀져도 좋은 변명거리 아닌가요? 만약 어머니가 저에게 채소를 먹도록 강요해도, 저는 제 DNA에 채소 유전자가 없다고 말할 수 있잖아요.
P   그건 그렇구나. 그 주제는 나에게도 재미있게 들리는데, 너의 프레젠테이션이 기다려지는구나.

(3) 문제 풀기 Tip

Tip 1.
문제가 나오면 전체 주제를 먼저 그린 뒤 보기를 읽어야 한다. 어떤 문제 유형이든 보기에 주제를 패러프레이징한 느낌이 있다면 정답일 가능성이 높다. 즉, 이 대화의 주제는 프레젠테이션의 주제이므로, 보기에 프레젠테이션과 관련된 것이 있다면 문제가 어떻든 정답이 된다.

Tip 2.
문제를 들을 때는 한 단어라도 놓치면 큰일나는 것처럼 하다가, 정작 문제가 나오면 읽지도 않고 바로 보기를 보는 학생이 많다. 이렇게 하지 말고, 먼저 문제를 읽은 뒤 전체적인 틀과 주제를 잡은 다음 보기를 읽는 연습을 하자. 문제 유형에 따른 오답 패턴을 알아 두면, 질문의 한 부분을 놓친다고 해도 나머지 보기를 오답 패턴에 적용해 하나씩 소거해서 정답을 선택할 수 있게 된다. 즉, 훈련 포인트를 무조건 정답 맞히기에 두기보다는 정답률을 올리는 데 중점을 두는 것이 좋다.

(4) 문제 풀기

01 Main Topic

What is the main topic of the conversation?

Ⓐ The importance of choosing the topic for the presentation
Ⓑ The student's topic for the class presentation
Ⓒ The research on people's genes
Ⓓ The effects of eating vegetables

대화의 주제는 무엇인가?

Ⓐ 프레젠테이션 주제 선정의 중요성
Ⓑ 학생의 수업 프레젠테이션 주제
Ⓒ 사람들의 유전자에 대한 조사
Ⓓ 채소를 먹는 것의 효과

오답 패턴 Ⓐ 주제어가 포함되어 정답인 듯 보이지만 한 단어 때문에 오답이 된다. importance 때문에 오답이 되었다.
Ⓒ Ⓓ 언급된 내용이지만 대화의 주제가 아니라 세부적인 내용이다.

02 Detail

According to the biologist's argument, why do some people dislike the bitter taste of vegetables?

Ⓐ Genetic predisposition
Ⓑ Their childhood experience
Ⓒ Trauma
Ⓓ Their thoughts

생물학자들의 주장에 따르면, 왜 어떤 사람들은 채소의 쓴맛을 싫어하나?

Ⓐ 유전적 원인
Ⓑ 그들의 어린 시절의 경험
Ⓒ 정신적 외상
Ⓓ 그들의 생각

오답 패턴 Ⓑ Ⓒ Ⓓ 언급된 내용이지만 질문에 대한 답이 아니다.

Tip 들었다고 무턱대고 정답으로 선택하면 안 된다. 보기의 난이도를 높이기 위해, 대화에서 언급된 내용으로 보기를 만들기 때문에 질문을 꼼꼼하게 읽어 출제 포인트를 잡아내야 한다.

03 Inference

Listen again to part of the conversation. Then answer the question.

> P: So, you mean a genetic predisposition prevents some people from enjoying the taste of vegetables? Isn't that just a made up story?

Why does the professor say this?
P: Isn't that just a made up story?

Ⓐ To encourage the student to make up stories to support the presentation
Ⓑ To emphasize some people don't like vegetables because of their genes
Ⓒ To imply that the research the student found might not be true
Ⓓ To encourage the student to do more research on this topic

대화의 일부를 다시 들으시오. 그러고 나서 질문에 답하시오.

> P: 그래서 네가 의미하는 게 유전적인 성향이 어떤 사람들이 채소의 맛을 즐기지 못하게 한다는 거야? 그냥 만들어진 이야기가 아닐까?

교수는 왜 이 말을 하나?
P: 그냥 만들어진 이야기가 아닐까?

Ⓐ 학생에게 프레젠테이션을 뒷받침하기 위해 이야기를 만들어낼 것을 권유하기 위해
Ⓑ 몇몇 사람들이 그들의 유전자 때문에 채소를 좋아하지 않는다는 것을 강조하기 위해
Ⓒ 학생이 발견한 연구가 사실이 아닐 수도 있다는 것을 암시하기 위해
Ⓓ 학생에게 이 주제에 대한 조사를 더 하라고 권유하기 위해

오답 패턴
Ⓐ 다시 들려 주는 부분에 들어간 made up을 이용해 보기를 만들었다.
Ⓑ 다시 들려 주는 부분과는 상관없는 부분에서 언급된 단어를 이용해 보기를 만들었다.
Ⓓ 정답에서 한 단계 더 나아간 오답을 만들었다. 예를 들어, 교수가 그 말을 한 의도는 학생이 발견한 게 사실이 아닐 수도 있기 때문인데, 여기서 한 단계 더 나아가서 '사실이 아니니까 연구를 더 해.'라고 만든 것이다.

Tip 다시 들려 주는 부분에 있는 단어가 그대로 들어가 있거나 다시 들려 주는 내용에서 한 단계 나아가면 오답일 가능성이 높다. 예) '어떤 도구에는 문제가 있다'라는 의도를 가지고 '어떤 도구에는 문제가 있으니 해결을 해야 한다.'까지 가면 오답이 된다.

2 강의

(1) 강의 듣기 Tip

Tip 1.

강의는 대화보다 상대적으로 어려운 내용을 다룬다. 대화라면 한번쯤 겪어 본 내용일 테니 어느 정도 예측을 할 수 있을 텐데, 강의는 주제부터 낯선 것들이 많다. 사실 이것은 영어의 문제가 아니라 주제 자체의 문제이다. 한국어로 된 다큐멘터리를 본다고 해도, 지구 온난화나 화학 작용 등을 다루는 내용이 나올 때, 그 분야에 관심이 없는 사람은 한쪽 귀로 듣고 다른 쪽 귀로 흘려보내게 된다.

따라서 토플 리스닝을 잘하기 위해서는 영어뿐만이 아니라 상식을 쌓아 두는 것이 좋다. 물론 백과사전이 된 듯이 모든 내용을 알 수는 없겠지만, 적어도 각 분야의 빈출 내용 정도는 정리해 두는 것이 좋다. 가령, 멸종한 동식물에 관한 문제에는 그에 대한 가설과 그 가설을 뒷받침하는 근거가 나온다. 지질학은 지구가 움직인다는 큰 그림에서 시작한다. 이처럼 대략적으로 배경지식을 정리해 둔다면, 리스닝을 들을 때 많은 도움이 될 것이다.

Tip 2.

노트 테이킹은 따로 연습할 필요가 없다. 우선 강의 내용 중 문제에 나오는 부분에 대한 감을 키우는 것이 중요하다. 문제가 나오는 부분에는 '중요하다' 등의 강조 어구가 들어가는데, 그런 어구를 시그널이라고 한다. 노트 테이킹보다는 시그널 부분에 집중해 무의식 중에도 반응이 일어나게 연습을 한다. 그렇게 이 부분이 문제로 나온다는 확신이 생기면 그 부분에 대해 한두 단어 정도는 자연스럽게 적어놓게 된다. 노트 테이킹은 따로 연습하는 게 아니라 자연스럽게 이루어져야 한다. 그리고 노트 테이킹의 양과 점수는 아무런 상관관계가 없다. 한 문제를 35초 전후로 해결해야 하고, 모니터를 보면서 문제와 보기를 보고 내용을 파악해 오답을 거르고 정답을 찍는 데도 시간이 빠듯하기 때문에 노트 테이킹은 최소한으로 하고, 그 전에 문제 포인트를 귀로 잡아내는 연습부터 한다.

Tip 3.

동굴에 오랜 시간 있다고 해서 동굴 내부가 밝아지는 것은 아니지만 어둠에 익숙해져 사물을 분별할 수 있게 된다. 강의 역시 마찬가지이다. 모든 분야를 아는 사람은 없기에 강의를 완벽히 듣고 문제를 푸는 것은 쉬운 일이 아니다. 하지만 잘 들리지 않는 것을 인정하면서 토플 리스닝의 흐름에 익숙해지게 되면 완벽히는 들을 수 없어도 정형화된 패턴의 문제를 푸는 방법을 알게 된다. 기억해야 할 것은 토플이 아무리 어렵다고 해도 결국 사지선다 형식이고, 문제 유형 역시 정해져 있다는 점이다. 이 시험은 미국 대학에서 수업을 듣는 데 도움을 주기 위한 시험이지, 미국에 못 가게 막기 위한 것이 아니다. 리스닝 역시 그런 관점에서 접근해야 한다. 연습을 이어 가다 보면 잘 들릴 때도 있고 그렇지 않을 때도 있는데, 그때마다 일희일비하지 말고 꾸준히 연습하자. 길은 열리게 되어 있다.

(2) 강의 듣기

Listen to part of a lecture in an ancient history class.

Today's focus will be on one of Rome's great technological developments. **01** What I'm talking about is the water distribution system known as aqueducts. Aqueducts are channels of water that permit the transport of water from its source to another location, usually a city.

04 I'm sure you are already aware that a reliable water supply is essential for cities. I mean people are not able to sustain their lives without the sufficient amount of water. So, it would be waste of time for me to add more comments on this. **03** Take Rome, for example. The city had an estimated 500,000 to one million people. That was a large city even by today's standards. Supplying all those people with water was a major engineering achievement. Over several hundreds of years, 11 aqueducts were constructed to bring water to Rome from as far as 90 kilometers away, providing 1,000 liters of water per day for every person. **03** The water brought by aqueducts was also used to keep the city clean by flushing out trash. Aqueducts paved the way for the Roman Empire to spread its power. I should point out that it would have been impossible for the Roman Empire to become one of the largest ancient empires without these advanced water distribution systems.

02 The aqueducts were built after first locating a water source. Roman people tried to find enough sources from which water could be diverted to the city. Also, they looked only for sources at a higher elevation than the city, in order for the water to flow down to the city through the aqueducts. You see, the source had to be at a higher elevation than Rome, since the system of aqueducts relied entirely on gravity to move the water down the pipes and channels. The aqueducts were made out of pipes and were laid underground in trenches that were then filled in. This allowed the land above to be utilized and the aqueducts to be kept safe from enemy attacks. When the geography demanded it the Romans would build tunnels deep under a mountain and build arcades over river valleys. It's still a mystery how the Romans created such an amazing engineering achievement.

고대 역사 강의 중 일부를 들어 보시오.

오늘의 주제는 로마의 위대한 기술 발달 중 하나입니다. **01** 내가 이야기하는 것은 수로교라고 불리는 물 분배 시스템이에요. 수로교는 물의 공급지에서 다른 장소, 대개 도시로 물을 이동시키는 길입니다.

04 여러분들도 이미 믿을만한 물 공급이 도시에 얼마나 중요한지 알고 있을 거라고 생각해요. 사람은 충분한 양의 물 없이는 생명을 유지할 수 없죠. 그래서 이 점에 대해 더 설명하는 건 시간 낭비일 것 같네요. **03** 로마를 예로 들어 보겠습니다. 이 도시는 대략 50만에서 100만 명 정도의 사람들이 살고 있었습니다. 오늘날의 기준에서 봐도 대 도시이죠. 이 모든 사람들에게 물을 공급하는 것은 아주 중요한 기술공학적 성취죠. 수백 년 간, 11개의 수로교가 지어져 90km까지 멀리 떨어져 있는 로마에 매일 1000L의 물이 공급되어 모든 시민들이 이용했습니다. **03** 수로교로 공급된 이 물은 쓰레기를 쓸어내어 도시를 깨끗하게 만드는 데도 이용되었어요. 수로교는 로마 제국 자신의 힘을 확산시키는 데에 큰 도움을 주었습니다. 이 선진적인 수로교가 없었다면 로마 제국이 가장 거대한 고대 제국이 되는 것은 불가능 했을 수도 있다는 것을 강조해야겠네요.

02 수로교는 첫 번째 물 공급지의 위치를 찾은 후에 지어졌어요. 로마인들은 도시에 도달할 만큼 충분한 물 공급지를 찾으려고 시도했습니다. 또한, 그들은 물이 수로를 따라 도시 밑으로 흘러갈 수 있도록 도시보다 높은 고도에서 공급지를 찾았습니다. 즉, 수로교의 원리는 물이 배수관과 수로를 따라 흘러 내려가기 위해 완전히 중력에 의존하기 때문에, 물 공급지는 로마보다 더 높은 곳에 위치해 있어야 한다는 말입니다. 수로교는 배수관으로 만들어졌으며 땅 아래 도랑에 놓인 후에 매장됩니다. 이로 인해, 수로교가 있는 곳 위의 땅도 활용가능할 뿐 아니라, 적의 공격에도 안전했어요. 지형적으로 필요가 있으면 로마인들은 산 아래에 터널을 깊게 만들기도 했고, 강 계곡에 아치형 통로를 짓기도 했습니다. 어떻게 로마인들이 이처럼 놀라운 업적을 만들어 냈는가는 여전히 수수께끼로 남아있어요.

(3) 문제 풀기 Tip

Tip 1.

늘 문제부터 정확하게 이해하도록 한다. 문제를 보고 유형을 파악하면 출제 의도를 분석할 수 있기 때문에, 몇 단어 놓쳤다고 너무 당황하지 않아도 된다. 중요한 것은 주제와 큰 흐름이다. 그리고 유형별로 오답이 패턴화되어 있기 때문에, 문제 유형 먼저 파악하고 보기를 읽도록 한다.

Tip 2.

때로는 놓친 부분을 물어보는 문제가 나오기도 한다. 학생들은 당황해서 보기 중 본인이 들었던 단어를 선택하는 경향이 있는데 결코 좋은 방법이 아니다. 왜냐하면 출제자는 정답을 최대한 숨겨 놓고, 들은 몇 개의 단어만으로는 찍어서 정답을 맞힐 수 없게 만든다. 오히려 들은 단어들을 덫으로 이용해 오답을 만들곤 한다. 만약 문제를 못 들어서 찍을 수밖에 없는 상황이 된다면, 단어보다는 주제와 가장 가까운 보기를 선택하는 것이 정답률을 높이는 비결이다.

(4) 문제 풀기

01 Main Topic

What is the main purpose of the lecture?

Ⓐ To explain the sophisticated construction process of arcades
Ⓑ To explain why the Roman people needed to build a water distribution system
Ⓒ To describe the difficult tasks the Roman people faced while building aqueducts
Ⓓ To describe the characteristics of an ancient Roman technology

강의의 주된 목적은 무엇인가?

Ⓐ 정교한 아케이드의 건설 과정을 설명하기 위해
Ⓑ 로마 사람들이 왜 배수 시설을 만들 필요가 있었는지 설명하기 위해
Ⓒ 수로를 짓는 동안 로마인들이 직면한 어려운 일들을 묘사하기 위해
Ⓓ 고대 로마 기술의 특징들을 묘사하기 위해

오답 패턴 Ⓑ 언급된 내용이지만 주제가 아니라 세부적인 내용이다.

02 Detail

According to the professor, what were two requirements for building an effective aqueduct?
Choose 2 answers.

Ⓐ An adequate water source
Ⓑ Strong water pipes to be safe from enemy attack
Ⓒ A large population
Ⓓ A down flow pathway

교수에 따르면, 효과적인 수로를 건설하기 위한 두 가지 필요 조건은 무엇인가?
2개의 답을 고르시오.

Ⓐ 충분한 수원
Ⓑ 적의 공격에 안전한 튼튼한 수도관
Ⓒ 많은 인구
Ⓓ 밑으로 흐르는 경로

오답 패턴 Ⓑ Ⓒ 대화에서 언급됐지만, 질문에 대한 답이 아니다.

Tip 세부 사항의 출제 포인트로는 '이유, 중요, 예시, 용어 설명'이 있고, 세부 사항은 듣는 것 자체를 확인하는 문제이기 때문에 보기를 그렇게 꼬아서 내지는 않는다.

03 Organization

Why does the professor mention the size of ancient Rome's population?

Ⓐ To explain why the water source was located at a high elevation
Ⓑ To point out why water was important for survival
Ⓒ To describe the various ways of bringing water into the city
Ⓓ To explain why the Romans built a specific water distribution system

교수는 왜 고대 로마의 인구 규모를 언급했나?

Ⓐ 수원이 높은 고도에 위치해야 하는 이유를 설명하기 위해
Ⓑ 물이 생존에 중요한 이유를 강조하기 위해
Ⓒ 도시에 물을 가져오는 다양한 방법을 묘사하기 위해
Ⓓ 로마 사람들이 특정 배수 시설을 지었던 이유를 설명하기 위해

오답 패턴 Ⓐ 수원에 대한 고도가 강의에서 언급됐지만, 질문에 대한 답이 아니다.
Ⓑ 물이 중요한 것은 맞지만 궁극적으로는 수로의 중요성에 대한 것이 오늘의 주제이다.

Tip 정답 같은 보기 두 개가 남으면, 둘 중에 좀 더 주제와 가까운 것을 선택해라!
예) 공상 과학 소설에 대해 말하겠어요. 공상 과학 소설은 과학의 발달에 직면하는 사람의 본성이 변하는 것을 심오하게 다룬 것입니다. 대표적인 예로는 《프랑켄슈타인》이 있습니다. 이 소설의 주제는 갈바니즘이라고 불리는 것인데, 갈바니즘은 죽은 사체의 부분을 모아다가 전기를 주입하면 생명체가 부활할 수 있다는 유행했던 허구 과학 개념이었죠.

교수는 왜 갈바니즘을 언급했나?
Ⓐ 공상 과학 소설을 설명하기 위해
Ⓑ 프랑켄슈타인을 설명하기 위해
Ⓒ 갈바니즘의 정의를 설명하기 위해

보기는 모두 들은 내용인데 문제를 보니 구조 문제이다. 이럴 때 기준은 주제와 가까운 순서이므로, Ⓐ를 정답으로 고른다. Ⓑ의 프랑켄슈타인과 Ⓒ의 갈바니즘도 결국은 주제인 공상 과학 소설을 설명하기 위한 것이기 때문이다.

04 Inference

Listen again to part of the conversation. Then answer the question.

> I'm sure you are already aware that a reliable water supply is essential for cities. I mean people are not able to sustain their lives without the sufficient amount of water. So, it would be waste of time for me to add more comments on this.

What does the professor mean when she says this:
So, it would be waste of time for me to add more comments on this.

Ⓐ She believes that the students don't need to know about the importance of water.
Ⓑ She doesn't want to waste her time.
Ⓒ She thinks that the students already have enough information about the importance of water.
Ⓓ She tries to explain in more detail about the importance of water.

강의의 일부분을 다시 들으시오. 그러고 나서 질문에 답하시오.

> 여러분들도 이미 믿을만한 물 공급이 도시에 얼마나 중요한지 알고 계실 거라고 생각합니다. 제가 의미하는 것은 사람은 충분한 양의 물 없이는 생명을 유지할 수 없습니다. 그래서 이 점에 대해 더 설명하는 건 시간 낭비일 거 같네요.

교수가 이 말을 할 때 의미한 것은 무엇인가?
그래서 이 점에 대해 더 설명하는 건 시간 낭비일 거 같네요.

Ⓐ 그녀는 학생들이 물의 중요성에 대해 알 필요가 없다고 믿는다.
Ⓑ 그녀는 시간을 낭비하기를 원하지 않는다.
Ⓒ 그녀는 학생들이 물의 중요성에 대해 이미 충분한 지식을 가지고 있다고 생각한다.
Ⓓ 그녀는 물의 중요성에 대해 더 자세하게 설명하려고 한다.

오답 패턴   Ⓑ 다시 들려 준 부분에 있는 단어들로 오답을 만들었다.

TOEFL iBT
LISTENING

영단기 TOEFL

ACTUAL TEST

TEST 01

TEST 1   Set 1 Conversation

Listen to part of a conversation between a student and a professor.

학생의 용건:
보고서 작성 시 출처 표시에 어려움이 있음

S   Professor, can I talk to you?
P   Hello. Yes, I am free right now. Is there something you don't understand in today's lecture?
S   Actually, it is about the assignment on Medieval England. 01 I am unsure about citing the sources.

개요 작성의 중요성

P   Alright. Can I first see your outline?
S   Well, I don't have it written down, but I planned it out in my mind. I already started writing the first draft.
P   Hmm... are you sure you can write your research paper without a written outline? You may not have enough information to finish your paper.
S   I'll be fine. I have planned out well how to develop it.
P   It really helps to write an outline. I strongly recommend you to write one. 02 The outline will help you see how much progress you have made in the paper and organize your information, guiding you to the right track. You know what I mean?
S   Yes. I get it. I think it will help me a lot because I will be writing about a whole bunch of information.

보고서의 소재 1:
성(城) 역할의 변화

P   Great idea. So, what is your topic again?
S   I want to write about castles in the 11th and 12th century.
P   Alright. What about castles exactly?
S   03 Um, I was thinking about the shift in the role of castles, such as the role of castles after being used as military forts.
P   Okay. I am just checking, but do you know what the military purpose of castles was?
S   Of course. When the Vikings were raiding England, people had to find themselves a place where they could be safe from enemies. So, rich aristocrats would often build high walls around their castles. The huge appearance of the structure clearly showed the owner's power.
P   Correct. Do you also remember what the rich aristocrats

Tip 과제의 주제가 언급되면, 세부 사항을 묻는 문제가 출제될 수 있으니 주의하며 듣는다.

S   교수님, 교수님과 말씀 좀 나눌 수 있을까요?
P   안녕. 그래, 지금은 시간이 있단다. 오늘 수업에서 이해가 안 간 것이 있니?
S   사실 중세 영국에 관한 과제에 대한 거예요. 01 출처를 표시하는 것에 대해 잘 모르겠어요.
P   그렇구나. 먼저 너의 개요를 좀 볼 수 있을까?
S   그게, 적어 놓지 않았지만, 머릿속에 정리했어요. 저는 벌써 초고를 쓰기 시작했거든요.
P   흠…… 개요 작성도 하지 않고 연구 보고서를 쓸 수 있을까? 보고서를 끝내기에는 정보가 충분하지 않을 수도 있을 텐데 말이야.
S   괜찮을 거 같아요. 어떻게 진행할지 계획을 잘 세워놨어요.
P   개요를 쓰는 것은 정말 도움이 된단다. 너에게 개요를 쓰는 것을 강력히 추천하마. 02 개요는 보고서가 얼마만큼 진행됐는지 파악하고 정보를 체계화하는 데에 많은 도움을 주어서, 네가 올바른 방향으로 갈 수 있게 도와줄 거야. 무슨 의미인지 알겠지?
S   네. 알겠습니다. 저는 굉장히 많은 정보에 대해서 쓸 예정이기 때문에 개요 작성이 많은 도움이 될 것 같네요.
P   좋은 생각이구나. 그래서 주제가 뭐라고 했지?
S   저는 11세기와 12세기의 성(城)에 관해서 쓰고 싶어요.
P   그렇구나. 정확히 성에 대한 어떤 것이니?
S   03 음, 저는 군사 요새로 쓰이고 난 이후의 성의 역할과 같은 성 역할의 변화에 대해 생각 중이에요.
P   좋아. 그냥 확인하는 것인데, 너는 성의 군사적 목적이 무엇이었는지 알고 있지?
S   물론이죠. 바이킹들이 잉글랜드에 침입했을 때, 사람들은 적으로부터 안전한 장소를 찾아야만 했어요. 그래서 부유한 귀족들은 종종 그들의 성 주변에 높은 성벽을 쌓곤 했어요. 건축물의 거대한 외관은 소유주의 힘을 분명하게 보여 줬어요.
P   맞아. 그럼 부유한 귀족들이 사람들에게 어떻게 불렸는지도 기억하니?
S   영주요. 그들이 침략을 받을 때, 모든 사람들이 성벽 뒤에 숨곤 했어요. 그래서 그 성벽들이 사람들을 보호했죠.

	were called by people?
S	Lords. When they were raided, all the people would hide behind the castle walls. So, the walls protected the people.
P	If they served such a good purpose, why did people stop living in castles?
S	The Vikings disappeared as well as dangerous wars. People eventually did not need protection. However, some people continued to build castles just for their reputation.
P	That is true. Anything else you were thinking of including in the paper?

보고서의 소재 2: 성(城)과 관련된 법

S	03 I was thinking of adding information about the law back then. The law was that the royal family could make use of any castle in the country whenever they wanted. In fact, the nobility living in castles took it as a great privilege to be required to act as hosts to the royal family.
P	04 I was worried that you might not be prepared enough, but now you are onto something.

학생에게 교내 글쓰기 센터의 워크숍에 참석할 것을 제안함

S	Thanks. But I am still stuck with citing the resources. You know, I am not even sure whether I should make a bibliography or add footnotes.
P	You should definitely make a bibliography.
S	Okay, but how do I make it? Is there some kind of set format or is it just listing titles and dates?
P	05 I'm afraid that I can't give you all the information. Bibliography entries must be written in a very specific format, but that format will depend on the particular style of writing you use. There are several formats employed in the different fields, and the writing center provides information related to this issue. I think it probably can help you. As far as I know, it has a weekly workshop to help students. If you take part in it, you can get much useful information you can refer to.
S	A weekly workshop?
P	Yes. The writing center is there to answer your questions.
S	I guess I should go there then.
P	Sounds great. Good luck with your paper. I am looking forward to reading it.

[**Vocabulary**] cite[sait] 인용하다   first draft 초고, 초안   a whole bunch of 매우 많은   military fort 군사 요새
raid[reid] 침략하다   aristocrat[ərístəkræt] 귀족   bibliography[bìbliágrəfi] 저서 목록, 참고 목록   entry[éntri] 항목
footnote[fútnout] 각주

01 Main Topic

Why does the student visit the professor? | 학생은 왜 교수를 찾아갔나?

Ⓐ To get some advice on citing the sources for a paper
Ⓑ To get some information about a paper outline
Ⓒ To ask about how to lay out a paper
Ⓓ To ask how to find sources for research

Ⓐ 보고서에 출처를 표시하는 것에 대한 조언을 얻기 위해
Ⓑ 보고서의 개요에 관한 정보를 얻기 위해
Ⓒ 보고서를 어떻게 구성해야 할지를 묻기 위해
Ⓓ 연구를 위한 자료를 어떻게 찾아야 할지를 묻기 위해

02 Detail

Why does the professor recommend writing an outline? | 교수는 왜 개요를 작성하는 것을 추천했나?

Ⓐ To see the development while writing the student's paper
Ⓑ To assure the topic of the student's paper is appropriate
Ⓒ To remember all information included in the student's paper
Ⓓ To change the student's paper format easily

Ⓐ 학생 보고서의 작성에 대한 진전을 확인하기 위해
Ⓑ 학생 보고서의 주제가 적절한지 분명히 하기 위해
Ⓒ 학생의 보고서에 담긴 모든 내용을 기억하기 위해
Ⓓ 학생의 보고서 형식을 쉽게 바꾸기 위해

오답 해설   Ⓒ 보고서의 모든 내용을 기억하기 위해서가 아니라 글의 체계화 및 진행 상태 등을 파악해, 보고서 작성에 대한 방향 제시에 도움이 되기 때문에 교수는 학생에게 개요를 작성할 것을 추천했다.

03 Detail

What information will the student include in the paper?
Choose 2 answers.

학생은 보고서에 어떤 정보를 포함할 것인가?
2개의 답을 고르시오.

Ⓐ The change in the roles of castles
Ⓑ The strength of castles when used for military purposes
Ⓒ The walls that lords built around castles
Ⓓ The law applied to privileged people

Ⓐ 성 역할의 변화
Ⓑ 군사적 목적으로 사용될 때 성의 장점
Ⓒ 영주가 성 주변에 만든 벽
Ⓓ 특권층에 적용된 법

04 Inference

Listen again to part of the conversation. Then answer the question.

> P: I was worried that you might not be prepared enough, but now you are onto something.

What does the professor imply when she says this:
P: ... but now you are onto something.

Ⓐ She thinks that more information should be included in the student's paper.
Ⓑ She expresses approval of the topic of the student's paper.
Ⓒ She believes that the student needs help to finish in the paper.
Ⓓ She pays a compliment about the student.

대화의 일부를 다시 들으시오. 그러고 나서 질문에 답하시오.

> P: 네가 충분히 준비하지 못했을까 봐 걱정했는데, 좋은 결론에 도달했구나.

교수가 이 말을 할 때 암시한 것은 무엇인가?
P: …… 하지만 너는 좋은 결론에 도달했구나.

Ⓐ 그녀는 학생의 보고서에 더 많은 정보가 포함되어야 한다고 생각한다.
Ⓑ 그녀는 학생의 보고서 주제에 대한 승인을 표현한다.
Ⓒ 그녀는 학생이 보고서를 끝내기 위해 도움이 필요하다고 생각한다.
Ⓓ 그녀는 학생을 칭찬한다.

어휘   be onto something (대단한 것을) 발견해(이뤄) 낼 가능성이 있다

05 Detail

Why does the professor suggest going to the weekly workshop?

Ⓐ She cannot provide details about the student's request.
Ⓑ She thinks that the student will find the workshop very interesting.
Ⓒ She knows that the student is busy writing a paper.
Ⓓ She wants the student to participate in school services.

교수는 왜 주간 워크숍에 갈 것을 제안했나?

Ⓐ 그녀는 학생의 요청에 대해 자세한 설명을 해 줄 수 없다.
Ⓑ 그녀는 학생이 워크숍을 매우 흥미로워 할 것이라고 생각한다.
Ⓒ 그녀는 학생이 보고서를 쓰느라 바쁜 것을 안다.
Ⓓ 그녀는 학생이 학교 서비스에 참여하기를 원한다.

오답 해설   Ⓓ 교수가 학생의 궁금증을 직접 해결해 줄 수 없기 때문에, 학생이 서비스에 참여할 것을 제안했다.

TEST 1　Set 1 Lecture 1

Listen to part of a lecture in a biology class.

P 06 Let's continue with our study of insect behavior by studying ants, focusing on their similarities with gardeners. Does this confuse you? How can ants be compared to gardeners? Well, the ant population has exercised a great amount of influence on the surrounding environment for over millions of years, which, most of the time, proved to be harmonious.

Why don't we look at one example? First, I want to discuss the ant species, M. schumanni. These ants inhabit Peru's Amazon rainforest as their chosen ecological niche. When I referred to ants as gardeners, I came up with these ants. You see, M. schumanni ants primarily consume a tree named D. hirsuta. You can think of this tree as their key source of sustenance. By the way, I would like to apologize for the strange names of the ant and the tree. Both names are unusual. Well, a scientist discovered that D. hirsuta is the dominant species among the plants in a particular part of the Peruvian rainforest. D. hirsuta is more abundant and widespread than any other tree in this region. Yes, Amy?

S I remember reading about the area. I thought it was something about the mysteries of the rainforest.

P It is quite a perplexing phenomenon, so I'm not surprised that it's referred to as a mystery. Usually, there are diverse numbers of plants in a normal rainforest due to its temperate climate. Warm and humid conditions found in rainforests foster growth and diversity of the plants. Apparently, no one could venture to postulate how a single species of a tree came to occupy such vast areas of the rainforest. Some wondered if this certain rainforest has something unique. They assumed that perhaps a certain trait of the rainforest promoted territorial divisions. However, it turned out that D. hirsuta was the only dominant species in the whole Peruvian rainforest, which means its dominance was not a result of its territorial trait, but rather a result of features of the species itself. At first, the botanists argued that the trees secret a toxic herbicide, a plant poison that kills the adjacent vegetation.

Yet, it turned out that M. schumanni ants were the organisms responsible for this enigma. ⁰⁷ The ants dwell in the hollow cavities of D. hirsuta trees, and they use their poisonous chemical to eradicate all other types of plants that grow around their food, D. hirsuta trees. In effect, the ants are cultivating or farming D. hirsuta, as if they were gardeners who weed the garden by restricting the growth of other types of plants in certain areas of the rainforest. And, they receive nourishment and a place to live from the trees.

S Can it be considered as a symbiotic relationship, where both species receive benefits? I guess without the competition, the tree will get more nutrients, water, and light while the ants get more territory and food.

P Exactly! In fact, this exemplary instance of a mutual relationship works out perfectly. Since we covered symbiotic relationships, such as parasitism, commensalism, and mutualism, I expect you to recall that out of these, mutualism denotes a relationship, which is advantageous for both parties involved. That being said, M. schumanni ants have enjoyed the upper hand over other species in the rainforest for nearly 850 years, accompanied by their botanical ally.

⁰⁸ As for the ants, I want to discuss another type of ant, the leafcutter ants, which have developed an analogous kind of relationship with a particular type of fungus. Similar to M. schumanni ants, the leafcutter ants have cultivated this fungus for a very long time, eventually becoming reliant on it. Of course, likewise, the fungus also grows by depending on the leafcutter ants. ⁰⁹ Actually, a queen ant brings a fragment of the fungus with her when she leaves to establish a new nest because this fungus is an essential part of new start. ¹⁰ The primary reason these ants developed such a relationship with the fungus is that the fungus is able to carry out a

function that the ants cannot achieve. The fungus decomposes the leaves into consumable nutrients through its metabolic pathway. **The ants can't digest the leaves themselves because they don't possess the enzymes to break down, so they have to rely on the fungus which metabolizes the leaves into a digestible nutrient. And the fungus receives nourishment and protection.**

가위개미가 유지하는 자연의 균형

S But, I've heard that the leafcutter ants are very dangerous and destructive. I think this symbiotic relationship may pose a threat to the rainforests.

P You are right! They are capable of ravaging plants at South American rainforests at breakneck speed. The species contains a population of up to eight million ants, so it is pretty easy to picture the kind of repercussions they can bring over to the local surroundings. However, it is also important to consider that they have been latent for a substantial duration of time and yet the Peruvian rainforest still flourishes. You see, the ants have a way to perpetuate the overall ecological equilibrium. ¹¹ Leafcutter ants get their food by assaulting and consuming large amounts of various plants. However, they refrain from attacking the plants again until they have fully recuperated from the previous attack. By taking such precautions, the ants preserve environmental balance, which benefits both their colony and the forest as a whole.

시킬 수 없어서 그들은 잎을 소화할 수 있는 영양소로 분해하는 이 균에 의지해야 해요. 그리고 그 균은 영양분과 보호를 받습니다.

S 하지만 제가 듣기로는 가위개미가 매우 위험하고 유해하다고 들었어요. 이런 공생관계가 우림에는 위협이 될 수도 있을 것 같아요.

P 맞아요! 이 개미는 맹렬한 속도로 남미 우림의 식물을 파괴할 능력이 있습니다. 이 종은 800만 개체를 가지고 있어서, 주변 지역 환경에 가져올 영향을 쉽게 상상할 수 있어요. 하지만 그들이 상당히 오랫동안 잠재해 왔는데도, 페루의 우림은 여전히 번창하고 있다는 사실을 고려하는 것 역시 중요합니다. 그러니까, 이 개미는 생태계의 전체적인 균형을 영구화하는 방법을 알고 있습니다. ¹¹ 가위개미는 많은 양의 다양한 식물을 공격하고 섭취하면서 그들의 음식을 얻습니다. 하지만 그들이 이전의 공격으로부터 완전히 회복하기 전까지 그들은 그 식물들을 다시 공격하는 것을 삼가해요. 이런 조치를 취함으로써 그 개미는 생태적 균형을 지키는데, 그것은 그들의 집단과 숲 전체에 이익을 줍니다.

[Vocabulary] niche[nitʃ] 적합한 환경 sustenance[sʌ́stənəns] 자양물 perplexing[pərpléksiŋ] 복잡한 temperate[témpərit] 온화한 postulate[pɑ́stʃəlit] 상정하다 promote[prəmóut] 촉진하다, 기르다 botanist[bɑ́tənist] 식물학자 herbicide[hə́ːrbisàid] 제초제 enigma[ənígmə] 수수께끼 cavity[kǽvəti] 구멍 eradicate[irǽdəkèit] 제거하다 symbiotic[sìmbaiɑ́tik] 공생의 parasitism[pǽrəsàitizm] 기생 commensalism[kəménslìzm] (편리) 공생 mutualism[mjúːtʃuəlìzm] 공생 denote[dinóut] 나타내다 the upper hand over ~ 보다 우위 analogous[ənǽləgəs] 유사한 decompose[dìːkəmpóuz] 분해시키다 enzyme[énzaim] 효소 ravage[rǽvidʒ] 황폐하게 만들다 breakneck speed 맹렬한 속도 repercussion[rìːpərkʌ́ʃn] (좋지 못한) 영향 latent[léitnt] 잠재하는 perpetuate[pərpétʃuèit] 영속시키다 equilibrium[ìːkwəlíbriəm] 균형 recuperate[rikjúːpərèit] 회복하다

06 Main Topic

What is the lecture mainly about?

Ⓐ The cooperative relationship shared among living organisms
Ⓑ The contentious methods employed by M. schumanni ants for D. hirsuta trees
Ⓒ The mutually advantageous relationship between the leafcutter ants and the fungus
Ⓓ The efforts to prevent the destruction of the environmental balance in nature

강의는 주로 무엇에 관한 것인가?

Ⓐ 생물들이 공유하는 상호 협력 관계
Ⓑ D. hirsuta 나무를 위해 M. schumanni 개미가 사용하는 논쟁적인 방법
Ⓒ 가위개미와 균 사이의 상호 이익이 되는 관계
Ⓓ 자연에서 환경 균형의 파괴를 막기 위한 노력

07 Detail

What does the professor say about the relationship between M. schumanni ants and D. hirsuta trees?
Choose 2 answers.

Ⓐ The ants impede the expansion of the trees by secreting a toxic herbicide.
Ⓑ The trees provide a shelter for the ants.
Ⓒ The ants stimulate the trees to absorb nutrients from the ground.
Ⓓ The ants weed away the surrounding area for the trees.

교수가 M. schumanni 개미와 D. hirsuta 나무의 관계에 대해 말한 것은 무엇인가?
2개의 답을 고르시오.

Ⓐ 개미는 독성의 제거제를 분비해서 그 나무가 확산되는 것을 방해한다.
Ⓑ 나무는 개미에게 안식처를 제공한다.
Ⓒ 개미는 나무가 땅에서 영양분을 흡수하는 것을 촉진시킨다.
Ⓓ 개미는 그 나무를 위해 주변 지역의 잡초를 제거한다.

08 Inference

Listen again to part of the lecture. Then answer the question.

> P: As for the ants, I want to discuss another type of ant, the leafcutter ants, which have developed an analogous kind of relationship with a particular type of fungus.

Why does the professor say this:
P: As for the ants...

Ⓐ To gradually transit into a different topic
Ⓑ To remind the students of the characteristics of various ants
Ⓒ To continue discussing another type of ant
Ⓓ To emphasize the difficulty of understanding ants

강의의 일부를 다시 들으시오. 그러고 나서 질문에 답하시오.

> P: 개미에 대해 더 이야기한다면, 특정 종류의 균과 유사한 유형의 관계를 발전시킨 다른 종류의 개미인 가위개미에 대해서 논하고 싶어요.

교수는 왜 이 말을 했는가?
P: 개미에 대해 더 이야기한다면……

Ⓐ 점차 다른 주제로 넘어가기 위해
Ⓑ 학생에게 다양한 개미들의 특징들에 대해 상기시키기 위해
Ⓒ 다른 종류의 개미에 대한 논의를 계속하기 위해
Ⓓ 개미를 이해하는 것의 어려움을 강조하기 위해

09 Organization

Why does the professor mention a queen leafcutter ant?

Ⓐ To describe the procedure for the formation of her colony
Ⓑ To emphasize the important role a fungus plays in the survival of leafcutter ants
Ⓒ To elaborate on the biological hierarchy that characterizes the social structure of ants
Ⓓ To emphasize the biological benefit to ants through chemical secretions

교수는 왜 여왕 가위개미를 언급했나?

Ⓐ 그것의 군집 형성 과정을 설명하기 위해
Ⓑ 가위개미의 생존을 위해 균이 하는 중요한 역할을 강조하기 위해
Ⓒ 개미의 사회 구조를 특징 짓는 생물학적 계층을 설명하기 위해
Ⓓ 화학 분비물로 개미가 얻는 생물학적인 이익을 강조하기 위해

정답 해설 Ⓑ 교수는 균이 여왕개미가 새 둥지를 꾸리는 데 중요한 부분이라고 말하며, 균의 중요성을 설명하기 위해 여왕개미를 언급했다.

10 Detail

What is the function of the fungus regarding its relationship with the leafcutter ants?

Ⓐ It provides the ants with nourishment by preparing leaves appropriate for ingestion.
Ⓑ It speeds up the digestive system of the ants.
Ⓒ It provides shelter for the ants from harsh climates and predators.
Ⓓ It forms a chemical concoction that improves the development and growth of ants.

가위개미와의 관계와 관련된 균의 기능은 무엇인가?

Ⓐ 이파리를 섭취용으로 만들어 개미에게 영양분을 제공한다.
Ⓑ 개미의 소화기 계통의 속도를 높여 준다.
Ⓒ 혹독한 기후와 포식자로부터 안전한 쉼터를 개미에게 제공한다.
Ⓓ 개미의 성장과 발전에 도움을 주는 화학적 혼합물을 만든다.

11 Inference

What does the professor imply about leafcutter ants?

Ⓐ The ants are destructive yet highly discerning, only attacking plants that threaten the environmental balance.
Ⓑ The ants adjust their levels of consumption temporally, hereby keeping the stability of the environment.
Ⓒ The aggressiveness of ants actually benefits the environment by getting rid of weeds.
Ⓓ The ants present a research opportunity since they secrete a special chemical.

교수가 가위개미에 관해 암시한 것은 무엇인가?

Ⓐ 이 개미는 파괴적이지만 매우 주의가 깊어, 환경 균형을 위협하는 식물들만 공격한다.
Ⓑ 이 개미는 그들의 섭취 수준을 일시적으로 조절하여 환경의 안정을 유지한다.
Ⓒ 개미의 공격성은 잡초를 제거해 사실상 환경에 도움이 된다.
Ⓓ 이 개미는 특별한 화학 물질을 분비하기 때문에 연구 기회를 제공한다.

TEST 1 Set 2 Conversation

Listen to part of a conversation between a student and a professor.

학생의 용건:
전공 선택에 어려움이 있음

P Hi. Tim, how may I help you?
S Hi, Professor Gray, actually, I came here to discuss something with you.
P Sure, go on.
S Um... as you know, I've always been interested in economics and taken many classes related to this major since I started studying in this school.
P Yes. I'm aware of it. So, do you have any problems with it?

Tip 전문 용어에 대한 설명을 하면, 세부 사항 문제로 출제될 수 있으니 주의하며 듣는다.

S 02 Actually, I took History 201 last semester, and I learned a very interesting concept called the "bottom-up" approach, which means to predict our future, we should focus on our past. The professor said history was not made up by only prominent figures such as kings and generals, and we should also consider the common people. Our history has always consisted of these mundane lives, and it projects our future as well. This idea really inspired me, and it was kinda interesting. You know in economics, we don't really care about the background stuff. 01 So, now I'm not really sure which major I should go for. Economics is always my favorite, but I'm also interested in analyzing historical backgrounds.

복수 전공을 제안함

P Oh. Right. That's the common situation most students come across. But, you already took many economics classes. It's not good to just change the major at this time. If so, you might end up staying one more year to graduate. Have you considered doing a double major? Like economics and history?
S Umm... I actually did. 03 But if I do a double major, I think I have to write two theses for each major in my senior year. So, I'm worried that the workload will be heavier than I bargain for. What if I can't handle that kind of workload?

복수 전공자를 위한 특별 논문 프로그램 소개

P The school provides a special program for students who decide to go for double majors. They are

학생과 교수의 대화 중 일부를 들어 보시오.

P 안녕. Tim, 뭘 도와줄까?
S 안녕하세요, Gray 교수님, 사실, 교수님과 상의할 게 있어서 왔어요.
P 그래, 말해 보렴.
S 음……아시다시피, 저는 항상 경제학에 관심이 있어서, 제가 이 학교에서 공부를 시작한 이래로 그 전공 관련 수업을 많이 들었어요.
P 그래. 잘 알고 있단다. 그런데 무슨 문제라도 있니?
S 02 사실 저는 지난 학기에 역사 201 수업을 들었는데, 우리의 미래를 예측하기 위해 우리는 우리의 과거에 초점을 맞추어야 한다는 상향식 접근이라는 매우 흥미로운 개념을 배웠어요. 그 교수님은 역사는 단지 왕이나 장군 같은 중요한 인물들에 의해서만 만들어지는 것이 아니라, 우리는 보통 사람들에게도 관심을 가져야 한다고 하셨어요. 우리 역사는 항상 이런 일상적인 삶으로 구성되었고 그것이 우리의 미래 또한 조명할 것이라고요. 이 생각은 정말로 저에게 영감을 주었고 꽤 흥미로웠어요. 아시다시피 경제학에서는 배경적인 문제에 대해서는 신경 쓰지 않잖아요. 01 그래서 저는 이제 제가 어떤 전공을 해야 할지 확신이 서지 않아요. 경제학은 언제나 제가 가장 좋아하는 과목이었지만, 저는 역사적 배경을 분석하는 것에도 관심이 있거든요.

P 아. 그렇구나. 그건 대부분의 학생들이 직면하는 흔한 상황이지. 하지만 너는 이미 많은 경제학 수업을 들었잖니. 지금 전공을 바꾸는 건 좋지 않아 보이는구나. 그렇게 한다면 너는 졸업하기 위해서 1년을 더 다녀야 할지도 몰라. 복수 전공을 하는 것은 생각해 보았니? 경제학과 역사학으로?
S 음……사실 생각해 보았어요. 03 하지만 만약 복수 전공을 하게 되면, 4학년에 전공별로 하나씩, 2개의 논문을 써야 해요. 그래서 그 학습량이 제가 예상했던 것보다 더 힘들까 걱정이 돼요. 만약에 제가 그 학습량을 다 감당할 수 없으면 어쩌죠?

P 학교에서는 복수 전공을 하기로 결정한 학생들을 위한 특별한 프로그램을 제공하고 있단다. 그들은 주제 하나에 전공 두 가지

permitted to turn in one senior thesis that covers both majors under one topic. But, you should keep in mind the topic has to deal with both fields.

S Oh, really? I didn't know about it. So, how can I apply for the program?

P First you need to get approval from both department heads, and they will require you to submit the proposal first to see if your topic is suitable for the purpose. 04 Just remember they are very picky about these kinds of theses. The evaluation process of your proposal will be much more critical than single major submissions. So, you need to prepare an outstanding paper outline to be approved.

학생을 격려함

S Oh, that sounds tough and a lot of work. I'm not sure where I should begin.

P 05 I know it's challenging, but it's also worth a try. And I wouldn't tell you about this program in the first place if I didn't think you were qualified for this. Considering your past performance, I believe you are well prepared for this.

S Thank you for saying that. Um, do you think you could check the thesis topic for me once I pick one out? I mean, it needs to be highly relevant to both economics and history, so...

참고 도서를 추천함

P So you think that my opinion could help you develop your topic, huh?

S Right, exactly! To be honest, I'm not even sure where to start looking for the topic.

P Hmm, there is a book that pops into my head. It's written by economic professors, but they don't just focus on the current market. They take a holistic look at the past and present social scene, and they even venture to guess about the future. Here, I'll give you the title. Try looking for it at the library.

S Wow, thanks, Professor Gray. This definitely puts a whole new spin on the situation for me.

P No problem. While writing a proposal, let me know if you have any problems.

[**Vocabulary**] prominent[prámənənt] 중요한   kinda(kind of) 약간, 어느 정도   come across 직면하다   thesis[θíːsis] 학위 논문(*pl.* theses)   bargain for ~을 예상하다, ~을 대비하다   picky[píki] 까다로운   evaluation[ivæ̀ljuéiʃən] 평가   submission[səbmíʃən] 제출   holistic[hòulístik] 전체론의   spin[spin] (상황에 대한) 의견 제시

01 Main Topic

Why does the student go to see the professor?

Ⓐ To discuss an interesting aspect of history class he took last semester
Ⓑ To talk about why he lost his interest in economics
Ⓒ To figure out how to choose a double major
Ⓓ **To discuss which major he should choose**

학생은 왜 교수를 만나러 갔나?

Ⓐ 지난 학기에 들은 역사 수업의 흥미로운 점을 상의하기 위해
Ⓑ 왜 경제학에 흥미를 잃었는지 이야기하기 위해
Ⓒ 복수 전공을 선택하는 방법을 알아내기 위해
Ⓓ 그가 어떤 전공을 선택해야 하는지 상의하기 위해

02 Detail

What is the "bottom-up" approach in history?

Ⓐ It is the idea that a few powerful people dominate history.
Ⓑ **It is the idea that various aspects of history are fundamental facts to understand our future.**
Ⓒ It is the idea that interesting events have happened throughout history.
Ⓓ It is the idea that ordinary people played more important roles than influential people in history.

역사학에서 상향식 접근은 무엇인가?

Ⓐ 그것은 영향력 있는 몇몇의 사람들이 역사를 지배한다는 개념이다.
Ⓑ 그것은 역사의 다양한 측면이 우리의 미래를 이해하는 근본적인 사실이라는 개념이다.
Ⓒ 그것은 흥미로운 사건들이 역사를 통해 발생해 왔다는 개념이다.
Ⓓ 그것은 역사에 있어서 평범한 사람들이 영향력 있는 사람들보다 중요한 역할을 했다는 개념이다.

03 Detail

Why is the student worried about double majoring?

Ⓐ **He thinks that the amount of work might be more than he can stand.**
Ⓑ He doesn't have enough time to complete two majors.
Ⓒ He wants to graduate as soon as possible.
Ⓓ He thinks he cannot decide the thesis topic on time.

학생은 왜 복수 전공을 하는 것에 대해 걱정하나?

Ⓐ 그가 감당할 수 있는 것보다 학습량이 많을 것이라고 생각하기 때문이다.
Ⓑ 그는 두 개의 전공을 끝낼 시간이 충분하지 않기 때문이다.
Ⓒ 그는 가능한 한 빨리 졸업하고 싶기 때문이다.
Ⓓ 그는 논문 주제를 제시간에 결정할 수 없을 거라고 생각하기 때문이다.

04 Detail

What does the professor say about writing a thesis for a double major?

Ⓐ The paper is judged by a higher standard than single major submissions.
Ⓑ The student is required to prepare a lengthy paper to cover both majors.
Ⓒ The student needs to speak to heads of department to choose the right topic.
Ⓓ It is possible that the student's proposal won't be approved due to the difficulty of choosing various topics.

교수가 복수 전공 논문을 작성하는 것에 관해 말한 것은 무엇인가?

Ⓐ 복수 전공 논문은 단일 전공보다 더 높은 기준으로 평가된다.
Ⓑ 학생은 두 개의 전공을 모두 다루기 위해 길이가 긴 논문을 준비해야 한다.
Ⓒ 학생은 올바른 주제를 정하기 위해 학과장들과 이야기해야 한다.
Ⓓ 다양한 주제를 선택하는 어려움 때문에 학생의 제안은 승인을 받지 못 할 수도 있다.

오답 해설 Ⓒ 학과장들에게 논문의 주제를 승인받아야 한다고 했지만, 학생이 그들과 이야기를 해야 한다고 하지는 않았다.
Ⓓ 주제가 승인을 받기 어렵다고 했지, 다양한 주제 선택을 하는 것이 어렵다고 하지는 않았다.

05 Inference

Listen again to part of the conversation. Then answer the question.

> P: I know it's challenging, but it's also worth a try. And I wouldn't tell you about this program in the first place if I didn't think you were qualified for this.

What does the professor mean when she says this:
P: And I wouldn't tell you about this program in the first place if I didn't think you were qualified for this.

Ⓐ She implies it is the first time to suggest a double major to students.
Ⓑ She thinks the student has a high chance to complete a double major program successfully.
Ⓒ She implies that doing a double major could be challenging to the student.
Ⓓ She thinks the student doesn't have to get help about doing a double major.

대화의 일부를 다시 들으시오. 그러고 나서 질문에 답하시오.

> P: 그것이 도전적인 것은 알지만, 시도할 만한 가치는 있지. 그리고 네가 이 프로그램에 자격이 없다고 생각했다면 나는 이 프로그램 얘기를 너에게 하지 않았을 거란다.

교수가 이 말을 할 때 의미한 것은 무엇인가?
P: 그리고 네가 이 프로그램에 자격이 없다고 생각했다면 나는 이 프로그램 얘기를 너에게 하지 않았을 거란다.

Ⓐ 그녀는 학생들에게 복수 전공을 제안한 것이 처음이라는 것을 암시한다.
Ⓑ 그녀는 학생이 복수 전공을 위한 프로그램을 성공적으로 끝낼 가능성이 높다고 생각한다.
Ⓒ 그녀는 학생에게 복수 전공을 하는 것이 힘들 수 있다고 생각한다.
Ⓓ 그녀는 학생이 복수 전공을 하는 것에 대해 도움을 받을 필요가 없다고 생각한다.

TEST 1 Set 2 Lecture 1

Listen to part of a lecture in an astronomy class.

P Let's see, where were we? We just finished talking about our solar system and the planets that are in it. The solar system, with the sun in the center, includes Earth, the planet on which we live. Planets, moons, stars, comets, asteroids, and everything we see in the sky are a part of the solar system. Planets travel in orbits around the sun and are affected by its strong gravitational pull. The sun plays the main character on the stage called the solar system, as the hottest and most massive component. I mean, it pulls all the parts together in the system, generates heat, and provides light.

06 Now, it's time to talk about planets that are outside our solar system, called exoplanets. An exoplanet or extrasolar planet is usually referred to as a stellar remnant or a *brown dwarf which orbits a star other than the sun. If it is located outside our solar system, around what does it orbit? It centers its orbit on other big stars, called host stars. As you know, technology plays a significant role in astronomy. Using advanced technology, the *Kepler space telescope has detected almost 500 exoplanets, since the mid-1990s. Some planets are so near to their host stars that they take only a few hours to orbit, and there are others so far away that they take thousands of years to orbit. Some are so far out that it is difficult to tell if they are gravitationally bound to the host stars. The interesting thing about the discovery of such stellar bodies outside our solar system is that it has sparked studies about life in outer space.

The discovery of exoplanets has intensified interest in the search for extraterrestrial life, especially on those that orbit in the host star's habitable zone, which is the region around a star with sufficient atmospheric pressure to facilitate liquid water on its surface. This ability to sustain life, called habitability, is dependent on several factors. 07 One of these requirements is known to be water. A habitable planet needs water as well as the atmospheric pressure that can maintain water in its liquid form. Also, it needs to have a rocky surface instead of being gas giants like Jupiter and Saturn. So, what I mean is that a potentially habitable planet implies a *terrestrial planet that has similar living conditions compared to those of Earth and thus potentially favorable to live.

Okay, let's return to exoplanets. A red dwarf star, named Gliese 581, was discovered to be an Earth-like exoplanet. The host star is not as massive as the sun, meaning that it's smaller and cooler than the sun. Gliese 581 orbits around this host star and other planets called Gliese 581b, c, d, and e rotate around Gliese 581. It's like the moon orbiting around Earth. But forget Gliese 581b and c for now. We're going to focus on Gliese 581d and e because astronomers reported in 2009 that these two exoplanets show some Earth-like characteristics.

09 Gliese 581d was found a few years ago, and it was initially thought to be too cold for life. Its orbit seemed too far from its host star at first, but later observations yielded information that indicated otherwise. This exoplanet, due to its location, has a surface temperature lower than that of Earth but is mild enough to maintain life. 08 Gliese 581d has a mass seven times that of Earth, and its radius is thought to be around twice that of Earth. So researchers predicted that the planet has a core made out of rock and iron, which is subsequently covered by an ice layer. It's a very dense planet, meaning that its ability to support life is relatively higher than that of less dense planets. That is because planets with low density exert weak gravitational forces. Consequently, planets with weak gravity have difficulty with atmosphere retention. Also, their atmospheres are susceptible to solar wind or collisions, since there is insufficient force keeping the surface intact. Thus, the high density of Gliese 581d suggests that it has a sufficient atmosphere to sustain life. Also, along with a life-sustaining atmosphere, an ocean may exist on top of the ice

layer around the planet. ⁰⁹ The reason why these conditions exist is because the planet has high gravitational forces which enable it to retain its atmospheres, and intact atmospheres are less likely to lose the water they contain to outer space. In fact, computer climate simulations have confirmed the possibility of the existence of surface water. The confirmation of such factors related to suitability for planetary habitability increases the possibility of discovering life forms on those types of planets.

Gliese 581e의 특징

Compared to Gliese 581d, Gliese 581e might seem more of an Earth-like exoplanet because its mass and volume are only two times that of Earth. ¹⁰ However, Gliese 581e has a very short orbit around its host star, which means that it is very close to the stellar body that resembles the sun. So, its temperature exceeds the boiling point for water, making it unlikely that liquid water exists on its surface. The high thermal energy on the surface of the planet ensures that any liquid water would evaporate immediately. Except for this complication, this planet shares remarkable physical similarities with Earth, which is why scientists continue to set their hopes on finding life there.

외계 생명체의 존재 가능성

However, because it is about 20 light years from Earth, conclusive determinations about the planet are subject to heated debates among scientists. Nevertheless, astronomers have remained intrigued by its size, which is relatively close to that of Earth's, while the technology to explore the possibility of life on this planet is still being developed. As a matter of fact, the confirmation of the existence of numerous exoplanets has raised the probability that extraterrestrials exist. ¹¹ Just as scientists have gained information in the past about the creation of the universe and the planets in our solar system, you can bet that with better technology and further observations, we will soon obtain more conclusive results about planets outside of our solar system.

[**Vocabulary**] comet[kάmit] 혜성　asteroid[ǽstərɔ̀id] 소행성　stellar[stélər] 별의　remnant[rémnənt] 잔존물　host star 호스트 항성　extraterrestrial[èkstrətəréstriəl] 외계인　exert[igzə́ːrt] (압력을) 가하다　susceptible[səséptəbl] 영향 받기 쉬운　intact[intǽkt] 온전한, 전혀 다치지 않은　conclusive[kənklúːsiv] 결정적인

43

[각주]
* **brown dwarf** 진홍색과 갈색 사이의 빛을 약하게 내는 항성이다. 크기가 작고 온도도 낮기 때문에 직접적인 관측은 어렵다.
* **Kepler space telescope** 독일의 천문학자인 요하네스 케플러(Johannes Kepler, 1571~1630)의 이름을 딴 망원경이다. 2009년 발사된 이후로 132개의 행성을 발견했고 그 중에는 생물 주거 가능성이 높은 행성도 포함되어 있다.
* **terrestrial planet** 구성 물질이 지구와 비슷한 행성을 가리키는데, 수성, 금성, 화성 등이 이에 속한다.

06 Main Topic

What is the lecture mainly about?

ⓐ Planets located outside the habitable zone
ⓑ Technology used to observe exoplanets
ⓒ Planets that can substitute Earth in the future
ⓓ Recent postulations concerning celestial bodies

강의는 주로 무엇에 관한 것인가?

ⓐ 주거 가능 지역 밖에 위치한 행성
ⓑ 태양계외행성을 관찰하는 데 사용된 기술
ⓒ 미래에 지구를 대신할 수 있는 행성
ⓓ 천체와 관련된 최근의 가설

07 Detail

According to the lecture, what are the two conditions for planetary habitability?
Choose 2 answers.

Ⓐ A host star with a mass equal to or larger than that of the sun
Ⓑ Sufficient pressure to maintain liquid water on the surface of the planet
Ⓒ Terrestrial composition of solid materials
Ⓓ A warm and constant temperature similar to that of Earth

강의에 따르면, 행성의 주거 가능성을 위한 두 가지 조건은 무엇인가?
2개의 답을 고르시오.

Ⓐ 태양과 질량이 같거나 그보다 큰 호스트 항성
Ⓑ 행성의 표면에 있는 액체 상태의 물을 유지할 수 있는 충분한 압력
Ⓒ 단단한 물질로 이루어진 지구형 구성
Ⓓ 지구와 유사한 따뜻하고 변함없는 온도

08 Organization

Why does the professor mention the mass and radius of Gliese 581d?

ⓐ To emphasize that a planet with high density is capable of maintaining its atmosphere
ⓑ To explain that a massive planet has more surface area to carry living organisms
ⓒ To illustrate a big planet has a wide orbit and keeps its distance from the host star
ⓓ To emphasize a planet with intense gravity is likely to contain water in a solid form

교수는 왜 Gliese 581d의 질량과 반지름을 언급했나?

ⓐ 밀도가 높은 행성은 대기를 유지할 수 있다는 점을 강조하기 위해
ⓑ 거대한 행성은 생명체가 살 표면 공간을 더 많이 가지고 있다는 점을 설명하기 위해
ⓒ 큰 행성은 넓은 궤도를 가지고 있어 호스트 항성과의 거리를 유지한다는 점을 설명하기 위해
ⓓ 중력이 강한 행성은 물을 고체 상태로 지니고 있을 가능성이 있다는 점을 강조하기 위해

09 Detail

In the lecture, the professor describes the characteristics of Gliese 581d. Indicate whether each of the following is the characteristic.

Put a check(✓) in the correct boxes.

	Yes	No
It yields results that do not comply with the initial assumption.	✓	
It has enough natural force that attracts matter to itself.	✓	
It is unlikely to contain water according to computer simulations.		✓
It is in a short orbital radius around the host star.		✓
It is difficult to observe the planet using current technology.		✓

강의에서, 교수는 Gliese 581d의 특징을 설명했다. 다음이 그 특징인지 표시하시오.

맞는 칸에 체크 표 하시오.

	예	아니오
초기 가설과는 일치하지 않는 결과를 가져왔다.	✓	
물질을 잡아당기는 충분한 힘을 가지고 있다.	✓	
컴퓨터 시뮬레이션에 따르면 물이 존재할 것 같지 않다.		✓
호스트 항성을 도는 궤도가 짧다.		✓
현재 기술을 이용해서는 이 행성을 관찰하기 어렵다.		✓

10 Inference

What can be inferred about the length of the orbit?

Ⓐ It is directly proportional to the mass of a planet.
Ⓑ It is directly proportional to the temperature of a planet.
Ⓒ It is inversely proportional to the mass of a planet.
Ⓓ **It is inversely proportional to the temperature of a planet.**

궤도의 길이에 관해 추론할 수 있는 것은 무엇인가?

Ⓐ 그것은 행성의 질량에 비례한다.
Ⓑ 그것은 행성의 온도에 비례한다.
Ⓒ 그것은 행성의 질량에 반비례한다.
Ⓓ **그것은 행성의 온도에 반비례한다.**

정답 해설 Ⓓ 행성의 궤도가 짧다는 것은 행성과 호스트 항성과의 거리가 가깝다는 것을 의미하고 이 때문에 표면 온도가 높다고 말했으므로, 궤도의 길이와 온도는 반비례 관계임을 알 수 있다.

11 Inference

What can be inferred about technology regarding astronomy?

Ⓐ Advanced technology increases the likelihood of the existence of extraterrestrial life.
Ⓑ **Advanced technology aids scientists with their research.**
Ⓒ Astronomy is flawed because of technological limitations.
Ⓓ Astronomers should study planets by using technology rather than just make conjectures.

천문학에 관련된 기술에 관해 추론할 수 있는 것은 무엇인가?

Ⓐ 발전된 기술은 외계 생명체의 존재 가능성을 높인다.
Ⓑ **발전된 기술은 과학자들의 연구에 큰 도움이 된다.**
Ⓒ 천문학은 기술적 한계로 인해 결함이 있다.
Ⓓ 천문학자들은 그저 추측을 하는 것 대신에 기술을 사용해서 행성을 연구해야 한다.

TEST 1 Set 2 Lecture 2

Listen to part of a lecture in a psychology class.

강의 주제: 의사 결정에 영향을 주는 요소

P People make thousands of decisions every day. These decisions range widely, from easy to difficult. From the moment we wake up, we have to choose what to eat, what to wear, what to ride to school and so on. These decisions are not only applied to our daily lives, but also to political and economic spheres, such as when you decide to vote for a certain political party wherein you carefully examine the candidates' qualifications and public pledges to reach an ideal decision. This is obvious, right? This process includes identifying and choosing alternatives based on the values and preferences of the decision-maker. So, a major part of decision-making involves the analysis of a finite set of alternatives described based on criteria. It is also common sense that one should go through more complex thinking processes when one does difficult decision-making. It just seems logical that hard decisions deserve careful consideration. This was evident to most people, and no one has ever questioned it. You all have heard of the old saying, "You should sleep on it when making a big decision." 12 But, some people wondered whether sleeping can actually help one to make a better decision. Interesting, right? Well, we will be talking about an experiment in order to solve this question.

의사 결정의 두 가지 유형

Before we go on, I would first like to mention the two main types of decisions people make in daily lives. There are simple decisions that have only a few variables to consider. Let's say you could choose a toothbrush at a supermarket. All you consider is the cost, and sometimes the brand. As you see, there are not many things that you take into account. 13 The other type is a complex decision. This might be a bit different. This decision is complicated because there are so many variables to consider. When you should decide which company you would apply for, you have to consider numerous things such as a location, a salary, the reputation of the company, and the

심리학 강의 중 일부를 들어 보시오.

P 사람들은 매일 수천 개의 결정을 합니다. 이러한 결정은 쉬운 것부터 어려운 것까지 다양하죠. 우리가 일어나는 순간부터 우리는 무엇을 먹을지, 무엇을 입을지, 무엇을 타고 학교에 갈지 등을 결정해야 해요. 이런 결정은 단순히 우리의 일상생활뿐만 아니라, 정치나 경제 상황에도 적용되는데, 이상적인 결정에 도달하기 위해 후보자의 자격이나 공약을 주의 깊게 분석해 어떤 정당에 투표할지를 결정할 때와 같은 때에도 생깁니다. 이것은 당연한 일이에요. 그렇죠? 의사 결정자의 가치 기준이나 선호도에 근거해 대안을 모색하고 선택하는 것이 이 과정에 포함됩니다. 따라서 의사 결정의 핵심은 평가 기준에 근거하여 만들어진 한정된 대안을 분석하는 일이 수반됩니다. 또한 사람이 어려운 의사 결정을 할 때 더 복잡한 사고 과정을 거치는 것은 상식이죠. 어려운 결정에는 심사숙고가 필요하다는 것은 당연한 논리처럼 보입니다. 이것은 대부분의 사람들에게 분명했고, 누구도 이것에 대해 의문을 품지 않았어요. 여러분 모두 '큰 결정을 할 때는, 하룻밤 자며 신중히 생각해야 한다.'는 속담을 들어 봤을 거예요. 12 하지만 몇몇 사람들은 잠을 자는 것이 더 나은 결정을 하는 데 실제로 도움이 될지 궁금해 했어요. 재미있어요, 그렇죠? 음, 우리는 이 문제를 해결하기 위해 한 실험에 대해 이야기할 거예요.

그 전에, 먼저 일상생활에서 사람들이 하는 두 가지의 주요한 결정에 대해 이야기할 거예요. 몇 가지 변수만 고려하면 되는 간단한 결정이 있죠. 예를 들어, 여러분이 슈퍼마켓에서 칫솔 하나를 고른다고 합시다. 여러분이 고려할 것은 가격뿐일 것이고 가끔 상표 정도겠네요. 보다시피 여러분이 고려해야 할 사항이 많지 않아요. 13 다른 유형은 복잡한 결정입니다. 이것은 약간 달라요. 이러한 결정은 고려할 변수가 너무 많아 복잡합니다. 여러분이 어떤 회사에 지원할 것인지 결정해야 할 때, 여러분은 위치, 급여, 회사의 평판, 그리고 회사의 분위기 등 수많은 것들을 고려해야 하죠. 여러분은 또한 여러분이 좋은 회사에 지원할 능력이 있는지 혹은 들어간 후에 승진을 할 수 있을지도 고려해야 합니

atmosphere of the company. You also have to consider whether you actually have the ability to apply for a good company or get promoted after you get hired. So, a complex decision presents many questions to answer although each of these questions may differ in its level of importance. Most of the time, we continuously engage in simple decisions, but sometimes, we have to rack our brains over a complex decision that is more consequential than several of the simple decisions added together. Then, how do we solve this complexity?

의사 결정 요인에 관련된 실험

Now that we have considered the two types of decisions, we can go over the experiment to analyze the decision-making processes. In this experiment, test subjects answered a simple question: choosing the best house out of eight houses. All they had to consider were four factors, such as location and price. The test subjects were divided into two groups and given four minutes to complete a task. But the difference is that one group was asked to select a house while watching a movie and another group was asked to select a house without being given any distractions. 14 The purpose was to inhibit the ability of half of the group to consciously think about the question by concentrating on watching the movie. The same task was given during the following experiment, but this group of people was told to consider twenty variables instead of four. In addition to the previous four factors, the group was given a longer list of variables to consider. Just like the previous experiment, half of the test subjects were asked to concentrate on the task, and the other half was asked to work on the task while watching a movie.

실험의 결과와 심리학자들의 결론

How do you think the experiment proceeded? What would you guess? The result was that people who were consciously thinking about the question were better at answering the simple question as you might expect. With only four variables, they didn't have a hard time figuring out which house was the smart choice, which means the group with no distractions, such as movies, was able to choose the best house by effectively analyzing the four variables. I mean

Tip 실험이 언급되면, 실험의 목적과 결과를 묻는 문제가 출제될 수 있으니 주의하며 듣는다.

this was not surprising, right? ¹⁵ However, umm, I know it sounds far-fetched but when it came to complex decisions, those who were watching a movie and thus unconsciously thinking over a problem made better decisions. ¹⁶ The researchers thought that the unconscious mind was actually a better fit to consider numerous variables and make better choices. When a person is faced with an enormous number of variables, an unconscious mind that is not overly aware of all the variables can actually result in a good decision. ¹⁶ On the other hand, the conscious mind puts unnecessary emphasis on unimportant variables when confronted by too many of them. So, this may distract people's ability to make the best decision for the best result. The researchers later concluded that this experiment should only be applied when making complex decisions.

¹⁵ 하지만, 음, 알아요. 말이 안 되게 들리기는 하겠지만 복잡한 결정에 관해서는, 영화를 보느라 그 문제에 대해 무의식적으로 생각한 사람들이 결정을 하는 데 더 나았어요. ¹⁶ 연구원들은 무의식이 많은 변수를 고려하고 더 나은 결정을 하는 데 더 알맞다고 생각했습니다. 사람이 막대한 변수에 직면하면, 모든 변수들에 대해 필요 이상으로 잘 알지 못하는 무의식이 실제로는 좋은 결정을 이끌어낼 수 있어요. ¹⁶ 반면에, 의식은 너무 많은 변수에 직면할 때 별로 중요치 않은 변수들을 강조하죠. 그래서 이것은 아마 최선의 결과를 위한 최고의 결정을 하는 사람들의 능력을 방해했을 거예요. 나중에 연구원들은 이 실험은 복잡한 결정을 내릴 때만 적용될 수 있다고 결론지었습니다.

실험 결과에 대한 교수의 의견

Tip 실험 결과에 대한 개인적인 의견이 언급되면, 태도를 추론하는 문제가 출제될 수 있으니 주의하며 듣는다.

They said that people should allow their unconscious minds to make only complex decisions with many variables. It seemed that people faced with a lot of variables were unable to focus their minds on important aspects, thus losing their ability to prioritize. ¹⁷ This is just my opinion, but I don't completely agree with their opinion. Think about it. I would hate it if my employer were to make recruitment decisions while watching movies.

그들은 사람들이 많은 변수가 있는 복잡한 결정을 내릴 때만 무의식을 사용해야 한다고 말했어요. 수많은 변수에 직면한 사람들은 중요한 부분에 집중할 수 없기 때문에, 우선순위를 결정하는 능력을 잃었을 수도 있습니다. ¹⁷ 이것은 단지 저의 의견입니다만, 저는 그들의 의견에 완전히 동의하지는 않아요. 생각해 보세요. 만약 제 고용주가 영화를 보면서 직원들을 선택한다면 저는 매우 싫을 것 같거든요.

[Vocabulary] political party 정당　　wherein [hwɛərín] 어떤 점에　　public pledge 공약　　finite [fáinait] 한정된, 유한한　　criterion [kraitíəriən] 기준 (pl. criteria)　　variable [vέəriəbl] 변수; 가변적인　　take into account 고려하다　　rack one's brain 깊이 생각하다　　consequential [kànsəkwénʃəl] 중대한　　subject [sʌ́bdʒikt] 실험 대상　　far-fetched 믿기지 않는, 설득력이 없는

12 Main Topic

What is the lecture mainly about?

(A) An experiment that deals with two types of decision-making
(B) Variables that people should consider in different decision-making situations
(C) A tendency that people show when making a difficult decision
(D) Comparison between an easy decision and a difficult decision

강의는 주로 무엇에 관한 것인가?

(A) 두 가지의 의사 결정 유형을 다룬 실험
(B) 다른 의사 결정 상황에서 사람들이 고려해야 할 변수
(C) 사람들이 어려운 결정을 할 때 보이는 경향
(D) 쉬운 결정과 어려운 결정의 비교

13 Organization

Why does the professor mention deciding which company to apply for?

(A) To criticize numbers of people who make decisions with their unconscious minds
(B) To provide an example of an important decision with a few variables
(C) To explain the way to achieve a better decision
(D) To illustrate complex variables involved in decision-making

교수는 왜 어떤 회사에 지원할지를 결정하는 것에 대해 언급했나?

(A) 무의식으로 의사 결정을 하는 많은 사람들을 비판하기 위해
(B) 변수가 많지 않은 중요한 결정의 예시를 제공하기 위해
(C) 더 나은 결정을 해내기 위한 방법을 설명하기 위해
(D) 의사 결정에 수반되는 복잡한 변수들을 묘사하기 위해

오답 해설   (D) 지원할 회사를 결정하는 문제와 관련된 복잡한 변수들을 나열하기 위해서가 아니라, 복잡한 변수가 있는 문제에 대한 의사 결정 과정을 설명하기 위해 그 예를 들었다.

14 Detail

Why did the researchers make half of the group watch a movie in the decision-making experiment?

(A) To pose constraints on making decisions consciously
(B) To improve their ability to make the right decisions
(C) To allow them to concentrate on their decision making
(D) To prove that watching a movie helps the decision-making process

의사 결정 실험에서 연구자들은 왜 절반의 그룹이 영화를 보게 했나?

(A) 의식적으로 결정을 하는 것에 제약을 가하기 위해
(B) 올바른 결정을 하는 그들의 능력을 향상시키기 위해
(C) 그들이 의사 결정을 하는 것에 집중하도록 하기 위해
(D) 영화를 보는 것이 의사 결정 과정을 돕는다는 것을 입증하기 위해

15 Inference

Listen again to part of the lecture. Then answer the question.

> P: However, umm, I know it sounds far-fetched but when it came to complex decisions, those who were watching a movie and thus unconsciously thinking over a problem made better decisions.

Why does the professor say this:
P: However, umm, I know it sounds far-fetched...

Ⓐ To indicate disagreement with the outcome of the experiment
Ⓑ To indicate that the result might be unexpected
Ⓒ To express uncertainty about the outcome
Ⓓ To remind the students of the result

강의의 일부를 다시 들으시오. 그러고 나서 질문에 답하시오.

> P: 하지만, 음, 알아요. 말도 안 되게 들리기는 하겠지만 복잡한 결정에 관해서는, 영화를 보느라 그 문제에 대해 무의식적으로 생각한 사람들이 결정을 하는 데 더 나았어요.

교수는 왜 이 말을 했나?
P: 하지만, 음, 알아요. 말도 안 되게 들리기는 하겠지만……

Ⓐ 실험 결과에 반대하기 위해
Ⓑ 그 결과가 예상치 못한 것일 수도 있다고 알려주기 위해
Ⓒ 결과에 대한 불확실성을 표현하기 위해
Ⓓ 학생들에게 결과를 상기시키기 위해

16 Detail

What are two characteristics of conscious and unconscious minds?
Choose 2 answers.

Ⓐ The unconscious mind is more efficient at sorting many variables.
Ⓑ The conscious mind puts more emphasis on unimportant factors.
Ⓒ People find it convenient to make decisions with their unconscious minds.
Ⓓ The conscious mind has an uncomplicated processing system.

의식과 무의식의 두 가지 특징은 무엇인가?
2개의 답을 고르시오.

Ⓐ 무의식은 많은 변수를 정리하는 데 더 효과적이다.
Ⓑ 의식은 중요하지 않은 요소들을 더 강조한다.
Ⓒ 사람들은 무의식적으로 결정을 하는 것이 편리하다고 생각한다.
Ⓓ 의식은 단순한 처리 시스템을 가지고 있다.

17 Inference

Which of the following describes the professor's attitude toward the conclusion of the study?

Ⓐ He thinks that the result of the study can be interpreted differently.
Ⓑ He shows an inclination to choose a conscious mind over an unconscious mind.
Ⓒ He criticizes that employers are fond of particular business tactics.
Ⓓ He doesn't think that the result of the experiment is applicable to all situations.

다음 중 연구 결과에 대한 교수의 태도를 묘사하는 것은 무엇인가?

Ⓐ 연구 결과가 다르게 해석될 수 있다고 생각한다.
Ⓑ 무의식보다 의식을 선호하는 경향을 보인다.
Ⓒ 고용주들이 특정 경영 전략을 좋아한다고 비난한다.
Ⓓ 실험 결과가 모든 상황에 적용할 수 있다고 생각하지 않는다.

영단기 TOEFL

ACTUAL TEST

TEST 02

TEST 2 Set 1 Conversation

Listen to a conversation between a student and a professor.

과제로 지정된 글이 도서관에 없음

S May I come in, Professor Simpson?
P Sure, Kathy! Do you need any help?
S I just visited a library to read the article on *Francis Bacon, our assignment.
P Yes, the article is very important to understand the history of western philosophy. As you know, Bacon laid out the foundation of modern scientific inquiry and this article gives you an idea of how he took up Aristotelian ideas, arguing for an empirical, inductive approach in the scientific field.
S 02 Well, the library system showed that there were actually a couple of books, but they have been checked out, so I couldn't get them.
P I would advise you to check regularly with the library desk. I'm sure that people have been checking out the copies. However, I strongly suggest you to read it because the article is important, you know.

과제로 지정된 글이 중요한 이유

S Is that so? Do you mind if I ask you why it is so essential?
P Most importantly, the article deals with Bacon's life in the early 1600's, a crucial point in Bacon's life. 03 It was the time when Bacon pursued his works in natural philosophy. He rejected the traditional scientific method being practiced in England, but arguing that scientific knowledge could be gained through empirical methods and the careful observation of events in nature.
S I remember from your class that science in the past mostly followed *Aristotle's ways of logic, and uh, also, that the truth would be derived from authority.
P You are right. Aristotle employed deductive logic. You are familiar with the process of reasoning based on one or more statements made in order to reach a logically certain conclusion. This philosophical movement was really influential, but Bacon adopted inductive reasoning, which was exactly the opposite approach. So, his life had to endure various challenges. 03 I mean another great thing about the

학생과 교수의 대화를 들어 보시오.

S 들어가도 될까요, Simpson 교수님?
P 물론이지, Kathy! 도움이 필요하니?
S 저는 방금 저희 과제인 프랜시스 베이컨에 관한 글을 읽기 위해 도서관에 다녀왔어요.
P 그래. 그 글은 서양 철학사를 이해하는 데 매우 중요하단다. 너도 알다시피, 베이컨은 현대 과학 연구의 기초를 닦았고, 이 글은 그가 과학 분야에서 경험적이고 귀납적인 접근을 주장하면서, 아리스토텔레스의 생각을 어떻게 받아들였는지에 대해 생각하게 해 줄 거야.
S 02 음, 도서관 시스템에는 책 두 세권이 있다고 나오는데, 책들이 대출되어서 구할 수 없었어요.
P 도서관 데스크를 정기적으로 확인하라고 조언하고 싶구나. 사람들이 책을 빌렸겠지. 그렇지만 너도 알다시피, 그 글이 매우 중요하기 때문에 나는 네가 그 글을 꼭 읽어야 한다고 권해주고 싶구나.
S 그런가요? 왜 그게 그렇게 중요한지 여쭤봐도 될까요?
P 가장 중요한 건, 그 글이 1600년대 초기의 베이컨의 삶을 다루는데, 그것은 베이컨의 삶에서 중요한 부분이란다. 03 그때는 베이컨이 자연 철학에서 그의 작업을 추구하던 때였단다. 그는 영국에서 적용되던 전통적인 과학적 방법을 거부했지만, 과학적 지식은 경험적인 방법과 자연 현상을 관찰하는 것을 통해 얻어질 수 있다고 주장했어요.
S 교수님 수업에서, 과거의 과학은 대부분 아리스토텔레스의 논리 방식을 그대로 답습했다는 것과, 어, 진리의 근원을 권위에서 끌어내려고 했다는 것이 기억이 나요.
P 맞아. 아리스토텔레스는 연역법을 사용했지. 너는 논리적으로 어떤 결론에 도달하기 위해, 한 개 이상의 진술에 기초한 논리 과정에 익숙할 거야. 이 철학적인 움직임은 굉장히 영향력이 있었지만, 베이컨은 정확히 정반대적 접근인 귀납법을 사용했지. 그래서 그의 인생은 다양한 도전을 버텨야 했단다. 03 그의 또 다른 좋은 점 한 가지는 과학에서뿐만 아니라 정치에 있어서도 그가 견뎌야 했던 다양한 비난들과 더불어 베이컨의 마음가짐에 대해서도 다룬다는 것이지.

article is that it discusses Bacon's mindset, including various adversities he had to endure not only in science but in politics, too.

S Well, I thought I should let you know about this missing article because I've heard that you are planning a quiz on Friday?

P 04 That's right, but I wouldn't worry about the quiz. You will be able to access the electronic version of the article via the Internet. The library always kept an online version of the article.

S Yes! I just remembered! I never thought about that!

P It's actually mentioned in the syllabus. Also, yesterday, I told everyone in class about the electronic version of the article. You should also know that Bacon devised a new approach to science by employing inductive reasoning which is still used widely today.

S Right, you told us about the scientific method in class.

P 05 Yeah, I did! Isn't it hard to imagine that the scientific method was rarely used for preserving data, acknowledging patterns, and drawing conclusions from observations in the past?

S Well, come to think about it, I have a lot of reading ahead of me to prepare for that quiz on Friday.

P Oh, you are right! I should let you get started on it!

S Oh actually, what I was trying to say was…I consider reading about Bacon to be crucial in preparing for the upcoming quiz. Unfortunately, as I said, it's difficult to get the article. Even though I could utilize the electronic version you recommended, I still think more time should be given for the task.

P So, what are you trying to say? 01 You want me to give out the quiz on another day, right?

S Honestly speaking, I actually came over to ask you about that. Also, the extended period for preparing the quiz would be really helpful to others who will not be able to get the article.

P I get your point, but I think I've made enough effort to make sure you guys get that article. I understand the books and copies in the library are all checked out, yet there's still enough time for you guys to read it by Friday. And it really isn't fair for those who have been reading.

S Okay.

[**Vocabulary**] lay out (주장을) 제시하다   inquiry [inkwáiəri] 연구, 탐구   empirical [empírikəl] 실증적인   inductive [indʌ́ktiv] 귀납적인   deductive [didʌ́ktiv] 연역적인   reasoning [ríːzəniŋ] 추론   mindset [máindset] 사고방식   via [váiə] 경유해서, 매개해서   syllabus [síləbəs] 교수요목   devise [diváiz] 고안하다

[각주]

* **Francis Bacon(1561 ~ 1626)** 영국의 철학자이자 정치인이다. '아는 것이 힘이다'라는 말을 남긴 것으로 유명하다. 그는 경험과 관찰을 중요하게 생각했기 때문에 귀납법을 중요시 여기고 고대의 유물론을 주장하기도 했다. 그는 일반 원리를 제시하는 스콜라 철학자나 연역 추론을 주장하는 아리스토텔레스를 비판하고, 더 나아가 관계 없는 사실만 늘어놓고 의미 있는 결론에는 도달하지 못하는 경험 철학을 비판했다. 베이컨은 그 당시의 학문은 권위에 지나치게 얽매여 자만과 논리적 오류에 빠져 있다고 생각하고, 이런 과거와의 단절이 중요하다고 생각했다.
* **Aristotle(B.C. 384 ~ B.C. 322)** 고대 그리스의 철학자이다. 소크라테스와 플라톤을 잇는 그리스 정치 철학 고전기의 마지막 인물이다. 체계적이고 방대한 양의 연구로 '실전 철학'이라는 고유한 개념을 완성했다. 그의 스승인 플라톤이 철인왕이 통치하는 이상적인 정치 체제를 주장했다면, 아리스토텔레스는 현실에서 이탈한 철학을 불신했고, 정의는 인간 관계를 초월한 것이 아니라 현실 세계의 다양한 관계에서 비롯된 것이라고 믿었다.

01 Main Topic

Why does the student go to see the professor?

Ⓐ To ask if the date of the quiz can be moved back
Ⓑ To complain that there are no articles on Francis Bacon in the library
Ⓒ To request for extra articles on Francis Bacon
Ⓓ To ask questions about Francis Bacon and his scientific methods

학생은 왜 교수를 찾아갔나?

Ⓐ 퀴즈 날짜가 뒤로 미뤄질 수 있는지 묻기 위해
Ⓑ 도서관에 프랜시스 베이컨에 관한 글이 없다는 것을 불평하기 위해
Ⓒ 프랜시스 베이컨에 관한 글을 요청하기 위해
Ⓓ 프랜시스 베이컨과 그의 과학적 방법에 관해 질문을 하기 위해

02 Detail

What is the student's problem?

Ⓐ The student thinks the article is difficult to understand.
Ⓑ The student cannot get the material that the professor assigned to read.
Ⓒ The student cannot understand why the article is so important.
Ⓓ The student does not know about the electronic version of the article.

학생의 문제는 무엇인가?

Ⓐ 그 글이 이해하기 어렵다고 생각한다.
Ⓑ 교수가 읽으라 지정한 자료를 얻지 못했다.
Ⓒ 그 글이 왜 그렇게 중요한지 이해하지 못하고 있다.
Ⓓ 그 글의 전자 버전이 있다는 사실을 모른다.

03 Detail

What does the professor say about Francis Bacon?
Choose 2 answers.

Ⓐ He built the foundation of western philosophy.
Ⓑ He did not choose the traditional approach to science.
Ⓒ His approach was very similar to Aristotle's.
Ⓓ He had to undergo various scientific and political adversities.
Ⓔ His deductive reasoning is adequate for preserving data and acknowledging patterns.

교수가 프랜시스 베이컨에 대해 말한 것은 무엇인가?
2개의 답을 고르시오.

Ⓐ 그는 서양 철학의 기초를 세웠다.
Ⓑ 과학에 대한 전통적인 접근법을 선택하지 않았다.
Ⓒ 그의 접근법은 아리스토텔레스의 것과 매우 유사했다.
Ⓓ 그는 다양한 과학적이고 정치적인 비난들을 겪어야 했다.
Ⓔ 그의 연역 추론은 데이터를 보존하고 특정한 행동 양식을 이해하는 데 적합했다.

04 Organization

Why does the professor mention the electronic version of the article on Francis Bacon?

Ⓐ To let her know that preparing the quiz requires a lot of time
Ⓑ To emphasize the convenience of reading the article in its electronic version
Ⓒ To suggest another way to prepare the student's upcoming task
Ⓓ To explain to her how to access the article online

교수는 왜 프랜시스 베이컨에 관한 글의 전자 버전을 언급했나?

Ⓐ 퀴즈를 준비하는 데 많은 시간이 요구된다는 것을 알려 주기 위해
Ⓑ 전자 버전으로 된 글을 읽는 것의 편리성을 강조하기 위해
Ⓒ 학생의 다가오는 과제를 준비할 수 있는 다른 방법을 제안하기 위해
Ⓓ 그 글을 온라인으로 찾을 수 있는 방법을 설명하기 위해

05 Inference

Listen again to part of the conversation. Then answer the question.

> P: Yeah, I did! Isn't it hard to imagine that the scientific method was rarely used for preserving data, acknowledging patterns, and drawing conclusions from observations in the past?
> S: Well, come to think about it, I have a lot of reading ahead of me to prepare for that quiz on Friday.

What does the student imply when she says this:
S: ...I have a lot of reading ahead of me to prepare for that quiz on Friday.

Ⓐ She does not want to waste her time talking with the professor.
Ⓑ She feels the quiz will be very hard with all the information from the reading.
Ⓒ She thinks she needs to start reading the article as soon as possible.
Ⓓ She tries to get some extra time to finish the reading for the quiz.

대화의 일부를 다시 들으시오. 그리고 나서 질문에 답하시오.

> P: 그래, 내가 그랬었지! 과거에는 데이터를 보존하고, 특정한 행동 양식을 인지하고, 그리고 관찰을 통해 결론을 이끌어 내는 데 과학적 방법이 거의 사용되지 않았다는 게 상상이 가니?
> S: 음, 생각해 보니, 저는 금요일에 있을 그 퀴즈를 준비하려면 읽어야 할 책이 많네요.

학생이 이 말을 할 때 암시한 것은 무엇인가?
S: ……저는 금요일에 있을 그 퀴즈를 준비하려면 읽어야 할 책이 많네요.

Ⓐ 교수와 이야기하면서 그녀의 시간을 낭비하고 싶지 않다.
Ⓑ 읽기 자료의 모든 정보를 포함하면 퀴즈가 어려울 것이라고 느낀다.
Ⓒ 최대한 빨리 사설을 읽기 시작해야 한다고 생각한다.
Ⓓ 퀴즈에 나오는 읽기 자료를 끝내기 위해 추가 시간을 요청하려 한다.

정답 해설 Ⓓ 학생은 퀴즈를 준비하는 데 어려움이 있으니 퀴즈를 미뤄 달라는 말을 하기 위해 교수를 찾아왔고, 대화 후반부에 이를 직접적으로 언급하기 전까지 지속적으로 퀴즈를 준비하는 데 시간이 부족함을 호소하고 있다.

TEST 2 Set 1 Lecture 1

Listen to part of a lecture in a U.S. history class.

P So, uh, a couple of centuries ago in 1783, to be specific, there was an urgent need to discuss the location of the capital city. Back then, eight cities served as the meeting places for the U.S. Congress and were, therefore, considered to be a capital city of the U.S. But during the early 1780s, the heart of the country was Philadelphia. It was considered to be the economic and financial center, the fashion and art district, and surprisingly, it turned out to be the geographical center of the country as well! With this being said, it was only logical to make Philadelphia the capital city, established in 1790. However, its designation as the capital didn't last for long. Umm, I will explain this later in a little while, but there is something I want you to know beforehand. The issue of the location of the capital city had a lot to do with the relations between the North and South. 06 So today I will talk about the situation of the country at that time—regarding how the states related to and interacted with each other and how this led to the establishment of the capital.

07 The 13 states were supposedly controlled by a central government, but this government was weak and had almost no power over them. This was because, uh, each state had its own government. So, the actual governing was done by the state itself. The result of this independent system was very poor cooperation among the states. Since each state had a different set of goals and objectives, they could never reach an agreement on anything. Suppose you are in a state bordering the Atlantic Ocean. Wouldn't you want to use the budget for improving fishing and shipping industries? Of course, you would! You don't even need to think about this one. Similarly, suppose the neighboring state proposes to invest in developing roads instead. How would you react to this proposal? With so many different states that were concerned about their own goals, the country

was unable to form a strong central government.

불평등했던 수도 선정

So, in order to reinforce the power of the central government, it took the initiative to select the capital city for the country. In the beginning, the capital city changed locations every once in a while, to escape from violent protesters asking for money after they fought in the war and as well as from the British government. So, while the capital city changed its location from time to time, the central government ultimately always chose to place it in the North. This decision was quite unfair for the Southern states, but the central government did not change its mind.

United States Funding Act of 1790

To make matters worse, in the middle of all this, the Northern states agreed to submit the Assumption Bill. After this bill was successfully legislated, the United States Funding Act of 1790 was enacted. Let me briefly explain what the Act is. 08 It was basically an Act making provision for the payment of the debt of the United States. With the establishment of the new government in 1789, the settlement of the Revolutionary War debt was a matter of prime importance. The Act proposed that the debts of the American Revolutionary War became a national issue. 10 This means that all the states must pay the debt equally. The thing was, with the Southerners' massive wealth, the Southern states had almost finished paying off their debts from the war. 9 If the bill had passed, then they would have had to pay their remaining debts as well as the obligations of the Northern states! Can you picture yourself as a Southerner reacting to this? Obviously, this Act would have made them furious!

The Compromise of 1790

10 So, in order to mediate disagreements over the issue of the Act, uh… in 1790, a compromise was reached between the North and South, suitably given the name, *The Compromise of 1790. This agreement addressed two major issues: first, it arranged for the capital to be placed in the South, and second, it assured the peaceful relations between the North and South, being able to avoid a major conflict like a civil war. So as to keep both sides pleased, the central government chose Philadelphia as the temporary capital city. At that time, Philadelphia was already the

nation's capital, and it was decided that the capital remained that way until another location was chosen.

수도 설립에 대한 북부와 남부의 입장 차

But in fact, the North believed that the South would never actually push through the plans of making a new location for the capital city, and that is the reason the North agreed to this compromise. Umm, put simply, Philadelphia had already been acting as the capital city for a while, and there were some government facilities that had been carrying out their responsibilities for supporting the country. So, the North thought that it would be unlikely that the central government would move to another location. Because, well... relocation of the capital city costs a lot of money and time. However, the Southern states obviously had a different mindset and didn't just wait for this to happen! [11] They actively bought large tracks of land for the new capital. They bought the land in every manner possible through private purchases using local bids, sometimes even paying for entire cities! I swear, the Southerners were more than eager to bring the capital city to the South, and they did everything they could to make it happen.

그러나 사실, 북부는 남부가 실제로 새로운 수도를 만드는 계획을 해낼 리 없다고 믿었고, 그것이 북부가 이 타협안에 동의한 이유였어요. 음, 간단하게 말하자면, 필라델피아는 이미 한동안 수도로서의 역할을 해 왔고, 몇몇의 정부 기관들이 이미 그곳에서 국가를 지원하는 역할을 하고 있었습니다. 그래서 북부는 중앙 정부가 다른 지역으로 옮겨질 수도 있다고 생각하지 않았어요. 음……수도의 이전은 많은 비용과 시간이 드는 일이니까요. 하지만 남부의 주들은 명백하게 다른 태도를 가지고 있었고 이것이 일어날 때까지 그저 기다리고 있지만은 않았어요! [11] 그들은 적극적으로 새로운 수도를 위한 거대한 땅을 구입했습니다. 그들은 지역 입찰을 이용한 사적인 구매를 통해서까지 가능한 모든 방법으로 땅을 구입했고 심지어 도시 전체를 구입하기도 했어요! 장담하건대, 남부 사람들은 수도를 남부로 가져오는 것을 무척이나 열망했고, 그러기 위해 할 수 있는 모든 것을 했어요.

수도 설립의 결과

So now you know about the events that led to the foundation of the nation's capital. In your books, you can take a look at the image of the Assumption Bill as well as the White House in Washington. The pictures are simply drawn by hand, but nevertheless, it will give you a good idea of the location of the capital city since the late 1700s.

이제 여러분들은 그 국가의 수도 설립을 야기한 사건들을 배웠습니다. 여러분들의 책에서, 워싱턴의 백악관뿐만 아니라 Assumption Bill의 이미지도 볼 수 있어요. 그 그림들은 단순하게 손으로 그려졌지만, 여러분들에게 1700년대 후반 이후 수도의 위치에 대한 좋은 이해를 제공할 거예요.

[Vocabulary] establish[istǽbliʃ] 제정하다, 설립하다　　designation[dèzignéiʃən] 지정　　objective[əbdʒéktiv] 목적, 목표
bordering[bɔ́:rdəriŋ] 경계해 있는　　initiative[iníʃətiv] 계획　　every once in a while 가끔　　protester[proutéstər] 시위자
Act[ækt] (국회를 통과한) 법률　　enact[inǽkt] 제정하다　　make provision for ~을 준비하다　　assure[əʃúər] 장담하다
relocation[rì:loukéiʃən] 이주　　bid[bid] 입찰

[각주]
* **The Compromise of 1790** 미국의 국가적인 분열을 극복하기 위한 법안으로 새로운 중앙 정부는 도시의 산업 발달 및 서부 평야 지대의 농업 확장 등을 통해 분열된 미국을 하나로 모으려 했다.

06 Main Topic

What is the lecture mainly about?

(A) A procedure of the establishment of the capital city in the United States
(B) The importance of Philadelphia as the capital city of the United States
(C) The reasons that the North was considered as a better place for the capital city than the South
(D) The relationship between the North and South in the United States

강의는 주로 무엇에 관한 것인가?

(A) 미국의 수도 설립의 절차
(B) 미국 수도로서 필라델피아의 중요성
(C) 북부가 남부보다 수도로 더 적합하다고 여겨진 이유
(D) 미국에서 남부와 북부의 관계

07 Detail

Why was the central government so weak?

(A) Because it lacked funds to gain the support of each state
(B) Because the British government opposed to its establishment
(C) Because each state was controlled by different entities
(D) Because the American Revolutionary War divided the country into the North and South

중앙 정부는 왜 그렇게 힘이 없었나?

(A) 각 주의 지지를 얻기 위한 자금이 부족했기 때문에
(B) 영국 정부가 중앙 정부의 설립을 반대했기 때문에
(C) 각 주들이 다른 독립체에 의해 통제되었기 때문에
(D) 미국 독립 전쟁이 나라를 북부와 남부로 나눴기 때문에

08 Detail

What did the United States Funding Act of 1790 aim to do?

(A) To treat the issue of outstanding payment as a national concern
(B) To pacify the frustration of the Southern states
(C) To unite various states into one strong nation
(D) To stimulate the national economy

United States Funding Act of 1790의 목적은 무엇인가?

(A) 부채를 국가적인 문제로 처리하는 것
(B) 남부 주들의 불만을 진정시키는 것
(C) 여러 주들을 하나의 강한 나라로 통합하는 것
(D) 국가 경제를 촉진하는 것

09 Inference

Listen again to part of the lecture. Then answer the question.

> P: If the bill had passed, then they would have had to pay their remaining debts as well as the obligations of the Northern states! Can you picture yourself as a Southerner reacting to this? Obviously, this Act would have made them furious!

What does the professor mean when she says this:
P: Obviously, this Act would have made them furious!

A She thinks the students have frequently heard about the Southerners' situation.
B She wants to find out whether the students would like her to review the Southerners' reaction.
C She thinks the students can likely deduce the Southerners' response.
D She wants the students to explain what they know about the Southerners.

10 Detail

Why was The Compromise of 1790 deemed necessary?

A Because the South was more populous and economically wealthy than the North
B Because the South had gained a foothold during the Revolutionary War
C Because the South was at a disadvantage regarding the payment of the national debt
D Because the South wanted to purchase actively large tracks of land for the new capital

11 Detail

According to the professor, how was the capital relocated from Philadelphia?

A The North and South chose a location where both sides were satisfied.
B The central government supported the South with funds and legislations.
C The South made other provisions for the new capital city.
D The North relinquished Philadelphia as the capital city in consideration of the situation of the South.

TEST 2   Set 1 Lecture 2

Listen to part of a lecture in a psychology class.

P   Okay, let's start with today's lesson, shall we? If you did your assignment, you should remember that the section on human personality is related to the emerging field of personality neuroscience as well as NIRS. Oh, NIRS—that's short for near infrared spectroscopy. [12] So today, I'm going to discuss how NIRS can be used to study personality. What NIRS does is to show us images of the brain while it receives information or stimuli. If our brains are exposed to some stimulus, hemoglobin starts to concentrate in a certain area of the brain. Near Infrared Spectroscopy or NIRS can track this change and visualize this concentration.

You may be reminded of an infrared camera or a thermographic camera, originally developed for military use during the war. NIRS and an infrared camera are similar in that both devices form an image using infrared radiation. Unlike an infrared camera, NIRS is used primarily for research. The difference between the two is that an infrared camera provides an internal view of the brain and its structure while NIRS actually gives us a glimpse of what the brain is doing. [13] More specifically, NIRS shows how the brain is reacting as it confronts a particular situation. NIRS allows researchers to more deeply examine the workings of the brain by observing its responses to stimuli, which makes it a better choice for research than infrared cameras.

Now, let's talk about the technology used in NIRS. It observes neuronal activity, which is linked to changes in localized cerebral blood flow. It utilizes infrared radiation to measure activity in distinct parts of the brain by measuring changes in blood flow and oxygen concentrations. [14] Once the observations are made, computers come into play. Information obtained from advanced computerized processing allows researchers to create a detailed map of the brain. Researchers then eventually develop a blueprint of the parts by recording the reactions to stimuli associated with each area.

NIRS가 이용되는 심리학의 분야

NIRS is a valuable tool for psychologists and is expected to lead to answers for some questions about human personalities. By the way, are you aware of what personality is? It is a set of psychological characteristics that stay constant over time. Researchers wanted to determine whether certain types of personalities existed and what they were. By using NIRS, they learned answers to questions such as whether people's personalities are defined by their DNA or whether they could shape their personalities after birth. It could be that NIRS showed connections in the brain areas that control personality.

NIRS를 이용한 실험과 입증

To have an answer to these questions, researchers conducted the study with the help of NIRS. 15 This experiment, concerning a portion of the brain called the frontal lobe, really benefited from the application of NIRS. The frontal lobe, named for its location in the brain, is located at the front of each cerebral hemisphere. This portion regulates the ability to project future consequences and make decisions about what to do. In one study, subjects were shown pictures of several situations and asked to make a decision what course of action would lead to the best result. The researchers then observed the subjects' brains responses. This decision-making process stimulated the frontal lobe of some of the test subjects, whose brain responses showed on NIRS. Researchers noted of the increases in blood flow, as some subjects were careful when making decisions, which caused blood to concentrate in the brain's decision-making hub, the frontal lobe. The subjects who showed high blood flow in their frontal lobe tended to be more careful and conscientious in this situation. On the other hand, the frontal lobe of other subjects reflected no stimulation, which showed that they were prone to be impetuous and impatient when they made decisions. After a year, the researchers repeated the experiment on the same group of people, and surprisingly, the result was the same. From this study, researchers have concluded that the way a person makes a decision which is an aspect of personality, doesn't change over time. That's consistent with the definition of personality I provided a while ago, right? So, it can be assumed that the portion of the brain that controls reactions has something to do with personality.

NIRS의 한계

However, I want to remind you that NIRS studies are not always dependable. A popular misconception resulting from over-reliance on NIRS is the association of personality neuroscience with the surge of blood flow. Our brains are sophisticated at the highest level, so simple images of blood flow cannot explain such neurobiological phenomena like personality entirely. You see, sudden concentration of blood flow doesn't necessarily reflect human personality. Another mistaken idea is that the brain maps from NIRS are complete explanations. Just like geographical maps, they are limited, although undoubtedly useful. For example, a geographical map tells you a lot about the region and helps us find a specific area but nothing about its inhabitants. So, through brain maps, we can see the activated part of the brain, but they don't account for people's behaviors.

NIRS를 보완하는 전통적인 설문 조사 방법

[16]When met with such barriers, scientists try to resolve the problem by utilizing basic research procedures like the questionnaire, gathering test subjects and asking them to fill out questionnaires about their personalities. I guess this is similar to how you might find out details about the inhabitants of a certain region questioning them door to door. As you know from your reading, psychological questionnaires have shortcomings. These research tools don't always reflect accurate information. What I mean is…people are subjective about themselves and easily influenced by extraneous factors including memory and self-image issues. They can't be expected to detach from their ego and evaluate their flaws and virtues objectively. You see, it's true that questionnaires can't be trusted entirely, but they do provide useful and relevant data. Scientists would be very wrong to piece together information from questionnaires as factual statements, but they can gain relatively credible data by outlining the information and forming a big picture. [17]In short, it's true that state of the art technologies such as NIRS have provided solutions to several questions, but traditional research methods shouldn't be discarded yet since they still serve a purpose.

하지만 여러분들에게 NIRS 연구가 항상 믿을 만한 것은 아니라는 것을 다시 한번 알려 주고 싶네요. NIRS에 과도하게 의존한 결과에 따른 일반적인 오해는 성격 신경 과학과 혈류 급증을 연관 짓는 거예요. 우리의 뇌는 고도로 정교하고, 간단한 혈류의 이미지로 성격과 같은 신경 생물학적 현상을 전적으로 설명할 수는 없어요. 즉, 갑작스런 혈류의 집중이 필연적으로 인간의 성격을 반영한다고 할 수는 없다는 것이죠. 또 다른 잘못된 생각은 NIRS로 얻은 뇌 지도가 완벽한 설명이라는 것이에요. 물론 의심의 여지 없이 유용하지만, 지리학적 지도와 마찬가지로 그것들도 한계는 있어요. 예를 들어, 지리학적 지도는 지역에 관해 많은 것을 이야기해 주고 특정 장소를 찾는 데 도움을 주지만, 거주자에 대해서는 아무것도 알려 주지 않아요. 그러니까 뇌 지도를 통해서 우리는 뇌의 활성화된 부분은 볼 수 있지만, 그것들이 사람들의 행동을 설명하는 것은 아니에요.

[16]이런 장벽을 만나게 된 과학자들은 설문지와 같은 기본적인 연구 방법으로 문제를 극복하려 노력했고, 실험 대상자들을 모아 그들에게 그들의 성격에 관한 설문지를 작성할 것을 요구했어요. 이것은 여러분들이 일일이 방문하면서 특정 지역 거주자들의 세부 사항을 조사하는 것과 유사하다고 말할 수 있어요. 여러분이 책을 읽어 알고 있듯이, 심리학적 설문지에는 단점이 있습니다. 이 조사 도구이 항상 정확한 정보를 반영하는 것은 아니에요. 내 말은……사람들은 그들 스스로에 대해 주관적이고 기억이나 자기 이미지 문제 같은 외부적 요소에 쉽게 영향을 받아요. 그들이 자아와 분리되어 그들의 단점이나 장점을 객관적으로 평가하기를 기대하는 건 어렵죠. 그래서 설문지를 완전히 믿을 수는 없지만, 그것들은 유용하고 적절한 정보를 제공하죠. 과학자들이 설문지에서 얻는 정보를 사실에 기반한 진술 같이 끼워 맞추는 것은 잘못일 수 있지만, 그들은 정보를 요약하고 큰 그림을 그려 비교적 믿을 만한 정보를 얻을 수는 있어요. [17]즉 NIRS 같은 최신 기술 덕에 많은 질문에 대한 답을 찾은 것은 사실이지만, 전통적인 연구 방법은 여전히 도움이 되기 때문에 버려져서는 안 됩니다.

[**Vocabulary**] neuroscience[njùərəsáiəns] 신경 과학　spectroscopy[spektráskəpi] 분광학　stimulus[stímjuləs] 자극 (pl. stimuli)　thermographic[θərmágrəfi] 체열의　come into action 실행되다, 참여하다　frontal lobe 전두엽　cerebral hemisphere 대뇌 반구　hub[hʌb] 중추　conscientious[kànʃiénʃəs] 양심적인, 성실한　be prone to~ ~하기 쉽다　impetuous[impétʃuəs] 성급한, 충동적인　misconception[mìskənsépʃən] 오해　neuroscience[njùərosáiəns] 신경 과학　surge[səːrdʒ] 급증; 급증하다　neurobiological[njùəroubàiəlàdʒikəl] 신경 생물학적　phenomenon[finámənàn] 현상 (pl. phenomena)　questionnaire[kwèstʃənɛ́ər] 설문지　extraneous[ikstréiniəs] 관계 없는　detach[ditǽtʃ] 분리되다　factual[fǽktʃuəl] 사실에 기반을 둔　discard[diskáːrd] 버리다

12 Main Topic

What does the professor mainly discuss? | 교수는 주로 무엇에 관해 논의하는가?

Ⓐ The recent developments in infrared radiation imaging
Ⓑ The reasons neurological research is important
Ⓒ The relationship between personal traits and inner areas of the brain
Ⓓ **The equipment used to detect activities that take place in the brain**

Ⓐ 적외선 영상분야의 최근의 진전
Ⓑ 신경학상 연구가 중요한 이유
Ⓒ 성격적 특징과 뇌의 내부의 관계
Ⓓ 뇌에서 일어나는 활동을 감지하는 데 사용되는 장비

13 Detail

What is the function of NIRS in neuroscience research? | 신경 과학 연구에서 NIRS의 기능은 무엇인가?

Ⓐ It shows a three-dimensional view of the brain.
Ⓑ It produces full-color images.
Ⓒ **It provides information about brain responses.**
Ⓓ It accurately reflects internal brain structures.

Ⓐ 뇌의 3차원적 영상을 보여 준다.
Ⓑ 전면 컬러 이미지를 만든다.
Ⓒ 뇌의 반응에 대한 정보를 제공한다.
Ⓓ 뇌의 내부 구조를 정확하게 나타낸다.

14 Detail

Why are computers used together with NIRS? | 컴퓨터는 왜 NIRS와 함께 사용되나?

Ⓐ To solve problems associated with NIRS
Ⓑ **To convert the collected data into a diagram**
Ⓒ To connect to the brain through wires
Ⓓ To quantify brain stimulation

Ⓐ NIRS와 관련된 문제를 해결하기 위해
Ⓑ 수집된 정보를 도표로 바꾸기 위해
Ⓒ 선을 통해 뇌와 연결하기 위해
Ⓓ 뇌 자극을 수치화하기 위해

15 Organization

Why does the professor mention a study involving the frontal lobe?

- (A) To illustrate the reason that NIRS became an effective method in psychology fields
- (B) To suggest that human personality is relatively constant
- (C) To emphasize an instrumental method used in psychology studies
- (D) To explain that the frontal lobe controls emotions

교수는 왜 전두엽과 관련된 연구를 언급했나?

- (A) 심리학 분야에서 NIRS가 효과적인 방법이 된 이유를 설명하기 위해
- (B) 인간의 성격이 상대적으로 변함 없다는 것을 제안하기 위해
- (C) 심리학 연구에서 쓰이는 기기 분석법을 강조하기 위해
- (D) 전두엽이 감정을 통제한다는 것을 설명하기 위해

정답 해설 (C) instrumental method는 NIRS를 가리킨다.
오답 해설 (A) 심리학 분야에서 NIRS가 효과적인 방법이 된 이유는 강의의 앞부분(적외선 카메라와의 비교 부분)에서 언급했다. 교수는 NIRS의 쓰임새 및 활용도를 강조하기 위해 전두엽과 관련된 연구를 언급했다고 보아야 한다.

16 Detail

According to the lecture, what is the similarity between brain maps and geographical maps?

- (A) They explain phenomena that cannot be directly observed.
- (B) They are often complemented by other methods.
- (C) They may be flawed by including outdated information.
- (D) They are utilized to locate a certain spatial region.

강의에 따르면, 뇌 지도와 지리학적 지도의 유사성은 무엇인가?

- (A) 직접적으로 관찰될 수 없는 현상을 설명한다.
- (B) 다른 방법에 의해 종종 보완된다.
- (C) 오래된 정보를 포함해 결함이 있을 수 있다.
- (D) 특정 공간의 위치를 찾기 위해 사용된다.

17 Inference

What can be inferred about NIRS?

- (A) Studies are being conducted to obtain accurate information using NIRS.
- (B) A lot of time is needed before NIRS can yield better results.
- (C) There is a limit to the information provided by NIRS.
- (D) It is too problematic to apply NIRS to the examination of brains.

NIRS에 관해 추론할 수 있는 것은 무엇인가?

- (A) NIRS를 이용해 정확한 정보를 얻기 위해 연구가 진행 중이다.
- (B) NIRS가 더 나은 결과를 내기 위해서는 많은 시간이 필요하다.
- (C) NIRS가 제공하는 정보에 한계가 있다.
- (D) NIRS를 뇌 연구에 적용하는 것은 너무 문제가 많다.

TEST 2 Set 2 Conversation

Listen to part of a conversation between a student and a university staff.

S Hello. I came here to ask some questions about a club I joined. It's about the Smoky Mountain Hiking Club.

US Oh. It's the club for mountain hiking and outdoor activities, right? I've seen it on a school bulletin board.

S Yes. We are a very active social group full of diverse students who enjoy hiking with others. Our club members meet once a month and go hiking.

US Yes, I'm aware of it. Actually, one of my friends is interested in joining the club. It sounds fun to me, too, so where do you hike?

S There are lots of wonderful places around the campus that we can enjoy. Our hikes range from very easy hikes on paved paths along gentle streams and lakes to very strenuous, steep climbs and rock scrambles. This activity can improve our health and give opportunities to make friends while enjoying the benefits of the great outdoors. Actually, I am the one who started the club, and 02 I was surprised that there weren't any clubs like this before.

US That's great. Umm, so where do I fit in?

S 01 Oh, here is the thing. Since we just started last semester, people aren't aware of the existence of the club. So we're planning to set up booths to advertise us. Also, we are designing flyers to give out to students on campus. I mean when the new semester starts, there are a whole bunch of students who are looking for a club they'd like to join, and we need to give them a chance to get to know about our club. So, I'd like to get some information about setting up the club booth and printing flyers at the school print center.

US 03 Aha, I got it. I mean, your club is a good way to expand the workout group of those who share a common interest, so I think gathering more people is better. First, you need to fill out this application and hand it back to me whenever you are ready. By the way, have you registered with the school as a club? ⁰⁴To set up a booth on campus, the school requires the official registration as a club.

S Yes. I did right after I started the club.

US That's good. That makes the process much easier. ⁰⁴You also need to go to the student services office in the main hall to find out which places are available for your booth and check the time as well. If staff at the office find any empty places your club can use them, they'll let you know the location and available time, and it's free of charge.

홍보물 인쇄 센터 안내

And here is a map to find a print center where you can make your flyers. The center usually offers discounts to new clubs.

S Really? That's good because we are tight on money, right now. ⁰⁵Do you know how much we can get a discount?

US Hmmm... I think they offer about 20 percent discount. I would ask them directly, though, just to be safe.

S I have one more question. We also need to redesign our flyer since it doesn't look professional. Does the print center provide any design services?

US Sorry again. I really don't know anything about their services. Why don't you contact them to get more details? They open until 8 p.m. weekdays.

S Oh, I will talk to them.

US OK, like I said, here is the application form, and just get back to me when it's done.

S Yes, I really appreciate your help.

[**Vocabulary**]   bulletin board 게시판   paved[peivd] 포장된   strenuous[strénjuəs] 힘이 많이 드는, 격렬한   steep[sti:p] 가파른   scramble[skrǽmbl] 기어가기, 오르기   flyer[fláiər] 광고지

01 Main Topic

Why does the student go to the office?

Ⓐ To organize a hiking club in the school
Ⓑ To plan to set up club booths
Ⓒ To try to advertise the club he joined
Ⓓ To complain that there are no hiking clubs on campus

학생은 왜 사무실을 찾아갔나?

Ⓐ 학교에 하이킹 클럽을 만들기 위해
Ⓑ 클럽 부스를 설치할 계획을 세우기 위해
Ⓒ 그가 가입한 클럽을 홍보하기 위해
Ⓓ 캠퍼스에 하이킹 클럽이 없다는 것을 불평하기 위해

02 Inference

Listen again to part of the conversation. Then answer the question.

> S: ...I was surprised that there weren't any clubs like this before.
> US: That's great. Umm, so where do I fit in?

What does the staff imply when she says this:
US: Umm, so where do I fit in?

Ⓐ She doesn't have any idea why the student came to the office.
Ⓑ She thinks that she is not a suitable person to help the student.
Ⓒ She doesn't intend to provide the information the student requested.
Ⓓ She doesn't know how to help the student.

대화의 일부를 다시 들으시오. 그러고 나서 질문에 답하시오.

> S: ……그 전에 이런 클럽이 없었다는 사실에 놀랐어요.
> US: 훌륭하네요. 음, 그런데 내가 어떻게 도와줄까요?

직원이 이 말을 할 때 암시한 것은 무엇인가?
US: 음, 그런데 내가 어떻게 도와줄까요?

Ⓐ 학생이 왜 사무실을 찾아왔는지 전혀 모른다.
Ⓑ 그녀가 학생을 돕기에 적절한 사람이 아니라고 생각한다.
Ⓒ 학생이 요구한 정보를 제공할 마음이 없다.
Ⓓ 학생을 도울 방법을 모른다.

> 오답 해설 Ⓐ 대화 도입부에서 학생은 본인이 가입한 클럽에 대해 몇 가지 질문이 있어 찾아 왔다고 방문 용건을 밝혔으므로, 직원은 학생이 사무실을 찾은 이유를 전혀 모르는 상태는 아니다. 추론 문제에서 not ~ any 또는 never 같은 '절대 부정' 표현은 오답이 될 가능성이 높다.

03 Inference

What can be inferred about the staff's attitude towards the student?

Ⓐ She tries to empathize with the student.
Ⓑ She thinks that the student is overly demanding.
Ⓒ She is annoyed by the student's lack of information.
Ⓓ She is not satisfied with the print center's service.

학생에 대한 직원의 태도로 추론할 수 있는 것은 무엇인가?

Ⓐ 그녀는 학생에게 공감하려고 노력한다.
Ⓑ 그녀는 학생이 과하게 요구가 많다고 생각한다.
Ⓒ 그녀는 학생의 정보 부족에 짜증이 난다.
Ⓓ 그녀는 인쇄 센터의 서비스에 만족하지 않는다.

04 Detail

What are the requirements to set up a booth on campus?
Choose 2 answers.

- [A] To enroll as an official club
- [B] To gather enough members to register
- [C] To visit the student services office to pay the service fee for setting up a booth
- [D] To visit the place providing student services

| 캠퍼스에 부스를 설치하기 위한 요건은 무엇인가?
2개의 답을 고르시오.

- [A] 공식 클럽으로 등록하는 것
- [B] 등록하기 위한 충분한 멤버를 모으는 것
- [C] 학생 서비스 사무실을 방문해서 부스 설치에 필요한 수수료를 지불하는 것
- [D] 학생 서비스를 제공하는 곳을 방문하는 것

05 Inference

Listen again to part of the conversation. Then answer the question.

> S: Do you know how much we can get a discount?
> US: Hmmm... I think they offer about 20 percent discount. I would ask them directly, though, just to be safe.

What does the staff mean when she says this:
US: I think they offer about 20 percent discount.

- Ⓐ She is not sure she understands the student's question.
- Ⓑ She thinks that the rate of discount is sufficient for the student.
- Ⓒ She implies that the information is incorrect.
- Ⓓ She is uncertain about the discount rate offered by the printing service.

대화의 일부를 다시 들으시오. 그러고 나서 질문에 답하시오.

> S: 저희가 얼마큼 할인을 받을 수 있는지 아시나요?
> US: 흠…… 내가 알기로는 그들은 20% 정도 할인을 제공해요. 하지만 혹시 모르니깐 직접 물어 보는 게 좋겠어요.

직원이 이 말을 할 때 의미한 것은 무엇인가?
US: 내가 알기로는 그들은 20% 정도 할인을 제공해요.

- Ⓐ 학생의 질문을 잘 이해했는지 확신하지 못한다.
- Ⓑ 할인율이 학생에게 충분하다고 생각한다.
- Ⓒ 그 정보가 부정확함을 암시한다.
- Ⓓ 인쇄 서비스가 제공하는 할인율에 대해 확신하지 못한다.

TEST 2 Set 2 Lecture 1

Listen to part of a lecture in an entomology class.

P   OK, let's get started. We've been talking about insects. Insects have various attributes that have helped them to adapt and survive in every environment imaginable. Their adaptations include the ability to fly, unique mouth structures, and the ability to molt. Imagine if all insects lived in exactly the same habitats and ate exactly the same food. Then, it would be hard for them to thrive, because members of the same species would compete too much over food and habitats. So, they need to differentiate their adaptive attributes to survive in different places to minimize the competition. Could someone elaborate on the different stages of a butterfly's life?

S   It starts off as an egg, then a caterpillar, forms a cocoon-like pupa, and finally becomes a butterfly.

P   Perfect! 06 In biology, this process is called metamorphosis. This is a very big word, but the process is very clear. Basically, metamorphosis is a biological process by which an insect changes its shape after birth or hatching, involving a conspicuous and comparatively abrupt transformation in the insect's body structure through cell growth and differentiation. In fact, we actually learned about butterfly metamorphosis when we were kids, right? So, did you know that there are various kinds of metamorphosis? The changing stage that you just described to me is classified as complete metamorphosis.

S   So if that's called complete metamorphosis, are you saying that there is something called incomplete metamorphosis?

P   Yes, actually there are two types of this process. Some insects undergo an incomplete or partial metamorphosis, and others go through complete metamorphosis, but many people mistakenly think that metamorphosis is a phenomenon limited to insects. In fact, some amphibians, mollusks, and some other species can also exhibit metamorphosis.

07 But I'm getting ahead of myself. Let's take a closer look at what insect metamorphosis is. As I was explaining, there are actually two types of metamorphosis, both of which involve a process called molting. That refers to an insect shedding its exoskeleton and forming a new set. Let me tell you about this exoskeleton more. Insects don't have internal bones, so this armor-like structure has a function to protect them. It not only protects internal organs, it also provides shape and structure to the insect's body and prevents water loss.

Now, I want to talk about "incomplete metamorphosis or partial metamorphosis", in which, an insect undergoes little change in its appearance or prey, except in terms of size. It includes three distinct stages: the egg, nymph, and the adult, which is also called imago. In this type, insects go through gradual changes and there is no pupal stage. The nymph somewhat resembles its imago but lacks wings and functional reproductive organs. Obviously, the adult will be bigger and will gain reproductive capabilities. **08** A good example of this is the grasshopper, which at first seems small and wingless, yet after it sheds its exoskeleton, the insect, and particularly its wings, grow larger and until, it finally possesses the full sized wings when it reaches its adult stage. Despite this growth, the grasshopper's diet remains unaltered as it changes between each phase. In fact, they don't change much aside from their size. However, some insects like dragonflies transforms in habitat and diet. Young dragonflies, in a phase called the naiad form, live and breathe under water and consume an aquatic diet, even including little fish. When a dragonfly is about to reach the adult stage, it crawls out of the water, shedding its exoskeleton to turn into an air-breathing, insect consuming, and winged adult. Even so, such a change is not as impressive as it sounds when compared to complete metamorphosis.

In complete metamorphosis, the young and the adult have completely different forms, habitats, and diets. **09** What's important here is that complete metamorphosis involves one more stage than incomplete metamorphosis, which is the pupal stage. At this stage, an insect seals itself in a cocoon and grows at on astonishing speed. A good example of an animal that does this is a butterfly. The first stage of a butterfly's life is as a larva, not a small-sized butterfly. For butterflies and moths, we refer to the larvae as caterpillars. On the other hand, we call fly larvae maggots. Whatever the name of the larva, it is different from its adult form. Larvae also have different diets and live in different environments compared to their adult form. [10]The only purpose of the larva is to eat and grow. Then, it turns into a pupa and changes into a worm-shaped object, and then into an adult insect. When the pupa reaches the adult stage, it becomes a full-grown insect with wings. It lives in a completely different ecosystem and has a new additional purpose—mating.

변태가 생존에 주는 이익

S But why is that so? What I'm trying to ask is...is there some biological or environmental benefit if there is a difference between the young and the adult?

P Yes, glad you brought that up. [11]What I was trying to explain is that these different stages each specialize in a different purpose. That is, in each phase, the insect species adapts to a different environment and learns to deal with it. The larva, while it's growing, might need more nutritional advantages so it lives underwater or underground where it gets more nourishment. And the adult has wings to get more mobility in order to mate with other adults. Another reason might be competition. In fact, there won't be any dietary competition between the adults and the young since they have different appetites, enhancing the survivability of the species.

[**Vocabulary**] caterpillar[kǽtərpìlər] (나비의) 애벌레　cocoon[kəkúːn] 고치　pupa[pjúːpə] 번데기　metamorphosis [mètəmɔ́ːrfəsis] 변태　amphibian[æmfíbiən] 양서류　mollusk[máləsk] 연체동물　molding[móuldiŋ] 주조　shed[ʃed] 내뿜다, 흘리다　exoskeleton[èksouskélitən] 외골격　nymph[nimf] (곤충의) 유충　naiad[néiæd] (잠자리 등 반변태 곤충의) 약충 시기　larva[láːrvə] 유충　maggot[mǽgət] 구더기

06 Main Topic

What is the main purpose of the lecture?

Ⓐ To examine the steps of metamorphosis by following the life of a butterfly
Ⓑ To discuss the advantages of complete metamorphosis over incomplete metamorphosis
Ⓒ To explain the significance of metamorphosis in the life cycles of various species
Ⓓ To describe a biological process by which insects develop and change their body structure

강의의 목적은 무엇인가?

Ⓐ 나비의 생애를 보고 변태의 단계를 면밀히 살피기 위해
Ⓑ 불완전 변태에 대한 완전 변태의 이점을 논의하기 위해
Ⓒ 다양한 종들의 생활 주기에서 변태의 중요성을 설명하기 위해
Ⓓ 곤충이 그들의 신체 구조를 발달시키고 변화시키는 생물학적 과정을 묘사하기 위해

07 Inference

Listen again to part of the lecture. Then answer the question.

> P: But I'm getting ahead of myself. Let's take a closer look at what insect metamorphosis is.

What does the professor mean when he says this:
P: But I'm getting ahead of myself.

Ⓐ He thinks that discussing other species is not worth the time.
Ⓑ He intends to return to what he was discussing.
Ⓒ He plans to explain the lecture at a slow pace.
Ⓓ He believes that the students need time to understand.

강의의 일부를 다시 들으시오. 그러고 나서 질문에 답하시오.

> P: 그러나 내가 앞서 나가고 있네요. 곤충의 변태가 무엇인지에 대해 자세하게 보도록 합시다.

교수가 이 말을 할 때 의미한 것은 무엇인가?
P: 그러나 내가 앞서 나가고 있네요.

Ⓐ 다른 종에 대해서 논의하는 것은 시간 낭비라고 생각한다.
Ⓑ 논의하고 있던 것으로 되돌아 갈 작정이다.
Ⓒ 천천히 강의를 설명하려고 한다.
Ⓓ 학생들이 이해할 시간이 필요하다고 믿는다.

08 Organization

Why does the professor mention grasshoppers and dragonflies?

Ⓐ To imply that they are the best-known examples of metamorphosis
Ⓑ To emphasize how they develop their reproductive ability
Ⓒ To illustrate that they evolve to stop competing for the same food and habitat
Ⓓ To explain that variations exist in incomplete metamorphosis

교수는 왜 메뚜기와 잠자리를 언급했나?

Ⓐ 그들이 변태 과정을 거치는 대표적인 예라는 것을 암시하기 위해
Ⓑ 어떻게 그들이 번식 능력을 개발하는지를 강조하기 위해
Ⓒ 그들이 같은 음식과 서식지에 대한 경쟁을 멈추기 위해 진화했다는 것을 설명하기 위해
Ⓓ 불완전 변태의 다양성이 존재한다는 것을 설명하기 위해

09 Detail

Which of the following is a crucial difference between complete metamorphosis and incomplete metamorphosis?

- Ⓐ The number of life cycle stages
- Ⓑ A change in mouth structure
- Ⓒ The ability to mate
- Ⓓ A susceptibility to weather

다음 중 완전 변태와 불완전 변태 사이의 주요한 차이점은 무엇인가?

- Ⓐ 생활 주기 단계의 수
- Ⓑ 입 구조의 변화
- Ⓒ 짝짓기를 할 수 있는 능력
- Ⓓ 날씨에 대한 민감성

10 Detail

What is the critical function of a larva stage?

- Ⓐ To feed and prepare for its growth
- Ⓑ To form a strong structure called the cocoon
- Ⓒ To develop preliminary wings
- Ⓓ To protect against predators

유충 단계의 중요 기능은 무엇인가?

- Ⓐ 먹이를 먹고 성장을 준비하는 것
- Ⓑ 고치라고 불리는 튼튼한 구조를 만드는 것
- Ⓒ 예비 날개를 발달시키는 것
- Ⓓ 포식자로부터 지키는 것

11 Detail

According to the professor, which of the following are biological benefits for insects that undergo metamorphosis? **Choose 2 answers.**

- Ⓐ It allows for insects to commit themselves to their aims.
- Ⓑ It allows larvae to live underwater or underground to protect themselves from predators.
- Ⓒ It makes mating and reproduction easier for adult insects because they live in different habitats from their larvae.
- Ⓓ It establishes less competition between adult insects and their larvae.

교수에 따르면, 다음 중 변태를 겪는 곤충의 생물학적 이점은 무엇인가? **2개의 답을 고르시오.**

- Ⓐ 곤충이 그들의 본연의 목적에 충실할 수 있게 해 준다.
- Ⓑ 애벌레들이 포식자로부터 스스로를 보호하기 위해 물속이나 땅 밑에 살게 해 준다.
- Ⓒ 그들의 애벌레와는 다른 서식지에 살기 때문에 성충이 짝짓기와 번식이 더 쉬워진다.
- Ⓓ 성충과 그들의 애벌레 사이의 경쟁을 줄이도록 한다.

영단기 TOEFL

ACTUAL TEST

TEST 03

TEST 3 Set 1 Conversation

Listen to part of a conversation between a student and a bookstore employee.

학생의 용건: 도서 환불 요청

S ⁰¹Hi, I was wondering if I could return this book. I don't need it anymore because I dropped my psychology class.
E Okay, when did you purchase this book?
S I think it was about a month ago if I remember correctly.
E A month ago? That's a few weeks before school started. Hmm, are you aware of the return policy here?
S Uh, what return policy?
E The one that's on the front door you came in. It's also on your purchase receipt. Could you take it out for me? I need to see the purchase date. Also, let's take a look at the return policy, too.
S My purchase receipt...here it is. Is there a problem?

환불 규정

E Take a look. The school allows students to return books only for a limited time. You could have returned it last week, until one week after the class started. Your psychology class started two weeks ago, right?
S That's right. ⁰²I realized that I could waive this class, only after the class had started. Apparently, the class is equivalent to the Introduction to Psychology class I took as an exchange student in France. But it took a while since I needed consent from the professor and the department. If all the processing didn't take so long, I would've returned this book ages ago! Is there anything I can do? The book is brand new, with no writing on it whatsoever.
E I can see it's in great condition. However, I can't bend the school policy for you. Sorry.
S The school policy seems a little unfair. For a busy student, one week is very short. Like I said, the process of withdrawing a class takes a long time. The time limit should be stretched to the middle of the semester since students can be pretty busy. You know, I don't think the school is too timely with their

학생과 서점 직원의 대화 중 일부를 들어 보시오.

S ⁰¹안녕하세요, 제가 이 책을 환불 받을 수 있는지 궁금해서요. 제가 심리학 수업을 취소해서 더 이상 이 책이 필요 없어졌거든요.
E 알겠어요. 언제 이 책을 구입했나요?
S 제가 제대로 기억한다면 한 달 전이에요.
E 한 달 전이요? 학기가 시작하기 몇 주 전이네요. 음, 여기 환불 정책에 대해서 알고 있나요?
S 어, 무슨 환불 정책이요?
E 학생이 들어온 정문에 붙어 있는 거요. 그건 구매한 영수증에도 있어요. 혹시, 꺼내 줄 수 있나요? 구입 날짜를 확인해야 해서요. 그리고 환불 정책도 확인하고요.
S 제 영수증이라……여기 있어요. 무슨 문제가 있나요?

E 보세요. 학교는 제한된 기간 동안만 학생들이 책을 환불할 수 있도록 허락하고 있어요. 학생은 수업이 시작하고 한 주 뒤인 지난 주까지만 환불이 가능했어요. 학생의 심리학 수업은 2주 전에 시작한 걸로 알고 있는데, 맞지요?
S 맞아요. ⁰²수업이 시작되고 나서야 이 수업을 면제 받을 수 있다는 사실을 알았어요. 보아하니 이 수업은 작년에 교환학생으로 갔던 프랑스에서 들었던 심리학 개론 수업과 동일해서요. 하지만 교수님과 학부의 승인을 받는 데 시간이 걸렸어요. 이 모든 과정이 오래 걸리지 않았다면, 이 책을 훨씬 전에 환불할 수 있었어요! 다른 방법은 없나요? 책에 어떤 것도 쓰이지 않은, 새 책이에요.
E 상태가 깨끗한 건 알겠어요. 하지만 학교 규정을 어길 수는 없어요. 미안해요.
S 학교 규정이 조금 불공평한 것 같아요. 바쁜 학생에게 한 주는 매우 짧아요. 아까 말씀 드린 것처럼 수업을 철회하는 과정이 오래 걸려요. 학생들이 꽤 바쁠 수 있기 때문에 기간 제한이 학기 중간까지 연장되어야 해요. 수업과 관련된 학교의 행정 처리도 시간을 딱 맞추는 거 같지 않던데요.
E 사실 학교 규정이 항상 이런 것은 아니었어요. 7~8년 전까지는 학생들은 학기 중 아무 때나 책을 환불할 수 있었지요. ⁰³하지만 어떤 학생들은 이 규정을 남용했어요.

processing regarding classes.

E Actually, the school policy wasn't always like this. Until 7~8 years ago, students could return books anytime during a semester. 03 But some students started taking unfair advantage of this policy. They would take a class for a whole semester, and then ask for a full refund of their books afterwards.

S Oh dear, that's awful. But I've never used this book. It seems unfair that I can't get a refund, though. Is there really no way to take care of this problem?

E Well, you could sell it at the buyback price. It's not a full refund, but it's better than nothing.

S The buyback price? How much would that be?

E Half the original price of the book. Also, there's a condition. The textbook must be required material for the class next semester. Would you like me to check?

S Oh, yes, please. The class is Psychology 201.

E Let's see. The psychology department apparently won't be using this book next semester. The department has posted that this book will be in use only for this semester. They're planning to use a new book afterwards. I'm sorry.

S So you won't buy back my book? What should I do with it then?

E Your last option is selling it to the book distributors. They'll buy back your book and sell it to another college that can use it for a class. 04 The downside is that their buy-back price is only a quarter of the original price.

S My book cost about a hundred dollars. Wait, are you telling me I would get back only 25 dollars?

E It's the best we can do. In fact, this option was recently made, in order to give the students a bit of their money back.

S This option wasn't available before?

E Before we made an agreement with the book distributors, students couldn't get any of their money back. So, what do you say?

S 05 You're right. It's better than nothing. Thanks for your help.

[**Vocabulary**] take out 꺼내다　　waive [weiv] 포기하다　　be equivalent to 맞먹다, 동일하다　　consent [kənsént] 동의
whatsoever [hwὰtsouévər] (whatever의 강조형) 무엇도, 어떤 것도　　bend [bend] 굽히다　　withdraw [wiðdrɔ́ː] 철회하다
stretch [stretʃ] (기간을) 연장하다　　post [poust] 게시하다, 공고하다　　afterwards [ǽftərwərdz] 그 이후에　　buyback [báibæk]
되사다　　book distributor 도서 배급업자　　downside [dáunsàid] 단점

01 Main Topic

Why does the student go to the bookstore?

Ⓐ To buy a textbook for his psychology class
Ⓑ To receive a refund for an unused book
Ⓒ To inquire about the store's return policy
Ⓓ To sell his textbook to a book distributor

학생은 왜 서점에 갔나?

Ⓐ 그의 심리학 수업 교재를 사기 위해
Ⓑ 사용하지 않은 책을 환불 받기 위해
Ⓒ 서점의 환불 정책에 대해 문의하기 위해
Ⓓ 도서 배급자에게 그의 교재를 팔기 위해

02 Detail

Why does the student go to return the book two weeks after the class started?

Ⓐ He needed to make sure that he could receive credits without taking the class.
Ⓑ He was delayed because of returning from France following his student exchange program.
Ⓒ He realized that the book was not one of the required materials for the class.
Ⓓ He discussed his situation with a professor who taught a similar class.

학생은 왜 수업이 시작되고 나서 2주일 후에 책을 환불하러 왔나?

Ⓐ 그 수업을 듣지 않고도 학점을 받을 수 있는지 확인해야 했다.
Ⓑ 교환 학생 프로그램 후에 프랑스에서 돌아오는 것이 지연됐기 때문에 늦었다.
Ⓒ 교재가 필수 수업 자료가 아니라는 것을 알게 되었다.
Ⓓ 비슷한 수업을 가르치는 교수님과 그의 상황을 논의했다.

03 Detail

Why did the school implement the one-week return policy?

Ⓐ To accommodate the schedules of busy students
Ⓑ To discourage students from practicing dishonesty
Ⓒ To stop students from getting refunds for their books
Ⓓ To retail new books instead of used ones

학교는 왜 일주일 환불 정책을 시행하나?

Ⓐ 바쁜 학생들의 스케줄을 수용하기 위해
Ⓑ 학생들이 부정을 저지르는 것을 막기 위해
Ⓒ 학생들이 그들의 책을 환불 받는 것을 막기 위해
Ⓓ 중고 책 대신에 새 책을 팔기 위해

04 Inference

Listen again to part of the conversation. Then answer the question.

> E: The downside is that their buy-back price is only a quarter of the original price.
> S: My book cost about a hundred dollars. Wait, are you telling me I would get back only 25 dollars?

What does the student imply when he says this:
S: Wait, are you telling me I would get back only 25 dollars?

Ⓐ He does not want to settle for anything less than a full refund.
Ⓑ He feels that the amount is a small fraction of the original price.
Ⓒ He thinks that the commission for the distributor is too much.
Ⓓ He wants to ensure how much he could receive a refund.

대화의 일부를 다시 들으시오. 그러고 나서 질문에 답하시오.

> E: 단점은 그들이 되사는 가격은 정가의 4분의 1밖에 안 된다는 것이에요.
> S: 제 책은 약 100달러였어요. 잠시만요, 제가 25달러만 받는다는 건가요?

학생이 이 말을 할 때 암시한 것은 무엇인가?
S: 잠시만요, 제가 25달러만 받는다는 건가요?

Ⓐ 전액 환불 이하의 금액으로는 합의하고 싶지 않다.
Ⓑ 그 금액이 정가에 훨씬 못 미치는 액수라고 생각한다.
Ⓒ 배급업자의 수수료가 너무 많다고 생각한다.
Ⓓ 얼마를 환불 받을 수 있는지 확인하고 싶다.

오답 해설 Ⓓ 25달러만 받는 것이 맞냐는 것은 환불을 얼마나 받을 수 있는지 확인하기 위한 것이라기 보다는 받을 금액이 생각보다 너무 적어 반문한 것으로 보아야 한다.

05 Inference

What can be inferred about the student?

Ⓐ He decides to concede to his present situation concerning the textbook.
Ⓑ He is glad about the fact that he can sell his book at a buyback price.
Ⓒ He continues to feel uncertain because he is unsatisfied with the woman's advice.
Ⓓ He is upset at the school because the psychology class is not offered next year.

학생에 대해 추론할 수 있는 것은 무엇인가?

Ⓐ 교과서와 관련된 그의 현재 상황을 수긍하기로 결정한다.
Ⓑ 되사는 가격에 그의 책을 판매할 수 있다는 사실에 기쁘다.
Ⓒ 여자의 조언에 만족하지 않기 때문에 그는 확신이 없다.
Ⓓ 심리학 수업이 다음 해에 개설되지 않기 때문에 그는 학교에 화가 난다.

TEST 3 Set 1 Lecture 1

Listen to part of a lecture in an archaeology class.

P   In the field of archaeology, one of the biggest challenges is the conservation of the original artifacts during excavation. Although an archaeologist's job is to restore ancient artifacts, the steps he or she takes in digging a site ultimately and systematically destroy them. So, obviously, archaeologists need sophisticated techniques that are non-destructive. Then, what about artifacts buried underwater? I mean…underwater areas are more difficult to navigate and dangerous than dry land, so excavating the regions requires more patience and effort. Excavation practiced underwater is called underwater archaeology, and it generally deals with the restoration of human settlements that have sunk underwater. Some areas of human occupation that were previously located on dry land may become submerged due to various seismic events or climate change. However, underwater archaeology is not limited just to the study and excavation of human settlements. The application of archaeology to underwater areas initially emerged from skills and tools developed in salvaging shipwrecks. 07 Umm, individual shipwrecks can be of historical importance because they offer unique insights into our populations past and into the lives of people who travelled by sea. As a bonus, pirate ships or treasure ships could contain precious artifacts that are well worth excavating.

06 In this sense, the discovery of the San Jose shipwreck has all the elements of a grand drama. This shipwreck was one of the richest, with her findings including treasures of gold and emeralds worth up to $17 billion. This ship was a galleon of the Spanish Navy, launched in 1698 and sunk in battle off the coast of Cartagena, Colombia in 1708. A U.S.—based salvage company, Sea Search Armada, found the ship, registered its location in 1982, and spent the next five years bringing parts of the ship

to the surface. This was very impressive work, since the vessel weighed over 1,400 tons.

08 After her recovery, many artifacts were found in the hull of the San Jose, such as weapons, tools, and coins, which were crucial for historians because they provided valuable information about naval warfare, shipbuilding techniques and day-to-day life at the turn of the 17th century. Since the San Jose's voyage was funded by the King of Spain, she was ornately decorated with adornments and sculptures to exhibit Spain's power and glory. The sculptures were carved with a considerable amount of effort and cost. I mean, this vessel was a valuable asset not only for her expensive cargo but also for conducting archaeological research. So, the salvage company and archaeologists worked together for her recovery.

Then, what caused this costly and beautiful ship to sink? Some historians argued that the cannons attached to each side of the ship were not tied tightly enough. I mean, they were not secured, so they rolled around the deck of the vessel as she started to move. The balance of each side collapsed, which caused her to tip over into the water suddenly. Moreover, others speculated the weight of the sculptures and tools was too heavy and the ship couldn't handle it. **09** However, after the recovery of the shipwreck, archaeologists figured out what the real cause of the ship's sinking was. The ship was tall, so it required a lot of ballast to keep it balanced. During those times, people used heavy stones as ballast, placed at the bottom of the ship. Unfortunately, the San Jose didn't contain enough ballast to stand against gravity. So the structure became unstable and tipped over.

Because the ship sunk in very cold water, she was well preserved. The low temperature prevented the ship from deteriorating, which would usually occur from mollusks and shipworm that pierce into the ship's woodwork. However, the San Jose posed an unprecedented challenge for archaeologists. The ship did suffer waterlogging because it was in the water for a long time. The water eventually damaged the organic components of the wood works. Even the rigid cellulose of the wood fibers decayed away over time. While it is true that the ship maintained her form, she still became very fragile. Due to her condition, it was extremely difficult to preserve her form when she was brought up to the surface. The instant the ship was raised to the surface, the water evaporated from the vessel. Astoundingly, 580 tons of water vanished from the ship. This meant the ship had to be kept wet constantly thereafter, so that it did not dry out and crack before it could be properly preserved. Drying out could cause enough damage to break the ship and literally collapse her.

To prevent such a calamity, researchers slowly applied a material called hydrophobic coating to the vessel. This waxy substance provided a protective shell for the ship and slowed down water evaporation. The more the water started evaporating, the more hydrophobic coating was sprayed onto the vessel. In fact, this actually worked pretty well, and the San Jose's shape was successfully preserved. [10]It was clear that hydrophobic coating was a very economical and efficient way to protect any artifacts that were retrieved from the water. And it didn't harm the ocean because it didn't contain any toxic materials. Also, this method was convenient. I mean all we had to do was spray this coating material onto the vessel. However, the process did take a very long time due to the ship's enormous size. They had to spray this material on the ship for over 17 years! [11]Now, if you want to talk about patience, talk to these archaeologists. Unfortunately, the ship became very fragile again because of the lengthy process. I mean, every bean has its black. There are several ways to recover something buried deep in the ocean, all of which have their own risks and limitations. So, I would like to conclude that the San Jose is still being worked on to preserve its magnificence.

[**Vocabulary**] conservation[kànsərvéiʃən] 보존　artifact[áːrtəfækt] 유물　excavate[ékskəvèit] 발굴하다　seismic [sáizmik] 지진의　shipwreck[ʃíprèk] 난파선　pirate ship 해적선　salvage company 난파선 인양 회사　hull[hʌl] 선체　day-to-day 그날 그날의　cannon[kǽnən] 대포　ballast[bǽləst] (균형을 잡기 위한) 균형 밸러스트, 무거운 짐　tip over ~을 뒤집어 엎다　deteriorate[ditíː(ː)əriərèit] 악화되다　mollusk[máləsk] 연체동물　shipworm[ʃípwəːrm] 좀조개　woodwork [wúdwəːrk] 목조부　unprecedented[ʌnprésidèntid] 전례 없는　waterlog[wɔ́ːtərlɔ̀(ː)g] 침수시켜 항행이 불가능하게 하다　cellulose[séljəlòus] 셀룰로우스, 섬유소　calamity[kəlǽməti] 재난

06 Main Topic

What does the professor primarily discuss?

Ⓐ The historical value of a warship called the San Jose
Ⓑ Archaeological aspects of a sunken ship
Ⓒ The method used for restoring a ship
Ⓓ The importance of excavating shipwrecks

교수는 주로 무엇을 논의하는가?

Ⓐ San Jose라고 불리는 군함의 역사적인 가치
Ⓑ 가라앉은 배의 고고학적인 측면
Ⓒ 배를 복구하는 데 사용되는 방법
Ⓓ 난파선 발굴의 중요성

07 Inference

What can be inferred about shipwrecks?

Ⓐ They are the main concern for archaeologists.
Ⓑ They are well-preserved because of underwater conditions.
Ⓒ They are connected to historical events.
Ⓓ Their discovery is more profitable than searching for artifacts on dry land.

난파선에 대해 추론할 수 있는 것은 무엇인가?

Ⓐ 고고학자들에게 주요 관심사이다.
Ⓑ 수중 환경 때문에 잘 보존된다.
Ⓒ 역사적 사건들과 연관이 있다.
Ⓓ 그것들의 발견은 육지에서 유물을 찾는 것보다 수익성이 좋다.

오답 해설 Ⓓ 해적선이나 보물선에 귀중한 유물이 있을 수 있지만 이를 난파선에 대한 일반적인 사항이라고 볼 수 없다. 또한 난파선이 수익성 측면에서 육지의 유물 발굴과 어떤 차이가 있는지는 언급되지 않았다.

08 Detail

Why were the artifact findings on the San Jose important?

Ⓐ Because the artifacts provided information on how people spent their ordinary lives at the time
Ⓑ Because archaeologists learned a new wartime technology through the weapons found on the ship
Ⓒ Because archaeologists were able to make huge economic gain by selling the artifacts that were discovered on the ship
Ⓓ Because the artifacts helped archaeologists determine about how the ship sank in 1628

San Jose호에서 발견된 유물은 왜 중요했나?

Ⓐ 그 당시 사람들이 어떻게 생활을 했는지에 대한 정보를 제공했기 때문에
Ⓑ 배에서 발견된 무기를 통해 고고학자들이 새로운 전쟁 기술을 배웠기 때문에
Ⓒ 고고학자들이 배에서 발견된 유물을 팔아서 막대한 경제적 이익을 얻을 수 있었기 때문에
Ⓓ 고고학자들이 1628년에 배가 어떻게 가라앉았는지 알아 내도록 도왔기 때문에

오답 해설 Ⓑ San Jose호에서 발견된 무기로 새로운 전쟁 기술을 배웠는지에 대해서는 언급되지 않았다.

09 Detail

According to the lecture, what was the actual reason for the sinking of the San Jose?

Ⓐ The cannons were not tied tightly to the deck, thereby rolling around and throwing the ship off-balance.
Ⓑ The ship cargo, such as sculptures and tools, was too heavy for the ship to handle.
Ⓒ It failed to contain the weight sufficiently to maintain its balance.
Ⓓ Cold sea water damaged the ship because it froze the wooden structures.

강의에 따르면, San Jose호 침몰의 진짜 이유는 무엇인가?

Ⓐ 대포가 갑판에 단단히 묶이지 않아, 굴러서 배의 균형을 무너뜨렸다.
Ⓑ 배가 지탱하기에 조각과 도구 같은 화물이 너무 무거웠다.
Ⓒ 그것의 균형을 유지할 수 있을 만큼 충분한 무게를 보유하는 데 실패했다.
Ⓓ 차가운 물이 나무로 된 배의 구조물을 얼려서 배를 손상시켰다.

10 Detail

In the lecture, the professor describes the benefits of hydrophobic coating. Indicate whether each of the following is an advantage.

Put a check(✓) in the correct boxes.

	Yes	No
Comparatively inexpensive to use	✓	
Immediately responsive		✓
Environmentally friendly	✓	
Relatively easy to apply	✓	
Continuously renewable		✓

강의에서 교수는 소수성 코팅제의 이점에 대해 설명한다. 다음이 장점인지 표시하시오.
맞는 칸에 체크 표 하시오.

	그렇다	아니다
사용하기에 비교적 저렴하다.	✓	
즉각적인 효과가 있다.		✓
친환경적이다.	✓	
상대적으로 사용하기 쉽다.	✓	
끊임없이 재생 가능하다.		✓

11 Inference

Listen again to part of the lecture. Then answer the question.

> P: Now, if you want to talk about patience, talk to these archaeologists. Unfortunately, the ship became very fragile again because of the lengthy process. I mean, every bean has its black.

What does the professor imply when she says this:
P: I mean, every bean has its black.

Ⓐ The method was not accepted because of its limitations.
Ⓑ The method was not completely satisfactory.
Ⓒ Other methods were adopted to restore the ship.
Ⓓ Archaeologists expected the method to yield different results.

강의의 일부를 다시 들으시오. 그리고 나서 질문에 답하시오.

> P: 그러니 만약 인내심에 대해 이야기하고 싶다면, 고고학자들에게 물어 보세요. 불행히도 이 긴 과정 때문에 배는 다시 약해졌죠. 그러니까 어떤 것이나 안 좋은 점은 있죠.

교수가 이 말을 할 때 암시한 것은 무엇인가?
P: 그러니까 어떤 것이나 안 좋은 점은 있죠.

Ⓐ 그 방법은 단점 때문에 받아들여지지 않았다.
Ⓑ 그 방법이 완벽하게 만족스럽지는 않았다.
Ⓒ 배를 복원하기 위해 다른 방법이 채택되었다.
Ⓓ 고고학자들은 이 방법이 다른 결과를 낳기를 기대했다.

TEST 3 — Set 2 Conversation

Listen to part of a conversation between a student and a professor.

S Hello, Professor. Do you have a moment?

P Hi, Anne. I'm not busy right now. How is your paper going?

S I think I'm doing quite well. I just finished my first draft, and I'm trying to polish it up now. I actually visited a writing center to get some help, and they took care of my outline so that I can prepare my paper better. By the way, I wanted to take the time to tell you that I do enjoy taking your philosophy course.

P That's good to hear. So, what is your paper about?

S 02 I'm writing about John Locke and his life. I found his life fascinating and he is considered as one of the most influential thinkers of modern politics. He also provided the foundation for *the Declaration of Independence. So I'm sure there are lots of aspects of him to research.

P Oh, he is one of my favorite philosophers as well. 02 If I were to give you a little something to think about, I would suggest that you focus on the principles of humanism and individual freedom that he argued for.

S Oh, definitely. Thank you for your advice. Um... 01 Anyway, the reason I dropped by is that I'm looking for a tutoring job like a TA. 03 So, I was wondering if there are any professors in the department looking for a TA for next semester.

P Um, as far as I know, you are only a sophomore, right? Unfortunately, only upper-class students can apply for a job in our department.

S 04 Really? But some of my friends who are second years are also doing TA jobs, so I thought that I might also be able to do it.

P I'm not sure which departments your friends are currently working in, but all the TAs in our department are graduate students. And they are all pursuing their academic career in Philosophy.

S   OK, but I'm going to major in Philosophy and even though I'm only a sophomore, I have taken several advanced Philosophy courses and some of them were actually graduate level ones.

P   I can see you have initiative and enthusiasm, but our TAs are in charge of some of the introductory level courses, which means they actually do some teaching in class. I'm sure you have already taken some basic courses taught by a TA. Anyway, that's why our department has a policy of not hiring undergraduates as TAs.

S   Oh, so that's why TAs taught some of my courses. I wasn't too sure about what TAs do, so it just seemed like such a great opportunity. So there aren't any ways that I can work in the department?

교수가 연구 보조 자리를 제안함

P   Actually, we are now hiring students to help with grading papers and preparing professors' researches. We don't call them TAs, but they are doing lots of work. If you are interested, I can recommend you as a potential candidate. But I'm not the one who is in charge of the screening process.

S   Wow, that sounds great. I'm really willing to do that. Then, how can I apply for it?

P   I don't know the procedures exactly, since the department takes care of this hiring process, so I think you should talk to other staff members. 05Talking about the hiring opportunities, I'm planning to start my research on *Jeremy Bentham's moral philosophy. If you recall, we discussed him in Introductory Philosophy 101.

S   Yes, I remember him. You said that his idea was to motivate people by giving compliments. And you mentioned that his goal is to maximize public happiness. It was a very interesting topic, so I still remember the lecture. But why did you bring him up all of a sudden?

P   05I'm glad you remember. I brought that up because a thought just passed my mind. I think I can give you an opportunity that you could help me with this project. Of course, you can get paid for this work. Are you interested?

S   Yea, sure! I'd love to. Thank you, professor!

P 너의 진취성과 열정은 알겠는데, 우리 조교들은 기초 수업들을 책임지고 있는데, 그 말은 그들이 실제로 수업을 진행한다는 거야. 너도 이미 조교가 가르치는 기초 과목들을 들었을 텐데. 어쨌든, 이런 이유로 우리 과에서는 대학생을 조교로 고용하지 않는다는 원칙을 갖고 있단다.

S 아, 그래서 제 수업 중 몇 개를 조교가 가르쳤던 거군요. 저는 조교가 하는 일이 무엇인지 잘 몰라서 그냥 좋은 기회처럼 보였어요. 그럼, 제가 이 학과에서 일할 수 있는 기회는 없는 건가요?

P 사실, 지금 우리는 시험지를 채점하는 걸 도와주고, 교수님들의 연구를 준비할 학생들을 고용하고 있단다. 그 학생들을 조교라고 부르지는 않지만, 많은 일을 한단다. 만약 관심이 있다면, 유력한 후보자로 너를 추천하고 싶구나. 그렇지만 나는 심사 과정의 책임자는 아니란다.

S 와, 좋은데요. 저는 정말 하고 싶어요. 그럼, 어떻게 지원해야 하나요?

P 학과가 그 고용 절차를 관리하고 있어서 나는 정확한 절차를 잘 몰라서, 내 생각에 네가 다른 직원과 얘기해야 될 거 같구나. 05고용 기회에 대해 말해 주자면, 난 Jeremy Bentham의 도덕 철학에 대한 조사를 시작할 계획이란다. 우리가 지난 기초 철학 101 수업에서 그에 대해 논의했던 걸로 기억하는데.

S 네, 기억해요. 그의 사상은 칭찬으로 사람들의 동기를 부여하는 것이라 하셨죠. 그리고 그의 목표가 대중의 행복을 극대화하는 것이라고도 말씀하셨죠. 매우 흥미로운 주제여서, 아직까지 그 강의를 기억하고 있어요. 그런데 갑자기 그에 대한 얘기는 왜 꺼내신 건가요?

P 05네가 기억을 해서 다행이구나. 갑자기 내 머릿속을 스친 생각이 있어서 꺼낸 얘기야. 내 생각에 너에게 이 프로젝트를 도울 수 있는 기회를 줄 수 있을 거 같아. 당연히 이 일로 돈을 지급받을 수 있고 말이야. 관심이 있니?

S 네, 물론이죠! 정말 하고 싶네요. 감사합니다, 교수님!

[**Vocabulary**] draft[dræft] 초안   polish[páliʃ] 다듬다   the Declaration of Independence 독립 선언문   TA(teaching assistant) 조교, 보조 교사   initiative[iníʃətiv] 진취성   introductory level course 기초 단계 수업   screening process 심사 과정

[각주]
* **the Declaration of Independence** 1776년 7월 4일, 12명의 식민지 대표들은 필라델피아에 모여 토머스 제퍼슨이 기초한 독립 선언서를 채택하고 미국의 독립을 선언하였는데, 이것이 미국 독립 선언서의 시작이다. 미국 독립 선언문은 천부 인권, 로크의 사회 계약설, 평등과 같은 내용을 포함한다.
* **Jeremy Bentham** 영국 출신의 철학자로서 공리주의와 공익주의를 주장하였다. 공리주의 중에서도 '최대 다수의 최대 행복'을 기초로 하는 양적 공리주의를 강조하였다.

01 Main Topic

Why does the student go to see the professor?

ⓐ To get some help with her paper on philosophy
Ⓑ To check if there are any chances to get hired
ⓒ To convince the professor that she is qualified as a TA
ⓓ To decide which major she should choose

학생은 왜 교수를 찾아갔나?

ⓐ 철학에 관한 그녀의 보고서에 도움을 얻기 위해
Ⓑ 일자리가 있는지 확인하기 위해
ⓒ 교수에게 그녀가 조교로서 자격이 있다는 것을 설득시키기 위해
ⓓ 그녀가 어떤 전공을 선택해야 할지 결정하기 위해

02 Inference

What can be inferred about how the student's paper will turn out to be?

ⓐ It will primarily concern the biography of John Locke.
ⓑ It will elaborate on how John Locke interacted with other influential thinkers of modern politics.
ⓒ It will describe how the Declaration of Independence affected the John Locke's philosophy.
Ⓓ It will focus on the John Locke's philosophy such as principles of humanism and individual freedom.

학생의 보고서가 어떻게 될지에 관해 추론할 수 있는 것은 무엇인가?

ⓐ John Locke의 전기를 주로 다룰 것이다.
ⓑ John Locke가 어떻게 다른 영향력 있는 현대 정치 사상가들과 교류했는지를 설명할 것이다.
ⓒ 독립 선언문이 John Locke 철학에 어떻게 영향을 주었는지 묘사할 것이다.
Ⓓ 인본주의 원칙과 개인의 자유와 같은 John Locke의 철학에 집중할 것이다.

오답 해설   ⓐ 학생은 원래 John Locke의 인생에 대해 쓰려 했지만 교수가 인본주의 원칙과 개인의 자유에 대해 집중할 것을 제안하자 알았다며 교수의 제안을 받아들였다.

03 Inference

Listen again to part of the conversation. Then answer the question.

> S: So, I was wondering if there are any professors in the department looking for a TA for next semester.
> P: Um, as far as I know, you are only a sophomore, right?

Why does the professor say this:
P: Um, as far as I know, you are only a sophomore, right?

Ⓐ To imply that the student is not qualified to be a teaching assistant
Ⓑ To disparage the student's lack of academic experience
Ⓒ To ask the student which grade she is currently in
Ⓓ To show his disappointment at not being able to hire the student

대화의 일부를 다시 들으시오. 그러고 나서 질문에 답하시오.

> S: 그래서, 다음 학기에 조교를 찾으시는 교수님이 혹시 있으신지 궁금해요.
> P: 음, 내가 알기로 너는 2학년인데, 맞지?

교수는 왜 이 말을 했나?
P: 음, 내가 알기로 너는 2학년인데, 맞지?

Ⓐ 학생이 조교가 되기에 부적합함을 암시하기 위해
Ⓑ 학생의 부족한 학습 경험을 폄하하기 위해
Ⓒ 학생이 현재 몇 학년인지를 묻기 위해
Ⓓ 학생을 고용할 수 없어 실망스러움을 보여 주기 위해

오답 해설 Ⓒ 교수는 학생이 몇 학년인지 이미 알고 있다.

04 Detail

What is the student's assumption about the TA position in the philosophy department?

Ⓐ It is suitable only for the graduate students with a major in Philosophy.
Ⓑ It has a similar hiring policy to other departments.
Ⓒ It is only for those students who have taken the advanced courses in the major.
Ⓓ Graduate experience is required to teach the basic courses.

철학과 조교 자리에 관해 학생이 추론한 것은 무엇인가?

Ⓐ 철학 전공을 한 대학원생들만 가능하다.
Ⓑ 다른 학과와 유사한 고용 정책을 갖고 있다.
Ⓒ 전공에서 심화 수업을 들은 학생들만 가능하다.
Ⓓ 기본 과정을 가르치기 위해 대학원 경험이 요구된다.

05 Organization

For what purpose does the professor mention Jeremy Bentham?

Ⓐ To discuss his moral philosophy
Ⓑ To check the student's knowledge and understanding of the philosopher
Ⓒ To ask the student's opinion of the philosopher
Ⓓ To remind the student that the philosopher was discussed in the Introductory Philosophy 101

교수는 어떤 목적에서 Jeremy Bentham을 언급했나?

Ⓐ 그의 도덕 철학에 대해 논의하기 위해
Ⓑ 철학자에 대한 학생의 지식과 이해를 확인하기 위해
Ⓒ 철학자에 대한 학생의 의견을 묻기 위해
Ⓓ 그 철학자가 기초 철학 101 수업에서 다루어졌다는 것을 상기시키기 위해

TEST 3 Set 2 Lecture 1

Listen to part of a lecture in an environmental science class.

P Surely, you have heard that fossil fuels are a key factor in global warming. When fossil fuels are used, they release greenhouse gases that trap heat in the atmosphere. Greenhouse gases, mainly CO_2, prevent heat from leaving the atmosphere, which leads to a global rise in temperature. Another problem in using fossil fuels is that they are not renewable resources. They were made naturally a long time ago at extremely high pressures and temperatures, and they're basically impossible to synthesize, which means that once they're all depleted, we won't be able to use them anymore.

06 Luckily, fossil fuels aren't the only possible energy source. There are some alternatives, one of which is called biofuel. Biofuels are fuels made directly or indirectly from organic substances, such as plants and animal waste. Unlike fossil fuels, they are renewable. Biofuel can be classified as either ethanol or biodiesel.

Ethanol is usually extracted from staple crops, namely sugar cane and corn. They can be grown anywhere and have lower carbon emissions than fossil fuels. U.S. law dictates that oil companies must include some ethanol in their gasoline, due to the facts that it is both environmentally safe and non-polluting. 07 Initially, you might think that ethanol could substitute completely for gasoline. This appears on the surface to be very positive, right? 08 Unfortunately, ethanol isn't as efficient as fossil fuels. Not enough land exists to power all of the cars in the U.S. with plant-based ethanol. You see, fossil fuels are bad for the environment, but they are very efficient sources of energy. It's no wonder why they have been in use for a good part of history and up until this present day.

On the other hand, biodiesel is just as energy-efficient as petroleum. Like ethanol, biodiesel is derived from plants. [09] Rapeseed biodiesel makes up over 50 percent of biodiesel because rape seed is adaptable to a variety of environments. Other plants hold more energy potential, but they're much harder to grow. Oil palm trees, for instance, would provide five times as much power as rapeseed, but these particular trees only grows in tropical climates. Cultivating oil palm trees would harm rain forests along with animals native to those areas. Biodiesel is an attractive energy source, but destroying the environment would only compound the problem. Another downside of biodiesel is that most cars in the U.S. can not be fueled by diesel because they don't run on diesel engines. You see...the U.S. government doesn't give any tax benefits on using diesel engines. Besides, there is a problem even if American cars start adopting diesel engines. There is still not enough energy to be harvested from oil palm trees to support all the cars in America.

Well, is there a way to produce enough fuel for our population while still preserving the environment? The answer probably lies with algae. It might be surprising, but algae may be a prime candidate for producing biodiesel. [10] Oil comprises about 40 percent of algae's weight, meaning that it's 30 times as energy-efficient as oil palm trees. Also, algae grow extremely fast, doubling in only a few hours, rather than the months needed for other conventional biodiesels. You can leave algae in ponds or lakes, and come back a while later to find vast amounts of them. In some parts of the world, algae grow so fast that they are considered environmental pests. They cover a whole area, consuming all of the oxygen and suffocating other organisms. Marine plants and animals die because algae use up all the nutrients and sunlight for themselves. I guess such instances show the proliferative ability of algae. But, using this plant is tricky business. Even though the growing time is short, processing algae into fuel requires a lot of effort and time. So, some people argue that biodiesel doesn't actually replace as much fossil fuel as we would expect because of its time-consuming extracting process.

However, there is one solution to harnessing this energy efficiently, and it involves isolated containers, referred to as bioreactors. When algae grow and increase in size, they fill in the entire container. Then the bottom of the container opens, allowing the cultivated algae to fall and be easily harvested. Another application that uses this energy is the combination of bioreactors and CO_2 emissions from cars. Since algae are plants, they need CO_2 to make food. If you recall from basic biology, plants have chlorophyll. Chlorophyll can convert sunlight and CO_2 into carbohydrates. Carbohydrates are sugars that plants use as food sources. By utilizing CO_2 emissions in this process, air pollution can be reduced while supporting algae growth. The bioreactors are transparent to receive sunlight, and they are filled with a chemical liquid that the algae utilize to photosynthesize. If CO_2 is injected into this liquid, then the algae can carry out photosynthesis, which converts the CO_2 into food. So, we could reduce the amount of this greenhouse gas in the atmosphere substantially. The bioreactor seems to be the perfect method, right? Despite all these advantages, it won't be commercialized for a long time because of financial difficulties. Bioreactors have been successfully tested in experiments, but they are still too costly for industrial use. Since bioreactors are new type of technology, we have to come up with a new, effective way to actually apply them, which is going to take some time. 11 Of course, it would be exciting to power cars using biodiesel produced by bioreactors. Can you imagine fossil fuels being thrown out and replaced by clean, renewable energy? I can, but it certainly won't be in near future.

[**Vocabulary**] fossil fuel 화석 연료　synthesize[sínθisàiz] 합성하다　deplete[diplí:t] 감소시키다, 고갈되다　biofuel[báioufjù:əl] 생물 연료　animal waste 가축 배설물　staple[stéipl] 주된, 주요한　sugar cane 사탕수수　rapeseed[réipsì:d] 유채씨　oil palm tree 기름야자나무　algae[ǽldʒi:] 해조류　proliferative[proulaifréitiv] 증식하는, 급증하는　harness[háːrnis] (동력원 등으로) 이용하다　chlorophyll[klɔ́:rəfil] 엽록소　carbohydrate[kàːrbouháidreit] 탄수화물　commercialize[kəmə́ːrʃəlàiz] 상업화하다, 대중화하다

06 Main Topic

What does the professor mainly discuss?

Ⓐ The possibility of opting for biofuel instead of fossil fuel
Ⓑ The sources for the production of biofuel
Ⓒ The advantage of biofuel as an energy source
Ⓓ The environmental importance of using biofuel

교수는 주로 무엇을 논의하는가?

Ⓐ 화석 연료를 생물 연료로 대체할 가능성
Ⓑ 생물 연료의 생산이 가능한 원료들
Ⓒ 에너지원으로써 생물 연료의 장점
Ⓓ 생물 연료 사용의 환경적 중요성

07 Inference

Listen again to part of the lecture. Then answer the question.

> P: Initially, you might think that ethanol could substitute completely for gasoline. This appears on the surface to be very positive, right?

Why does the professor say this:
P: This appears on the surface to be very positive, right?

Ⓐ To express strong agreement on the use of ethanol
Ⓑ To show doubt about the application of ethanol
Ⓒ To remind the students of the positive aspects of ethanol
Ⓓ To express reservations about the disadvantages of using ethanol

강의의 일부를 다시 들으시오. 그리고 나서 질문에 답하시오.

> P: 처음에, 여러분들은 에탄올이 가솔린을 전적으로 대체할 수 있다 생각할 지도 몰라요. 이것은 표면적으로 굉장히 좋아 보여요, 그렇죠?

교수가 이 말을 한 이유는 무엇인가?
P: 이것은 표면적으로 굉장히 좋아 보여요, 그렇죠?

Ⓐ 에탄올 사용에 대한 강한 동의를 표현하기 위해
Ⓑ 에탄올 적용에 대한 의심을 보여 주기 위해
Ⓒ 학생들에게 에탄올의 긍정적인 측면을 상기시키기 위해
Ⓓ 에탄올 사용의 단점에 대한 의구심을 표현하기 위해

08 Detail

Why is ethanol insufficient to replace gasoline?

Ⓐ Ethanol is extracted from a restricted range of staple crops like sugar cane and corn.
Ⓑ Ethanol is required in greater quantities than traditional fuels, in order to produce the same energy output.
Ⓒ Ethanol increases people's dependence on fossil fuels.
Ⓓ Ethanol is not a stable source of energy because its use as a fuel is still at an experimental stage.

에탄올은 왜 휘발유를 대체하기에 불충분한가?

Ⓐ 에탄올은 사탕수수나 옥수수 같은 제한된 주곡에서 추출된다.
Ⓑ 동일한 양의 에너지를 생산하기 위해서는 화석 연료보다 더 많은 에탄올이 필요하다.
Ⓒ 에탄올은 화석 연료에 대한 사람들의 의존도를 높인다.
Ⓓ 연료로써의 사용이 아직 실험 단계이기 때문에 에탄올은 안정적인 에너지원이 아니다.

09 Detail

Why is rapeseed the leading source of biodiesel?

A) Rapeseed has a high percentage of oil in its weight.
B) Rapeseed is the most plentiful plant in the U.S.
C) Rapeseed cannot be consumed by humans or livestock.
D) Rapeseed is not difficult to cultivate.

유채씨는 왜 바이오 디젤의 주 원료인가?

A) 유채씨는 그 씨앗 내에 다량의 기름을 가지고 있다.
B) 유채씨는 미국에서 가장 흔한 식물이다.
C) 유채씨는 사람이나 가축이 먹을 수 없다.
D) 유채씨는 재배하기 어렵지 않다.

10 Detail

According to the lecture, why are algae useful as a fuel source?
Choose 2 answers.

A) They contain a high oil proportion.
B) They multiply quickly.
C) They are technologically feasible.
D) They can be harvested from nature.
E) They are rapidly converted into oil.

강의에 따르면, 해조류는 왜 좋은 연료 자원으로 사용될 수 있나?
2개의 답을 고르시오.

A) 기름 함유량이 많다.
B) 빠르게 증식한다.
C) 기술적으로 가능하다.
D) 자연에서 수확될 수 있다.
E) 빠르게 기름으로 전환된다.

11 Inference

What is the professor's attitude towards biodiesel?

A) He believes that biodiesel cannot replace fossil fuels.
B) He thinks people should concentrate more on various problems concerning biodiesel.
C) He is skeptical about the production of biodiesel because of its high maintenance cost.
D) He thinks biodiesel would eventually become an alternative source of traditional fuels.

바이오 디젤에 대한 교수의 태도는 무엇인가?

A) 바이오 디젤이 화석 연료를 대체할 수 없다고 믿는다.
B) 사람들이 바이오 디젤에 관련된 다양한 문제들에 더 집중해야 된다고 생각한다.
C) 높은 유지비 문제 때문에 바이오 디젤의 생산에 대해 회의적이다.
D) 바이오 디젤이 언젠가 전통적인 연료를 바꾸는 대체 에너지원이 될 것이라 생각한다.

TEST 3 Set 2 Lecture 2

Listen to part of a lecture in an ecology class.

P   The Amazon Basin spreads out over a vast area in South America, covering some countries. This region includes territory belonging to nine nations. The Amazon River Basin is home to the largest rainforest on Earth, and this moist broadleaf forest covers most of the Amazon Basin. The Amazon River is the most voluminous river in the world, which is eleven times to size of the Mississippi, and covers an area equivalent in size to the United States. Because of its considerable size, it is made up of the largest and most species-rich tract of tropical rainforest in the world.

So, how is it that such numerous types of organisms inhabit the Amazon? What distinct features make it possible for diverse species to live here? Also, a remarkable fact is that the organisms found in the Amazon are unique to the area, unfound in other parts of the world. What is the reason behind this? **12 The answers to such questions are the main theme of my lecture today...the concept of species allocation or speciation, which happens especially in this area.** Species allocation is an, uh, event that occurs when a particular species gets divided into several groups by a geographic barrier, causing a group of one species to evolve into multiple distinct species. For example, a group of one species would be allocated to the different mountain-region elevation and evolve separately according to the altitude of the location which they inhabit. Since different altitudes provide entirely different surroundings to living organisms, animals living at altitudes are often different from ones living at low altitudes. **13 As a result, even if the two groups begin as a single species, they will follow their own line of evolution over many years and change so much to the point that they are incapable of procreating with one another. In the end, a new species is created, which is fundamentally different from its parent** species as a result of species allocation. This phenomenon is called speciation.

종 분화의 조건

¹⁴Given a second glance, there are two requisites for successful species allocation: isolation of one group of a single species from another for a prolonged period of time and an adequately large geographic barrier to make this isolation possible. ¹⁵It is interesting that such type of barriers cannot be found in the Amazon Rainforest. ¹⁶Typical geographic barriers are such as high mountains and huge oceans that will limit the interaction between two groups of a single species, none of which are present in the Amazon. An example of this type of barrier is the Isthmus of Panama which divides the Pacific Ocean and the Caribbean Sea. This long, thin strip of land limited the interaction between snapping shrimp populations living in these two bodies of water. As a result, the two groups were isolated from each other for many years and eventually evolved into two different types of organisms unable to reproduce with each other. This example is quite easy to understand, but we could not find such examples of speciation which have occurred in the Amazon Rainforest.

Alfred Wallace의 연구

Such phenomenon remained without a clear explanation until a naturalist named Alfred Wallace came up with an answer. Okay, let me tell you more about him. He was a British naturalist, geographer, and biologist. He formulated the theory of evolution by natural selection, which predated Charles Darwin's published contributions on the matter. In fact, no one before Wallace had ever noticed that species with similar characteristics live relatively close to one another. He also carried out research to explain the biodiversity of the Amazon area. During his time there, he spent almost two years travelling in the region and did extensive research on biodiversity in the Amazon. He realized that there were so many different species living in the area and wanted to find the reason behind its phenomenon.

Alfred Wallace의 연구 결과

In pursuit of the answer, Wallace investigated various isolated regions in the Amazon for the first time in history and discovered that a geographic barrier did in fact exist. I realized that this finding is against what had been previously believed. However, such boundaries did exist and it was undersized, yet large enough to separate some organisms. Also, Wallace was the first to note that rivers could be considered as geographic barriers, unlike previous scientists who envisioned barriers as being other kinds of geographical features. I mean, before him, people believed that only enormous obstacles, such as oceans and mountains, could act only as geographic barriers. Wallace's explanations were ignored or criticized.

Anyhow, there are numerous waterways in the Amazon, ranging from small streams to wide rivers. Such waterways have divided species of tiny creatures, such as leafcutter ants, serving as geographic barriers, causing the divided species to become two separate species. The Amazon Rainforest and its distinct natural habitat enabled the development of different, unique types of organisms that cannot be found anywhere else in the world. Through such studies, Wallace successfully confirmed that even small streams can act as geographic barriers, a fact which was ignored by other geographers. These small waterways served their purpose in creating the perfect barrier for separating groups of a species from one another for many years and allowed them to evolve into distinct species. In fact, this temperate area provides ideal habitats for organisms. They can settle down and adapt quickly in a new area, so they don't need to hurdle even the very small barriers. 17Had it not been for Alfred Wallace and his pursuit to answer the question behind the biodiversity of the Amazon Basin, the issue might still remain a mystery.

[Vocabulary] basin[béisən] (강의) 유역 broadleaf forest 활엽수림 species-rich 종(種)이 풍부한 allocation[æləkéiʃən] 할당 speciation[spìːʃiéiʃən] 종 분화 procreate[próukrièit] 새끼를 낳다 requisite[rékwizit] 필요 조건 prolonged[prəlɔ́ːŋd] 오래 계속되는 adequately[ǽdikwitli] 적절히, 충분히 the Isthmus of Panama 파나마 지협 snapping shrimp 딱총새우 predate[priːdéit] ~ 보다 먼저 오다 envision[invíʒən] 마음 속에 그리다 temperate[témpərit] 온화한

12 Main Topic

What is the lecture mainly about?

(A) The evolution of living organisms into various distinct species
(B) The requisites for the occurrence of species allocation
(C) The effect of waterways in the Amazon Basin on living organisms
(D) The explanation behind speciation in the Amazon Rainforest

강의는 주로 무엇에 대한 것인가?

(A) 생물의 다양한 종으로 진화
(B) 종 할당의 발생을 위한 필요 조건
(C) 아마존 유역의 수로가 생물에 미치는 영향
(D) 아마존 우림의 종 분화에 대한 설명

13 Detail

What is the outcome of speciation?

(A) A particular species gets divided into several groups.
(B) Species are located far away from each other.
(C) The divided groups of species are unable to reproduce with one another.
(D) The evolution of species is confronted by geographical barriers.

종 분화의 결과는 무엇인가?

(A) 특정 종이 여러 그룹으로 나뉜다.
(B) 한 종이 다른 종으로부터 고립된다.
(C) 분리된 그룹들 간 서로 번식할 수 없다.
(D) 종의 진화가 지형적 장벽에 부딪치게 된다.

오답 해설 (A) (B)는 종 분화의 요건이다.

14 Detail

What are the two requisites for species allocation?
Choose 2 answers.

(A) Frequent contact among species
(B) The separation of species for an extended period of time
(C) High mountains and large oceans
(D) The presence of geographic barriers

종 할당을 위한 두 가지 필수 조건은 무엇인가?
2개의 답을 고르시오.

(A) 종들 간의 빈번한 접촉
(B) 오랜 기간 동안의 종의 분리
(C) 높은 산과 넓은 바다
(D) 지형적 장벽들의 존재

15 Detail

Why did speciation seem to be a mystery in the Amazon Rainforest?

Ⓐ Because the Amazon Rainforest is oversized
Ⓑ Because typical geographic barriers are not found in this area
Ⓒ Because the Caribbean Sea is too large for speciation
Ⓓ Because thin strip of land is appropriate for speciation

아마존 우림의 종 분화는 왜 미스터리인 듯 보였나?

Ⓐ 아마존 우림은 거대하기 때문에
Ⓑ 이 지역에서는 전형적인 지형적 장벽이 발견되지 않기 때문에
Ⓒ 카리브 해는 종 분화에 너무 넓기 때문에
Ⓓ 땅이 얇은 지대가 종 분화에 적합하기 때문에

16 Organization

Why does the professor mention the Isthmus of Panama?

Ⓐ To explain the long, thin strip of land divides the Caribbean Sea and the Pacific Ocean
Ⓑ To give an example of a natural formation that segregates an area
Ⓒ To emphasize the importance of various types of geographic barriers
Ⓓ To indicate that the Isthmus of Panama is an area with repeated speciation

교수는 왜 파나마 지협을 언급했나?

Ⓐ 땅의 길고 얇은 지대가 카리브 해와 태평양을 나누는 것을 설명하기 위해
Ⓑ 지역을 분리하는 자연 형성물에 대한 예를 제시하기 위해
Ⓒ 다양한 종류의 지형적 장벽의 중요성을 강조하기 위해
Ⓓ 파나마 지협이 반복되는 종 분화 지역임을 나타내기 위해

정답 해설 Ⓑ a natural formation은 지형적 장벽을 가리킨다.

17 Inference

Listen again to part of the lecture. Then answer the question.

> P: Had it not been for Alfred Wallace and his pursuit to answer the question behind the biodiversity of the Amazon Basin, the issue might still remain a mystery.

What can be inferred about the professor when he says this?

Ⓐ He wants to prove that Alfred Wallace's accomplishments were mocked by the scientific community.
Ⓑ He shows respect for Alfred Wallace's efforts in solving the curiosity about speciation.
Ⓒ He criticizes the scientific community for ignoring Alfred Wallace's studies.
Ⓓ He emphasizes the need for further scientific research regarding speciation in the Amazon.

강의의 일부를 다시 들으시오. 그러고 나서 질문에 답하시오.

> P: 아마존 유역의 생물 다양성에 대한 이유를 연구했던 Alfred Wallace의 노력이 없었다면, 아직까지 이 주제는 미스터리로 남아 있었을 것입니다.

교수가 이 말을 할 때, 그에 대해 추론할 수 있는 것은 무엇인가?

Ⓐ Alfred Wallace의 성취가 과학계로부터 무시를 받았다는 것을 증명하기를 원한다.
Ⓑ 종 분화에 대한 호기심을 풀어 낸 Alfred Wallace의 노력에 대해 존경을 표한다.
Ⓒ Alfred Wallace의 연구를 무시한 과학계를 비난한다.
Ⓓ 아마존의 종 분화와 관련된 더 많은 과학적 연구의 필요성을 강조한다.

영단기 TOEFL

ACTUAL TEST

TEST 04

TEST 4 Set 1 Conversation

Listen to a conversation between two students in a chemistry class.

W I don't think I'm doing a very good job at this.
M What's wrong?
W 01 This reaction is supposed to produce ammonia gas, but all I'm getting is just air.
M Uh, how can you tell?
W We learned that ammonia gas, which is alkaline, colors the red *litmus paper blue, but nothing's happening.
M Aha. Right. So, explain the procedure of the experiment to me?
W First, I mixed nitric acid with water in this test tube. Next, I put sodium carbonate in it. This theoretically causes a chemical reaction and produces ammonia gas. The ammonia gas that comes out of the glass tubing here is then supposed to go into the test tube there. But for some reason this is not happening for me.
M Are you telling me that the reaction didn't take place?
W Well. This gas is supposed to have a characteristic pungent smell, and turn moistened litmus paper from red to blue and moistened *universal indicator paper to blue since it is alkaline. Also, I tested with hydrogen chloride gas, which is supposed to be reacted with ammonia and form a white smoke. But nothing has happened yet. I do not see any smoke.
M So, do you mean that ammonia gas necessarily has to turn the paper to blue?
W Yes, it was supposed to. I mean I cannot rely solely on smoke produced since it has no color. I just figured that the easiest way to identify ammonia gas would be by the indicator paper.
M I see. 02 Well, how about repeating your experiment and hoping something turns out differently?
W Sure, can you make sure I'm doing everything

correctly? It's my third time now, so I really want to make this happen.

M No problem. We need clean test tubes first, right? Here are two. And there's a glass tubing with a rubber stopper. What else do we use?

W A graduated cylinder and the Bunsen burner. I have them right here, along with the nitric acid and the sodium carbonate.

M Everything seems to be ready. Wait, what about taking the sodium carbonate and the acid from those reagent bottles on the other lab table? I just realized that your materials could be contaminated from being out in the open for so long.

W I never thought of that. I guess you're right.

M All done. Let's start the experiment, shall we? You repeat what you've been doing all long, and I'll observe your process.

W I start by fixing the test tube on a stand, and then I pour about five milliliters of the nitric acid in it.

M 03 Did you say "about" five milliliters? That's not very scientific, is it?

W Jeez, Mr. Scientist. Exactly five milliliters of nitric acid. Happy?

M Better. Go on, then.

W I then place the sodium carbonate into the acid.

M And you just need to drop it into the acid?

W Yeah. See? You get an immediate bubbling kind of reaction!

M That's pretty neat!

W Then I have to close the test tube with this rubber stopper.

M To trap the gas inside the test tube, I see.

W That's right. Then I wait for the gas to move through the glass tubing into the other test tube. By now, all the ammonia gas should have moved into the other test tube. Can you check if the paper changes its color?

문제점을 발견함

M Yikes! What in the world are you thinking?

W What's the matter?

M 04 You can't collect gas when you're holding the test tube under the mouth of the tube like that!

W Why? I don't get it.

M I guess you forgot something about ammonia gas. Which is lighter, ammonia or air?

W Ammonia. What's that got to do with this?
M ⁰⁴Ammonia gas, which is lighter than air, is floating up. It's rising from the mouth of the tube, not falling into your container. You forgot that fact, which is why you were unable to collect ammonia gas.
W Oh! I should've held it over the test tube! I get what I've been doing wrong all this time. What would I have done without you? Will you hold this paper at the mouth of this tube, please?
M Okay. Here's your paper changing.
W Wow! Look at it change its color.
M That's a very nice experiment. And you finally get to prove ammonia gas is present. Nice going!
W Well, I really appreciate your help. Thanks, Mike. ⁰⁵Now I'm going to write a report for this experiment.
M That's the not-so-exciting part of an experiment. Do you have any future experiments in plan?
W Yeah, I think I want to try something using sodium and water.
M This time, try to remember everything we learned in class!

W 암모니아지. 그게 이거랑 무슨 관계인데?
M ⁰⁴암모니아 가스는 공기보다 가볍기 때문에 떠오른단 말이야. 그게 용기로 떨어지지 않고 시험관 입구로 올라간단 말이지. 네가 그 사실을 잊고 있어서 암모니아 가스를 모으지 못했던 거야.
W 아! 시험관 위로 가도록 그걸 잡았어야 했구나! 내가 내내 뭘 잘못했는지 알겠네. 네가 없었으면 어쩔 뻔 했어? 시험관 입구에 이 종이 좀 잡고 있어 줄래?
M 그래. 여기 종이 색깔이 바뀌었네.
W 우와! 색깔 바뀐 것 좀 봐.
M 정말 멋진 실험이야. 그리고 넌 마침내 암모니아 가스가 존재한다는 것을 증명했어. 잘했는 걸!
W 음, 도와줘서 정말 고마워. 고맙다. Mike. ⁰⁵이제 이 실험 보고서를 작성해야겠다.
M 그건 실험에서 정말 재미없는 부분이야. 다른 실험도 계획한 거 있어?
W 응. 나트륨이랑 물로 뭔가를 좀 해보려고 생각 중이야.
M 이번에는 우리가 수업에서 배웠던 것들을 잘 기억하면서 해 봐!

[**Vocabulary**] litmus paper 리트머스 시험지   nitric acid 질산   sodium carbonate 탄산 나트륨
theoretically[θìːrétikəli] 이론적으로   pungent[pʌ́ndʒənt] 톡 쏘는 듯한   universal indicator paper 만능 지시약 시험지
hydrogen chloride gas 염화수소 가스   rubber stopper 고무 마개   graduated cylinder 눈금 실린더
Bunsen burner 분젠 버너   reagent[riéidʒənt] 시약

[각주]
* **litmus paper** 용액의 산성, 알칼리성을 판단하는 데 쓰이는 리트머스 수용액을 이용해 물들인 종이이다. 이 시험지를 산성 용액에 넣으면 청색지가 붉은색으로 변하고, 알칼리성 용액에 넣으면 적색지가 청색으로 변한다.
* **universal indicator paper** 만능 지시약을 거름종이에 스며들게 한 시험지의 일종이다. 색이 변하는 pH 범위가 넓기 때문에 실험하는 대상의 pH를 대략적으로 파악할 수 있다는 것이 장점이다.

01 Main Topic

What is the goal of the woman's experiment?

Ⓐ To demonstrate the characteristics of ammonia gas
Ⓑ To prove that a litmus paper reacts with ammonia gas
Ⓒ To show the formation of a particular gas
Ⓓ To determine a mistake in the experiment

여자의 실험 목표는 무엇인가?

Ⓐ 암모니아 가스의 특징들을 입증하는 것
Ⓑ 리트머스 시험지가 암모니아 가스에 반응한다는 것을 증명하는 것
Ⓒ 특정 가스의 형성을 보여 주는 것
Ⓓ 실험에서 한 실수를 알아내는 것

오답 해설   Ⓓ 실험에서 한 실수를 알아내서 암모니아 가스의 존재를 증명하는 것이 여자가 한 실험의 궁극적인 목표이다.

02 Detail

What does the man suggest to the woman?

Ⓐ She should watch him repeating the experiment.
Ⓑ She should receive an explanation of the experiment.
Ⓒ She would be better off getting information about hydrogen gas.
Ⓓ She can redo her task under his observation.

남자가 여자에게 제안한 것은 무엇인가?

Ⓐ 여자는 남자가 실험을 반복하는 것을 봐야 한다.
Ⓑ 여자는 실험의 설명을 들어야 한다.
Ⓒ 여자는 수소 가스에 대한 정보를 얻는 것이 더 좋다.
Ⓓ 여자는 그의 관찰 하에 과제를 다시 할 수 있다.

03 Inference

Listen again to part of a conversation. Then answer the question.

> M: Did you say "about" five milliliters? That's not very scientific, is it?

Why does the man say this:
M: That's not very scientific, is it?

Ⓐ To indicate that the woman needs to be more precise
Ⓑ To imply that the woman should use a different acid
Ⓒ To suggest a different experiment for the woman
Ⓓ To discourage the woman from becoming a scientist

대화의 일부를 다시 들으시오. 그러고 나서 질문에 답하시오.

> M: 너 5밀리미터 정도라고 했어? 그건 별로 과학적인 자세가 아닌데?

남자는 왜 이 말을 했나?
M: 그건 별로 과학적인 자세가 아닌데?

Ⓐ 여자가 더 정확해질 필요가 있음을 나타내기 위해
Ⓑ 여자가 다른 산을 사용해야 함을 넌지시 나타내기 위해
Ⓒ 여자에게 다른 실험을 제안하기 위해
Ⓓ 여자가 과학자가 되는 것을 막기 위해

04 Detail

What mistake does the woman make during her experiment?

Ⓐ A characteristic concerning a gas was overlooked.
Ⓑ Test tubes were confused and mixed up.
Ⓒ Materials used in the experiment were contaminated.
Ⓓ Nitric acid mixture with sodium carbonate failed to react.

실험을 하는 동안 여자가 한 실수는 무엇인가?

Ⓐ 특정 가스에 관한 특성이 간과됐다.
Ⓑ 시험관들이 서로 혼동되고 섞였다.
Ⓒ 실험에 사용된 물질들이 오염됐다.
Ⓓ 질산 혼합물과 탄산 나트륨이 반응하는 데 실패했다.

오답 해설 Ⓓ 질산 혼합물과 탄산 나트륨이 반응하는 데 실패한 것은 여자의 실수의 결과이다.

05 Inference

What will the woman do next?

Ⓐ She will clean the lab apparatus she used.
Ⓑ She will review her notes on ammonia gas.
Ⓒ She will write an official record for the experiment.
Ⓓ She will conduct another chemistry experiment.

여자는 다음에 무엇을 할 것인가?

Ⓐ 그녀가 사용한 실험 도구를 정리할 것이다.
Ⓑ 암모니아 가스에 관한 그녀의 필기를 복습할 것이다.
Ⓒ 실험에 관한 공식 기록을 할 것이다.
Ⓓ 다른 화학 실험을 할 것이다.

TEST 4 Set 1 Lecture 1

Listen to part of a lecture in a psychology class.

P ⁰⁶Alright, class. Today I'm going to explain the concept of emotional intelligence. Some of you might already know what it is, but I will define it for the rest of the class. Emotional intelligence is the ability to understand both one's own emotions and the emotions of other people and to discriminate between different feelings and label them appropriately. By looking at a person's facial expressions, gestures, and posture nonverbal cues, someone with high emotional intelligence can sense how that person is currently feeling. Studies have shown that persons with high EQ have greater mental health, exemplary job performance, and stronger leadership skills. I mean they are better at retaining positive social relations and psychological well-being. But of course, if your EQ level is low, you have a hard time understanding whether your friends are not in a good mood, or your co-workers are angry. Also, you often feel like others don't get the point and it makes you frustrated and impatient. So, consequently, you might have a hard time getting along with others. I mean EQ plays an important role in society.

There are two aspects of emotional intelligence. The first aspect is understanding your own emotions through your own thoughts. By reflecting on your emotions, you can control and adjust them as you wish. The second aspect is controlling how you react to different situations, using your thoughts to regulate your emotions. If you know someone who is prone to becoming very happy or very mad and can't control their emotions, well, it's possible that person might have little emotional intelligence. [07]Throughout most of history, psychologists scoffed at the idea of emotional intelligence. They argued that these two words could not be used together, believing that the two forces of emotion and intelligence were in constant conflict. The idea that passion or rage could exist in unison with intellectual thought was a ridiculous one.

OK, let me explain first how emotional intelligence has been gradually accepted in psychology fields. It was such a preposterous concept that it wasn't until recently that the phrase was first used. In 1966, the possibility of emotional intelligence was proposed in a paper written by a German psychologist. But...well, no one seemed to care about it, and the psychologist's article went largely unnoticed. It wasn't until 1990 that emotional intelligence was discussed again, this time by two other psychologists. They went further than the German psychologist and created a working theory of emotional intelligence. This theory explained what it was and how it developed in humans. Once again, however, this study failed to grab anyone's attention. Apparently, emotional intelligence was not something people cared about. Finally, in 1995 a well-respected psychologist named Daniel Goleman published a book titled Emotional Intelligence: *Why It Can Matter More Than IQ.* [08]Having written many articles in various science journals, Goleman had unassailably established himself as a knowledgeable individual. So when he released his book on emotional intelligence, people went crazy over it. It sold five million copies and was so popular that it was even translated into various languages. He has followed up with several further popular sequels of a similar subject matter that reinforce the use of the term. As a result, there have since been hundreds of studies focused on emotional intelligence.

Researchers have developed tests to gauge an individual's emotional intelligence. Though there are many different trials, I'm only going to talk about two of them today. The first one is the Self-Report Assessment. It is a type of psychological test in which an individual fills out a questionnaire. The individual is then able to calculate his or her own emotional intelligence by answering basic yes or no questions such as, "Do I have difficulty controlling my anger when something bad has happened to me?" Each answer to a question is worth a certain amount of points. Once you have finished the test, you add up your points and check your total score against a provided chart to see where you lie on the spectrum of emotional intelligence. ⁰⁹An especially great aspect of the test is that people enjoy taking it and learning about themselves. Also, since there are only two answers to each question to choose from, the test allows researchers to use it when examining for large groups of people with few staff.

감성 지능을 평가하는 방법 2

¹⁰The second test requires an individual to look at various pictures of explicit scenes. For example, you could be shown an image of someone smiling. You would then be asked to rate your agreement with the statement "I can see the anger in this person's expression," by ticking one of the choices: "very much," "a little bit," and "not at all." The more accurately you match a person's emotions with their faces, the higher your ability to read other people's emotions.

감성 지능에 대한 연구 전망

¹¹I know these tests are rather simplistic ones because emotional intelligence is still a brand new science. However, as science becomes more and more advanced, we can expect to have access to well-developed tests to measure our own emotional intelligence. After acquiring more accurate methods to evaluate it, we could demonstrate the issue with the belief that EQ is a more desirable personality quality than IQ, especially in managing successful lives.

고 여러분의 총 점수를 확인해요. ⁰⁹이 테스트가 특별히 좋은 점은 사람들이 그것을 하면서 자신에 대해 알아 가는 것을 즐긴다는 거예요. 또한 각 질문에 대해 선택할 수 있는 답변이 두 개뿐이기 때문에, 연구자들은 적은 직원을 데리고 사람이 많은 그룹을 테스트할 때 그것을 쓸 수 있어요.

¹⁰두 번째 테스트는 개인들에게 특정한 상황에 대한 다양한 사진을 보여 줍니다. 예를 들어, 당신은 누군가가 웃는 이미지를 볼 수 있어요. 그리고 나서 '매우', '약간', 그리고 '전혀'라는 선택지 중 하나를 선택해서 "이 사람의 표정에서 화를 읽을 수 있습니다."라는 문장에 얼마나 동의하는지 점수 매길 것을 요청 받을 수 있어요. 여러분이 사람의 감정을 그들의 얼굴과 더 정확하게 연결시킬수록 여러분은 다른 사람의 감정을 읽는 능력이 더 높아요.

¹¹감성 지능은 아직 새로운 과학 분야이기 때문에 이 테스트들은 꽤 간단한 형태예요. 하지만 과학이 더 발전하면 할수록, 우리는 우리의 감성 지능을 측정할 수 있는 잘 개발된 테스트를 사용할 수 있을 거라고 기대하고 있죠. 그것을 평가하는 더 정확한 방법들이 갖춰지면, 특히 성공적인 삶을 위해 IQ보다 EQ가 더 이상적인 성격이라는 믿음과 같은 문제를 증명할 수 있을 거예요.

[**Vocabulary**] discriminate[diskrímənit] 구별하다　posture[pástʃər] 자세　exemplary[igzémpləri] 모범적인　reflect on 숙고하다　be prone to ~의 경향이 있다　scoff[skɔ(:)f] 조롱하다, 비웃다　unison[júːnisən] 조화　preposterous[pripástərəs] 비상식적인　unassailably[ʌnəséiləbli] 공격할 수 없게, 견고하게　sequel[síːkwəl] 후속 편　gauge[geidʒ] 측정 기준; 측정하다

06 Main Topic

What is the main purpose of this lecture?

Ⓐ **To inform about emotional intelligence's history and development**
Ⓑ To explain how to evaluate emotional intelligence through various tests
Ⓒ To discuss the necessity of emotional intelligence in the field of psychology
Ⓓ To discuss reactions to emotional intelligence in the society

이 강의의 목적은 무엇인가?

Ⓐ 감성 지능의 역사와 발전을 알리는 것
Ⓑ 다양한 테스트들을 통해 감성 지능을 평가하는 방법을 설명하는 것
Ⓒ 심리학 분야에서 감성 지능의 필요성을 논의하는 것
Ⓓ 사회에서 감성 지능에 대한 반응을 논의하는 것

07 Detail

Why did early psychologists reject emotional intelligence?

Ⓐ They believed that emotion and intelligence were separated from one concept.
Ⓑ **They believed that emotion and intelligence were at variance with each other.**
Ⓒ They believed that neither emotion nor intelligence could be evaluated by a simple test.
Ⓓ They believed that emotion and intelligence required another condition if they were to work together.

초기 심리학자들은 왜 감성 지능을 거부했나?

Ⓐ 감정과 지성이 하나의 개념에서 분리된 것이라고 믿었다.
Ⓑ 감정과 지성이 서로 상충된다고 믿었기 때문이다.
Ⓒ 감정과 지성은 간단한 테스트로 평가될 수 없는 개념이라 믿었다.
Ⓓ 감정과 지성이 함께 작용하기 위해서는 다른 조건이 필요하다고 믿었다.

08 Organization

Why does the professor mention Daniel Goleman?

Ⓐ To show that he was the first to discuss emotional intelligence, and how the study of it developed through history
Ⓑ **To explain how emotional intelligence has been widely accepted by the public**
Ⓒ To demonstrate how his work was largely mocked
Ⓓ To emphasize that his book is an important work in the development of study of emotional intelligence

교수는 왜 Daniel Goleman을 언급했나?

Ⓐ 그가 역사상 첫 번째로 감성 지능을 논의했으며, 연구를 어떻게 발전시켰는지 보여 주기 위해
Ⓑ 감성 지능이 어떻게 대중들에게 널리 수용됐는지 설명하기 위해
Ⓒ 그의 연구가 어떻게 무시되었는지 증명하기 위해
Ⓓ 그의 책이 감성 지능 연구의 발달에서 중요한 작업임을 강조하기 위해

09 Detail

According to the professor, what are the advantages of using the Self-Report Assessment?
Choose 2 answers.

Ⓐ It is the most accurate way of measuring emotional intelligence.
Ⓑ People can calculate their score on emotional intelligence.
Ⓒ People like taking it because they enjoy learning about themselves.
Ⓓ Researchers can easily evaluate many participants with simple answers.

교수에 따르면, 자기 보고 평가를 사용하는 것의 이점은 무엇인가?
2개의 답을 고르시오.

Ⓐ 감성 지능을 측정하는 가장 정확한 방법이다.
Ⓑ 사람이 감성 지능에 대한 그들의 점수를 계산할 수 있다.
Ⓒ 사람들은 스스로의 상태를 알 수 있는 즐거움 때문에 그것을 좋아한다.
Ⓓ 연구자들은 간단한 답변으로 많은 참가자들을 수월하게 평가할 수 있다.

오답 해설 Ⓑ 자기 보고 평가에 대한 설명이다. 점수를 계산하는 것 자체는 자기 보고 평가의 이점이 아니다.

10 Organization

Why does the professor mention an image of someone smiling?

Ⓐ To show the importance of understanding others' feelings
Ⓑ To suggest another method to measure emotional intelligence
Ⓒ To explain the difficulty of perceiving what emotion is being portrayed in the pictures
Ⓓ To emphasize how recently emotional intelligence has been developed

교수는 왜 미소 짓는 사람의 이미지를 언급했나?

Ⓐ 다른 사람의 감정을 이해하는 것의 중요성을 보여 주기 위해
Ⓑ 감성 지능을 측정할 수 있는 다른 방법을 제안하기 위해
Ⓒ 사진에 어떤 감정이 묘사되어 있는지 인지하는 것의 어려움을 설명하기 위해
Ⓓ 감성 지성이 최근에 얼마나 발전했는지 강조하기 위해

11 Inference

What can be inferred about the lecture?

Ⓐ The study of emotional intelligence has been accepted and established for a long time.
Ⓑ Psychologists have yet to fully develop assessment systems of emotional intelligence.
Ⓒ People like to learn more about themselves by judging various images shown by psychologists.
Ⓓ Society values emotional intelligence over IQ.

강의에 관해 추론할 수 있는 것은 무엇인가?

Ⓐ 감성 지능에 대한 연구는 오랫동안 받아들여지고 발전되어 왔다.
Ⓑ 심리학자들은 감성 지능의 평가 시스템을 아직은 완벽하게 발전시키지 못했다.
Ⓒ 심리학자들이 보여 주는 다양한 사진을 판단하면서 사람들은 그들 스스로에 대해 배우는 것을 좋아한다.
Ⓓ 사회는 IQ보다 감성 지능에 더 가치를 둔다.

TEST 4 Set 1 Lecture 2

Listen to part of a lecture in a business class.

경영학 강의 중 일부를 들어 보시오.

강의의 주제:
우편 번호와 마케팅의 관계

P So far we have covered the definition of marketing and how it is an essential part of any commercial organizations. **12 However, not all marketing is effective, so it's imperative that we discover exactly what effective marketing is.** Up until the 1960's, marketing wasn't the sophisticated system we know of today. Before then, it was a relatively random and unmanaged process. Then the U.S. Postal Service created something called the ZIP codes in the 60's. ZIP codes were assigned to every geographical area in the U.S. based on their numerical order. Now who can answer how ZIP codes are connected to marketing?

S Um, wouldn't it be because ZIP codes help postal service systems organize and send mail to the destination as quickly as possible? And also, I think good marketing requires the skillful use of geographic information in the distribution of commercial advertising.

P That's right. Interestingly, large corporations required the government to creat ZIP codes for planning their marketing more efficiently. With the ZIP codes, they were able to distribute their advertising effectively. Several marketing companies have stumbled upon the advantages of being able to analyze the regional demographics of their customers. Let's look at an example. **13 Let's say a company is selling a farming tool, such as a cultivator.** Would it want to send the advertisements to places like New York City or farmland areas like Kansas? What kind of farm tools do people need in Texas? What about California? **13 By analyzing the demographics of the country through ZIP codes, companies were able to determine where they needed to advertise and areas where they didn't.** This process allowed them to save money by focusing on advertising in areas where there were a large number of potential buyers.

P 지금까지 우리는 마케팅의 정의와 그것이 어떻게 모든 기업에서 필수적인 요소로 자리잡았는지에 대해 다뤘어요. 12 하지만 모든 마케팅이 효율적인 것만은 아니라서, 그래서 효과적인 마케팅이 무엇인지 정확히 아는 것은 필수적이에요. 1960년대까지 마케팅은 우리가 오늘날 알고 있는 것 같은 정교한 시스템이 아니었어요. 그 전까지 그것은 비교적 두서 없고 관리되지 않는 과정이었어요. 그런데 60년대에 미국 우편국은 우편 번호라고 불리는 것을 만들어 냈어요. 우편 번호는 번호 순서대로 미국의 모든 지리학적 지역에 매겨졌죠. 이제 누가 우편 번호와 마케팅이 어떻게 연결되는지 대답해 볼까요?

S 음, 우편 번호가 우편 제도를 조직화하게 했고 편지를 목적지까지 최대한 빨리 보낼 수 있게 했기 때문일까요? 그리고 상업 광고를 할 때 좋은 마케팅은 지리 정보를 능숙하게 사용할 필요가 있다고 생각해요.

P 맞아요. 흥미롭게도 대기업들은 그들의 마케팅을 더 효율적으로 계획하기 위해 정부에 우편 번호를 만들어 달라고 요구했습니다. 우편 번호로, 그들은 그들의 광고를 더 효과적으로 배포할 수 있었어요. 몇몇의 마케팅 회사들은 그들 고객의 지역별 인구 통계 자료를 분석할 수 있는 이점을 얻었어요. 예를 하나 봅시다. 13 어떤 회사가 경운기와 같은 농기구를 판다고 가정해 봅시다. 그 회사는 뉴욕 같은 곳에 광고를 보내고 싶을까요, 아니면 캔자스 같은 농경지에 광고를 보내고 싶을까요? 텍사스에 있는 사람들은 어떤 농기구가 필요할까요? 캘리포니아는 어떨까요? 13 우편 번호를 통해 나라의 인구 통계 자료를 분석해, 기업은 그들이 광고를 해야 할 곳과 하지 않아도 될 곳을 결정할 수 있었죠. 이 과정은 그들이 잠재 고객이 많이 있는 지역에 광고를 집중할 수 있어서 비용을 절약할 수 있게 했어요.

Then the Internet emerged. With this advanced technology, these companies were able to target their markets even more effectively. These more targeted advertising methods came to benefit not only corporations but also politicians. Can anyone tell me how politicians can use computers to market themselves? Yes, Jenny?

S I'll take a guess. The survey can be done in large regions by using the Internet. And then, the politicians can use the information to target potential voters.

P That's spot on. As Jenny said, the Internet provides easier access to potential voters. According to an online Gallup survey, people in the eastern states such as Virginia and New York usually vote for Democratic politicians while Utah is traditionally considered to be the Republican state. So, politicians would be able to plan their campaigns based on this demographic research. 14Of course, there are more examples of politicians utilizing demographic research in their campaigns, but I don't want this class to turn into a political science class. So back to the corporations. 15Companies now use the Internet to collect a considerable amount of information. Thanks to the marvels of technology, companies have increased the amount of consumer details they know and utilized such demographics when choosing where to advertise their products or services in order to increase sales.

What they use here is something called a lifestyle cluster. 16A lifestyle cluster is a group of people with similar demographics who live together in specific neighborhoods. These lifestyles can reflect various factors, such as the socio-economic status, and education level. 17There are almost 100 types of such clusters and they can be amazingly detailed. Companies try to meet customers' needs and desires by tailoring their products to their lifestyle. This strategy can enhance companies' sales by turning non-consumers into consumers and existing consumers into better consumers.

생활 방식 클러스터에 대한 예시

Now we will look at an example. ¹⁷Take a look at our little town. What could be the lifestyle cluster here?

S So, we are a university town where most of the people are students or faculty members, so we mostly buy books and go to school. We like to hang out in the sports bar after exams, and don't usually purchase expensive items.

P Very good. I took some time to research this town beforehand. The lifestyle cluster for this town is mostly people who are under the age of 30, of which the majority are single, and live in rented properties rather than owning a home. Many enjoy outdoor activities, and they spend their money mostly on books and food. There is a higher demand for fast food and coffee than other towns. People usually don't have their own cars. There's a lot more, but I won't go into them in the interest of time. This pretty much describes a typical college town.

효율적인 마케팅을 위한 정보 조사

S Oh my gosh, that's a lot more specific than I would have thought. But with so much information, I want to ask if it's actually relevant. Isn't there a danger of it just turning out to be a ton of unnecessary detail?

P That's hardly the case. The more data you get, the better you are able to analyze that data. For example, if you are planning to open a restaurant in this college, you probably consider various aspects. You would research on the demographics of potential customers and would want to advertise in the most effective areas to maximize your revenue. Now, how would you have come up with all of the information required to make these decisions in the first place? Surveys, such as those done by Gallup, are a good option. They can be done on the street, door-to-door, through phone calls or the Internet. There are many ways that companies can gather information. This influx of information actually helps to determine which information is valid to adopt and can be used to figure out how to advertise, what to advertise, and to whom to advertise. These steps should be planned carefully to attract potential customers as efficiently as possible.

[**Vocabulary**] numerical [njuːmérikəl] 숫자와 관련된　stumble upon 우연히 만나다　demographics [dèməgrǽfiks] 인구 통계 자료　Democratic [dèməkrǽtik] 민주당의　Republican [ripʌblikən] 공화당　marvel [máːrvəl] 경이로운 업적　lifestyle cluster 생활 방식 클러스터　tailor [téilər] 맞추다　venue [vénjuː] 장소　in the first place 우선　influx [ínflʌks] 유입

12 Main Topic

What is the lecture mainly about? | 강의는 주로 무엇에 대한 것인가?

Ⓐ The factors involved in identifying specific marketing groups
Ⓑ The reason corporations are interested in the development of marketing campaigns
Ⓒ **The reason lifestyle clusters can be useful in marketing a company's products**
Ⓓ The methods used when setting up a market strategy to promote sales

Ⓐ 특정 마케팅 집단을 식별하는 데 포함되는 요소들
Ⓑ 기업이 마케팅 활동을 개발하는 데 관심을 갖는 이유
Ⓒ 생활 방식 클러스터가 기업의 상품을 광고하는 데 유용한 이유
Ⓓ 판매를 촉진시키기 위해 시장 전략을 세울 때 사용되는 방법들

13 Organization

Why does the professor mention cultivators? | 교수는 왜 경운기를 언급했나?

Ⓐ To make sure that students understand cultivators can be used on farms
Ⓑ **To support the idea that companies use the demographic information to sell their products**
Ⓒ To demonstrate the different criteria that can be included in demographics
Ⓓ To illustrate how ZIP codes categorize regions easily

Ⓐ 경운기가 농업에 사용된다는 것을 학생들에게 확실히 이해시키기 위해
Ⓑ 기업이 그들의 상품을 팔기 위해 인구 통계 자료를 사용한다는 것을 뒷받침하기 위해
Ⓒ 인구 통계에 포함될 수 있는 다른 기준을 설명하기 위해
Ⓓ 우편 번호가 지역을 어떻게 쉽게 구분하는지 설명하기 위해

14 Inference

Listen again to part of the lecture. Then answer the question. | 강의의 일부를 다시 들으시오. 그러고 나서 질문에 답하시오.

> P: Of course, there are more examples of politicians utilizing demographic research in their campaigns, but I don't want this class to turn into a political science class.

> P: 물론 정치인들이 인구 통계 데이터를 그들의 선거 활동에 어떻게 이용하는지에 관한 예가 더 많지만, 저는 이번 시간을 정치과학 시간으로 만들고 싶진 않네요.

What does the professor imply when he says this:
P: ...but I don't want this class to turn into a political science class.

교수가 이 말을 할 때 암시한 것은 무엇인가?
P: ……하지만 저는 이번 시간을 정치과학 시간으로 만들고 싶진 않네요.

Ⓐ He thinks students learn more about demographics in political science.
Ⓑ He thinks that the political examples he mentioned are not relevant.
Ⓒ **He wants to focus on the commercial situation related to the topic.**
Ⓓ He wants students to cover political information in another class.

Ⓐ 학생들이 정치과학 시간에 인구 통계에 대해 더 배워야 한다고 생각한다.
Ⓑ 그가 언급한 정치적 예시가 적절하지 않다고 생각한다.
Ⓒ 주제와 관련된 상업적 상황에 집중하기를 원한다.
Ⓓ 다른 수업에서 학생들이 정치적 정보에 대해 다루기를 원한다.

15 Detail

What is the main advantage of using the Internet to analyze target markets?

Ⓐ It increases the chance for politicians to be elected.
Ⓑ It provides large amounts of data for companies to market their goods.
Ⓒ Companies can advertise their products to large regions.
Ⓓ Companies can make their products effectively using "lifestyle clusters" with the help of the Internet.

표적 시장을 분석할 때, 인터넷을 이용하는 것의 가장 큰 장점은 무엇인가?

Ⓐ 정치인들이 당선될 가능성을 높여 준다.
Ⓑ 기업이 그들의 상품을 광고하기 위한 많은 양의 정보를 제공한다.
Ⓒ 기업은 넓은 지역에 그들의 상품을 광고할 수 있다.
Ⓓ 기업은 인터넷으로 생활 방식 클러스터를 이용해 효과적으로 상품을 만들어낼 수 있다.

16 Detail

According to the lecture, what is "lifestyle cluster"?

Ⓐ It means people with shared backgrounds reside in similar areas.
Ⓑ It means that the population can be segmented by several factors.
Ⓒ It means that computers can be used to analyze buying patterns.
Ⓓ It means that a college town is segmented by many factors.

강의에 따르면, 생활 방식 클러스터는 무엇인가?

Ⓐ 배경을 공유하는 사람들이 비슷한 지역에 거주하는 것을 의미한다.
Ⓑ 인구가 여러 요소로 나누어질 수 있다는 것을 의미한다.
Ⓒ 컴퓨터가 소비 패턴을 분석하는 데 사용될 수 있다는 것을 의미한다.
Ⓓ 대학가가 여러 요소로 분리된다는 것을 의미한다.

17 Organization

Why does the professor mention a university town?

Ⓐ To analyze the buying pattern of customers in a university town
Ⓑ To demonstrate how difficult demographics can be applied to marketing
Ⓒ To explain market segmentation for promoting sales
Ⓓ To question that every region has its own lifestyle cluster

교수는 왜 대학가를 언급했나?

Ⓐ 대학가의 소비자 구매 패턴을 분석하기 위해
Ⓑ 인구 통계 자료가 마케팅에 적용되는 것이 얼마나 어려운지를 설명하기 위해
Ⓒ 판매를 촉진시키기 위한 시장 분할을 설명하기 위해
Ⓓ 모든 지역이 그만의 생활 방식 클러스터가 있다는 것에 대한 의구심을 표현하기 위해

정답 해설 Ⓒ lifestyle clusters가 market segmentation으로, marketing이 promoting sales로 패러프레이징 됐다.

TEST 4 Set 2 Conversation

Listen to part of a conversation between a student and a professor.

S Hello, Dr. Robinson. Can I talk to you for a second?

P Oh. Hi there, Mike. What brings you here? Do you have any questions about the class materials today?

S 01 No, actually, I came here to discuss my paper. I've decided to focus on the organization of craft unions in the late 1800s. You know it's like a labor organization in a manner that seeks to unite craftsmen, in a specific industry.

P OK. Could you tell me more details so that I can understand where I can fit in?

S Sure. It basically established better working conditions, such as higher wages, safety standards, and shorter working hours. 02 Also, the main purpose of craft unions was to protect workers, especially craftsmen against discrimination, but ironically to take part in the union, the member had to be qualified as a skilled craftsman. So, I mean the union itself discriminated against unskilled workers. Actually, I can't understand this point, and it's really bothering me.

P Right. You bring an interesting point, and this is a common issue that students come across. At that time, some people argued for more inclusive unions. They claimed the union had to redesign for open admittance to provide equal opportunity to people who wanted to join. I think you should find more information regarding this using some primary sources.

S I'm sorry, Professor. But what is a primary source?

P 03 A primary source can include a diary, letters, autobiography, official document or other source of information that was recorded or created at the time, event or with the person under study. It was produced during the time when events actually happened. Of course, these materials have not been distorted or altered. I think the best example you are probably

		aware of is *The Diary of Anne Frank*, which consisted of real experiences of a Jewish family during WWII. For your paper, you can find some speeches and news articles created while the union was actually organized.
2, 3차 자료	S	Then, are there probably second sources?
	P	Of course, these involve analysis, interpretation, or generalization of the original information. There are also tertiary sources. These are the textual consolidation of primary and secondary sources. But you should keep in mind that some tertiary sources are not to be used in certain academic fields. Obviously, some of them are taken from derived forms of the original source, which lessens the credibility of their data. So, I think you should contemplate if you decide to use one.
	S	Oh, I got it. So could you elaborate more on what I should look for?
	P	You can find some information such as news articles and speeches by a union leader or president during that time.
자료를 찾을 수 있는 곳	S	That sounds interesting, but where can I find the information?
	P	04 You should dig around. I think the Internet provides a wide variety of information, and you can visit an archive in the library. Do you know what the archive is? It is a place where historical records and documents are stored. So, you might find some useful information as well. 04 But it might be difficult for you as an undergraduate student to enter and find the right information there, so if you try to use it, you'd better ask for some help from the library staff.
	S	05 Then, I think I should check a website first.
	P	That could be a good idea, but that might be easier said than done. You should keep in mind that some of the information provided by websites might not be reliable. 04 So you need to look into various resources to establish this more.
	S	OK, I can see what you mean by digging around. I will gather information as much as possible. Thank you very much.
	P	No problem. If you have any questions, feel free to stop by my office.

S 그럼, 아마도 2차 자료도 있겠네요?
P 물론이지. 이것들은 원래 정보에 대한 분석, 해석이나 일반화를 포함한단다. 또한 3차 자료도 있단다. 이것들은 1차와 2차 자료들의 원문을 통합한 것들이야. 하지만 몇몇의 3차 자료들은 특정 학계에서는 사용되지 않는다는 사실을 명심해야해. 분명히, 그것들 중 일부는 원본의 파생물이어서, 그 자료의 신뢰도를 떨어뜨리지. 그래서 만약 네가 그 자료 중 하나를 사용하려고 결정했으면, 이 부분을 고려해야 할 거야.
S 오, 이해했어요. 제가 무엇을 찾아야 하는지 더 자세히 알려 주시겠어요?
P 그 당시의 신문 기사나 조합의 지도자나 조합장이 했던 연설문 같은 정보들을 찾을 수 있을 거야.
S 그거 매우 흥미로운데, 제가 어디서 그 정보를 찾을 수 있을까요?
P 04아마 좀 더 둘러봐야 할 거야. 인터넷은 다양한 정보를 제공해 줄 거고, 도서관의 기록 보관소도 방문할 수 있겠지. 참고로, 기록 보관소는 오래된 기록과 서류가 보관되어 있는 곳이란다. 그래서, 네가 유용한 정보를 찾을 수 있을지도 몰라. 04하지만 학부생인 네가 거기 들어가서 맞는 정보를 찾는 일이 어려울 수도 있으니, 만약 사용하고 싶다면, 도서관 직원에게 도움을 청하는 것이 더 나을 것 같구나.
S 05그렇다면, 저는 먼저 웹 사이트를 확인해 봐야겠네요.
P 그것도 좋은 생각일 수 있지만, 말처럼 쉬운 일이 아닐 수도 있단다. 웹 사이트에서 제공하는 몇몇 정보들은 믿을 수 없다는 점을 명심하렴. 04그러니 이것을 더 확실하게 하기 위해서는 다양한 자료를 조사해야 할 거야.
S 알겠어요, 이제 교수님이 좀 더 둘러보라고 하신 게 무슨 뜻인지 알겠어요. 제가 모을 수 있는 최대한의 정보를 모아야겠어요. 감사합니다.
P 천만에. 다른 질문이 있다면 언제든지 내 사무실로 오렴.

[**Vocabulary**] craft union 직능 조합　　craftsman[kræftsmən] 장인, 기술자　　inclusive[inklú:siv] 폭 넓은, 포괄적인　　admittance[ədmítəns] 입장, 들어감　　primary source 1차 자료　　autobiography[ɔ̀:təbaiágrəfi] 자서전　　distort[distɔ́:rt] 왜곡하다, 비틀다　　tertiary source 3차 자료　　consolidation[kənsàlidéiʃən] 통합, 합병　　lessen[lésən] 줄이다　　credibility[krèdəbíləti] 신뢰도　　contemplate[kántəmplèit] 고려하다　　elaborate[ilǽbərit] 정교한　　archive[á:rkaiv] 기록 보관소

01 Main Topic

Why does the student visit the professor?

Ⓐ To discuss how important primary sources are
Ⓑ To get some help in doing research for a paper
Ⓒ To learn how to use sources to complete a paper
Ⓓ To get approval for the topic for a paper

학생은 왜 교수를 찾아갔나?

Ⓐ 1차 자료가 얼마나 중요한지 논의하기 위해
Ⓑ 보고서를 위한 자료를 조사하는 데 도움을 받기 위해
Ⓒ 보고서를 완성하기 위해 자료를 어떻게 사용할지 배우기 위해
Ⓓ 보고서 주제에 대한 승인을 받기 위해

02 Detail

What does the student think about the craft union?

Ⓐ It played a decisive role in protecting skilled workers.
Ⓑ It was unable to empower craftsmen.
Ⓒ It discriminated against skilled workers.
Ⓓ It had a paradoxical policy.

학생은 직능 조합에 대해 어떻게 생각하는가?

Ⓐ 숙련된 노동자들을 보호하는 데 결정적인 역할을 했다.
Ⓑ 기술자들에게 힘을 실어 주지 못했다.
Ⓒ 숙련된 노동자들을 차별 대우했다.
Ⓓ 자기모순적인 조항이 있었다.

03 Organization

Why does the professor mention *The Diary of Anne Frank*?

Ⓐ To explain how the student could find valuable information
Ⓑ To provide an example of a primary source
Ⓒ To emphasize how important sources are when writing a paper
Ⓓ To compare the book with the student's paper

교수는 왜 《안네의 일기》를 언급했나?

Ⓐ 학생이 중요한 정보를 어떻게 찾을 수 있는지 설명하기 위해
Ⓑ 1차 자료에 대한 예시를 제공하기 위해
Ⓒ 보고서를 작성할 때 자료가 얼마나 중요한지 강조하기 위해
Ⓓ 그 책과 학생의 보고서를 비교하기 위해

04 Detail

What does the professor suggest the student to do?
Choose 2 answers.

A. To keep from using tertiary sources for academic research
B. To get help to access to a place academic materials are located
C. To talk to the library staff to find the right website
D. To search for various kinds of information related to the topic

교수가 학생에게 하라고 제안한 것은 무엇인가?
2개의 답을 고르시오.

A. 학술 연구에 3차 자료를 사용하지 않을 것
B. 학술 자료들이 있는 곳에 접근하기 위해 도움을 받을 것
C. 도서관 직원에게 맞는 웹 사이트를 찾아 달라고 말할 것
D. 주제와 관련된 다양한 종류의 정보를 찾을 것

오답 해설 A 몇몇 3차 자료가 특정 학계에서 사용되지 않기도 하니 사용할 때 주의하라고 했지만 그것이 3차 자료를 사용하지 말라는 의미는 아니다.

05 Inference

Listen again to part of the conversation. Then answer the question.

> S: Then, I think I should check a website first.
> P: That could be a good idea, but that might be easier said than done. You should keep in mind that some of the information provided by websites might not be reliable.

Why does the professor say this:
P: ...but that might be easier said than done.

A. To commend the student on bringing up a good idea
B. To indicate that the student needs to be concerned with other aspects
C. To emphasize that using the Internet is an easy way to find sources
D. To advise the student not to find sources on the Internet

대화의 일부를 다시 들으시오. 그리고 나서 질문에 답하시오.

> S: 그렇다면 저는 먼저 웹 사이트를 확인해 봐야겠네요.
> P: 그것도 좋은 생각일 수도 있지만, 말처럼 쉬운 일이 아닐 수도 있단다. 웹 사이트에서 제공하는 몇몇 정보들은 믿을 수 없다는 점을 명심하렴.

교수는 왜 이 말을 했나?
P: ……하지만 말처럼 쉬운 일은 아닐 수도 있단다.

A. 학생이 좋은 생각을 한 것을 칭찬하기 위해
B. 학생이 다른 부분도 신경을 써야 한다는 것을 나타내기 위해
C. 인터넷을 이용하는 것이 자료를 찾는 쉬운 방법임을 강조하기 위해
D. 학생에게 인터넷에서 자료를 찾지 말라고 조언하기 위해

TEST 4 Set 2 Lecture 1

Listen to part of a lecture in an ecology class.

P Hello, class. Today we will be continuing our discussion on the marine ecosystem. Last time, I gave you a general overview of the ecosystem of our ocean, defining the boundaries of marine ecosystems and giving you some characteristic examples of them. [06] Let's go more in-depth, and focus on a particular type of marine ecosystem—California kelp forests. First, most of you may not be familiar with kelp. Kelp is somewhat like seaweed. So, they're the grassy algae that grow on the ocean's floors and they come in different color varieties—red, green, and brown. In most species of kelp, the body is made up of flat or leaf-like structures called blades. California kelps are large plants found all over the Pacific Ocean. In fact, the kelps are the largest marine plant living in the Pacific. These plants stick to the bottom of the ocean and extend all the way up to the surface of the ocean. They are sometimes as tall as 200 feet, or 60 meters. I mentioned they were somewhat like seaweed because they grow very close together and form something that looks like forests. They even grow remarkably fast, just like weeds in your garden.

Based on their tendency to accumulate into dense masses and to grow very quickly, they are in fact very similar to tropical rainforests. [07] Kelp forests and tropical rainforests are alike in that they both have different layers. If you recall what you learned about tropical rainforests before our discussion moved into the marine habitat, rainforests provide several havens, which are distinguished by the amount of sunlight that reaches them. Likewise, because the amount of sunlight differs from various layers of the sea based on depth, each of these layers supports different types of sea animals, making distinctive ecosystems comparable to tropical rainforests. Each layer provides unique habitats to a particular set of animals that cannot be found in other areas. Because of these layers, there are numerous different species of sea animals that relate to kelp forests. These living organisms find food, shelter, and other necessities of life in kelp forests. 08 It is interesting how even Charles Darwin, a well-known naturalist who famously theorized about evolution, studied these marine forests. In fact, he was the first one to make note of the high complexity of and the vast number of sea animals residing in the kelp forests. He even mentioned that if the kelp forests disappeared, more see animals would lose their homes than if the whole rainforests vanished. We often surmise that the tropical rainforests are the ecosystems that contain the most animals per area, but think again! There is actually a much higher density of living creatures in the kelp forests. In fact, this area is a valuable asset in ecological research, so many ecologists and botanists have denoted research in these areas for years.

켈프 숲에 위협을 가하는 요인 1: 엘니뇨

However, unfortunately there are many dangers threatening kelp. It may not be able to survive and to sustain its robust animal populations if such negative factors continue to endanger its existence. 09 For example, *El Niño is one of the main causes affecting kelp. Does anyone here speak Spanish? El Niño refers to the Christ child, and was so named because this weather phenomenon is often noticed around Christmas. Basically, El Niño is the periodic warming in the Pacific near South America that creates increased rainfalls and the mighty wind gusts from east to west. And, due to the high concentration of water in the clouds, the rain pours. I mean, it literally pours. This phenomenon occurs once every three to seven years. It has been associated with catastrophic ecological conditions. You see, forests of giant kelp depend on cool, nutrient-rich water for survival and growth. 10 However, El Niño carries enormous amounts of rainwater, which is warm and does not contain much nutrition. So this nutrient depletion related to the influx of warm water has resulted in massive declines in the size of kelp forests. Also, this process could eliminate the abundance and diversity of life associated with the forests. This is a disastrous outcome, since, as I mentioned a while ago, the kelp forests are critical in the marine ecosystems.

사실 그는 켈프 숲에 살고 있는 해양 생물의 고도의 복잡성과 많은 수에 주목한 첫 번째 사람이었어요. 그는 심지어 만약 켈프 숲이 사라진다면, 열대 우림 전체가 사라지는 것보다 더 많은 해양 생물들이 서식지를 잃을 것이라고도 언급하기도 했죠. 우리는 종종 열대 우림이 지역당 가장 많은 동물들이 사는 생태계라고 생각하지만, 생각을 다시 해 봐야 해요! 실제로는 켈프 숲에 훨씬 고밀도로 생명체가 존재합니다. 사실상 이 지역은 생태학 연구에도 굉장히 중요한 자산이기도 해서, 많은 생태학자들과 식물학자들이 수년 동안 연구를 진행하고 있어.

하지만, 불행히도 켈프를 위협하는 많은 위험 요소들이 있어요. 만약 부정적인 요소들이 그것의 존재에 계속해서 위협을 가한다면, 이 건강한 해양 생물들을 유지하고 살아가게 할 수 없을 지도 몰라요. 09예를 들어, 엘니뇨는 켈프에 영향을 주는 가장 큰 원인 중 하나예요. 여기 스페인어를 할 수 있는 사람이 있나요? 엘니뇨는 아기 예수를 뜻하는데, 이 날씨 현상이 주로 크리스마스 시기에 발생하기 때문에 지어진 이름이죠. 기본적으로 엘니뇨는 강우량 증가와 동쪽에서 서쪽으로 부는 강한 돌풍을 만들어 내는 남미 근처 태평양에서 주기적으로 발생하는 온난화 현상입니다. 그리고 구름 안에 축적된 고농도의 물 때문에, 비를 퍼부어요. 정말 말 그대로 퍼부어요. 이러한 현상은 3에서 7년마다 발생합니다. 이 현상은 재앙적인 생태학적 상황과 연관이 있어요. 거대한 켈프 숲은 생존과 성장을 위해 시원하고 영양분이 풍부한 물에 의존해요. 10하지만 엘리뇨는 많은 양의 비를 동반하는데, 그것은 미지근하면서 영양분이 많지 않아요. 미지근한 물의 유입과 관련된 이 영양분의 감소는 켈프 숲 크기의 대량 감소로 이어집니다. 또한 이 과정은 그 숲과 관련된 생명의 다양성과 풍부함을 없앨 수 있어요. 앞에서 얘기했듯이, 켈프 숲은 해양 생태계에서 중요하기 때문에, 이것은 비참한 결과예요. 하지만 다행히, 이러한 현상은 켈프 숲에 영구적인 피해를 입힐 정도로 자주 발생하지는 않아요. 그래서 그것들은 이 연약한 식물을 뿌리채 뽑을 수도 있는 폭풍 같은 물리적인 폐해로부터 빠르게 회복할 수 있습니다.

Fortunately, however, this phenomenon does not often happen enough to damage the kelp forests permanently. So, they can recover quickly from physical disturbances such as storms that might uproot the fragile plants.

However, if humans and other factors started profoundly damaging the kelp it would not be able to return to its original condition. For instance I would like to focus on sea otters. They are marine mammals and the heaviest members of the weasel family. They are one of the many species that live near kelp forests in the Pacific Ocean. Although they don't have any direct connection with kelp, they do feed on sea hedgehogs and sea hedgehogs eat kelp, so the otters help maintain a sort of balance. Sea hedgehogs greedily graze on kelp when otters are not around, but the presence of the predators keeps sea hedgehog populations in check, which helps maintain kelp populations. This situation is an example of how different species are of varying importance in maintaining ecosystem functions. In these relationships between species they actually affect each other profoundly, which is why people should not thoughtlessly tamper with the food web. [11] But the problem is that the number of sea otters is dropping because of environmental pollution from human activities, including commercial and industrial disposal, oil spills, and fertilizer runoff that contaminate bodies of water. Pollutants eventually find their way into the seas and destroy habitats for various marine species including sea otters. If sea otters all disappear, then you can guess what will happen to the kelp, right?

[**Vocabulary**] kelp [kelp] 켈프(해초의 일종)　　grassy [grǽsi] 풀로 덮인　　seaweed [síːwiːd] 해조류　　naturalist [nǽtʃərəlist] 동식물학자, 박물학자　　theorize [θíː(ː)əraiz] 이론을 제시하다　　surmise [sərmáiz] 추적하다　　robust [roubʌ́st] 튼튼한　　gust [gʌst] 돌풍　　amass [əmǽs] 모으다, 축적하다　　uproot [ʌprúːt] 뿌리채 뽑다　　sea otter 해달　　sea hedgehog 바다 성게　　greedily [gríːdili] 탐욕스럽게, 게걸스럽게　　graze [greiz] 풀을 뜯어 먹다　　keep something in check ~을 억제하다, 억누르다　　thoughtlessly [θɔ́ːtlisli] 생각 없이　　tamper [tǽmpər] 쓸데없는 참견을 하다, 간섭하다　　food web 먹이 그물

[각주]
* **El Niño** 사람이 만들어 내는 공해로 기상 상태가 변하고 있다. 대표적으로 지구 온난화 현상이 있는데, 이것은 태양으로부터 받는 복사 에너지가 지구를 둘러싸고 있는 이산화 탄소 층 때문에 지구 밖으로 배출이 되지 않아 지구의 온도가 점점 올라가는 것을 말한다. 이런 온난화 현상은 바다에도 영향을 주는데 그 대표적인 예가 엘니뇨이다. 이것은 페루와 칠레 연안에서 일어나는 해수 온난화 현상으로 보통 12월 말경에 발생하기 때문에 크리스마스와 연관시켜 스페인어로 '어린 아이(아기 예수)'라는 뜻인 엘니뇨라고 이름을 붙였다. 이 현상이 일어나면 적도 부근의 해수 온도가 평년에 비해 0.5도 이상 올라가는 상태가 5개월 이상 지속되고 많은 양의 폭우를 동반한다. 이 결과로 바닷속 생태계 환경이 갑자기 변하고 많은 물고기가 죽어 근처의 어장이 황폐화돼 홍수가 발생해 농업과 수산업 전반에 큰 피해를 준다.

06 Main Topic

What is the lecture mainly about?

Ⓐ A comparison between kelp forests and other marine ecosystems
Ⓑ The several biological species that inhabit kelp forests
Ⓒ The characteristics of different layers of kelp forests
Ⓓ The role and condition of kelp forests

강의는 주로 무엇에 관한 것인가?

Ⓐ 켈프 숲과 다른 해양 생태계 비교
Ⓑ 켈프 숲에서 사는 다양한 생물 종
Ⓒ 켈프 숲의 다양한 층의 특성
Ⓓ 켈프 숲의 역할과 상태

07 Detail

According to the professor, what are the similarities between tropical rainforests and kelp forests?
Choose 2 answers.

A Both provide distinctive layers because of their environmental traits.
B Both provide protection and shelter from harsh surroundings.
C Both foster the variety and variability of life in their ecosystems.
D Both consist of the largest plants in their areas.
E Both are affected by natural disasters.

교수에 따르면, 열대 우림과 켈프 숲의 유사성은 무엇인가?
2개의 답을 고르시오.

A 환경적인 특성 때문에 독특한 층을 제공한다.
B 거친 환경으로부터 보호와 안식처를 제공한다.
C 그들의 생태계에 있는 생명체의 다양성과 가변성을 키운다.
D 그들 지역에서 가장 큰 식물들로 구성된다.
E 자연재해로부터 영향을 받는다.

08 Organization

Why does the professor mention Charles Darwin?

Ⓐ To describe what Charles Darwin found while researching kelp forests
Ⓑ To sympathize with Charles Darwin's concern for the consequence of dying kelp forests
Ⓒ To illustrate the beneficial relationship between kelp forests and the species in the marine ecosystem
Ⓓ To emphasize the biological complexity and ecological importance of kelp forests

교수는 왜 찰스 다윈을 언급했나?

Ⓐ 찰스 다윈이 켈프 숲을 연구하는 동안 발견한 것을 설명하기 위해
Ⓑ 죽어가는 켈프 숲의 결과에 관한 찰스 다윈의 우려를 지지하기 위해
Ⓒ 해양 생태계에서 켈프 숲과 종들 사이의 이로운 관계를 묘사하기 위해
Ⓓ 켈프 숲의 복잡성과 생태학적 중요성을 강조하기 위해

09 Inference

Listen again to part of the lecture. Then answer the question.

> P: For example, El Niño is one of the main causes affecting kelp. Does anyone here speak Spanish?

Why does the professor say this:
P: Does anyone here speak Spanish?

Ⓐ To check if students actually understand the meaning of El Niño
Ⓑ To introduce the Spanish meaning of the term
Ⓒ To get help with the Spanish meaning of El Niño
Ⓓ To inform where El Niño originated

강의의 일부를 다시 들으시오. 그러고 나서 질문에 답하시오.

> P: 예를 들어, 엘니뇨는 켈프에 영향을 주는 가장 큰 원인 중 하나예요. 여기 스페인어를 할 수 있는 사람이 있나요?

교수는 왜 이 말을 했나?
P: 여기 스페인어를 할 수 있는 사람이 있나요?

Ⓐ 학생들이 엘니뇨의 뜻을 실제로 이해했는지 확인하기 위해
Ⓑ 이 용어의 스페인어 뜻을 설명하기 위해
Ⓒ 엘니뇨의 스페인어 뜻과 관련해 도움을 받기 위해
Ⓓ 엘니뇨 현상이 어디에서 유래했는지 알려주기 위해

10 Detail

According to the professor, what impact does El Niño have on kelp forests?

Ⓐ It causes sudden flood, which eradicates habitats of marine species.
Ⓑ It destroys the food web existing in kelp forests.
Ⓒ It thins out some nutrients in a certain area of the ocean.
Ⓓ It raises the water level and impedes kelp forests from reaching sunlight.

교수에 따르면, 엘니뇨는 켈프 숲에 어떤 영향을 미치는가?

Ⓐ 급작스런 홍수를 야기하고, 그것은 해양 종들의 서식지를 없앤다.
Ⓑ 켈프 숲에 존재하는 먹이 그물을 파괴한다.
Ⓒ 바다의 특정 지역의 영양분이 줄어들게 만든다.
Ⓓ 수위를 높이고 켈프 숲에 햇빛이 닿는 것을 방해한다.

11 Organization

Why does the professor mention sea otters?

Ⓐ To specify one of the many animal species that inhabits kelp forests
Ⓑ To elaborate on the environmental significance of sea otters in kelp forests
Ⓒ To highlight the damage caused by human intervention in kelp forests
Ⓓ To explain the relationship between people and the animals

교수는 왜 해달을 언급했나?

Ⓐ 켈프 숲에 서식하는 많은 동물 중 하나를 명시하기 위해
Ⓑ 켈프 숲에서 해달의 환경적인 중요성을 자세히 설명하기 위해
Ⓒ 인간의 개입이 켈프 숲을 손상시킬 수 있다는 것을 강조하기 위해
Ⓓ 인간과 이 동물 간의 관계를 설명하기 위해

영단기 TOEFL

ACTUAL TEST

TEST 05

TEST 5 Set 1 Conversation

Listen to part of a conversation between a student and a professor.

S Evening, Professor Smalls. Do you mind if I come in?
P Sure thing, Kate! Do you need any help?
S Yes, today in class, you told us to watch a film on *Thomas Jefferson...
P Yes, I did! Is there a problem?
S The thing is, I wanted to know if the film is about how Thomas Jefferson organized the *Lewis and Clark expedition.
P Err...not really. It focuses on Jefferson's political philosophy during his presidency. It is a very important film because it elaborates on the kind of influence that Jefferson's policy...
S Oh, actually, we are supposed to choose an influential event that happened in U.S. history as a topic for the term paper. I selected the Lewis and Clark expedition, so I wanted to know if the film contains content about the expedition.
P Huh? Sure, why not! The film does include a segment about the expedition. Talking about the expedition, do you know why this carried such a tremendous meaning for our country? 02 Lewis and Clark explored uncharted regions to map out the continent. I mean, this was the first American expedition to cross what is now the western part of the United States. They also spent a great deal of time among Native Americans to learn about their lives and culture. In fact, President Thomas Jefferson himself commissioned the expedition shortly after the Louisiana Purchase in 1803 and this was an important event in his presidency, but the film deals mostly with how Jefferson motivated American colonists to break from Great Britain and we are not going to cover the expedition separately for the rest of the semester.
S Oh, I'm aware of that. 03 But, well, in my botany class, I learned that Lewis and Clark did more than just that. They even discovered lots of new species of

plants, collected numerous plant specimens and recorded information such as the plants' habitats and uses by Native Americans. Most of the newly discovered plant species were named by Lewis and Clark themselves! Moreover, the voyage of discovery added to the world's supply of food crops and plants beneficial to humankind. This was the source of my inspiration to write a paper on the expedition. Unfortunately, I'm stuck with this one problem.

P Really? What problem?

S You see...there are a countless number of websites containing various information about the expedition. [04]The trouble is that most of the time, the information on an individual website is so radically different from that on other websites to the point where I'm very confused as to which website contains the correct and precise information.

P Well, that's not surprising. Of course, the Internet contains some extremely valuable, high-quality information sources, but at the same time, it contains some very unreliable, biased sources of misinformation. I mean, that's its nature.

S Yes, but I think I still have to use the Internet for research.

P I mean, not necessarily. Did you check the textbook? It contains a big chapter about the Lewis and Clark expedition.

S [01]I understand, but what I was trying to say is, I wanted a broad spectrum of resources. Is it possible to check if the information on a website is correct?

P I guess you can infer them from various clues. First, you should check the main purpose of the site. I mean, you should figure out if this site is maintained for selling a product, promoting a personal hobby, or providing general information. For example, commercial websites are not obligated to post historically precise contents; they are just selling a product. So, you might want to refer academic websites or government-related websites because they provide more reliable sources. [05]Also, you need to find out who authored the site. You can check this information at the top, bottom or sidebar of the web page. Then, you need to make sure the author

    provides his or her credentials and what type of expertise he or she has on the subject. You can always try googling the author.
S Thanks, I just wanted my paper to contain correct information.
P Well, keep up your good work! Ask questions, and when you try to judge the credibility of sources, simply trust your instinct. If the information seems strange or unreliable, don't use it. 05 Also, remember that you don't have to use only a single online resource. I wouldn't worry too much and I feel confident that you are on the right track!
S Thanks again for your help. I'll try my best!

가지고 있는 전문 지식의 종류도 확인해야 해. 작가에 대한 정보는 언제든 인터넷에서 찾아 볼 수 있지.
S 감사합니다. 저는 제 보고서에 정확한 정보를 넣고 싶었거든요.
P 음, 계속 열심히 하렴! 질문하고, 자료의 신뢰도를 판단할 때는 네 직감을 믿어보렴. 만약 그 정보가 이상하거나 못 믿겠다 싶으면 사용하지 말고. 05 그리고 하나의 온라인 자료만 사용할 필요가 없다는 점도 기억하렴. 내가 많이 걱정하지 않아도 네가 잘 진행하고 있다는 확신이 드는구나!
S 도와주셔서 다시 한번 감사 드려요. 최선을 다할게요!

[**Vocabulary**] expedition[èkspidíʃən] 탐험, 여행   segment[ségmənt] 부분   uncharted[ʌntʃɑ́ːrtid] 미지의   commission[kəmíʃən] 의뢰하다   botany[bátəni] 식물학   radically[rædikəli] 급진적으로   biased[báiəst] 편향된   misinformation[mìsinfərméiʃən] 오보   infer[infə́ːr] 추론하다   refer[rifə́ːr] 참고하다   credential[kridénʃəl] 자격   credibility[krèdəbíləti] 신뢰도   instinct[ínstiŋkt] 직감

[각주]
* **Thomas Jefferson** 미국의 정치가이자 교육자, 철학자이다. 미국 독립선언문의 기초 위원이었다. 1800년 제3대 대통령에 당선되었고 1804년 재선되었다. 생전에 자신이 직접 정해 놓았다는 묘비명인 "미국 독립 선언의 기초자, 버지니아 신교자유법의 기초자, 버지니아대학교의 아버지 토머스 제퍼슨 여기에 잠들다"라는 글귀가 잘 알려져 있다.
* **Lewis and Clark expedition** 미국의 대통령 토머스 제퍼슨의 명령으로 메리웨더 루이스와 윌리엄 클라크가 진행했던 탐험이다. 미국 대륙을 가로질러 태평양에 이르는 경로를 따라서 1804에서 1806년 사이에 진행됐다. 탐험의 목표는 미국 대륙의 서쪽을 가로지르는 경로를 찾아내어 다른 나라들에게 그 땅이 미국의 영토임을 주장하는 것이었다. 탐험대는 이 탐험에서 그 지역에 거주하는 수많은 아메리카 원주민들과 교류하면서 많은 강과 호수의 위치 등 지형적 정보를 얻을 수 있었고, 그 과정 동안 그린 그림들, 여행 기록과 지도를 1806년 토머스 제퍼슨 대통령에게 전달했다.

01 Main Topic

What is the conversation mainly about?

Ⓐ A film about Thomas Jefferson
Ⓑ Various places to find resources for a paper
Ⓒ A student's concern about finding reliable online sources
Ⓓ Questions about the Lewis and Clark expedition

대화는 중점적으로 무엇에 대한 것인가?

Ⓐ 토마스 제퍼슨에 대한 영화
Ⓑ 보고서 자료를 찾을 다양한 장소들
Ⓒ 믿을 만한 온라인 정보를 찾는 것에 대한 학생의 우려
Ⓓ 루이스 클라크 탐험에 대한 질문

오답 해설 Ⓐ 대화의 서두에 영화에 대해 언급을 하긴 했지만, 학생은 그 영화가 과제의 주제와 관련이 있다고 생각해 그에 대한 이야기를 꺼냈다.
Ⓑ 학생은 이미 인터넷에서 자료를 찾고 있었다. 자료를 찾다 인터넷 자료의 신뢰성에 대한 문의를 하기 위해 교수를 찾았다.

02 Detail

According to the professor, what are two achievements of the Lewis and Clark expedition?
Choose 2 answers.

Ⓐ Spreading Thomas Jefferson's policy throughout the western United States
Ⓑ Finding out the undiscovered regions of the country
Ⓒ Studying the daily lives and culture of Native Americans
Ⓓ Discovering new animal species

교수에 따르면, 루이스 클라크 탐험의 성과 두 가지는 무엇인가?
2개의 답을 고르시오.

Ⓐ 미국 서부에 토마스 제퍼슨의 정책을 전파하는 것
Ⓑ 나라의 발견되지 않은 지역을 발견한 것
Ⓒ 아메리카 원주민들의 일상과 문화를 연구하는 것
Ⓓ 새로운 동물 종을 발견한 것

03 Detail

Why did the student choose to write about the Lewis and Clark expedition?

Ⓐ The student wants to learn more than is covered in class.
Ⓑ The student considers it more interesting than the Jeffersonian philosophies.
Ⓒ The student has written about it in the botany class.
Ⓓ The student found its various aspects in the botany class.

학생은 왜 루이스 클라크 탐험대에 대해 쓰기로 결정했나?

Ⓐ 학생은 수업 시간에 다루는 것보다 더 배우기를 원한다.
Ⓑ 학생은 그것이 제퍼슨식 철학보다 더 재미있다고 여긴다.
Ⓒ 학생은 식물학 수업에서 그것에 대해 쓴 적이 있다.
Ⓓ 학생은 식물학 수업에서 그것의 다양한 측면을 발견했다.

04 Inference

Listen again to part of the conversation. Then answer the question.

> S: The trouble is that most of the time, the information on an individual website is so radically different from that on other websites to the point where I'm very confused as to which website contains the correct and precise information.
> P: Well, that's not surprising.

What does the professor imply when he says this:
P: Well, that's not surprising.

Ⓐ The professor can easily deduce the problem which is related to the Internet.
Ⓑ The professor feels that the Internet contains unsurprising information.
Ⓒ The professor seems indifferent about the student's comment.
Ⓓ The student should have been aware of the fact that the Internet is not reliable.

대화의 일부를 다시 들으시오. 그러고 나서 질문에 답하시오.

> S: 문제가 무엇이냐 하면, 어떤 웹 사이트의 정보가 다른 웹 사이트에 있는 정보와 근본적으로 달라서, 어떤 웹 사이트가 옳고 정확한 정보를 담고 있는 건지 모르겠다는 거예요.
> P: 음, 그건 놀랍지 않구나.

교수가 이 말을 할 때 암시한 것은 무엇인가?
P: 음, 그건 놀랍지 않구나.

Ⓐ 교수는 인터넷과 관련된 문제를 쉽게 추측할 수 있다.
Ⓑ 교수는 인터넷이 놀랍지 않은 정보를 포함한다고 느낀다.
Ⓒ 교수는 학생의 말에 대해 무관심한 듯하다.
Ⓓ 학생은 인터넷이 믿을 만하지 않다는 것을 알았어야 했다.

정답 해설 Ⓐ 교수가 놀랍지 않다고 말한 것은 그 문제에 대해 이미 알고 있다는 뜻이다.
오답 해설 Ⓓ should have p.p.는 '~ 했어야 했는데, 하지 않았다'라는 뜻이다. 교수는 학생이 인터넷의 신뢰성과 관련된 문제에 대해 인지하지 못한 점에 대해 언급하지 않았다.

05 Detail

What does the professor suggest the student to do?
Choose 2 answers.

Ⓐ To refrain from using the Internet sources
Ⓑ To refer to government websites for checking reliability of information
Ⓒ To verify the qualification of the creator of the website
Ⓓ To take into account that various kinds of information exist

교수가 학생에게 하라고 제안한 것은 무엇인가?
2개의 답을 고르시오.

Ⓐ 인터넷 자료 사용을 삼가할 것
Ⓑ 정보의 신용도를 확인하기 위해 정부 웹 사이트를 참고할 것
Ⓒ 웹 사이트를 만든 사람의 자격을 확인할 것
Ⓓ 다양한 정보가 존재한다는 것을 고려할 것

TEST 5 Set 1 Lecture 1

Listen to part of a lecture in an economics class.

P Okay, let me ask you a pretty random question. Where do you keep your precious money? You can't keep all of it in your pockets or your wallet, so what do you do? Well, I'm sure that most of you here keep it safe and sound in a bank. A bank is a financial institution that is primarily engaged in lending money to borrowers and creating deposits. Normal people like us borrow money from a bank when we use credit cards, and big companies borrow money for business purposes. As you can imagine, starting or maintaining a company requires huge sums of money. As ordinary bank users, we put our money in banks because we want to keep our savings in a secure place.

However, banks weren't always so trustworthy. There was a time when the public confidence in banks dropped to so low a level that they had to close entirely. During this coerced bank holiday, people had no access to the money in their bank accounts. This brings us to my lecture today. [06] Our topic for today is banking panic. In particular, we'll be talking about the banking panics that swept the United States during the Great Depression in the 1930s. [07] A banking panic occurs when a financial crisis causes multiple banks to close simultaneously as people rush to cash out all of their savings. In other words, a banking panic happens when people no longer trust banks.

Due to some unforeseen situation such as a long economic recession, bank users worry that their banks are going to close, disappearing along with their precious savings. So, they immediately demand the return of their deposits in cash. Thus, the panic starts. Do you see the problem associated with this event? For one thing, banks do not typically carry such vast amounts of cash, especially not the amount that arises when so many people want to withdraw their savings simultaneously. So, banks have to force loan borrowers to pay off their debts, but companies and individuals that have borrowed money cannot readily respond to this pressure because they are financially insecure. So, they start liquidation, which is the process of closing a business and distributing its assets to claimants. Once the procedure is complete, the business is dissolved. Then, the banks will consequently face bankruptcy as well because entities that have to settle bank loans disappear. These rush requests like immediate demands for cash by the public can cause even the most stable banks to fail. The banking system thus suffers from the loss of the public's confidence in financial security.

대공항

The first banking panic took place during the fall of 1930. Many more followed, such as in the spring and, the fall of 1931, and again in the fall of 1932. Over this brief moment almost 10,000 banks collapsed. However, the Great Depression, an economic slump that critically affected the financial situation of the United States, is said to have started with something else, apart from banking panics. In fact, banking panic is more likely a result than a cause. 08 I am sure that you have heard of the infamous event * "Black Thursday", which refers to the first day of the stock market crash in 1929. The sudden and substantial market crash dealt a terrible blow to the staggering American economy. Oh, but don't be mistaken. You should remember that the stock-market crash wasn't the only cause of the Great Depression. It was just one of the economic problems that acted as a factor.

미국 정부의 공항 회복 노력 1: 긴급은행법

So, how did the banking panic end? The panic was resolved by President Franklin Delano Roosevelt, who declared a national bank holiday 1933. He assumed the presidency during the Great Depression and took on the responsibility of saving America from its economic crisis. After his inauguration as president, Roosevelt passed the Emrgency Banking Act in 1933. After its enactment, beginning on February 14 of that year, Michigan, which suffered severely in the Great Depression, declared an eight-day bank holiday, the first in US history. This bank holiday led to the closure of banks. They were subsequently allowed to reopen after government inspectors confirmed their financial security. This eight-day relief period restored the public's confidence in banks. Three days after the legislation was enacted, 5,000 banks were declared secure, and the panic finally passed.

09 Later, the Emergency Banking Act was fortified with the Banking Act of 1933. You see, the Emergency Banking Act had only acted like a Band-Aid, patching the fiscal emergency for only a limited time.

The Banking Act of 1933 presented a more lasting solution. This policy prohibited commercial banks from participating in the business of investment banking. The purpose behind this legislation was to strengthen banks and to immunize them from engaging in baseless guesswork. To achieve such a goal, there was a separation between commercial and investment banking, and the Federal Deposit Insurance Corporation or FDIC was created. 10 Okay, today the FDIC provides a form of insurance that guarantees bank deposits up to an amount of 250,000 dollars for each person. Even if a bank fails, the FDIC ensures bank users that not all of their deposits will be lost. The FDIC functions as a preventative measure against future banking panics. 11 These various acts constituted *Roosevelt's New Deal, a series of programs focused on saving the country from the Great Depression. From 1933 to 1938, the New Deal aimed to institute short-term and long-term solutions for the economy of the United States. Eventually, they succeeded, and to say the least; the United States has been free from severe banking panics since 1933.

[**Vocabulary**] deposit[dipázit] 예금   coerce[kouə́ːrs] 강압하다   banking panic 은행 공황   sweep[swiːp] 휩쓸다   cash[kæʃ] 현금으로 바꾸다   recession[riséʃən] 불황   readily[rédəli] 손쉽게, 순조롭게   liquidation[lìkwidéiʃən] 청산   claimant[kléimənt] 청구인   dissolve[dizálv] 청산하다, 끝내다   infamous[ínfəməs] 악명 높은   stock market 주식 시장   stagger[stǽgər] 큰 충격을 주다   presidency[prézidənsi] 대통령 직(임기)   inauguration[inɔ̀ːgjəréiʃən] 취임(식)   legislation[lèdʒisléiʃən] 법률의 제정   fortify[fɔ́ːrtəfài] 강화하다   fiscal emergency 재정 비상 사태   immunize[ímjənàiz] 면역력을 갖게 하다

[각주]
* **Black Thursday** 1930년 미국의 대공황을 야기한 주식 시장의 붕괴가 시작된 날을 의미한다. 당시 미국의 금융 시장은 실질 화폐가 부족했기 때문에 주식 폭락으로 은행들이 문을 닫으면서 많은 사람들이 재산을 잃게 되었다.
* **Roosevelt's New Deal** 루스벨트 대통령이 대공황을 해결하기 위해 내세운 정책이다. 케인즈 학파의 주장을 받아들여 정부 지출을 늘리는 등 정부가 경제 문제에 개입하였다는 데 의의를 둔다.

06 Main Topic

What is the main topic of the lecture?

Ⓐ The circumstances that led to banking panic
Ⓑ The strategies that were used to end banking panic
Ⓒ The effect of banking panic on the Great Depression
Ⓓ An economic disaster in American history

강의의 주제는 무엇인가?

Ⓐ 은행 공황을 초래한 상황
Ⓑ 은행 공황을 끝내기 위해 사용된 전략
Ⓒ 은행 공황이 대공황에 미친 영향
Ⓓ 미국 역사의 경제적 재앙

07 Detail

According to the lecture, why does a banking panic begin?

Ⓐ Because people demand liquidation of assets
Ⓑ Because people suddenly try to convert their deposits into cash
Ⓒ Because people refrain from using cash
Ⓓ Because people sell their stocks until the market crashes

강의에 따르면, 은행 공황은 왜 시작되나?

Ⓐ 사람들이 자산의 청산을 요구하기 때문에
Ⓑ 사람들이 갑자기 그들의 예금을 현금으로 바꾸려고 하기 때문에
Ⓒ 사람들이 현금을 사용하는 것을 삼가기 때문에
Ⓓ 시장이 붕괴될 때까지 사람들이 주식을 팔기 때문에

08 Detail

What does the professor state about Black Thursday?

Ⓐ It directly caused the series of banking panics.
Ⓑ It was one of the reasons for the Great Depression, but not the only one.
Ⓒ It was induced by sudden stock-market investments.
Ⓓ It led to a lack of cash in the banks.

교수가 Black Thursday에 대해 언급한 것은 무엇인가?

Ⓐ 일련의 은행 공황을 직접적으로 야기했다.
Ⓑ 대공황의 원인 중 하나이지만, 유일한 것은 아니다.
Ⓒ 급격한 주식 시장 투자에서 초래되었다.
Ⓓ 은행의 현금 부족을 야기했다.

09 Inference

Listen again to part of the lecture. Then answer the question.

> P: Later, the Emergency Banking Act was fortified with the Banking Act of 1933. You see, the Emergency Banking Act had only acted like a Band-Aid, patching the fiscal emergency for only a limited time.

Why does the professor say this:
P: You see, the Emergency Banking Act had only acted like a Band-Aid, patching the fiscal emergency for only a limited time.

- Ⓐ To imply that the Emergency Banking Act permanently affected the economy
- Ⓑ To emphasize that the Emergency Banking Act was not as successful as it seemed
- Ⓒ To illustrate the importance of the Emergency Banking Act on recuperating the American economy
- Ⓓ To note that the Emergency Banking Act was a helpful but short-term solution

강의의 일부를 다시 들으시오. 그러고 나서 질문에 답하시오.

> P: 이후에 긴급은행법은 1933년 은행법으로 강화되었어요. 알다시피, 긴급은행법은 재정 비상 사태를 시한부로 보수하는 미봉책에 불과했거든요.

교수가 이 말을 한 이유는 무엇인가?
P: 알다시피, 긴급은행법은 재정 비상 사태를 시한부로 보수하는 미봉책에 불과했거든요.

- Ⓐ 긴급은행법이 영구적으로 경제에 영향을 주었다는 것을 암시하기 위해
- Ⓑ 보이는 것만큼 긴급은행법이 성공적이지 않다는 것을 강조하기 위해
- Ⓒ 미국 경기 회복에 대한 긴급은행법의 중요성을 설명하기 위해
- Ⓓ 긴급은행법이 효과적이었지만 단기적인 해결책이라는 것을 언급하기 위해

10 Detail

Which of the following is the function carried out by the FDIC?

- Ⓐ It stops existing banking panics from escalating.
- Ⓑ It guarantees bank users a portion of their savings.
- Ⓒ It separates commercial banks from investment banks.
- Ⓓ It gives an incentive to bank users in the form of cash.

다음 중 FDIC가 수행하는 기능은 무엇인가?

- Ⓐ 끝나지 않은 은행 공황의 확대를 멈춘다.
- Ⓑ 은행 이용자들에게 그들의 예금의 일부를 보장한다.
- Ⓒ 상업 은행과 투자 은행을 분리한다.
- Ⓓ 현금의 형태로 은행 이용자들에게 혜택을 준다.

오답 해설   Ⓒ 상업 은행과 투자 은행의 분리는 1933년 은행법의 결과이다.

11 Inference

What can be inferred about Roosevelt's economic solutions?

- Ⓐ They were not as primary as the New Deal programs.
- Ⓑ They backfired on the fiscal problem.
- Ⓒ They turned banks into powerful institutions in the U.S.
- Ⓓ They paved the way for a sound economy.

루스벨트의 경제 해결책에 대해 추론할 수 있는 것은 무엇인가?

- Ⓐ 뉴딜 정책만큼 주요한 것은 아니었다.
- Ⓑ 국가 재정 문제에 역효과를 낳았다.
- Ⓒ 은행을 미국에서 힘 있는 기관으로 만들었다.
- Ⓓ 건실한 경제를 위한 토대를 마련했다.

TEST 5 Set 2 Conversation

Listen to a conversation between a student and an English literature professor.

S Professor Flores? It's Mike. May I come in?
P Of course. 01 Please come in, Mike. I called you in today because, well, I wanted to talk about your essay on *Oscar Wilde.
S My essay? What about it, Professor?
P 02 I wanted to comment on this part here. Let me read it to you. "In his major work *The Importance of Being Earnest*, Wilde drives into the mind the issues of personality and responsibility, attempting to reveal an individual's intellect and sentiments." I couldn't agree with it more. That's a very acute observation, and you phrased it very well. Could you explain how you came up with the idea?
S Oh, that. Um, I guess reading helped. I did a lot of reading, you know, about Wilde and his plays. So I was just thinking really hard about my topic for the essay, and it occurred to me.
P Ah. Then how about the play? May I assume that you've read the entire *The Importance of Being Earnest*?
S Err...not exactly. I wanted to, but I couldn't because of time constraints. 03 I did read all of Act One, though, and I think I got the gist of the ending, and I read reference books conscientiously.
P So you read only the beginning and the ending, and still came up with such a poignant assessment of the essence of the play?
S Uh...
P If so, that's a pretty impressive feat.
S Well, um...that's nice of you to say, Professor.
P What grabbed my attention, in particular, was your choice of words. Aside from the opinion, which is superb, the phrasing...your wording seemed familiar as if I'd read it before. It was the phrase, "Wilde drives into the mind the issues of personality and responsibility." This expression immediately caught my eye.

S Oh, um...really? I guess I might have put a lot of thought into that part.
P Well then, if that's true, you sure have a knack with words! But I wonder, why do you think I found it familiar? Perhaps you've used that phrase in one of your previous papers?
S I think, in my opinion, it might be that...hmm...
P But oddly, this is the first time we've discussed Wilde. So that can't be a possibility, right?
S I guess, um...
P It's a powerful statement, and I don't think I would just skim over something like that. By any chance, did you receive any help from someone for this essay? Or was it entirely your work?
S I definitely wrote it! That's right, I wrote every single word in this essay, but well...

의도적으로 표절을 한 것은 아님

P Oh, then maybe you happened to find sources you liked. It could have been a book that agreed with your opinion. Then you decided to borrow its wording.
S That sounds possible. Yes, that might be the case.
P If so, that's understandable, Mike.
S It is, Professor?
P Yes, it's a common occurrence, with time-consuming essays. We don't mean to, but when we read an individual material repeatedly, it can confuse us into thinking that it's our own opinion.
S I think that's maybe because I did read a certain reference book about it over and over again. It just really coincided with my thoughts about Wilde. It was as if the author was echoing my exact sentiments!
P Oh, I know that feeling. When a book voices our idea, in a nice phrase, we write it down. Then, we work it into our essay. 04 But because we're busy, we forget to add a footnote to it. That could happen, right?
S Yes, Professor. Especially when the essay is nearing its due date.
P So this phrase, "Wilde drives into the mind the issues of personality and responsibility," was probably taken from a book that evaluated Wilde's work. When something like that happens, the phrase should be set in quotation marks, followed by a citation. I noticed that the book you took the phrase from is actually in your of bibliography.

표절에 대한 주의

S So that's why you called me in. But if I may say so, I didn't mean to plagiarize. I know it's something all students and scholars should always be wary of. I'm so sorry, Professor. I had so many things to turn in at once, and my brain got frazzled. Would you please allow me to correct this essay?

P That's why I called you into my office. I'm glad to hear it was a one-time accidental mistake. Plagiarism should never become a habit. 05 Now, go to the library and find your reference book. If any expressions or phrases catch your eye, jot it down along with their sources.

S From now on, I'll be very careful about the academic sources I use. Professor, I can't thank you enough for this lesson.

S 그래서 절 부르신 거군요. 하지만 그렇다고 해서 제가 표절을 하려고 했던 건 아니에요. 모든 학생들과 학자들이 항상 조심해야 하는 점이란 걸 알아요. 정말 죄송해요, 교수님. 한번에 제출할 일들이 너무 많아서 제 뇌가 지쳤어요. 제가 이 에세이를 고쳐도 될까요?

P 그게 내가 너를 사무실로 부른 이유란다. 의도치 않은 한 번의 실수라니 다행이구나. 표절은 습관이 되어서는 안 돼. 05 이제, 도서관에 가서 너의 참고 문헌을 찾도록 하렴. 만약 표현이나 문구가 네 눈에 들어 끌면, 출처와 함께 적어놔야 해.

S 앞으로는 학문 자료를 참고하는 일에 대해서 정말 신경 쓸게요. 교수님, 정말 감사드려요.

[Vocabulary] drive into 몰아넣다　constraint[kənstréint] 통제, 제한　conscientiously[kànʃiénʃəsli] 꼼꼼하게　poignant[pɔ́injənt] 가슴 아픈　feat[fi:t] 솜씨, 재주　skim over 대충 훑어 보다　quotation[kwoutéiʃən] 인용(구)　citation[saitéiʃən] 인용구(문)　bibliography[bìbliágrəfi] 참고문헌　plagiarize[pléidʒəràiz] 표절하다　wary[wέ(:)əri] 경계하는, 조심하는　frazzled[frǽzld] 기진맥진한　jot down 쓰다, 적다　quote[kwout] 인용문　cite[sait] 인용하다　pore[pɔ:r] 숙고하다, 골똘히 생각하다　jumbled[dʒʌmbld] 무질서한　procrastination[proukræstənéiʃən] 미루는 버릇; 연기

[각주]
* **Oscar Wilde** 아일랜드에서 태어난 극작가이자, 소설가, 에세이 작가, 시인이다. 1880년대에 다양한 작품을 발표한 후 1890년대 초반에 런던에서 가장 유명한 극작가 중 한 명이 되었다. 성공한 지식인이였던 부모님 덕분에 프랑스어, 독일어 등을 유창하게 할 수 있었으며 예술의 본질은 미라고 생각한 심미주의에 영향을 많이 받았다.

01 Main Topic

Why does the student go to see the professor?

Ⓐ The student is struggling to come up with a topic for the essay.
Ⓑ The student was summoned by the professor.
Ⓒ The student needs to change certain words in the essay.
Ⓓ The student wants to improve the essay.

학생은 왜 교수를 찾아가는가?

Ⓐ 학생은 에세이 주제를 떠올리는 데 어려움을 겪고 있다.
Ⓑ 학생은 교수의 호출을 받았다.
Ⓒ 학생은 에세이의 특정 단어를 바꿔야 한다.
Ⓓ 학생은 에세이를 개선하고 싶다.

02 Organization

Why does the professor mention the play *The Importance of Being Earnest*?

Ⓐ To suggest seeing the complete play for writing an essay
Ⓑ To provide a creative and accurate summary of the play
Ⓒ To imply that the student should recognize the importance of honesty
Ⓓ To discuss a part of the student's essay that describes the play

교수는 왜 희곡 〈The Importance of Being Earnest〉를 언급했나?

Ⓐ 에세이를 쓰기 위해 완전한 희곡을 볼 것을 제안하기 위해
Ⓑ 희곡에 대한 창의적이고 정확한 요약을 제공하기 위해
Ⓒ 학생이 정직의 중요성을 인식해야 한다는 것을 암시하기 위해
Ⓓ 그 희곡을 묘사한 학생의 에세이 일부에 대해 논의하기 위해

03 Inference

Listen again to part of the conversation. Then answer the question.

> S: I did read all of Act One, though, and I think I got the gist of the ending, and I read reference books conscientiously.
> P: So you read only the beginning and the ending, and still came up with such a poignant assessment of the essence of the play?

What does the professor imply when she says this:
P: So you read only the beginning and the ending, and still came up with such a poignant assessment of the essence of the play?

Ⓐ She is accusing the student openly.
Ⓑ She is subtly expressing skepticism.
Ⓒ She is expressing surprise at the student's talent.
Ⓓ She is asking a simple question.

대화의 일부를 다시 들으시오. 그러고 나서 질문에 답하시오.

> S: 그렇지만 1막은 모두 읽어서 결론의 요지는 파악한 것 같고, 참고 문헌들은 꼼꼼하게 읽었어요.
> P: 그럼 넌 도입부와 결론만 읽었는데, 그 희곡의 본질에 대해서 그런 감명 깊은 평가를 떠올린 거니?

교수가 이 말을 할 때 암시한 것은 무엇인가?
P: 그럼 넌 도입부와 결론만 읽었는데, 그 희곡의 본질에 대해서 그런 감명 깊은 평가를 떠올린 거니?

Ⓐ 교수는 솔직하게 학생을 비난하고 있다.
Ⓑ 교수는 미묘하게 의심을 표현하고 있다.
Ⓒ 교수는 학생의 재능에 대해서 놀라움을 표현하고 있다.
Ⓓ 교수는 간단한 질문을 하고 있다.

04 Detail

What was the problem with the student's essay?

Ⓐ It included false information about Wilde's play.
Ⓑ The student failed to cite its sources properly.
Ⓒ The student used confusing words and phrases.
Ⓓ It was turned in after the due date.

학생 에세이의 문제점은 무엇이었나?

Ⓐ Wilde의 연극에 대한 잘못된 정보를 포함했다.
Ⓑ 자료의 출처를 바르게 밝히지 않았다.
Ⓒ 혼동을 주는 단어와 문구를 사용했다.
Ⓓ 기한이 지나 제출되었다.

05 Detail

Which of the following lessons does the professor primarily emphasize?

Ⓐ Students need to read their books meticulously before writing essays.
Ⓑ Students should avoid making careless mistakes by keeping records of information.
Ⓒ Students should never turn in their tasks after the due date.
Ⓓ Students need to practice creativity when writing literary essays.

다음 교훈 중 교수가 주로 강조한 것은 무엇인가?

Ⓐ 학생들은 에세이를 작성하기 전에 책을 꼼꼼히 읽어야 한다.
Ⓑ 학생들은 정보를 기록해 부주의한 실수를 하는 것을 피해야 한다.
Ⓒ 학생들은 절대로 기한이 지난 후에 과제를 제출해서는 안 된다.
Ⓓ 학생들은 문학 에세이를 쓸 때 창의성을 연습해야 한다.

TEST 5 Set 2 Lecture 1

Listen to part of a lecture in a biology class.

강의의 주제: 악어의 소통법

P Today, we will cover the chapter on the reptiles. Well, first of all, we must discuss crocodiles in order to study these predators that have been around over seventy million years. So, crocodiles...they are large aquatic reptiles that live throughout the tropics in Africa, Asia, and the Americas. Crocodiles' physical characteristics enable them to be successful predators. Their streamlined bodies allow them to swim swiftly. They also push their feet to the side while swimming, which enables them to swim faster by decreasing water resistance. Also, their communication skills increase their survivability. 07 For some reason, a lot of people consider crocodiles to be solitary predators that hide in swamps. However, crocodiles are actually far from solitary. They communicate with each other very actively. 06 One of the most common interaction techniques that they use is vocalization. They generate various types of sounds such as hisses or cries. In fact, every branching species of the crocodile family interacts with each other this way.

Tip 사람들이 흔히 하는 일반적인 오해가 언급되면, 문제로 출제될 수 있으니 주의하여 듣는다.

악어가 내는 소리의 기능 1: 짝짓기

I think an American crocodile would be a good example. During the mating season in the swamps, male crocodiles make a very unique set of sounds, using a variety of hissing, grunting, and so forth. 08 One function of this vocalization is to make a strong enough sound in order to send vibrations through the water as a warning to rival males to stay away from their territory. Due to its very low frequency, this sound wave would not be able to be heard by human ears. 08 However, it can be heard by other crocodiles and when a female crocodile picks up this sound, she will take it as a mating signal and will venture out to find the male who made the sound.

악어가 내는 소리의 기능 2: 구조 요청

Vocalization also has other functions. Another purpose is to get the attention of nearby crocodiles and to convey a message such as a distress call. Let's take the infant crocodiles and hatchlings as an example and see how they use vocalization to interact with their mothers. You see, newborn crocodiles are very vulnerable to predators, especially swamp birds and mammals. Now, these baby crocodiles will continually make a muffled cry within their nests so that the mother in the vicinity of the nest will consistently listen to these cries. If the cries change in frequency, the mother crocodile will be alerted that the babies are calling for help and she will move them to another safe location or protect them. Although the individual cries are muffled, in fact, this really is a loud process. When all of the eggs hatch, a mother crocodile has to look after up to 40 infant crocodiles at once. When a mother uses her mouth to carry infants to the safety, she will be able to move about 15 babies at a time. During this process, the remaining babies will consistently make their rescue cries, which is why the process becomes phenomenally loud. I guess it is a kind of "Don't forget about me." message. The hatchlings can perform more complicated distress calls when they get separated far away from their family. They will make a call that will be delivered to the nearest siblings. Then, the siblings make another call and so on that would eventually reach their parents.

언론 매체의 정보를 받아들일 때 주의할 점

Well, last week, I actually came across a documentary on television that showed this spectacle. Did anyone get to see it? 09 It looked kind of interesting, but if you are going to watch it, just remember to carefully examine what is being shown on the television. You never really know where they find these so-called "reptilian experts." I mean, this is one of the aspects to be aware of when choosing from which media source you get your information. We need to select carefully television programs or books with credible producers or authors.

새끼 악어가 내는 소리에 대한 다른 의견

Anyway, some people argue that crying just makes the situation worse. They claim that it is reasonable to assume that prey do their best to keep low profiles by using camouflage, silence, or other various tactics so predators cannot recognize them. They speculate that noise would instead attract these predators, which is not good for infant crocodiles. So, they argue that the call doesn't function effectively as protection. **10 This might be true, but, in fact, the mother always stays in the vicinity of the nest. Also, if it were you, would you want to mess with the mother crocodile?** The call obviously grabs the mother's attention, not the attention of predators.

Now, after the mother brings all of the hatchlings to safety, the babies will continue to make the calls and cries to their mother. This vocalization develops throughout the crocodile's development into adulthood when the crocodile will come to possess 18 different types of signal calls. Ironically, this behavior is more common for mammals to do than for reptiles. **11 We all know that other types of mammals such as dogs, make different calls to interact with each other. But some of you may not have known that crocodiles also know how to get their point across. They have more developed and sophisticated vocalization than the domesticated dog.** In fact, their calls vary widely depending on species, age, size, and sex, varying from noticeable hissing sounds to inaudible infrasound.

악어의 정교한 발성법

[Vocabulary] streamlined [strí:mlàind] 유선형의   swiftly [swíftli] 신속하게   solitary [sáliteri] 혼자 하는   vocalization [vòukəlizéiʃən] 발성   hiss [his] '쉬' 하는 소리를 내다   grunting [grʌntiŋ] '끙' 하는 소리   distress call 조난 호출, 구원 요청   hatchling [hǽtʃliŋ] 갓 부화한 동물   muffle [mʌ́fl] 소리를 죽이다, 약하게 하다   vicinity [visínəti] 부근, 인근   phenomenally [finάmənli] 경이적으로, 극도록   spectacle [spéktəkl] 구경거리, 볼거리   keep a low profile 자세를 낮추다, 눈에 띄지 않게 하다   camouflage [kǽməflàːʒ] 위장   mess with something (부정적으로) 얽히다   infrasound [ínfrəsàund] 초저주파

06 Main Topic

What is the lecture mainly about?

Ⓐ Discussing various physical characteristics of crocodiles
Ⓑ Describing crocodiles' various survival techniques
Ⓒ Emphasizing the importance of crocodiles' sound signals in their survival
Ⓓ Analyzing an interactive method used by crocodiles

강의는 주로 무엇에 관한 것인가?

Ⓐ 악어의 다양한 신체적 특징들을 논의하는 것
Ⓑ 악어의 다양한 생존 기법들을 묘사하는 것
Ⓒ 생존을 위한 악어의 소리 신호의 중요성을 강조하는 것
Ⓓ 악어가 이용하는 상호 작용 방법을 분석하는 것

07 Detail

What is a common misconception about crocodiles?

Ⓐ Crocodiles do not make cries to signal different situations and conditions.
Ⓑ Crocodiles behave individually and do not interact with each other.
Ⓒ Only a few species of crocodiles are capable of making sound signals.
Ⓓ Crocodiles are very interactive animals that live others of their species.

악어에 대한 일반적인 오해는 무엇인가?

Ⓐ 악어는 다른 상황이나 조건을 알리기 위해 소리 내지 않는다.
Ⓑ 악어는 서로 교류가 없고 개별적으로 행동한다.
Ⓒ 악어의 몇몇 종만이 소리 신호를 만들 능력이 있다.
Ⓓ 악어는 종끼리 모여 사는 매우 상호적인 동물이다.

08 Detail

According to the lecture, what are two functions of American Alligator's signal calls during the mating season?
Choose 2 answers.

Ⓐ Preventing competition from other male alligators
Ⓑ Attracting female alligators with a cry
Ⓒ Calling for help from nearby alligators
Ⓓ Protecting newborn babies from predators

강의에 따르면, 번식기 동안 미국 악어의 신호음의 두 가지 기능은 무엇인가?
2개의 답을 고르시오.

Ⓐ 다른 수컷 악어와의 경쟁을 막는 것
Ⓑ 울음소리로 암컷을 끌어들이는 것
Ⓒ 근처 악어에게 도움을 구하는 것
Ⓓ 포식자로부터 갓 부화한 새끼를 지키는 것

09 Inference

What can be inferred about the television program on crocodiles?

Ⓐ Its credibility has to be checked by experts.
Ⓑ It contains crocodile contents programmed with the help of reptile experts.
Ⓒ It sometimes contains unreliable information.
Ⓓ It should be analyzed critically and developed by students.

악어에 대한 TV 프로그램에 대해 추론할 수 있는 것은 무엇인가?

Ⓐ 그것의 신뢰성은 전문가에 의해 확인돼야 한다.
Ⓑ 그것은 파충류 전문가들의 도움으로 제작된 악어에 대한 내용을 포함하고 있다.
Ⓒ 그것은 때때로 신뢰할 수 없는 정보를 포함한다.
Ⓓ 그것은 학생들에 의해 비판적으로 분석되고 개발되어야 한다.

정답 해설 Ⓒ so-called는 사물이나 사람을 묘사할 때 사용된 단어나 표현이 사실은 잘못됐다고 생각할 때 쓰는 표현이므로, 교수는 그 프로그램이 파충류 전문가에 의해 만들어졌다고 생각하지 않음을 추론할 수 있다.

10 Inference

Listen again to part of the lecture. Then answer the question.

> P: This might be true, but, in fact, the mother always stays in the vicinity of the nest. Also, if it were you, would you want to mess with the mother crocodile?

Why does the professor say this:
P: Also, if it were you, would you want to mess with the mother crocodile?

Ⓐ To emphasize how brave it is to challenge a fully matured female crocodile
Ⓑ To discuss how mother crocodiles are capable of protecting their young
Ⓒ To ask the students about the problems faced by a mother crocodile
Ⓓ To indicate disagreement with the previous argument about the function of crocodiles' calls

강의의 일부를 다시 들으시오. 그러고 나서 질문에 답하시오.

> P: 이것은 맞는 말일 수도 있지만, 사실, 어미는 항상 보금자리 근처에 있어요. 당신이라면, 어미 악어와 안 좋게 마주치고 싶겠어요?

교수는 왜 이 말을 했나?
P: 당신이라면, 어미 악어와 안 좋게 마주치고 싶겠어요?

Ⓐ 다 성장한 암컷 악어에 도전하는 것이 얼마나 용감한 것인지 강조하기 위해
Ⓑ 어미 악어가 그들의 새끼를 보호하는 데 얼마나 능력이 있는지 논의하기 위해
Ⓒ 어미 악어가 직면한 문제에 대해 학생들에게 묻기 위해
Ⓓ 악어 울음소리의 기능에 대한 앞선 주장에 대한 반대를 표시하기 위해

11 Organization

Why does the professor mention dogs?

Ⓐ To emphasize crocodiles share similar organ structures that resemble other mammals
Ⓑ To explain crocodiles have the most diverse set of signals and calls among reptiles
Ⓒ To emphasize the interactive strategy that crocodiles have developed
Ⓓ To show crocodiles are similar to dogs regarding level of biological sophistication

교수는 왜 개를 언급했나?

Ⓐ 악어가 다른 포유류와 유사한 장기구조를 가지고 있다는 것을 강조하기 위해
Ⓑ 악어가 파충류 중에 가장 다양한 신호음과 울음소리를 가지고 있다는 것을 설명하기 위해
Ⓒ 악어가 발달시킨 상호 작용 전략을 강조하기 위해
Ⓓ 생물학적 정교함의 수준에 관해 악어가 개와 비슷하다는 것을 보여 주기 위해

TEST 5 Set 2 Lecture 2

Listen to part of a lecture in a literature class.

P   Alright, let's get started. I'm going to assume that you all have already read the poems I gave you to study for homework. Very well. **12**If you have done the assignment, then Gertrude Stein and her use of language should be nothing new. However, before we go into more detail, do any of you have questions regarding her poems?

S   Professor, could you explain a bit more about the poems? I had a hard time figuring out the message she wanted to convey through her poems. In fact, I am still trying to figure out her intention in using repetition throughout her work. In particular, I was puzzled by the section where the word "would" appears repeatedly. For instance, the one with the phrase "would, would, would you..." I didn't understand what she wanted to say.

P   **13**I see what you are trying to say, but this is also one of the reasons behind her reputation. Umm, don't get me wrong. She became a valuable writer not merely for her vague writing style, but also for her abstract form of literature.

Her works, including plays, novels, and stories, had a playful, humorous, and repetitive style. Typical quotes include, "Rose is a rose is a rose is a rose." The thing is, she pursued her career in a way that had never been seen before during her time. She focused on abstract ideas in her writings. In the beginning, her writing was criticized and ignored by the public because her writing style was very distinct from what was common at the time. However, Stein didn't begin writing in this abstract form from the very start. You see, she was inspired by reputable artists such as Picasso and Cezanne, who specialized in abstract paintings, more specifically, *"Cubism." This genre is characterized by a three-dimensional viewpoint by which its objects are analyzed, broken up, and interpreted in an abstracted form instead of illustrating objects from a regular flat viewpoint.

Such a name originated from the fact that individual parts of drawings appeared to be similar to parts of a cube put together. Cubists considered every part of the canvas was equally important and drew objects repeatedly in order to achieve a solid look. If you've seen Picasso's cubist works, you'll get what I'm trying to say. In any case, Stein strived to write in a similar manner to Cubism. Cezanne especially influenced Stein's ideas about equality, which often resulted in Stein using the entire text as a field in which every element mattered and in which she chose each word carefully to try to convey equal amounts of meaning. On a somewhat related note, Stein was fascinated by abstract art, and collected pieces in this genre over the years.

S I still can't grasp the concept of Stein's writing style. I mean, I have no problem understanding Cubism, but I cannot imagine how an author can convey it through her writings. I believe that looking at a painting to understand equality and repetition makes a lot of sense, [14] but it is quite difficult to figure out what the author is trying to say through a piece of writing.

P I can see the point you are trying to make, but the matter concerning which of these works can deliver meanings more effectively, well, that's a matter of debate. Some people thought that Stein encapsulated the idea of Cubism in her work pretty successfully, which led her to become an influential figure in literature. [15] But, of course, at first, when Stein was just beginning to incorporate Cubism to her writings, she wrote pieces such as *Three Lives* that could be quite confusing to understand. Of course, this was a new type of literary work to the public. I mean it was hard to gain the recognition from the beginning. Even though this work was denounced at first, people came to appreciate its merits later on as she became an influential author. [16] Her unique style even inspired other famous writers such as *Ernest Hemingway. As I said before, Cubism had a big impact on her writings and, in particular, she was moved by how the blending of colors and precisely illustrated expressions worked together to depict a theme that remained intact throughout the years. Stein attempted to replicate such images in her

다음 시간 수업 내용 예고

writings by utilizing recurring sentences that little by little created the essence of the characters and plot in her compositions. Of course, this was a new style to the public at the time.

S Ah, now I think I sort of understand her and the message she was trying to convey. Her intentions were to gradually construct characters, plots, and ideas through the use of repetitions. But in reality, I am not quite captivated by her repetitive techniques. As I said, the way she presented her work seems very vague to me. Umm, I am concerned that literature might not be my cup of tea.

Tip 다음 시간에 배울 내용이나 과제에 대해 언급되면, 미래 행동을 묻는 문제로 출제될 수 있으니 주의하며 듣는다.

P In that case, there is nothing to worry about. 17In the following classes, we will take a close look at John Milton's *Paradise Lost*, which is one of his masterpieces, with its *blank verse writing style. I am quite certain that most of you will find this poem about the fall of a man quite enjoyable, thanks to its simple use of language and straightforward plot.

S 아, 이제 그녀와 그녀가 전달하려 했던 메시지를 이해할 수 있을 것 같아요. 그녀의 의도는 반복을 이용해서 등장인물, 줄거리, 개념들을 점차적으로 만들어 나가는 것이었군요. 그러나 실은, 저는 그녀의 반복적인 기법에 별로 매혹되지는 않네요. 제가 말씀 드렸듯이, 그녀가 작품을 표현하는 방법이 저에게는 매우 애매모호하네요. 음, 문학이 제가 좋아하는 분야가 아닌가 하는 염려가 되네요.

P 그렇다면, 그런 것은 전혀 걱정할 필요가 없어요. 17다음 시간에, 우리는 존 밀턴의 대표작 중 하나인 《실낙원》과 그것의 무운시 기법에 대해 자세히 알아볼 거예요. 확신하건대 여러분은 그 단순한 언어의 사용과 간단한 줄거리 덕에 인간의 몰락에 관한 그 시를 꽤 재미있다고 생각할 거예요.

[**Vocabulary**] quote[kwout] 인용문   reputable[répjətəbl] 평판이 좋은   three-dimensional 삼차원적인   cube[kju:b] 정육면체   strive[straiv] 분투하다   encapsulate[inkǽpsəlèit] 요약(압축)하다   incorporate[inkɔ́:rpərit] 포함하다, 설립하다   denounce[dináuns] 맹렬히 비난하다, 고발하다   appreciate its merits 가치를 인정하다   intact[intǽkt] 온전한   recur[rikə́:r] 되돌아가 말하다   captivate[kǽptəvèit] ~의 마음을 사로잡다, 매혹하다   one's cup of tea ~의 취향   blank verse 무운시   straightforward[strèitfɔ́:rwərd] 복잡하지 않은, 솔직한

[각주]

- **Cubism** 20세기 초 프랑스 파리에서 시작된 예술 장르로, 사물을 객관적이고 입체적으로 나타내려고 한 예술 관점이다. 사물의 본질을 파악하기 위해 다양한 각도에서 관찰한 사물의 모습을 한 작품에 그렸다. 피카소와 세잔이 대표적인 입체파 화가이다.
- **Ernest Hemingway** 미국의 소설가로서 《노인과 바다》로 퓰리처상과 노벨 문학상을 수상하였고, 그 외에 《무기여 잘 있거라》 《누구를 위하여 종은 울리나》 등의 작품이 있다. 그는 인간의 비극적인 모습을 간결한 문체로 묘사했다. 1차 세계 대전 이후 해외 특파원으로 파리에 간 그는 수많은 작가들과 교류하며 많은 작품을 집필했다.
- **blank verse** 16세기 이후로 영미시에서 가장 영향력 있고 일반적으로 사용된 시의 형태 중 하나이다. 모든 운문 형식 중 영어 대화체의 본래의 리듬을 잘 살려서 표현했고, 융통성이 있어 대중들에게 시를 친근하게 느끼게 했다. 극시나 대서사시에 많이 사용되었고, 괴테가 《파우스트》의 원전인 《포스터스 박사》에서 이 형식을 사용했고 셰익스피어에 이르러 완성되었다.

12 Main Topic

What is the lecture mainly about?

Ⓐ The influence of renowned artists on Gertrude Stein
Ⓑ The distinct writing style of a well-known author
Ⓒ An artistic figure who later became a writer
Ⓓ The application of Cubism to a literary work

강의는 주로 무엇에 대한 것인가?

Ⓐ Gertrude Stein에 대한 유명한 예술가의 영향
Ⓑ 잘 알려진 작가의 독특한 문체
Ⓒ 후에 작가가 된 예술가
Ⓓ 문학 작품에 입체파의 적용

13 Detail

Why did Gertrude Stein become famous?

Ⓐ Because of her vague use of language
Ⓑ Because of her humorous writings
Ⓒ Because of incorporating Cubism in her poems
Ⓓ Because of her unique literary style

Gertrude Stein은 왜 유명해졌나?

Ⓐ 그녀의 모호한 언어 사용 때문에
Ⓑ 그녀의 재미있는 글 때문에
Ⓒ 그녀의 시에 입체파를 적용시킨 것 때문에
Ⓓ 그녀의 독특한 문체 때문에

오답 해설 Ⓒ Gertrude Stein은 입체파의 영향을 받아서 독특한 문체를 구사하게 되었고 이 독특한 문체 때문에 유명해졌다. 단지 입체파를 적용했기 때문에 유명해진 것은 아니다.

14 Inference

Listen again to part of the lecture. Then answer the question.

> S: ...but it is quite difficult to figure out what the author is trying to say through a piece of writing.
> P: I can see the point you are trying to make, but the matter concerning which of these works can deliver meanings more effectively, well, that's a matter of debate.

Why does the professor say this:
P: ...well, that's a matter of debate.

Ⓐ To show the agreement with the student's opinion
Ⓑ To imply that the student's opinion needs to be revised
Ⓒ To emphasize the professor doesn't understand the student's opinion
Ⓓ To indicate the professor needs to debate with the student

강의의 일부를 다시 들으시오. 그러고 나서 질문에 답하시오.

> S: ……한 편의 글을 통해 작가가 말하고자 하는 것을 알아내는 것은 꽤 어려워요.
> P: 학생이 무슨 말을 하려는지는 이해했지만, 어떤 것이 의미를 더 효율적으로 전달하는지에 관한 문제는, 음, 그것은 논쟁 거리가 되겠네요.

교수는 왜 이 말을 했나?
P: ……음, 그것은 논쟁 거리가 되겠네요.

Ⓐ 학생의 의견에 동의함을 보여 주기 위해
Ⓑ 학생의 의견이 수정될 필요가 있다는 것을 암시하기 위해
Ⓒ 교수가 학생의 의견을 이해하지 못한다는 것을 강조하기 위해
Ⓓ 교수가 학생과 토론해야 한다는 것을 나타내기 위해

15 Inference

What can be inferred about Stein's *Three Lives*?

ⓐ It was a creative literary work that brought popularity to Stein.
ⓑ It was an example that clearly showed Stein's artistic ability.
ⓒ It was met with different reactions from its primary and later audiences.
ⓓ It was repeatedly exposed to the public.

Stein의 《세 사람의 생애》에 대해 추론할 수 있는 것은 무엇인가?
ⓐ Stein을 유명하게 만들어 준 창의적인 문학 작품이다.
ⓑ Stein의 예술적 능력을 분명하게 보여 주는 예이다.
ⓒ 초기와 후기의 독자들에게서 다른 반응을 얻었다.
ⓓ 대중에 여러 차례 노출되었다.

오답 해설 ⓐ Stein이 영향력 있는 작가가 되고 나서 작품의 가치를 인정받은 것이지 이 작품 덕에 그녀가 유명해진 것은 아니다.

16 Organization

Why does the professor mention Ernest Hemingway?

ⓐ To elaborate on his works that incorporated Cubism into literature
ⓑ To highlight how influential a literary figure was
ⓒ To emphasize that Cubism had influence on Stein's writings
ⓓ To explain some authors who made social contact with Gertrude Stein

교수는 왜 어니스트 헤밍웨이를 언급했나?
ⓐ 문학에 입체파를 접목시킨 그의 작품을 설명하기 위해
ⓑ 한 문학적인 인물이 얼마나 영향력이 있었는지 강조하기 위해
ⓒ 입체파가 Stein의 작품에 영향을 주었다는 것을 강조하기 위해
ⓓ Gertrude Stein과 친분이 있던 몇몇 작가들을 설명하기 위해

오답 해설 ⓓ Gertrude Stein이 어니스트 헤밍웨이와 친분이 있었는지에 대한 것은 언급되지 않았다.

17 Inference

What will the professor discuss in the following class?

ⓐ Another work of literature by Gertrude Stein
ⓑ A literary work by an author who was influenced by Gertrude Stein
ⓒ Another type of writing style distinguished from Stein's one
ⓓ A particular type of literary work with a complicated plot

교수가 다음 수업에서 논할 것은 무엇인가?
ⓐ Gertrude Stein의 또 다른 문학 작품
ⓑ Gertrude Stein의 영향을 받은 작가의 문학 작품
ⓒ Stein의 것과 구별되는 다른 유형의 문체
ⓓ 복잡한 줄거리를 가진 특정 유형의 문학 작품

영단기 TOEFL

ACTUAL TEST

TEST 06

TEST 6 Set 1 Conversation

Listen to part of a conversation between a librarian and a student.

학생의 용건: 연극 논평 찾기

L   Hello. How may I assist you today?

S   01 I am here to find reviews for my English class. My professor told us to find reference materials of the play we are studying. And the reviews have to have been written when the play was first staged, so I'd like to know where I can get information about those reviews, such as a newspaper article from that time.

L   So you mean contemporary reviews, right? Can I get the name of the play?

S   It's *The Death of a Salesman* by *Arthur Miller. It was written in 1949 and this work had an enormous influence on American theater. So, we need to research why it played such an important role in American literature as well as theater art.

L   I can see why your professor asked you to read some of the old reviews. This play was successful and premiered on Broadway in February 1949, running for 742 performances. It won the three major drama prizes including *Pulitzer Prize for Drama.

연극에 대한 이례적인 논평

Many critics had comments on the play. When it was first performed, they described the play as the first great American tragedy. I guess that's why your professor wanted you to examine these critiques carefully. 02 I mean that critics usually say harsh things about plays, especially when they dealt with traditional themes. The theme of *The Death of a Salesman* was the American dream, which was very typical at that time. Even with this cliché the critics couldn't help but acclaim the work. So, I think it was exceptional.

S   Wow, the play must have really been a hit!

L   Yes. Especially the critics' reactions made people curious about it.

학생에게 논평을 찾을 곳을 제안함

S   OK, that sounds interesting. 03 So, how can I find reviews related to the play? I mean there was certainly no Internet back then. I guess the only publications I can rely on are newspapers, but I have been digging around for hours, and still don't have a clue about how to find them.

L   We have copies of newspapers in the basement since we have limited space to store all periodicals. 04They are primarily sorted out by dates, and if you need a shortcut, I also recommend our intranet. I think you should start from 1949. So if you have the year and a search word in the search engine, it will extract out all the information it can find related to your request.

Ah, I remember when I visited Broadway last year and watched the play there.

S   Oh, really? How was it?

L   I was impressed. There were famous actors and it was the first time that I went to a real theater. It was quite distinguished from the other plays that we usually saw in high school. The way they arranged props on the stage tended to be very classical.

S   Well, I've never been to one, but, according to my reading, it seemed pretty interesting to me. The story is told in a dramatic manner, and each character has its own interpretations of what the American dream means. Personally speaking, it sounds very inspiring.

L   Yeah, I understand your enthusiasm. To me, the play was everything you expect it to be. I remember a lot of laughter and clapping, and I also remember crying as well. I felt like a part of the play.

I would recommend doing more than just the reading. Students taking a theater major regularly put on the play *The Death of a Salesman* as a part of their project. 04I recommend you borrow one of those recordings of th play performed by students on the campus. I'm pretty sure that we have it in our registry.

S   Sounds like an interesting idea. It will help me get a new perspective on the play.

L   If you carefully examine the tape, I am sure that you will most likely agree with the critics who found the play laudable. At the same time, you will understand why people thought this work sounded fresh and vital.

S   05Right, I'm sure there is more to it than meets the eye. Perhaps, that's why the professor assigned this particular play. We'll see what happens.

[**Vocabulary**] premiere[primjíər] 초연되다　critique[kritíːk] 평론　cliché[kliːʃéi] 진부한 생각　periodical[pìəriɑ́dikəl] 정기 간행물　prop[prɑp] 소도구, 버팀목　clapping[klǽpiŋ] 박수　perspective[pərspéktiv] 관점, 시각　laudable[lɔ́ːdəbl] 칭찬(감탄)할 만한　meet the eye 눈에 보이다

[각주]
- **Arthur Miller** 미국의 극작가로 세계 2차 대전 중 군수 산업 경영자와 아들 간의 대립을 다룬 〈모두가 나의 아들〉로 큰 호평을 받았다. 뒤이어 발표한 〈세일즈맨의 죽음〉은 퓰리처상 및 비평가 단체상 등을 수상하면서, 브로드웨이에서 2년간 장기 공연을 했다.
- **Pulitzer Prize** 미국에서 가장 권위있는 보도, 문학, 음악상으로 컬럼비아 대학이 주최하며 매년 4월에 수상자를 발표하고 5월에 시상한다. 언론인 J.Pulitzer가 남긴 유산 50만 달러를 기금으로 하여 1917년에 창설되었다. 언론 분야는 미국 신문사에서 활동하고 있는 사람이어야 하며 다른 분야는 반드시 미국 시민권을 가지고 있어야 수상자가 될 수 있다.

01 Main Topic

Why does the student visit the librarian?

Ⓐ To get information about a play
Ⓑ To find ways of completing a task
Ⓒ To discuss reactions to a play
Ⓓ To hear about the experience of watching a play

학생은 왜 사서를 찾아갔나?

Ⓐ 연극에 대한 정보를 얻기 위해
Ⓑ 과제를 완수하기 위한 방법을 찾기 위해
Ⓒ 연극에 대한 반응을 논의하기 위해
Ⓓ 연극을 관람한 경험을 듣기 위해

02 Detail

Why does the librarian think that the critics' reaction to the play is exceptional?

Ⓐ Because critics don't like plays with a tragic theme
Ⓑ Because critics are generally skeptical about conventional themes
Ⓒ Because critics make disparaging remarks about plays
Ⓓ Because critics are usually objective when writing reviews about plays

사서는 왜 연극에 대한 비평가들의 반응이 이례적이라고 생각하나?

Ⓐ 비극적 주제의 연극을 싫어하기 때문에
Ⓑ 일반적으로 보편적인 주제에 비판적이기 때문에
Ⓒ 연극에 대해 폄하하는 발언을 하기 때문에
Ⓓ 연극에 대한 논평을 쓸 때 대개 객관적이기 때문에

03 Organization

Why does the student mention the Internet?

Ⓐ To emphasize the difficulty of finding resources
Ⓑ To show the reason why he chose to check out other resource materials
Ⓒ To explain how he looked up the newspaper resources
Ⓓ To emphasize how the Internet is different from a newspaper

학생은 왜 인터넷을 언급했나?

Ⓐ 수업에 관련된 자료를 찾는 어려움을 강조하기 위해
Ⓑ 그가 다른 자료들을 찾기로 한 이유를 보여 주기 위해
Ⓒ 그가 신문 자료를 어떻게 찾았는지 설명하기 위해
Ⓓ 인터넷이 신문과 어떻게 다른지 강조하기 위해

오답 해설　Ⓑ 인터넷으로는 자료를 찾을 수가 없어 다른 자료를 찾는다고 했지만, 이는 과제의 어려움을 강조하기 위해서이다.

04 Detail

What does the librarian advise the student to do?
Choose 2 answers.

- [A] To read one of the positive reviews of the play
- [B] To access to a private network as an alternative way
- [C] To attend one of the school's plays that are currently being performed
- [D] To see video footage of the play
- [E] To check out various periodicals about the play

사서가 학생에게 조언한 것은 무엇인가?
2개의 답을 고르시오.

- [A] 연극에 관한 긍정적인 논평을 읽을 것
- [B] 대안책으로 전용망을 이용할 것
- [C] 현재 공연 중인 학교 연극 중 하나에 참석할 것
- [D] 연극의 비디오 자료를 볼 것
- [E] 연극에 대한 다양한 간행물을 확인할 것

05 Inference

Listen again to part of the conversation. Then answer the question.

> S: Right, I'm sure there is more to it than meets the eye. Perhaps, that's why the professor assigned this particular play. We'll see what happens.

What does the student imply when he says this:
S: Right, I'm sure there is more to it than meets the eye.

- Ⓐ The student thinks that there is a profound intention behind the assignment.
- Ⓑ The student wants to find a positive review of the play among many negative ones.
- Ⓒ The student thinks that watching plays is important to gain understanding the director's intentions.
- Ⓓ The student believes that the play seems to be attractive to people.

대화의 일부를 다시 들으시오. 그러고 나서 질문에 답하시오.

> S: 맞아요, 눈에 보이는 것보다 무언가 더 있을 거라고 확신해요. 아마도, 그래서 교수님이 특정 연극을 지정하셨나 봐요. 어떻게 되는지 우선 해 봐야겠어요.

학생이 이 말을 할 때 암시한 것은 무엇인가?
S: 맞아요, 눈에 보이는 것보다 무언가 더 있을 거라고 확신해요.

- Ⓐ 과제 수행 이면에 깊은 의도가 있다고 생각한다.
- Ⓑ 연극에 관한 많은 부정적인 논평 중에서 긍정적인 논평을 찾고 싶어한다.
- Ⓒ 연극을 보는 것은 감독의 의도를 이해하기 위해 중요하다고 생각한다.
- Ⓓ 비평가들의 과격한 반응에 반해서 연극에 중대하고 다른 뭔가 있다고 생각한다.

TEST 6 Set 1 Lecture 1

Listen to part of a lecture in a biology class.

강의의 주제: 자연 선택

P   Okay, class, let's get started. 06So we've covered natural selection and its details, right? Can anyone tell me about it?

S   Yes, Professor. 06It is a mechanism of evolution, the change in heritable traits of a population over time. Those living organisms, which happen to be best suited to an environment, survive and reproduce most successfully, producing many similarly well-adapted descendants. I was very impressed at how natural selection plays a vital role for each species to survive in their respective environment. As the name implies, organisms could select traits that are appropriate for the environment. Animals might develop to gain certain physical changes that raise their chances of survival.

P   I'm glad to hear that you recall so much from last time! As we know, offspring inherit their genes from their parents, but the children's genes are not an exact copy of their parents'. Sometimes in the process of being made, the children's DNA changes. Do you remember how scientists have coined this phenomenon?

S   Mutation?

변이의 개념

P   Mutation, yes, exactly. Umm, such as birds' wings and bones. These unique structures developed from a species of dinosaurs, called theropods, which gradually moved from the terrestrial environment into the air. As you know, dinosaurs were reptiles, meaning that birds actually evolved from reptiles. Now, these birds' wings and bones play key roles in helping them to flee and feed. But before we discuss birds even further, I want to provide you with a general definition of mutation. It is a natural alteration of a DNA structure. When the parents endow genetic information to their young, a lot of copying errors occur randomly. These transmission errors also happen to plants. For most of the time, these genetic errors are not easily noticed and have no significant effect on the organism's prosperity, so these just disappear. 07 However, sometimes, a certain error may produce an effect that is advantageous for an organism's survival, thus resulting in its transmission to the next generation. Usually, these traits accumulate and their benefits eventually appear on the surface. This process is called mutation. This is a method which allows organisms to best survive in their environment. 08 So, does anyone know the story about monkeys and artwork? Well, you bring a million monkeys and have them paint random brushstrokes on their canvases. After a million years, these monkeys will be able to produce great works of art as they evolve. Of course, all of it would happen through the random brushstrokes. What I'm trying to say is that mutation is a phenomenon that can be observed when small changes accumulate over a long period of time.

08 This evolution is very similar to how birds' biological structures developed except for the fact that the birds spent more than a hundreds of millions of years to do so. Now the question is how the bones were actually formed. The best way to look at it is to observe the difference between ancient bird fossils and ancient theropods fossils. Theropods are a genus of bird-like dinosaurs that is in the transitional state between non-avian dinosaurs and modern birds. 09 You see, birds have light bones, which are made up of cartilage. Cartilage is soft tissue, which gives flexibility. The bone structure of theropods also consisted largely of cartilage. This type of body structure is especially suited for flying animals since it minimizes weight. Also, the bones of theropods were hollow like those of birds today. Because the bones of both birds and theropods consisted of the same materials and exhibited a similar structure, it can be concluded that their bones are related.

S 10 But isn't that strange? Isn't it too hasty to conclude that bird bones originated from reptile bones just based on the fact that they're made from the same material and designed in a similar way?

P This is where the other evidence comes in. Visually speaking, the anatomy of theropods looked very similar to the anatomy of birds today. ⁰⁹Theropod's bone structure, with its long upper limbs looks remarkably like the wings of a bird. Moreover, the muscle formation of this dinosaur resembled the muscle structure of the bird, allowing its body parts to move up and down, in an action similar to the birds' wings.

S But birds also have feathers on their wings. Does that also have something to do with the transition from dinosaur to bird as well?

P Yes, you're right. The feathers... Let me tell you an interesting fact about their feathers. A feather consists of a central shaft from which a series of slender barbs extends, each sprouting smaller barbules. Their functions are flight, insulation, and camouflage. Theropods had something like feathers as well, but these were made up of materials like reptilian scales. Their scale-covered wings were durable and hard like crocodile scales, protecting them from the surrounding environment. The feathers of birds today, though, develop on the soft skin, not hard scales, leaving the bird vulnerable. Their functions are to insulate the bird and help it fly, not to help the bird to resist attacks. ¹¹It is unknown why bird feathers did not develop from theropod scales. However, feathers would have been much more durable and sturdy if they retained some of the characteristics of scales. Feathers could provide protection, in addition to assisting with flight, if they were somewhat scaly.

However, that is the important aspect of natural selection; it is not always possible to make these changes appear on demand. ¹¹Natural selection doesn't proceed in the direction that makes animals somehow perfect. It simply allows animals to take advantage of their condition a little better. By this unique pattern of genetic development, species improve their chances of survival in the harsh environment.

[**Vocabulary**] heritable[hérɪtəbl] 유전인   coin[kɔin] (새로운 단어를) 만들다   mutation[mju(:)téiʃən] 변이, 변화
theropod[θíərəpàd] 수각류   terrestrial[təréstriəl] 땅위의, 육상의   alteration[ɔ̀:ltəréiʃən] 변화, 개조
transmission[trænsmíʃən] 전이, 전달   avian[éiviən] 조류의   cartilage[ká:rtəlidʒ] 연골, 물렁뼈   anatomy[ənǽtəmi]
(해부학적) 구조   limb[lim] 팔, (새의) 날개   shaft[ʃæft] 깃촉   slender[sléndər] 가느다란   barb[ba:rb] 깃가지
sprout[spraut] 자라나다, 나오다   barbule[bá:rbju:l] 작은 가지   insulation[ìnsəléiʃən] 단열   scaly[skéili] 비늘로 뒤덮인

06 Main Topic

What is the main topic of the lecture?

Ⓐ The advantage that arises from the gradual change of genetic traits
Ⓑ The biological factors that influence mutation
Ⓒ The bone structure of birds compared to that of dinosaurs
Ⓓ The evolutionary mechanism behind the physical features of birds

강의의 주된 주제는 무엇인가?

Ⓐ 유전 형질의 점진적 변화에서 발생하는 이점
Ⓑ 변이에 영향을 끼치는 생물학적 요소들
Ⓒ 공룡의 뼈 구조와 비교한 조류의 뼈 구조
Ⓓ 조류의 신체적 특징 뒤에 있는 진화 메커니즘

07 Detail

Which of the following correctly describes genetic mutation?

Ⓐ All random genetic changes that occur naturally in the DNA of living organisms
Ⓑ Unnoticeable copy errors that occur when genes are passed onto the next generation
Ⓒ The accumulated output that increases an organism's chances of survival
Ⓓ A scientific jargon that describes behavioral adaptation to a given environment

다음 중 유전적 변이를 바르게 설명한 것은 무엇인가?

Ⓐ 생물들의 DNA에서 자연적으로 발생하는 모든 무작위의 유전적 변화
Ⓑ 유전자가 다음 세대로 전달될 때 발생하는 눈에 띄지 않는 복제 오류
Ⓒ 생물체의 생존 가능성을 높이는 누적된 결과물
Ⓓ 주어진 환경에 행동 적응하는 것을 설명하는 과학 용어

오답 해설   Ⓓ 유전적 변이는 행동 적응이 아니라 유전 형질의 변화이다.

08 Organization

Why does the professor mention monkeys and artwork?

Ⓐ To elaborate on the intelligence of monkeys that sets them apart from other animals
Ⓑ To explain how monkeys can learn to produce artworks through training
Ⓒ To provide an example of natural selection that occurred a long time ago
Ⓓ To illustrate the process of natural selection through an analogy

교수는 왜 원숭이와 예술 작품을 언급했나?

Ⓐ 다른 동물보다 돋보이게 만드는 원숭이의 지능을 상술하기 위해
Ⓑ 훈련을 통해 원숭이가 예술 작품을 만드는 것을 배우는 방법을 설명하기 위해
Ⓒ 오래 전에 발생한 자연 선택의 예를 제시하기 위해
Ⓓ 비유를 통해 자연 선택 과정을 분명히 보여 주기 위해

09 Detail

According to the professor, why is the body structure of birds thought to have been developed from that of theropods?
Choose 2 answers.

[A] Both had bones that consisted of an elastic substance.
[B] Both had a light body with a small number of bones.
[C] Both had feathers that are made up of similar material.
[D] Both showed similar movement patterns.
[E] Both had durable and sturdy bones.

교수에 따르면, 왜 조류의 신체 구조가 수각류에서 진화했다고 여겨지나?
2개의 답을 고르시오.

[A] 둘 다 주로 유연한 물질로 구성된 뼈를 가졌다.
[B] 둘 다 소수의 뼈로 구성된 가벼운 몸통을 가졌다.
[C] 둘 다 비슷한 재질로 구성된 깃털을 가졌다.
[D] 둘 다 비슷한 행동 패턴을 보인다.
[E] 둘 다 견고하고 단단한 뼈를 가졌다.

10 Inference

Listen again to part of the lecture. Then answer the question.

> S: But isn't that strange? Isn't it too hasty to conclude that bird bones originated from reptile bones just based on the fact that they're made from the same material and designed in a similar way?

Why does the student say this:
S: But isn't it strange?

[A] To indicate that he is astounded by the unexpected evolutionary relationship between bird bones and dinosaur bones
[B] To point out that the professor's explanation seems to be insufficient
[C] To emphasize his belief that the evolution of dinosaur bones into bird bones is an unlikely event
[D] To show that he did not understand the professor's explanation about the concept of the evolution

강의의 일부를 다시 들으시오. 그러고 나서 질문에 답하시오.

> S: 그렇지만 좀 이상하지 않은가요? 단지 그 둘이 같은 물질로 만들어졌고 비슷한 형태라는 사실 때문에 조류의 뼈가 수각류의 뼈에서 유래했다고 결론 내리는 것은 너무 성급하지 않은 가요?

학생은 왜 이 말을 했나?
S: 그렇지만 좀 이상하지 않은가요?

[A] 그가 조류와 공룡 뼈 사이의 예상치 못한 진화적 관계에 대해 놀랐음을 나타내기 위해
[B] 교수의 설명이 부족해 보인다는 것을 지적하기 위해
[C] 공룡 뼈가 조류 뼈로 진화한 것은 발생 가능성이 적다는 그의 신념을 강조하기 위해
[D] 그가 진화의 개념에 대한 교수의 설명을 이해하지 못했음을 보여 주기 위해

정답 해설 [B] 그것만으로 결론을 내리는 것은 너무 성급하지 않냐는 학생의 말에 교수가 다른 증거를 언급했다. 이는 학생이 교수의 설명이 불충분하다 생각했다는 것임을 알 수 있다.

11 Inference

What can be inferred about birds?

[A] Birds would find it easier to maintain their populations if their wings were made up of other material.
[B] Birds' wings have increased in hardness and strength.
[C] Birds chose not to develop feathers from scales as they evolved.
[D] Birds' feathers would have evolved from scales, had there been enough scales.

조류에 대해서 추론할 수 있는 것은 무엇인가?

[A] 그들의 날개가 다른 물질로 만들어졌다면, 조류는 개체 수를 유지하기 쉬웠을 것이다.
[B] 조류의 날개는 단단함과 힘을 증가시켜 왔다.
[C] 조류는 진화하면서 비늘에서 깃털을 발전시키지 않기로 선택했다.
[D] 충분한 비늘이 있었더라면 조류의 날개는 비늘에서 진화됐을 것이다.

TEST 6 Set 1 Lecture 2

Listen to part of a lecture in an anthropology class.

P **12**As I am aware, you were assigned to read about the ancient people who inhabited the eastern Canadian Arctic and the northern Greenland over the past few thousand years. Today, we will discuss both of them. Well, these regions experienced very low temperatures, and surviving such environments can be very punishing, even with today's technological aids. But there were two groups of people, who had once flourished in these very harsh environments. What is very interesting and significant to note about these peoples is that while one of the cultures survived the other disappeared. Anyhow, why don't we start off by looking at the map of the two places, northeastern North America and Greenland?

Anthropologists named this first group of people, the Dorset. What have you learnt from the reading about the Dorset?

S Well, I know they were a Paleo-Eskimo people, meaning that they inhabited the Arctic before the Inuit people, who presently inhabit the area. They developed unique life patterns to adapt in this harsh condition. For example, they used snow to build their houses, and they hunted everything except whales.

P Correct, they liked to hunt animals in the area, including bears, birds, and sea mammals like walruses and seals. And you are also right that they did not hunt whales.

13However, contrary to what you have said, snow houses weren't always built out of snow. The Dorset frequently migrated along with their animals, moving to different areas each season. Thus, their shelters had to be temporary, and they often used animal skins or sod to build their houses. Basically, they were not the prevalent structures that you have speculated them to be. While following the animals, the Dorset might come across an environment where they couldn't find these materials, and they had to use snow instead.

Dorset 민족이 사용한 철기 도구

Scholars credit the Dorset with a profound understanding of their environment, but securing the enough food supply in the harsh habitat was another story. ¹⁴So, they needed an effective tool for hunting. The Dorset used iron to make their tools. They mined iron ore from iron meteorites near the area. Let me tell you more about these rocks. Iron meteorites are metal materials that mainly consist of an iron-nickel alloy known as meteoric iron. The iron found in meteorites was one of the earliest sources accessible to humans, before the evolution of smelting, which also signaled the beginning of the Iron Age. The Dorset were highly skilled at making refined iron tools by distinctive burins. So they were able to make robust tools to hunt huge land animals and survive in the cold over thousands of years.

Thule 민족의 우세한 특성

S Well, but they somehow disappeared, right?

P As for that, uh, the Dorset were essentially extinct by 1500, maybe because of difficulties in adapting to the Medieval Warm Period, or defeat in warfare with other groups. Over a few centuries, they were completely gone. As their population declined, another group of people started to replace the Dorset. This other group, the Thule, is the people that I also wanted to discuss today. At this point, it is not clear if the Thule's arrival was the primary cause of the Dorset's decline. The Thule migrated from western Alaska. They began to expand their reach to the Canadian Arctic, and after 200 years, they reached Greenland in AD 1200.

S So what you are trying to say is that the Thule's arrival is not the main cause of the Dorset's decline?

P It certainly could have contributed, but we just don't know exactly. The Thule possessed a more advanced technology than the Dorset, that's for sure. ¹⁵The Thule could use and build boats, which the Dorset couldn't, and, therefore, were able to hunt huge whales. ¹⁶Whales were the important incentives that motivated the Thule to continue expanding eastward into Canada and then to Greenland. About a thousand years ago, the Arctic climate began to rise in temperature, melting a lot of the ice and thereby causing the whales to migrate to the eastern Arctic oceans. The Thule simply followed the whales' eastward migrating. ¹⁵ The Thule also invented special spears with floats attached to them, which allowed the hunters to retrieve the spears and reuse them easily. There were a lot of other things that the Thule had which the Dorset didn't, for example, the bow and arrow or dog-pulled sleds. These were the kinds of advantages that helped the Thule to occupy the Dorset territory. Do you have a question, Kathy?

Thule 민족이 Dorset 민족에게 빌려 온 생각들

S I remember from the reading that the Thule actually took various good ideas from the Dorset, right?
P Yes, for instance, uh...
S For instance, snow houses and some tools?
P The snow house, right! It most likely did a great deal of help to the Thule because the warm period in Greenland ended as the Thule began to settle in the Dorset territory. In any case, the Thule had to build snow houses. They could have also taken the Dorset's idea of making iron tools, prospecting for iron from meteorites. Anyway, you made a really good point about the Thule borrowing ideas. That was the exact subject that I wanted to discuss. But we still don't know how the Dorset declined. ¹⁷ Well, I mean the appearance of the Thule may have had something to do with the Dorset's extinction. But there's one thing for sure, and that is that the Thule were more advanced and adaptable. The Thule took advantage of the changing environment and borrowed ideas from different people. This ultimately proved to be an important factor in their survival.

[**Vocabulary**] Arctic[ɑ́ːrktik] 북극 punishing[pʌ́niʃiŋ] 극도로 힘든, 살인적인 anthropologist[æ̀nθrəpɑ́lədʒist] 인류학자 term[təːrm] 칭하다 walrus[wɔ́ːlrəs] 바다코끼리 sod[sɑd] 잔디 prevalent[prévələnt] 만연한, 일반적인 credit[krédit] 믿는다 ore[ɔːr] 원석 meteorite[míːtiəràit] 운석 alloy[ǽlɔi] 합금 smelting[smeltiŋ] 제련 burin[bjú(ː)ərin] (금속 조각용의) 끌 eastward[íːstwərd] 동쪽으로

12 Main Topic

What is the main idea of the lecture?

Ⓐ The Thule's migration to the Dorset territory
Ⓑ The reason that the two peoples competed each other
Ⓒ The comparison between two ancient civilizations
Ⓓ The ways two civilizations used to survive

강의의 주제는 무엇인가?

Ⓐ Thule 민족의 Dorset 민족의 영역으로의 이주
Ⓑ 두 민족이 서로 경쟁한 이유
Ⓒ 고대의 두 문명에 대한 비교
Ⓓ 두 문명이 살아남기 위해 사용한 방법들

13 Inference

What can be inferred about the Dorset's shelters?

Ⓐ Snow houses provided effective protection against the cold weather of the Arctic.
Ⓑ Their shelters were easier to build out of materials other than snow.
Ⓒ Their shelters were built using a unique method that they developed.
Ⓓ The Dorset generally lived in structures that were not composed of snow.

Dorset 민족의 거주지에 대해 추론할 수 있는 것은 무엇인가?

Ⓐ 눈 집은 북극의 추운 기후에 대한 효율적인 보호를 제공했다.
Ⓑ 그들의 거주지는 눈 이외의 다른 재료로 만들기 더 쉬웠다.
Ⓒ 그들의 거주지는 그들이 발달시킨 독특한 방법으로 지어졌다.
Ⓓ Dorset 민족은 대개 눈이 아닌 다른 재료로 만들어진 구조물에서 살았다.

14 Detail

Which of the following functions did iron meteorites serve for the Dorset?

Ⓐ They were used to smelt strong weapons to prepare for wars.
Ⓑ They were turned into durable devices for everyday activities such as farming.
Ⓒ They were fashioned into implements that facilitated food provision.
Ⓓ They were used to build houses in order to resist the cold.

철질운석이 Dorset 민족에 도움이 된 기능은 다음 중 무엇인가?

Ⓐ 전쟁을 준비하기 위한 강한 무기로 제련되곤 했다.
Ⓑ 농사 같은 일상 생활을 위한 내구성 있는 장치로 만들어졌다.
Ⓒ 음식 공급을 용이하게 해 준 도구로 만들어졌다.
Ⓓ 추위를 견디기 위한 집을 만드는 데 사용되었다.

15 Detail

According to the professor, which activities were practiced by the Thule but not by the Dorset?
Choose 2 answers.

- [A] Building snow houses
- [B] Making iron tools
- [C] Hunting whales
- [D] Using equipment with a special function

교수에 따르면, Thule 민족이 했지만 Dorset 민족은 하지 않은 활동은 어떤 것인가?
2개의 답을 고르시오.

- [A] 눈 집을 만드는 것
- [B] 철 기구를 만드는 것
- [C] 고래를 사냥하는 것
- [D] 특별한 기능이 있는 장비를 사용한 것

16 Inference

What can be inferred about the migration of the Thule into northeastern Canada and Greenland?

- [A] They migrated to find a better and warmer environment.
- [B] They were short on food and had to find a new territory for food.
- [C] They tried to conquer the Dorset's territory.
- [D] They followed their sustenance.

Thule 민족이 캐나다 북동쪽과 그린란드로 이주한 것에 대해 추론할 수 있는 것은 무엇인가?

- [A] 그들은 더 좋고 따뜻한 환경을 찾기 위해 이동했다.
- [B] 그들은 음식이 부족해졌고 음식을 위해 새로운 영토를 찾아야만 했다.
- [C] 그들은 Dorset 민족의 영토를 정복하려 했다.
- [D] 그들은 먹거리를 따라갔다.

정답 해설 [D] Thule 민족은 사냥감인 고래를 따라 이동했다고 했다. sustenance는 '(음식·물 등) 생명을 건강하게 유지시켜 주는 것, 자양물'이라는 뜻이다.

17 Inference

Listen again to part of the lecture. Then answer the question.

> P: Well, I mean the appearance of the Thule may have had something to do with the Dorset's extinction. But there's one thing for sure, and that is that the Thule were more advanced and adaptable.

Why does the professor say this:
P: ...I mean the appearance of the Thule may have had something to do with the Dorset's extinction.

- [A] To explain how one of the people had an effect on the other
- [B] To assert that the mystery about the Dorset's decline must be solved
- [C] To introduce another reason for the Dorset's disappearance
- [D] To express uncertainty about the Thule's involvement in a phenomenon

강의의 일부를 다시 들으시오. 그리고 나서 질문에 답하시오.

> P: 음, 그러니까 Thule 민족의 출현이 Dorset 민족의 멸종과 관련이 있을 수 있다는 거예요. 하지만 Thule 민족이 더 발전됐고 환경 적응력이 더 우수했다는 것 하나는 확실해요.

교수는 왜 이 말을 했나?
P: ……그러니까 Thule 민족의 출현이 Dorset 민족의 멸종과 관련이 있을 수 있다는 거예요.

- [A] 어떻게 한 민족이 다른 민족에게 영향을 줬는지를 설명하기 위해
- [B] Dorset 민족의 쇠퇴에 대한 미스터리가 해결돼야만 한다고 주장하기 위해
- [C] Dorset 민족이 사라진 다른 이유를 소개하기 위해
- [D] 어떤 현상에 대한 Thule 민족의 개입에 대한 불확실성을 표현하기 위해

TEST 6 Set 2 Conversation

Listen to a conversation between a professor and a student.

S So sorry, Professor Murphy! I'm late!
P It's okay, Jim. **01**Did you say you wanted to ask me some questions about the requirements of your senior thesis?
S Yes, mam. I do have some questions. First of all, we usually write the thesis during the first semester of the school year, right? That is, of course, during our senior year.
P Correct.
S The thing is...I have already decided to use that time to tutor students at Belgrade High School. **02**My dream is to teach English in an educational institution after I graduate so, I was so pleased when I finally got placed at this school for a tutoring position. As you know, it's a really popular school among students in our department. There's fierce competition to get accepted there! Anyway, I'm planning to get some teaching experience at this institution for a semester. **03**So, I am worried about how to do all this when I have to write up a 40-to 50-page senior thesis. Apparently, writing a thesis is not an easy task.

P Right. But I don't think it will be a problem.
S Why not?
P Well, a lot of students who major in English go after the teaching certification. I've seen a lot of people finish their senior theses successfully after securing some tutoring experience. **04**I mean that the experience proved to be useful because they could base their paper on the specific things that they have tutored their students in. It's like killing two birds with one stone. So you can write your thesis during the second semester, after completing your teaching experience, which I think should leave you enough time.

논문에 도움을 줄 교수님의 부재	S	Wow, that is good to know. But this brings up another problem. The focus of my study has always been Renaissance literature. I also want to go after a graduate degree on this particular topic. This is why I had planned to write my senior thesis on the *Petrarchan sonnet because it could be relevant to my future studies and all.
	P	Right, but, you see, Professor Howard, the most knowledgeable expert in that area, will be away on sabbatical.
	S	Yes, I'm aware of that. Without Professor Howard, I thought it would be hard to write a paper on the Petrarchan sonnet. I mean, this is a topic that is most relevant to Professor Howard's experience.
논문의 주제를 바꿀 것을 제안	P	I understand what you are saying. 05 Then, do you mind if I provide you with a Plan B?
	S	Sure, why not? I really can't think of another topic for my thesis, though.
	P	You see, during the first semester, I am going to teach a course on an introduction to Shakespeare during the Renaissance era. The class meets late during the day so it won't bother your tutoring schedule. Moreover, it's been a while since the school offered this course, so I'm pretty sure that this is a new kind of study for someone like you.
	S	Yes, I have never heard of the class.
	P	05 If you are interested in such a topic and are willing to take the course, I feel confident that I can help you out with your senior thesis. The Petrarchan sonnet you are interested in and the Shakespeare's sonnet have much in common. Francesco Petrarch was the first to significantly solidify *sonnet structure in the beginning of the Renaissance era, and Shakespeare further developed this unique style of poetry in his own love poems, making it more attractive to the public. So, to broaden your perspective of this literary work, you need to first understand Shakespeare's sonnets. 05 I mean you could write about the similarity of these two sonnets.
	S	I really appreciate your suggestion. It does seem like a great idea, though I have to think it over. Actually I've never dabbled in Shakespeare, so I need to look thoroughly before I decide.

S 와, 좋은 이야기네요. 하지만 다른 문제도 있어요. 제 학업의 초점은 르네상스 문학이었어요. 저는 이 분야에 대해 대학원 학위도 받고 싶거든요. 이건 제가 제 졸업 논문을 Petrarchan 소네트에 관해 쓰는 이유이기도 한데, 그것이 제 미래의 학업에까지 관련이 있을 수도 있기 때문이에요.

P 그래, 하지만, 너도 알다시피, 이 분야에서 최고로 권위 있는 Howard 교수님이 안식년에 들어가서 학교에 안 계실 텐데.

S 네, 알고 있어요. Howard 교수님이 안 계시면 Petrarchan 소네트에 관한 논문 작성이 어려울 것 같아요. 그러니까 이 주제는 Howard 교수님의 경험과 가장 연관이 되어있으니까요.

P 네가 무슨 말을 하는지 알겠구나. 05 그럼 내가 다른 제안을 해도 되겠니?

S 네, 물론이죠! 전 새로운 논문 주제에 대해서는 생각조차 못했는걸요.

P 자, 첫 번째 학기에, 내가 르네상스 시대의 셰익스피어 입문에 대해 가르칠 거란다. 수업은 늦은 시간에 있으니까 네 교생 실습 시간과 겹치지 않을 거야. 게다가, 학교에서 이 수업이 개설됐던 게 꽤 오래돼서, 아마 너와 같은 사람들에게는 새로운 종류의 수업이 될 것 같구나.

S 네, 한번도 그 수업에 대해 들어본 적이 없어요.

P 05 네가 이 주제에 관심이 있고, 수업을 수강할 생각이 있다면, 내가 네 졸업 논문을 도와줄 수 있을 것 같은데. 네가 흥미있어 하는 Petrarchan 소네트와 셰익스피어의 소네트는 공통점이 많단다. Francesco Petrarch가 르네상스 시대 초기에 소네트의 구성을 확고히 한 최초의 사람이고, 셰익스피어는 이 독특한 시 스타일을 그의 연애시에서 더 발전시켜, 그것을 대중들에게 더 매력적이게 만들었단다. 그래서 이 문학 작품에 대한 너의 관점을 넓히기 위해서 셰익스피어의 소네트를 먼저 이해할 필요가 있는 거지. 05 그러니까, 네가 이 두 개의 소네트의 유사성에 대해서 쓸 수 있을 거 같구나.

S 제안 정말 감사합니다. 그건 정말 좋은 생각 같은데, 한 번 더 생각해 봐야할 거 같아요. 사실 전 한번도 셰익스피어에 대해서 깊이 공부해본 적이 없어서, 결정하기 전에 꼼꼼하게 봐야할 것 같아요.

P 좋아! 네가 르네상스 시대의 문학에 대해서 논문을 쓰기로 결정하면, 가능한 빨리 나에게 말해 주렴. 졸업 논문은 일이 많고, 네가 현명하다면 이번 여름 방학을 이용하는 게 좋을 거야. 내가 시작하도록 도와주마.

P Alright! If you make your mind up to write your paper on Renaissance-era literature, make sure to let me know as soon as possible. The senior thesis is a lot of work, and if you are wise, you should take advantage of this summer break. I'm sure I can help you get started.

[**Vocabulary**] senior thesis 졸업 논문   spanning [spæn] ~에 포괄하는   sabbatical [səbǽtikəl] 안식 기간
plan B 제 2안(첫째 안이 성공하지 못할 경우에 진행할 계획)   love poem 연애시   dabble [dǽbl] 조금 해 보다, 관여하다

[각주]
* **Petrarchan sonnet** 페트라르카의 서정시로, 페트라르카는 이탈리아의 시인으로서 교황청에서 일하면서 라우라라는 여자를 위해 연애시를 쓰기 시작했다. 뛰어난 자연 묘사와 함께 아름다운 운율을 구사하면서 단테의 〈신곡〉과 더불어 14세기 시의 걸작으로 불린다.
* **Sonnet** 13세기 이탈리아 민요에서 나온 14행시로, 대부분이 개인적인 사랑을 주제로 다루며 짧은 운을 통해 시적 기교를 보여주는 작품들이다. 단테나 페트라르카에 의하여 완성되었고, 르네상스 시대에 널리 퍼져 영국에서도 독자적인 소네트를 완성하였다.

01 Main Topic

Why does the student visit the professor's office?

Ⓐ To find an appropriate topic for a senior thesis
Ⓑ To receive help about planning tutoring schedules
Ⓒ To get information about the chosen senior thesis topic
Ⓓ To get advice regarding a senior thesis

학생은 왜 교수의 사무실을 방문했나?

Ⓐ 졸업 논문에 적합한 주제를 찾기 위해
Ⓑ 교생 실습 일정을 짜는 데 도움을 얻기 위해
Ⓒ 선택한 논문 주제에 대한 정보를 얻기 위해
Ⓓ 졸업 논문에 대한 조언을 구하기 위해

02 Inference

What can be inferred about the tutoring position at Belgrade High School?

Ⓐ The student applied for the position because of his senior thesis.
Ⓑ The student is able to earn credits by joining the position.
Ⓒ The student considers getting the placement as a stroke of luck.
Ⓓ The student will need to spend more time working compared to other tutoring jobs.

Belgrade 고등학교에서의 교생 실습 자리에 대해 추론할 수 있는 것은 무엇인가?

Ⓐ 학생은 졸업 논문 때문에 그 자리에 지원했다.
Ⓑ 학생은 그 자리에 참여하는 것으로 학점을 받을 수 있다.
Ⓒ 학생은 그 자리를 얻은 것을 뜻밖의 행운이라고 생각한다.
Ⓓ 학생은 다른 지도 업무와 비교해 더 많은 시간을 소비해야 할 것이다.

03 Detail

Why is the student worried about writing a thesis during the first semester of his senior year?

Ⓐ The student might be swamped with heavy workload.
Ⓑ A professor would show unwillingness to help the student.
Ⓒ The student has to gain teaching experience to prepare for writing a thesis.
Ⓓ It takes time to prepare a topic for the senior thesis.

학생은 왜 4학년 1학기에 논문을 작성하는 것에 대해 걱정하나?

Ⓐ 학생은 과중한 일에 시달릴 수도 있다.
Ⓑ 교수가 학생을 돕는 것을 꺼릴지도 모른다.
Ⓒ 학생은 논문을 쓰기 위해 교수 경력을 쌓아야만 한다.
Ⓓ 졸업 논문의 주제를 준비하는 데 시간이 걸린다

04 Inference

Listen again to part of the conversation. Then answer the question.

> P: I mean that the proved to be useful because they could base their paper on the specific things that they have tutored their students in. It's like killing two birds with one stone.

Why does the professor say this:
P: It's like killing two birds with one stone.

Ⓐ To imply that the student doesn't have to worry about writing a thesis
Ⓑ To assure that the student will meet the thesis deadline
Ⓒ To emphasize that the topic of his thesis is appropriate
Ⓓ To express that writing a paper helps some tutoring experience

대화의 일부를 다시 들으시오. 그러고 나서 질문에 답하시오.

> P: 실제로 그 경험은 유용하다고 증명되었는데, 학생들을 지도할 때 사용한 수업 자료의 특정 내용을 바탕으로 논문의 뼈대를 세울 수 있었기 때문이란다. 일석이조라고 할 수 있지.

교수는 왜 이 말을 하나?
P: 일석이조라고 할 수 있지.

Ⓐ 학생이 논문을 쓰는 것에 대해 걱정할 필요가 없다는 것을 암시하기 위해
Ⓑ 학생이 논문 마감 기한을 맞출 것임을 장담하기 위해
Ⓒ 그의 논문 주제가 적합하다는 것을 강조하기 위해
Ⓓ 보고서를 쓰는 것이 교생 경험에 도움이 된다는 것을 표현하기 위해

05 Detail

What does the professor suggest the student do?

Ⓐ To take a course directly related to the chosen thesis topic
Ⓑ To apply for various internship positions
Ⓒ To change the thesis topic to match the student's situation
Ⓓ To consult with a leading expert on the thesis topic

교수가 학생에게 제안한 것은 무엇인가?

Ⓐ 선택한 논문 주제와 직접적으로 관계가 있는 수업을 듣는 것
Ⓑ 다양한 인턴쉽에 지원하는 것
Ⓒ 논문 주제를 학생의 상황에 맞게 바꾸는 것
Ⓓ 논문 주제에 저명한 전문가에게 상담을 받는 것

TEST 6 — Set 2 Lecture 1

Listen to part of a lecture in an environmental science class.

P Let's continue with our discussion on the effects of global warming on the environment. Global warming is a term for the observed century-scale rise in the average temperature of Earth and its related effects. This problem occurs when the carbon emissions are released into the air by the production and consumption of fossil fuels, manufactured goods, materials and services. This eventually leads to the problematic "greenhouse effect", where the carbon dioxide that is inside the Earth's atmosphere captures solar heat and raises the planet's temperature. Consequently, this phenomenon has interrupted the balance of our ecosystem by causing phenomena such as melting ice caps in the polar region. Melting glaciers and early snowmelt cause more abrupt water shortages and increase the risk of wildfires globally. We are already familiar with the serious consequences of this environmental disaster and why we care about it.

06 This time, we will further discuss how the ocean is affected by this environmental disaster and its aftermath. First off, let us rewind our discussion to the Introduction of Physics that we covered previously. The most important point to keep in mind is the concept of how electrical properties work in water molecules. 07 The fact that one part of each water molecule has a negative charge while the other has a positive charge makes it like a magnet such that one can say that water molecules are dipolar. This bipolarity results in each molecule being drawn to another as they form a compact structure inside the greater mass of water.

S I apologize to interrupt, but I am a bit confused about our subject here. I thought we were going to discuss the ocean and its relation to global warming. And how does what you just explained have anything to do with it?

P Let me explain. When water molecules are tightly bound with each other, more energy is required to increase or decrease water temperature because water molecules tend to be compact. For instance, 145 degrees Celsius is the greatest recorded difference between the lowest and highest temperatures on land.

08 However, in the ocean, the greatest recorded temperature difference is only 40 degrees Celsius, which is much smaller than the greatest recorded temperature difference on land. As the ocean is composed of water, its temperature is much more stable than the temperature on land as more energy is required to change the water's temperature, which is why the ocean water usually maintains a lower temperature even on a hot summer day. Surprisingly, carbon dioxide is prone to be absorbed by water, especially cold water. Because of this, the ocean also absorbs a large amount of carbon dioxide that is in the air. The increased uptake of carbon dioxide into the ocean affects the temperature on land considerably because this phenomenon decreases the amount of greenhouse gases. The ocean acts as a massive carbon sink, and has taken up about a third of carbon dioxide emitted by human activity.

Now, you probably think it could be a great thing because this drops the temperature of the atmosphere on land. 07 As great as it sounds, there is a negative side to this.

S So what is the negative side?

P The negative aspect is that, uh, 09 if you're a clam chowder fan, you should be alarmed. The carbon dioxide we are pumping into the atmosphere is also changing our oceans into shell-eating acid. As mentioned before, the ocean takes in and absorbs the carbon dioxide, but when water and carbon dioxide combine, it results in the production of carbonic acid. 10 Importantly, carbonic acid generally prevents the production of the material called calcium carbonate that is a substance, which water naturally contains, and which is also an essential ingredient used to make the shells of shellfishes. As pollution emits an excessive amount of carbon dioxide, more than the amount that would be created naturally by the Earth, the ocean takes in more carbon dioxide to produce more carbonic acid and hampers sea animals' ability to generate calcium carbonate.

The augmenting production of carbon in the air causes more acidic ocean. Larger animals are less affected by this for now, but the increased acidity now has begun to take effect on the small sea animals that are at the bottom of the food chain, such as various planktons, sea snails, and small shellfish. Due to the enormous amount of pollution absorbed by the ocean, the amount of calcium carbonate has also decreased, so there is not enough of this material for shellfish to utilize in order to build their shells. With the ocean continually becoming more acidic, the tiny creatures will eventually be incapable of constructing their shells, which will obviously result in death.

11 The consequences have already hit coastal shell fishing towns hard. According to the Natural Resources Defense Council, ocean acidification has already cost the oyster industry in the U.S. Pacific Northwest nearly U.S. 100 million dollars and directly or indirectly jeopardized about 3,200 jobs. A bigger tragedy has yet to take place. If small creatures such as oysters are unable to build shells, this event will also affect the other sea creatures that are higher on the food chain, as we know that the smaller sea animals are what they primarily consume. So, it is important that you realize and understand what kind of effect carbon dioxide pollution has on Earth.

[Vocabulary] problematic[pràbləmǽtik] 문제가 많은　　ice cap 만년설　　snowmelt[snoumelt] 해빙
aftermath[ǽftərmæθ] 여파　　negative charge 음전하, 음극　　positive charge 양전하, 양극　　biopolarity[báioupouláerəti]
2극성, 양극성　　inland[ínlənd] 내륙으로, 내륙에 있는　　carbonic acid 탄산　　calcium carbonate 탄산 칼슘
hamper[hǽmpər] 막다, 방해하다　　augmenting[ɔːgméntiŋ] 증대시키는, 증대하는　　sea snail 바다 우렁이
acidification[əsìdəfikéiʃən] 산성화

06 Main Topic

What is the main purpose of the lecture?

- Ⓐ To explain the factors that affect the amount of carbon dioxide in the ocean
- Ⓑ To identify the relationship between the ocean and climate change
- Ⓒ To explain how human activities cause global warming
- Ⓓ To discuss the effects of climate change on the ocean, and how they can be mitigated

강의의 주된 목적은 무엇인가?

- Ⓐ 바다에 있는 이산화 탄소 양에 영향을 주는 요소들을 설명하는 것
- Ⓑ 바다와 기후 변화와의 관계에 대해 알아보는 것
- Ⓒ 인간의 활동이 어떻게 지구 온난화를 야기했는지 설명하는 것
- Ⓓ 바다에 미치는 기후 변화의 영향과 어떻게 그 영향을 경감시킬 수 있는지를 논의하는 것

07 Inference

What can be inferred about the fact that water molecules are dipolar?

- Ⓐ It can explain the importance of how electrical properties work in molecules.
- Ⓑ It shows how closely the water molecules are connected to each other at an atomic level.
- Ⓒ It proves the reason the water absorbs carbon dioxide, which subsequently causes environmental destruction.
- Ⓓ It can be used to understand the concept of the molecular structure of the water.

물 분자가 쌍극이라는 사실에 대해 추론할 수 있는 것은 무엇인가?

- Ⓐ 분자의 전기적 특성이 작용하는 방법의 중요성을 설명할 수 있다.
- Ⓑ 원자 단계에서 물 분자들이 서로 얼마나 가깝게 연결돼 있는지 보여 준다.
- Ⓒ 물이 이산화 탄소를 흡수해서, 결과적으로 환경 파괴를 야기하는 이유를 증명한다.
- Ⓓ 물의 분자 구조의 개념을 이해하는 데 사용될 수 있다.

08 Detail

What does the professor say about the difference in temperatures in the ocean and land?

- Ⓐ It explains the reason organisms become more sensitive to their environment.
- Ⓑ The temperature in the ocean is limited because more energy is required to alter it.
- Ⓒ The vast difference in temperatures on land signifies that it is more easily affected by global warming.
- Ⓓ This fact is proof that the ocean has a greater capability to deter global warming.

교수가 땅과 바다의 온도 차에 대해 말한 것은 무엇인가?

- Ⓐ 그것은 생물들이 그들의 환경에 더 민감해 지는 이유를 설명한다.
- Ⓑ 온도를 변화시키는 데 더 많은 에너지가 필요해 바다의 온도가 제한된다.
- Ⓒ 땅의 큰 온도 변화는 그것이 지구 온난화에 더 쉽게 영향 받을 수 있다는 것을 의미한다.
- Ⓓ 이 사실은 바다가 지구 온난화를 막을 더 큰 능력이 있다는 것에 대한 증명이다.

09 Inference

Listen again to part of the lecture. Then answer the question.

> P: ...if you're a clam chowder fan, you should be alarmed. The carbon dioxide we are pumping into the atmosphere is also changing our oceans into shell-eating acid.

Why does the professor say this:
P: ...if you're a clam chowder fan, you should be alarmed.

(A) To imply that the increase of a particular material might cause an adverse consequence to nature
(B) To emphasize there are many challenges the clam chowder industry faces
(C) To encourage students to look for ways to recover the environmental balance
(D) To explain how a species of shellfish affects the environment

10 Detail

What is the result of carbonic acid?

(A) The amount of carbon dioxide in the environment is decreased.
(B) It deters the creation of the material that comprises a sea animal.
(C) Water takes in and consumes carbon dioxide.
(D) Water molecules are more closely compressed.

11 Organization

Why does the professor mention 3,200 jobs?

(A) To emphasize how many people lost jobs in the U.S.
(B) To show that people should repair the damage they have been doing to environment
(C) To explain the number of people is needed to cultivate shellfishes
(D) To arouse attention to an aftermath of grave damage to environment

영단기 TOEFL

ACTUAL TEST

TEST **07**

TEST 7 Set 1 Conversation

Listen to a conversation between a student and a director of the Student Activity Center.

D Hi, Jack. **01 How are all the preparations for visiting the exhibition in New York taking place?**

S Great. Fifteen students signed up for the trip so far, and I made posters to advertise the event. So hopefully there will be more students who sign up for it. I'm pretty sure everything's ready.

D Including transportation?

S Of course. We decided to take the train. We'll arrive in the city at noon, so we'll have plenty of time to visit the art gallery downtown.

D Wow, I can tell you've really thought this through. It's exciting that the artwork done by one of our students will be there at that exhibition. It's a huge achievement for the lucky artist and will bring prestige to our school.

S No kidding! Actually, that lucky student is my roommate. I thought he'd appreciate it if I organized a student event for his big event. **02 I mean, I work at the Student Activity Center, and the activities we organize are always so popular.** I expect a lot of people to sign up. It's a great way to visit New York and check out the art scene while supporting a good friend. This exhibition is in collaboration with Jessy Harris, a new and rising American artist, so a lot of people are really excited by it. As you probably know, she is a renowned artist for sculptures and site-specific installations in New York City.

D We are definitely looking forward to it. It's an unbelievable opportunity for your friend since it actually raises his chances of getting into a good graduate school. It'll make him stand out from other applicants for sure. He must be glad to have a thoughtful roommate like you, who supports him during such an important event. He'll be thrilled to see these posters you've made!

S That's nice of you to say. I guess you've checked them

out? I made sure to put the posters where other students often pass by, so they would be easily seen. Oh, and I really want to thank you for the funds you've approved for us. You've been such a big help in making this trip work out.

High Line

D You're very welcome. So, I understand that the plans are finished? No last-minute changes?

S Well, I have been thinking about the bus lately. Instead of riding the bus from the station into the city, we could just walk. I checked the weather forecast a few days ago, and sunshine is predicted for the big day. Wouldn't it be a waste to miss a chance to walk the High Line?

D I'm sorry. The High Line?

S Oh, I guess you might know what it is. Um, it's kind of like a park in the sky. 03 At first, it was a railroad track for trains carrying freight, not passengers. Then, it was replaced by a road for trucks to cut costs, and then it was abandoned for a while. It was unused for decades until the city came up with a project to take advantage of the area and turned it into a mile-long park. Now, it's filled with flowers and trees, and is a place where people can enjoy fantastic views of the city. On top of all that, I thought it would be perfect since it leads from the train station to downtown, where the gallery is.

이동 계획에 문제가 있음

D I agree it sounds fabulous, but don't you think some people might mind walking? There might be complaints about not having a bus.

S I didn't realize that some people might object to the walk. How about dividing the group into two? One group could take the High Line with me, and the other group could ride the bus in comfort.

D 04 That could work but as the poster says, you're in charge of the whole tour. That means you need to plan out every part of the trip. If you're with those people who want to walk on the High Line, who's going to lead the people on the bus?

S Hmm, you raise a very good point. Do you have any suggestions?

대안책을 고민해 보기로 함

D 05 Oh well, I might be able to recall my way around the city. It's where I got my graduate degree. I did stay three years in the city, although that's nothing

175

compared to you since you spent your whole childhood there. Still, I want to help out as much as I can, since it's not every day that a student from our school gets to exhibit at an art gallery. I'll skim over the city map, and let you know alternatives.
S Thanks, you're such a big support. I really appreciate your help.

보낸 너와 비교하면 아무것도 아니지만. 그렇지만 우리 학교 학생이 미술관에 전시를 하게 되는 경우가 매일 있는 일이 아니니 내가 최대한 돕도록 하마. 도시 지도를 한번 훑어 보고, 대안책을 알려 주마.
S 감사합니다. 정말 큰 의지가 되요. 도움 정말 감사 드려요.

[Vocabulary] signe up for ~을 등록하다   think it through (문제에 대해) 충분히 생각하다   collaboration[kəlǽbəréiʃən] 공동 작업   renowned[rináund] 유명한   stand out from ~중에 두드러지다   site-specific installation 설치 미술   pass by ~을 지나치다, 스쳐가다   skim over 대충 훑어보다

01 Main Topic

What is the conversation mainly about?

Ⓐ Transportation arrangements for a school trip
Ⓑ The exhibition at an art gallery
Ⓒ Fundraising activities for the school
Ⓓ Details of a student activity

대화는 주로 무엇에 대한 것인가?

Ⓐ 수학여행을 위한 교통편 마련
Ⓑ 미술관의 전시회
Ⓒ 교내 기금 모집 행사들
Ⓓ 학생 활동에 관한 세부 사항

02 Detail

What does the student say about the Student Activity Center?

Ⓐ It manages fundraising activities for field trips.
Ⓑ It introduces students to various job opportunities.
Ⓒ It supports students starting their careers after school.
Ⓓ It is known for organizing school activities for students.

학생이 학생 활동 센터에 대해 말한 것은 무엇인가?

Ⓐ 현장 학습을 위한 기금 마련 행사를 관리한다.
Ⓑ 학생들에게 다양한 직업 기회를 소개한다.
Ⓒ 학생들이 졸업 후에 일을 시작할 수 있도록 지원한다.
Ⓓ 학생들을 위한 학교 활동을 기획하는 것으로 알려졌다.

03 Detail

What two features does the student mention about the High Line?
Choose 2 answers.

Ⓐ Its function has been changed.
Ⓑ It shouldn't be used to transport passengers.
Ⓒ It was transformed into a park by public demand.
Ⓓ It was not always in active use.

학생이 High Line의 두 가지 특징으로 언급한 것은 무엇인가?
2개의 답을 고르시오.

Ⓐ 용도가 바뀌었다.
Ⓑ 승객 수송용으로 사용되어서는 안 된다.
Ⓒ 대중의 요구에 따라 공원으로 바뀌었다.
Ⓓ 항상 이용이 많은 것은 아니었다.

04 Detail

Why does the director emphasize the information in the poster?

Ⓐ Because the poster needs to be updated to attract more students
Ⓑ Because the poster should present the plan for the entire tour
Ⓒ Because the poster includes a name of the person in charge of the activity
Ⓓ Because the poster indicates that a bus is available for transportation

센터장은 왜 포스터에 있는 정보를 강조했나?

Ⓐ 더 많은 학생들을 모으기 위해 포스터가 업데이트 될 필요가 있기 때문에
Ⓑ 포스터가 투어 전체의 계획을 보여 줘야 하기 때문에
Ⓒ 포스터가 활동 책임자의 이름을 포함하기 때문에
Ⓓ 포스터에 버스가 이동 수단으로 가능하다고 언급되어 있기 때문에

05 Inference

Listen again to part of the conversation. Then answer the question.

> D: Oh well, I might be able to recall my way around the city. It's where I got my graduate degree.

Why does she say this:
D: It's where I got my graduate degree.

Ⓐ To inform the student that she had graduated from a school in New York
Ⓑ To indicate that she is aware of the city
Ⓒ To suggest that she can be of some help to the student
Ⓓ To emphasize that she knows people living in New York

대화의 일부를 다시 들으시오. 그리고 나서 질문에 답하시오.

> D: 어, 글쎄, 내가 도시를 다녔던 길을 떠올려 볼 수 있을 것 같구나. 내가 석사 학위를 취득한 곳이거든.

그녀가 이 말을 한 이유는 무엇인가?
D: 내가 석사 학위를 취득한 곳이거든.

Ⓐ 그녀가 뉴욕에서 학교를 졸업했다는 사실을 학생에게 상기시키기 위해
Ⓑ 그녀가 그 도시에 대해 안다는 사실을 나타내기 위해
Ⓒ 그녀가 학생에게 도움이 될 수 있다는 사실을 말하기 위해
Ⓓ 그녀가 뉴욕에 사는 사람들을 안다는 것을 강조하기 위해

TEST 7 Set 1 Lecture 1

Listen to part of a lecture in a zoology class.

P Okay, here's a question. 07What would you do if someone next to you started to choke on some food? I guess you could call 911 or hit that person on the back to help him cough the food up. Whatever you do, it's probably not because you want a reward. 08Helping someone in need is usually an instinctive action. That is called altruism. What is altruism exactly? It's basically the principle or practice of being concerned for the welfare of others. Simply put, altruism is selflessness, or the opposite of selfishness. The French philosopher Auguste Comte coined the word altruism as an antonym of egoism. The term can be traced to the Italian term altrui, which can then be traced to the Latin term alteri, meaning "other people" or "somebody else." Altruism can be observed in biological organisms, when they perform an action, which sacrifices their well-being, such as quality of life, time, and probability of survival or reproduction, in order to benefit another, whether directly or indirectly, another third-party. The altruistic individual doesn't expect a reciprocal or compensatory reaction in return.

That's enough explanation for this psychological concept. 06Let me ask you another question. Do you think animals exhibit this kind of selfless action? That is, do you think animals help other animals without expecting anything in return? Some people believe that only humans feel a compulsion to help others, but this isn't true. We can find so many examples of various animals exhibiting selflessness. 06Primates, because they possess the intellectual capacity and social behavior similar to humans, are particularly interesting subjects for this study.

To further answer the questions surrounding animal altruism, researchers have conducted an interesting experiment using chimpanzees. This experiment was designed to explore the possibility of animal altruism. First, a chimpanzee was placed in a room with only one small hole. There was a banana outside the hole, but the chimpanzee needed a stick to reach the banana. A second chimpanzee was placed in a room with no banana and only two tools: a stick and a ball. There was a small opening in between the chimpanzees' rooms so that the second chimp could pass a tool to the first chimp if it wanted to. Do you see what this experiment wanted to test? Researchers wanted to see if the second chimp would help the first chimp by passing a necessary tool, even if the second chimp wouldn't get anything in return. I mean this experiment was designed to see if the second chimp handed an ideal stick to the first chimp. 09 Obviously, a ball is not the best tool for reaching the banana, but researchers gave the second chimp access to this tool to ensure that it had intent to help shown by sending the correct tool, instead of just handing over whatever was available without a specific intent. The results of this experiment delighted the researchers. If the second chimp were just giving tools at random to the first chimp, then it would have given the stick only 50 percent of the time. However, the second chimp handed the stick to the first chimp 90 percent of the time! Researchers were able to conclude that the second chimp selected and gave the necessary tool to the first chimp with intent to help.

침팬지에 대한 추가 실험

Researchers then added two more conditions in order to see whether the ability to understand the goal of another individual affected a chimp's behavior. In half of the experiments, the second chimp's room had transparent walls and in the other half, the room had completely opaque walls. The hypothesis was that if chimpanzees modulated their responses to a help request based on whether or not they could see the goal of another individual, then they would give the appropriate tool more often when the room's walls were transparent. 10 Again, the experiment was successful and researchers concluded that chimpanzees were more likely to offer up the appropriate tool when their room's walls were transparent. So, in addition to indicating the existence of animal altruism, the experiment proved that chimpanzees were able to understand which tool their partner would need in order to solve a given task. Another interesting aspect of this experiment was that 90 percent of the time, the second chimpanzee offered a tool only after the first chimpanzee requested for help. This suggested that chimpanzees may not spontaneously engage in helping behaviors, but that direct requests are effective in soliciting assistance.

Before we move on, let me tell you a little about the results from when the room walls were opaque to provide some insight into how chimpanzees determine which tools to provide when asked for help. [10] The second chimpanzee did act differently during the different opacity conditions. When opaque walls blocked its view, it could not see what was happening in the other room and acted a bit more passively except for a chimpanzee named Ayumu. Ayumu actually peered through the small opening into the other room, effectively overcoming the visual limitation.

As we can see from these experiments, primates like chimpanzees feel compelled to help other members of their species. Also, they make more active efforts to help if they are able to see the situation. The chimpanzees modulated the level of the altruistic behaviors they engaged in based on their environmental conditions. Notably, an exception to this trend was observed when a certain chimpanzee actively overcame a visual limitation in order to help another chimpanzee. [11] What can we infer about humans based on the results of these experiments? Like primates, our level of altruistic behaviors changes based on the conditions we face. For example, studies found that altruism is especially strong when people know each other. In a similar sense, people who are community-oriented may show more altruistic behavior than individualists.

[**Vocabulary**] choke[tʃouk] 숨이 막히다, 질식하다   cough up 토해내다   instinctive[instíŋktiv] 본능에 따른   altruism[ǽltru(:)ìzəm] 이타주의   welfare[wélfɛ̀ər] 안녕, 행복   selflessness[sélflisnis] 자기를 돌보지 않음, 사심이 없음   selfishness[sélfiʃnis] 이기적임   coin[kɔin] (새로운 낱말·어구를) 만들다   antonym[ǽntənim] 반의어   egoism[íːgouìzəm] 자기중심주의, 이기주의   altruistic[æ̀ltru(:)ístik] 이타적인   reciprocal[risíprəkəl] 상호 간의   compensatory[kəmpénsətɔ̀ːri] 보상의   compulsion[kəmpʌ́lʃən] 강요, 충동   opaque[oupéik] 불투명한   modulate[mɑ́dʒulèit] 조절하다, 바꾸다   solicit[səlísit] 간청하다, 얻으려고 하다   passively[pǽsivli] 수동적으로   compel[kəmpél] 강요하다, ~하게 만들다   notably[nóutəbli] 특히, 현저히

06 Main Topic

What is the lecture mainly about?

ⓐ The intellectual ability and social behavior of primates
ⓑ A psychological concept illustrated through experiments involving primates
ⓒ Levels of altruistic behavior difference depending on environmental conditions
ⓓ The reasons behind altruistic behaviors of primates

강의는 주로 무엇에 대한 것인가?

ⓐ 영장류의 지적 능력과 사회적 행동
ⓑ 영장류에 대한 실험을 통해 설명되는 심리적 개념
ⓒ 환경 조건에 따라 다른 이타주의 행동의 정도
ⓓ 영장류의 이타주의 행동의 이유

07 Organization

How does the professor introduce the lecture?

ⓐ By explaining that the term altruism originally stems from a Latin term
ⓑ By suggesting that altruism is universally observed, even in animals
ⓒ By discussing widespread misconceptions about animals
ⓓ By coming up with a relatable, but imaginary example

교수는 강의를 어떻게 소개했나?

ⓐ 이타주의의 개념이 원래는 라틴어에서 흘러왔다는 것을 설명하면서
ⓑ 이타주의가 동물들에게도 보편적으로 관찰된다는 것을 제안하면서
ⓒ 동물에 대한 보편적인 오해를 논의하면서
ⓓ 관련이 있는 가상의 예를 언급하면서

08 Detail

According to the professor, what is altruism?

ⓐ Sacrificing one person in order to save more than one person
ⓑ Offering beneficence when being observed by others
ⓒ Weighing the advantages of a situation and taking the best action
ⓓ Being considerate about the needs of another person

교수에 따르면, 이타주의는 무엇인가?

ⓐ 한 명 이상의 사람을 구하기 위해 한 명을 희생하는 것
ⓑ 다른 사람들이 관찰할 때 선행을 베푸는 것
ⓒ 상황에 대한 이점을 재서 가장 최선의 행동을 취하는 것
ⓓ 다른 사람의 필요에 대해 배려하는 것

181

09 Detail

Why did the researchers give two types of tools, a stick and a ball, to the second chimpanzee?

Ⓐ To confirm that chimpanzees selected tools with specific intent
Ⓑ To test the intellectual capacity of chimpanzees
Ⓒ To observe the use of different tools by chimpanzees
Ⓓ To make sure that chimpanzees were willing to hand over tools

연구자들은 왜 두 번째 침팬지에게 막대기와 공이라는 두 종류의 도구를 주었나?

Ⓐ 침팬지가 특정한 의도로 도구를 선택했다는 것을 확인하기 위해
Ⓑ 침팬지의 지적 능력을 시험해 보기 위해
Ⓒ 침팬지가 다른 도구를 사용하는 것을 관찰하기 위해
Ⓓ 침팬지가 도구를 기꺼이 건네주는 것을 확실히 하기 위해

10 Inference

Which of the following can be inferred from the chimpanzee experiment?
Choose 2 answers.

Ⓐ Chimpanzees are more likely to respond to a help request if they know what is happening.
Ⓑ Chimpanzees tend to actively overcome barriers in order to assist others more effectively.
Ⓒ Chimpanzees exhibit different levels of altruism depending on given conditions.
Ⓓ Chimpanzees show a strong willingness to sacrifice themselves for the betterment of their species.

다음 중 침팬지 실험을 통해 결론 내릴 수 있는 것은 무엇인가?
2개의 답을 고르시오.

Ⓐ 침팬지들은 만약 무슨 일이 일어나는 지를 안다면 도움 요청에 더 반응할 것이다.
Ⓑ 침팬지들은 더 효과적으로 다른 침팬지를 돕기 위해 적극적으로 방해물을 극복하는 경향이 있다.
Ⓒ 침팬지들은 주어진 상황에 따라 다른 정도의 이타주의를 보인다.
Ⓓ 침팬지들은 그들 종족의 개선을 위해서 스스로를 희생시키려는 강한 의지를 보인다.

11 Inference

What does the professor probably believe about altruism in animals and humans?

Ⓐ Animal altruism has evolved by imitating human altruism.
Ⓑ Animals are more active in expressing their altruism than humans are.
Ⓒ Animals and humans act similarly with an unselfish regard for others.
Ⓓ Human altruism depends a lot on situations compared to animal altruism.

교수가 동물과 인간의 이타주의에 대해 믿는 것은 무엇이겠는가?

Ⓐ 동물의 이타주의는 사람의 이타주의를 모방하면서 진화했다.
Ⓑ 동물은 사람보다 그들의 이타주의를 표현하는 데 더 적극적이다.
Ⓒ 동물과 사람은 비슷하게 다른 이들에게 이기심 없는 배려의 행동을 한다.
Ⓓ 사람의 이타주의는 동물의 이타주의와 비교해서 상황에 많이 의존한다.

TEST 7   Set 2 Conversation

Listen to a conversation between a student and a financial aid officer.

학생의 용건:
학자금 지원

S Good afternoon. I have some questions about tuition fees and related issues. Is this a right place?
O Yes. Here we are in charge of fiscal services and I am responsible for student finances.
S Awesome! I have no idea on how to apply for financial aid.
O I will be happy to help you in everything I can. What would you like to know?
S 01 Umm, I have no clue on how to apply for financial aid in the situation I am in now. Even if I get a part-time job, I do not have enough money to pay for textbooks and my rent. Ah, and also the insurance for my car. Insurance costs have risen a lot recently.
O Hmm, definitely. I paid my insurance a few days ago and I had to pay loads of money. It is unbelievable that you have to pay so much just to drive your own car! Anyhow, we do have some programs to help a student who...

근로 장학
프로그램

S In fact, I came across a thing like a work-study program. What is this exactly?
O Ah, the work-study program is quite straightforward. This program employs students for on-campus jobs. The students are given posts in the library, swimming pool, radio station, and other university facilities. The salaries they earn are used to pay for their tuition fees, so the students don't actually receive salaries. What's more is that school usually pays minimum wage. 02 So I would not suggest you take this option since you seem to need quite a lot of money to support yourself.

학교 밖에서
일을 구하거
나 장학금을
신청할 것을
제안함

S I see. If that's the case, what would be the best option for me?
O 03 In my opinion, it would be best for you to simply look for off-campus jobs. Not only will you get higher salaries, but also you will be able to spend them on things like books, rent, and so on. And I also

학생과 재정 지원 사무관과의 대화를 들어 보시오.

S 안녕하세요. 학비와 관련된 사안에 대해 몇 가지 질문이 있는데요. 여기에 문의해도 되나요?
O 맞아요. 우리는 재정 서비스를 담당하고 있고 나는 학생 재정을 맡고 있어요.
S 잘됐네요! 학자금 지원을 어떻게 신청해야 할지 모르겠어요.
O 가능한 범위 내에서 다 도와줄게요. 문의 사항이 뭐예요?
S 01 음, 저는 제 상황에서 학자금 지원을 어떻게 신청해야 하는지 전혀 모르겠어요. 아르바이트를 하고 있는데도, 책이나 집세를 낼 돈이 없거든요. 아, 그리고 자동차 보험도요. 요즘 자동차 보험료가 엄청나게 올랐거든요.
O 흠, 정말 그래요. 저도 며칠 전에 보험료를 냈는데, 거금이 들어갔어요. 단지 자가용을 운전하는 것 뿐인데 그렇게 많은 돈을 지불해야 되는 것이 말이 안 돼요! 어쨌든, 우리가 학생을 도와줄 프로그램이 있는데······.
S 사실, 제가 우연히 근로 장학 프로그램이라는 것을 알게 됐거든요. 이게 정확히 무엇인가요?
O 아, 근로 장학 프로그램은 꽤 간단해요. 이 프로그램은 교내에서 하는 일에 학생들을 고용해요. 학생들은 도서관, 수영장, 라디오 방송국, 그리고 대학의 다른 시설에서 일자리를 얻어요. 그들이 받는 급여는 그들의 학자금을 갚는 데 사용되서, 학생들은 사실상 급여를 받지 않아요. 게다가 학교는 대개 최저 임금을 지급해요. 02 그래서 별로 이 선택을 추천하진 않는데, 학생이 상당히 많은 돈을 필요로 하는 것처럼 보이기 때문이에요.
S 알겠어요. 만약 그러면, 저에겐 뭐가 제일 좋을까요?
O 03 내 생각으로는, 학교 밖에서 직업을 구하는 게 제일 좋을 것 같아요. 급여를 더 많이 받을 수 있을 뿐만 아니라, 책이나, 집세 등에 그것들을 쓸 수도 있잖아요. 그리고 이런 비용들을 지불하는데 도움이 되는 몇몇 장학금에 지원해 볼 걸 추천해요.

183

recommend applying for some scholarships to help you pay for those things.

S   Scholarships sound great, but I'm not sure if I meet the requirements. I have never actually applied for them.

O   That's OK, you can always give it try. I am sure there are scholarships you can get for the accomplishments you have at the moment. As a matter of fact, scholarships are given according to either your background or academic performance. Several large companies even prefer giving scholarships to the children of their employees, particularly to those who are studying the same major as their parents did, so these children can be prospective employees for the same company someday.

S   Oh wow! This is the first time I've heard of something like this. My dad is an accountant in a well-known firm so, I might have a good chance at this scholarship, right?

O   Of course! As I said, some companies offer scholarships based on merit, so if your GPA is high enough, you could try that. 04 But, will you be working as an accountant after college like your father? What's your major?

S   Umm, I major in biology, and I'm thinking about studying dentistry after my graduation. One of the basic abilities that an accountant need is analysis of numbers, but I have never been confident with mathematics and numbers and all that. What's more, I would like to work hard to give people a beautiful smile!

O   You have a well-planned life ahead of you. 05 As for the scholarships, I think you'd better do some research on private organizations and other entities that offer scholarships for dentistry majors. I am quite sure various organizations give out scholarships for soon-to-be dentists.

S   This is such a good idea. But I think it would be much better to put this down on the catalog to make it easier to find, don't you think?

O   You're right, but then the catalog will become too bulky. Just imagine all the trouble you would have carrying it around in your bag! 05 Also, you can easily find all this information and related issues in the

library. Ah, and a friendly reminder: the librarian knows where to look for this information, so be sure to ask for help. It will be much faster that way.
S I see. Thank you for your help.
O No problem. It's my job to help.

O 천만에요. 돕는 게 제 일인데요.

[Vocabulary] fiscal[fískəl] 재정의   post[poust] 직책   prospective[prəspéktiv] 유망한   merit[mérit] 우수한 평점(성적)
GPA 평점   dentistry[déntistri] 치과의학   entity[éntəti] 기업체, 회사   soon-to-be 곧, 머지않아

01 Main Topic

What is the main topic of this conversation?

ⓐ Looking for methods to deal with financial problems
ⓑ Planning a career after graduation
ⓒ Applying for a work-study program
ⓓ Earning money by working part-time

이 대화의 주제는 무엇인가?

ⓐ 재정 문제를 해결할 방법을 찾는 것
ⓑ 졸업 후 진로 계획을 세우는 것
ⓒ 근로 장학 프로그램에 지원하는 것
ⓓ 시간제 근무로 돈을 버는 것

02 Inference

What is the officer's opinion about a work-study program?

ⓐ It does not seem attractive to the student.
ⓑ Students rarely apply for it.
ⓒ The student may not qualify for it.
ⓓ It is not helpful towards the student's studies.

근로 장학 프로그램에 대한 사무관의 의견은 무엇인가?

ⓐ 학생에게는 매력적인 제안으로 보이지 않는다.
ⓑ 학생들이 거의 지원을 하지 않는다.
ⓒ 학생은 자격 요건에 안 맞을 수도 있다.
ⓓ 학생의 공부에 도움이 안 된다.

03 Detail

What is the benefit of off-campus jobs for the student?

ⓐ A wide selection of job types and locations
ⓑ A high possibility of getting a job
ⓒ Competitive wages
ⓓ A variety of methods of salary payment

학교 밖의 일은 학생에게 어떤 장점이 있나?

ⓐ 다양한 직업 종류와 위치
ⓑ 높은 구직 가능성
ⓒ 경쟁력 있는 임금
ⓓ 다양한 급여 방식

04 Inference

Listen again to part of the conversation. Then answer the question.

> O: But, will you be working as an accountant after college like your father? What's your major?

Why does the officer say this:
O: What's your major?

Ⓐ To encourage the student to change the major
Ⓑ To inform that the student's major makes it difficult to get a scholarship
Ⓒ To ask which major the student is currently interested in
Ⓓ To come up with an alternative way

대화의 일부를 다시 들으시오. 그러고 나서 질문에 답하시오.

> O: 그런데 아버지처럼 졸업 후에 회계사로 일할 건가요? 학생 전공이 뭐예요?

사무관은 왜 이 말을 했는가?
O: 학생 전공이 뭐예요?

Ⓐ 학생에게 전공 변경을 권유하기 위해
Ⓑ 그의 전공 선택으로 장학금을 받기 어렵다는 것을 알려주기 위해
Ⓒ 학생이 현재 관심을 갖고 있는 전공을 묻기 위해
Ⓓ 대안책을 고안하기 위해

05 Detail

What are two suggestions the officer gives to the student?
Choose 2 answers.

Ⓐ Search for a suitable work-study program for the student
Ⓑ Request an application form from the accounting firm
Ⓒ Look for entities related to a prospective career
Ⓓ Visit a place where the student can find the information

사무관이 학생에게 한 제안 두 가지는 무엇인가?
2개의 정답을 고르시오.

Ⓐ 학생에게 적절한 근로 장학 프로그램을 찾을 것
Ⓑ 회계 회사로부터 지원서를 요청할 것
Ⓒ 미래의 직업과 관련된 기업체를 찾아볼 것
Ⓓ 학생이 정보를 찾을 수 있는 장소를 방문할 것

TEST 7 Set 2 Lecture 1

Listen to a part of a lecture in a music class.

P Although genres of music vary between times and places, it is an integral component found in every culture and society, whether in the past or present. People have listened to music since ancient times. Even primitive people listened to music and enjoyed the feelings that it provided. Since most groups of people, including very isolated tribes, have a form of music, it is plausible that music has been ubiquitous for most of history. This field has been a part of our society for a long time. 06 When you listen to music, you can feel your emotions being affected by the song. A study of music and emotion seeks to understand the psychological relationship between the human brain and music.

Music stimulates the brain in ways that can be observed scientifically. It prompts reactions in certain areas that lie in and around the cerebrum. For example, when sound moves from a low frequency to a high frequency, our brain reacts to the change and produces electronic signals that may be detected through digital imaging. Speaking of the music and the brain, there are interesting studies pertaining to the use of Magnetoencephalography or MEG. A MEG scan creates an image that identifies brain activity and measures small magnetic fields produced in the brain. Usually, this scan is used to make medical diagnoses, but it can also be a valuable tool for psychological studies.

In one study, MEG scans showed that the auditory cortex which is the part of the temporal lobe of the brain that responds to sounds. But that wasn't all. Researchers were amazed to find that the visual region lit up as well. The study suggested that music stimulated the brain area called midbrain, a small central part of the brainstem. The midbrain serves important functions in motor movement, particularly movements of the eye, and in visual and auditory processing. There is a visual cortex in each hemisphere of the brain. The visual cortex in the left hemisphere processes information from the right eye, and vice versa. [07]The visual cortexes are located in the midbrain and the MEG scan makes it possible to pick up the activity of the areas because the brain attempts to create images that match the music that an individual is listening to. Isn't that interesting? This suggests that the brain does not passively process music, rather, it actively generates thoughts that can be connected to the music. In addition to the cerebral cortex, music even stimulates the deeper areas of the brain. [08]The important function of these areas from the limbic system is associated with an individual's memory and emotion. This system is responsible for recalling familiar memories or feelings when someone listens to an old, favorite song, or bringing the upbeat feeling one experiences when he or she listens to dance music. You see, music has a bearing on our visual images and emotions. That may explain why there is evidence of people writing and playing music since the beginning of civilization. People can express their emotions by playing music and music may arouse similar emotions from other people. Thus, our appreciation for music may be contributed to the sense of empathy and stimulation that it produces.

음악의 기원

Another question is what initiated the birth of the music. Of course, without sufficient evidence, it is impossible to identify exactly when music was birthed. However, the beginning of music can be estimated using the remains of fossilized instruments. The oldest known instrument resembles a pipe and was first discovered when researchers were studying a modern human settlement in a cave called Geissenklosterle in southern Germany. [09]The researchers determined that this bone pipe was nearly 30,000 to 40,000 years old. That was an especially remarkable discovery, as it indicates that the instrument is older than even agriculture. This also suggests that music has been a deep-seated culture in human history. I mean most people would guess that farming came before music. So, this shows people realized the importance of music that *elicited emotional reactions.* Let me explain a little bit more about the ancient pipe. It was 13 inches long with five finger holes, made from the naturally hollow wing bond of a griffon vulture. There were two deep, V-shaped notches, carved on the end of the mouthpiece. According to experts, it was possible for people to play a wide range of sounds using the pipe. [10]Whenever I talk about this pipe I try to imagine why primitive people made it. Why do you think someone took a mammoth tusk, made it hollow, cut it in half, and gave it holes? And then the person sealed the two halves back together and completed the instrument. Although the purpose of the pipe is unknown, it is clear that its inventors took great care and effort in its creation.

Now, why did people put a lot of effort into making the instrument? In my opinion, it's because music is important in many aspects of life. I mentioned that music stimulates our brain, but there's more. Let's take the people of ancient civilizations for example. For hunters, music was part of a crucial ritual for their hunts and combats. [11]Hunters chanted in unison and danced to bring good luck to their hunts and to strengthen their teamwork. I think music increases social cohesion of a group. Humans have a "need to belong" and a strong motivation to maintain interpersonal attachments.

[**Vocabulary**] ubiquitous [juːbíkwitəs] 어디에나 있는, 아주 흔한　cerebrum [səríːbrəm] 대뇌　pertain [pərtéin] 적용되다
magnetoencephalography [mægniːtouenséfələgræm] 뇌자기도기록, 뇌자기도검사　auditory cortex 청각 피질
temporal lobe 측두엽　midbrain [mídbrèin] 중뇌　brainstem [breinstem] 뇌간　vice versa 거꾸로, 반대로, 역도 또한 같음
cerebral cortex 대뇌 피질　limbic system 변연계　upbeat [ʌpbìːt] 긍정적인, 낙관적인　bearing [bɛ́(ː)əriŋ] 관련, 영향
deep-seated 뿌리 깊은　elicit [ilísit] 끌어내다　finger hole (목관 악기의) 바람 구멍　griffon vulture 그리폰 독수리
notch [nɑtʃ] 흠, 표시　mouthpiece [máuθpìːs] (악기에) 입을 대는 부분　tusk [tʌsk] 상아　unison [júːnisən] 조화, 화합
cohesion [kouhíːʒən] 화합, 결합, 응집력　need to belong 소속 욕구

06 Main Topic

What does the professor mainly discuss?

Ⓐ The activation of visual regions, caused by music
Ⓑ The development of music in society
Ⓒ Various reactions provoked by music
Ⓓ **The effect music has on people**

교수는 주로 무엇에 관해 논하나?

Ⓐ 음악으로 야기된 시각 영역의 활동
Ⓑ 사회에서 음악의 발달
Ⓒ 음악이 불러일으키는 다양한 반응들
Ⓓ 음악이 사람들에게 주는 영향

07 Detail

Why does the visual cortex become active when people listen to music?

Ⓐ Because the brain is divided into left and right hemispheres
Ⓑ Because people enjoy writing and playing music
Ⓒ **Because people come up with perceptions corresponding to music**
Ⓓ Because the outer layer of the cerebral cortex is stimulated

사람들이 음악을 들을 때, 시각령은 왜 활성화 되나?

Ⓐ 뇌가 좌·우반구로 나뉘기 때문에
Ⓑ 사람들은 음악을 연주하고 작곡하는 것을 즐기기 때문에
Ⓒ 사람들이 음악에 상응하는 생각을 떠올리기 때문에
Ⓓ 대뇌 피질의 외층이 자극 받았기 때문에

08 Detail

What function does the limbic system carry out in the human brain?

Ⓐ It causes people to have different tastes in music.
Ⓑ **It is associated with stored information and feelings.**
Ⓒ It helps people to produce music from individual memories.
Ⓓ It controls motor movement of the eye.

사람의 뇌에 있는 변연계가 수행하는 기능은 무엇인가?

Ⓐ 사람들이 음악에 관한 다른 취향들을 갖게 한다.
Ⓑ 저장된 정보와 감정에 관여한다.
Ⓒ 사람들이 개인적인 기억에서부터 음악을 만들어 낼 수 있게 도와준다.
Ⓓ 눈의 운동 신경의 움직임을 통제한다.

09 Organization

Why does the professor mention the bone pipe?

Ⓐ To highlight the technical ability and the hard work of ancient people
Ⓑ To suggest that music swayed people emotionally even during ancient times
Ⓒ To discuss the history behind the creation of musical instruments
Ⓓ To give an example of the musical accomplishments of ancient people

교수는 왜 뼈로 만든 피리를 언급했나?

Ⓐ 고대 사람들의 기술 능력과 고된 노동을 강조하기 위해
Ⓑ 고대에도 음악이 사람들을 감정적으로 동요시켰다는 것을 말하기 위해
Ⓒ 악기 창작에 대한 역사를 논의하기 위해
Ⓓ 고대 사람들의 음악적 성취의 예를 들기 위해

10 Inference

Listen again to part of the lecture. Then answer the question.

> P: Whenever I talk about this pipe I try to imagine why primitive people made it. Why do you think someone took a mammoth tusk, made it hollow, cut it in half, and gave it holes?

Why does the professor say this:
P: Whenever I talk about this pipe I try to imagine why primitive people made it.

Ⓐ To accentuate the value of an activity's influence on ancient people
Ⓑ To gauge the time and energy required for the production of the instrument
Ⓒ To describe the various materials used to make the pipe
Ⓓ To encourage students to share their opinions about the ancient instrument

강의의 일부를 다시 들으시오. 그러고 나서 질문에 답하시오.

> P: 이 피리에 대해 말할 때마다 왜 원시인들이 이것을 만들었을까를 상상해요. 왜 누군가가 매머드의 상아를 가져와, 상아의 속을 비운 후, 반으로 잘라 구멍을 뚫었다고 생각하나요?

교수는 왜 이 말을 했나?
P: 이 피리에 대해 말할 때마다 왜 원시인들이 이것을 만들었을까를 상상해요.

Ⓐ 고대 사람들에게 영향을 준 활동의 가치를 강조하기 위해
Ⓑ 악기의 제작에 요구되는 시간과 에너지를 측정하기 위해
Ⓒ 피리를 만드는 데 사용된 다양한 재료들을 묘사하기 위해
Ⓓ 학생들이 고대 악기에 대한 의견을 공유할 것을 장려하기 위해

11 Detail

According to the professor, why did ancient people use music?

Ⓐ To increase productivity when farming
Ⓑ To intimidate the animals they hunted
Ⓒ To increase their aggression
Ⓓ To induce collaborative relationships

교수에 따르면, 고대 사람들은 왜 음악을 사용했나?

Ⓐ 농사를 지을 때 생산성을 높이기 위해
Ⓑ 그들이 사냥하는 동물들을 위협하기 위해
Ⓒ 그들의 공격성을 증가시키기 위해
Ⓓ 협업 관계를 끌어내기 위해

TEST 7 Set 2 Lecture 2

Listen to part of a lecture in a biology class.

화학 생태학의 정의

P Since last week, we have been discussing chemical ecology. Does any of you remember what we talked about last class? Yes, the definition of chemical ecology. Chemical ecology is the study of chemicals involved in the interaction of living organisms. Social insects, including ants, secrete chemicals such as pheromones to communicate with each other. [12]Some insects use chemicals to defend themselves or to deter potential predators or pathogens from attacking a wide variety of species. In addition to being poisonous, defensive chemicals may have a foul smell or taste.

강의의 주제: 불나방

So I want to spend today's lecture going further into this mechanism, and looking at an interesting example, a garden tiger moth, which is also known as the great tiger moth. Everyone has seen moths, right? They look very similar to glamorous and colorful butterflies; the primary difference is that moths are rather dull brownish or beige in color. Unlike butterflies, moths usually fly at night. In addition, butterflies have club-shaped antennae while moths have what can be described as feathery antennae. More importantly moths have dense scales on their wings, which are a special defensive mechanism against predators, especially spiders, their greatest enemies. These scales are only loosely attached to the wings, so that the scales can easily detach. If a human rubs a moth's wings, his or her finger will be coated with what appears to be a dust or powder. This is actually the scales from the wings. When moths fly into a spider's web, they are able to leave only the scales on the sticky strings and get away. [13]By the way, in case you're curious, it's not only moths that are able to use this mechanism. Other organisms such as fish and reptiles have scales as well.

불나방의 독특한 행동 방식

14 Anyway, great tiger moths act very differently to other moths. This is what I really wanted to talk about. When these great tiger moths get caught in a spider web, they just lie still until a spider finds them. You may think that staying still is not a good idea, right? I mean if you put yourself in this situation, it's just better to fly away as soon as possible before you get eaten.

구역질 나는 맛이 나는 불나방의 날개

15 But here is the thing: great tiger moths have poisonous wings. The toxic chemical in their wings makes the moths taste foul. When a spider first bites a great tiger moth, it immediately realizes that it would be dangerous to eat the moth. Through this unpleasant imprint, spiders refuse to consume this prey, and they will, in fact, help the moth to fly out of the web. This tactic also works well on other predators. Even insectivorous bats don't eat great tiger moths because of the unpalatable taste that characterizes their poison. Can you believe that? Of course, the first moth is sacrificed in order for the predator to learn, but this sacrifice saves the entire species.

색이 밝은 불나방의 날개

15 Another unique factor of great tiger moths is that their wings have bright colors while other moths tend to have wings with dull colors. I bet you'd be surprised by the range of the colors. These bright colors include pink, orange, yellow, or white, accompanied by black markings. While it may seem that such bright colors would attract the attention of other animals, they actually function as a warning to predators. It is like saying, "You don't want to eat me. I am very dangerous." In the ecosystem, great tiger moths along with, monarch butterflies, coral snakes, and poisonous insects display their poison and signal danger to their predators by using their bright colors. This protective mechanism is a form of warning coloration known as "aposematism". Its signals give both the prey and predator a chance to avoid an unfortunate encounter.

불나방의 독성에 대한 실험

I want to add one more interesting fact about this insect. Scientists found out that at the larva stage, the larvae of the great tiger moth eat the leaves of the oleander plant. What is more interesting is that the leaves of the oleander plant contain a chemical toxin which is also found in the wings of the great tiger moths. The larvae store the poison, and the poison eventually accumulates on the wings of the adult moth. **16**There were actually some experiments carried out in order to discover whether the plant was truly the source of the toxin. Scientists fed the larvae bean plants that contained no toxin, instead of the oleander plant. Surprisingly, the grown-up moths had no toxin in their wings. **17**Even in nature, great tiger moth larvae would not have been poisonous and so would have readily been eaten by spiders had the larvae not fed on oleander plants. The chemical ecology shown here is that the great tiger moth relies on the oleander plant leaves to survive in nature. Furthermore, the moth's habitat is where the plants grow. Because the oleander plant is their primary food source, great tiger moths establish their habitat where the plants grow. Some of you might be curious about whether or not the larvae destroy the oleander plants by eating them. In fact, they do, but the great tiger moths are not classified as pests that we have to eliminate. The plant they consume is a weed. Its leaves are so poisonous that it can harm people. As you know, weeds compete with crops in the area for the nutrition in the soil, and their tenacity prevents the healthy growth of other surrounding plants. So, people appreciate the moths for getting rid of these poisonous weeds.

[**Vocabulary**] chemical ecology 화학 생태학   secrete[sikríːt] 분비하다   deter[ditə́ːr] 그만두게 하다   pathogen [pǽθədʒən] 병원균   foul[faul] 역겨운, 악취 나는   garden[great] tiger moth 불나방   brownish[bráuniʃ] 갈색의 띤   observant[əbzə́ːrvənt] 관찰력이 있는   club-shaped 곤봉 모양의   antennae[ænténiː] 더듬이   feathery[féðəri] 솜털 같은   imprint[ímprint] 각인   insectivorous[ìnsektívərəs] 곤충을 먹는   unpalatable[ʌnpǽlətəbl] 불쾌한   monarch butterfly 제주왕나빗과(科)의 나비의 일종   coral snake 산호뱀   aposematism[æpəsəmǽtizm] 경계색   oleander[òuliǽndər] 협죽도 (강한 독성을 가진 식물)   tenacity[tənǽsəti] 강인함

12 Main Topic

What is the professor mainly discussing?

Ⓐ The reason that great tiger moths consume a particular plant
Ⓑ The adaptation that allows great tiger moths to evade a predator
Ⓒ Different strategies used by various moths to survive
Ⓓ Physical traits of great tiger moths to increase their ability to survive

교수는 주로 무엇에 관해 논하고 있나?

Ⓐ 불나방이 특정 식물을 먹는 이유
Ⓑ 불나방이 포식자를 피하게 해 주는 적응력
Ⓒ 생존을 위해 사용하는 다양한 나방들의 여러 가지 전략
Ⓓ 생존 가능성을 높인 불나방의 신체적 특징

13 Inference

Listen again to part of the lecture. Then answer the question.

> P: By the way, in case you're curious, it's not only moths that are able to use this mechanism. Other organisms such as fish and reptiles have scales as well.

Why does the professor say this:
P: By the way, in case you're curious...

Ⓐ To solve the curiosity of the students about other organisms
Ⓑ To express that the students would not believe the statement
Ⓒ To indicate that the following statement is unimportant
Ⓓ To imply that the students don't understand the lecture

강의의 일부를 다시 들으시오. 그리고 나서 질문에 답하시오.

> P: 그건 그렇고, 여러분이 혹시 궁금해 할까봐 말하는데, 나방만이 이러한 기제를 사용하는 것은 아닙니다. 물고기나 파충류 같은 다른 생물체들도 비늘을 가지고 있죠.

교수는 왜 이 말을 했나?
P: 그건 그렇고, 여러분이 궁금해 할까봐 말하는데……

Ⓐ 다른 생물체들에 대한 학생들의 궁금증을 해결하기 위해
Ⓑ 학생들이 그 설명을 믿지 않을 수도 있다는 것을 표현하기 위해
Ⓒ 다음의 설명이 중요하지 않다는 것을 나타내기 위해
Ⓓ 학생들이 강의를 이해하지 못한다는 것을 암시하기 위해

정답 해설 Ⓒ 교수는 강의의 주제인 나방과 직접적인 관련이 없는 물고기, 파충류에 대해 보충 설명을 하면서 참고로만 알아 두라는 의도로 이 말을 했다.

14 Organization

Why does the professor mention the way normal moths react when caught in spider webs?

Ⓐ To demonstrate how moths use their scales to escape from spider webs
Ⓑ To emphasize how great tiger moths are different from other moths
Ⓒ To discuss how moths evolved into having scaled wings
Ⓓ To show the difference between moths and butterflies

교수는 왜 보통의 나방들이 거미줄에 걸렸을 때 반응하는 방식을 언급했나?

Ⓐ 나방이 거미줄에서 빠져나가기 위해 비늘을 어떻게 사용하는지 설명하기 위해
Ⓑ 불나방이 다른 나방들과 어떻게 다른지 강조하기 위해
Ⓒ 나방이 비늘이 있는 날개를 갖도록 진화한 방법에 대해 논의하기 위해
Ⓓ 나방과 나비의 차이점을 보여 주기 위해

15 Detail

According to the professor, what are the two unique characteristics of the great tiger moth?
Choose 2 answers.

Ⓐ Accumulation of poison in its wings
Ⓑ A foul odor that signals predators to flee
Ⓒ Wings that feature conspicuous hues
Ⓓ The ability to blind its predators by spraying powder

교수에 따르면, 불나방의 두 가지 독특한 특징은 무엇인가?
2개의 답을 고르시오.

Ⓐ 날개에 축적된 독
Ⓑ 포식자들을 도망가게 만드는 역겨운 냄새
Ⓒ 눈에 확 띄는 날개의 색조
Ⓓ 가루를 뿌려 포식자들의 눈을 멀게 하는 능력

16 Detail

What did the experiment mentioned in the lecture try to prove?

Ⓐ The toxin in the wings of great tiger moths is caused by their larvae diet.
Ⓑ The oleander plants are not harmful to moths.
Ⓒ The oleander plants are poisonous to spiders and should be removed.
Ⓓ Great tiger moth larvae like oleander plant leaves more than other plant leaves.

강의에서 언급된 실험은 무엇을 증명하려 했나?

Ⓐ 불나방의 날개에 있는 독소는 유충의 시기에 섭취한 먹이에 의한 것이다.
Ⓑ 협죽도는 나방에 해롭지 않다.
Ⓒ 협죽도는 거미에게 해롭기 때문에 제거되어야 한다.
Ⓓ 불나방 유충은 다른 식물 잎보다는 협죽도 잎을 좋아한다.

17 Inference

What can be inferred about great tiger moths?

Ⓐ They are hard to find around oleander plants.
Ⓑ They would not need oleander plants if they didn't have their natural enemies.
Ⓒ They need to be eliminated because they kill off oleander plants.
Ⓓ They intelligently choose oleander plants leaves over other plant leaves as their diet.

불나방에 대하여 추론할 수 있는 것은 무엇인가?

Ⓐ 그들은 협죽도 근처에서 발견하기 어렵다.
Ⓑ 그들의 천적이 없었다면 그들은 협죽도를 필요로 하지 않았을 것이다.
Ⓒ 그들은 협죽도를 죽이기 때문에 제거되어야 한다.
Ⓓ 그들은 영리하게 다른 식물 잎이 아니라 협죽도 잎을 그들의 먹이로 선택한다.

정답 해설 Ⓑ 불나방이 협죽도 잎을 먹어서 독성을 갖고 이로 인해 천적에게 잡아 먹히지 않는 것이다. 만약 불나방에게 천적이 없었다면 불나방은 협죽도를 먹을 필요도 없었을 것이다.

영단기 TOEFL

ACTUAL TEST

TEST 08

TEST 8 Set 1 Conversation

Listen to part of a conversation between a student and a professor.

S   Hello, Professor Smith. I was told to visit your office.

P   Hi, Julie. Yes, I asked you to come here. I think I misplaced your paper you handed in last class. I saw it somewhere on the desk, but I couldn't find it. So, if you saved the file on your computer, I think you should print out again or just e-mail it to me. I'm really sorry for the inconvenience.

S   Oh, that's not a big deal. I have one on my laptop, so I'll bring it tomorrow. I was going to visit your office anyway. The thing is I'm going to do my internship at McKay Elementary School next semester. **01 I was wondering if you could explain a teaching technique called consensus method, which we covered in our last class.** I think this strategy will be very helpful while I'm doing my internship.

P   OK, the consensus method is a way to encourage students to take part in meaningful conversations and discussion with their peers. This activity encourages students to critically analyze and rationalize a topic. The goal is for students to form an agreement to proposed topics through discussing.

S   You said in class that this method includes some steps. Could you elaborate more?

P   Oh, yes. There are some steps. **02 First, you, I mean, a teacher or instructor selects a topic to implement discussion.** Write down questions related to the topic on the board. The questions can be framed to stimulate deeper reflection of the topic. Then, the instructor asks students to write down their own opinions or thoughts about it. After completing this task, the instructor divides the students into small groups and inspires their discussion about the statement from each participant's point of view. **02 In addition, encourage them to support their claims using examples from the content based on given material or even from real life.** If groups are not capable of reaching a consensus, teachers can assist them to reach an agreement. Each student group is asked to select a representative to present their group decision to the rest of the class. In this technique, 03 the teacher's role is to guide their discussion and prepare some unexpected stressors like over-heated arguments or a fire alarm activated by mistake. The important thing is that students themselves are the active participants and leaders in the whole process. This strategy has some advantages. It can develop students' understanding, analytical skills and cooperative learning.

S Thanks, professor. This will be a great help for me in doing my job.

P By the way, what's your plan after the internship? There is a fellowship opportunity for which I think you are a competent candidate, so if you are interested, I will recommend you for that position.

S Oh, this is sudden. What is the project about?

P 04We are going to research methods for improving self-directed learning. You know, learning can be challenging even for the smart and motivated students, so students need a variety of skills and attitudes for successfully completing independent study. We are going to study which specific skills they need and how to hone these skills. You are planning to apply for a graduate school, right? This opportunity will help the application process and your career.

S 05That's true. I planned to pursue my master's degree at a graduate school, but I don't think that's my cup of tea, so I haven't made up my mind yet.

P Look, Julie. You are an outstanding student and school is the right place for such a talented student like you. If you successfully finish this project, a graduate school admission is practically guaranteed. I think blowing this opportunity is not a good idea. Please take your time and think over.

S I really appreciate your concern and I'll consider it.

[Vocabulary] consensus [kənsénsəs] 의견 일치, 합의   rationalize [rǽʃnəlàiz] 합리화하다, 합리적으로 생각하다
elaborate [ilǽbərət] 자세히 설명하다   fellowship [félouʃip] 특별 연구원   self-directed learning 자기 주도 학습
hone [houn] (기술을) 연마하다   my cup of tea 내가 좋아하는 것

01 Main Topic

What is the conversation mainly about?

Ⓐ An assignment that the professor mistakenly lost
Ⓑ A student's plan after graduation
Ⓒ An internship opportunity the student should take part in
Ⓓ A teaching approach the student learned

대화는 주로 무엇에 관한 것인가?

Ⓐ 교수가 실수로 잃어버린 과제물
Ⓑ 학생의 졸업 후 계획
Ⓒ 학생이 참여해야 하는 인턴십 기회
Ⓓ 학생이 배운 교수법

02 Detail

Which of the following are included in the consensus method?
Choose 2 answers.

Ⓐ Choosing resources for discussion
Ⓑ Writing down students' thoughts if they don't reach a consensus
Ⓒ Asking an instructor to take active participation in a discussion
Ⓓ Using examples to support students' own ideas
Ⓔ Following the majority's opinion

다음 중 의견 일치 방법에 포함되는 것은 무엇인가?
2개의 답을 고르시오.

Ⓐ 논의의 재료를 선택하는 것
Ⓑ 만약 학생들이 합의에 도달하지 않는다면 학생들의 생각을 적는 것
Ⓒ 강사에게 논의에 적극적으로 참가하도록 요청하는 것
Ⓓ 학생들 스스로의 생각을 뒷받침하는 예시를 사용하는 것
Ⓔ 대다수의 의견을 따르는 것

03 Organization

Why does the professor mention a fire alarm?

Ⓐ To explain an instructor's role
Ⓑ To warn about a situation which can happen while teaching students
Ⓒ To emphasize the importance of a teacher's duty
Ⓓ To see if the student recognizes a teacher's responsibility

교수는 왜 화재 경보기를 언급했나?

Ⓐ 강사의 역할을 설명하기 위해
Ⓑ 학생들을 가르치는 동안에 발생할 수 있는 상황에 대해 경고하기 위해
Ⓒ 교사 직무의 중요성을 강조하기 위해
Ⓓ 학생이 교사의 책임을 인식하고 있는지를 확인하기 위해

04 Detail

Which of the following is true about the fellowship opportunity?

Ⓐ It is designed for students who apply for a graduate school.
Ⓑ It will focus on a process by which individuals develop an ability for learning.
Ⓒ It includes leading a group discussion and guiding students.
Ⓓ Only outstanding students are allowed to participate in it.

다음 중 특별 연구원 기회에 대해 사실인 것은?

Ⓐ 대학원에 지원하는 학생들을 위해 계획되었다.
Ⓑ 개인들이 학습 능력을 개발하는 과정에 집중할 것이다.
Ⓒ 그룹 논의를 이끌고, 학생들을 지도하는 것을 포함한다.
Ⓓ 뛰어난 학생들만 참여할 수 있다.

오답 해설   Ⓐ 특별 연구원 기회는 대학원 지원을 위해 계획된 것이 아니라 거기서 잘하면 대학원에 들어갈 기회가 높아진다고 언급했다.

05 Inference

Listen again to part of the conversation. Then answer the question.

> S: That's true. I planned to pursue my master's degree at a graduate school, but I don't think that's my cup of tea, so I haven't made up my mind yet.

Why does the student say this:
S: ... but I don't think that's my cup of tea,

Ⓐ To explain why the student decided not to go to a graduate school
Ⓑ To show the student's uncertainty about an academic career
Ⓒ To emphasize the student's interest in the internship
Ⓓ To emphasize how hard it is to apply for a graduate school

대화의 일부를 다시 들으시오. 그러고 나서 질문에 답하시오.

> S: 맞아요. 대학원에서 석사 학위를 딸 계획이었어요. 하지만 이게 저한테 맞는 일이라는 생각이 안 들어서요. 아직 마음의 결정을 내리지 못했어요.

학생은 왜 이 말을 했나?
S: … 하지만 이게 저한테 맞는 일이라는 생각이 안 들어서요.

Ⓐ 학생이 왜 대학원에 가지 않기로 결정했는지를 설명하기 위해
Ⓑ 학업 진로에 대한 학생의 불확실성을 보여 주기 위해
Ⓒ 인턴십에 대한 학생의 흥미를 강조하기 위해
Ⓓ 대학원에 지원하는 게 얼마나 힘든지를 강조하기 위해

TEST 8 Set 1 Lecture 1

Listen to part of a lecture in an anthropology class.

P   The development of agriculture was critical for the early human population. After starting to grow their own food, people would settle in an area for extended periods of time. Traditional hunters and gatherers were nomadic tribes, who continually moved as they followed the migration of wild animals. The beginnings of agriculture can be traced to…about 10,000 years ago. It originated separately in the Middle East, Southeast Asia, and parts of the Americas. At first, the early farmers merely sowed seeds and waited for them to sprout. As agricultural techniques developed, farmers were able to implement ideas such as irrigation, crop rotation, and fertilizers. After these ideas were developed, agriculture spread to other parts of the world. So, it can be generally said that agriculture spread as people observed and copied developing agricultural practices.

06 However, an exception can be found in New Guinea. Some archaeologists think that in New Guinea, agriculture developed independently instead of being brought from other areas. Researchers argue that the people in this region developed agricultural practices without any influence from other people. On the map, you can see that New Guinea is a huge island in the southwest Pacific, above the continent of Australia. At first, it was thought that agriculture and the domestication of animals were introduced to New Guinea from Southeast Asia, roughly 3,500 years ago. But in the 1960s and 70s, researchers came up with the theory that agriculture had developed independently in New Guinea, and so they set off to the island to learn more. They inspected its terrain, looking for evidence to support their theory. Despite their search, they didn't find any concrete evidence, and were unable to prove their hypothesis. However, they did observe that deforestation had taken place about 7,000 years ago, but the researchers couldn't

be sure that the land had been cleared to facilitate farming. That is, the forest might have been cleared in order for hunters to hunt more easily, not for farmers to grow crops. If they had found plant remains, such as seeds and fruits, these would have been regarded as evidence for agriculture. 07 But because organic molecules contain carbon, they soon decompose in swampy ground, and New Guinea is known for its humidity. So the researchers had difficulty with their endeavors. I mean it would have been too hasty to conclude that a clear-cut part of the forest alone could be taken as evidence of agriculture.

But archaeologists examining a certain site discovered something encouraging. This site, called the Kuk swamp, had been inspected before, but it didn't produce any serious evidence. However, they decided to make a return visit and at this time they were rewarded for revisiting the site. The swamp is a wetland located in the Wahgi Valley, north of the New Guinea highlands. The archaeologists found what seemed to be evidence of a succession of phases of agricultural development while they were exploring the area. They found sedimentary layers placed on top of each other like cake layers. 08 The discovery was exciting because it dated from far in the past, way before agricultural influence could have come from Southeast Asia. Modern archaeological methods were used to carefully scrutinize the soil and analyze each layer of sediment at the swamp that was analyzed for data.

The oldest soil layer was determined to be approximately 9,000 years old. Surprisingly, the archaeologists found some agricultural remains in this ancient layer of earth such as pits, potholes, and irrigation drainage ditches. The researchers could logically deduce from these features that agriculture was present, even back then. The layer above the oldest layer, the second phase, displayed mounds that were separated by equal spaces in between. 09 Some crops aren't compatible with wet soil, like bananas, requiring mounds in order to grow well. Since Kuk is a mushy soggy marsh, farmers constructed mounds for plants that couldn't tolerate swampy conditions. In the third phase, on top of the second phase, archeologists found irrigation channels. The layer held ditches and drains that spread out in an extensive network, greatly aiding with agriculture.

Using various techniques, archaeologists examining the site even detected microfossils in the soil where banana trees had been planted. The sediment samples dated to about 7,000 years ago carried a high number of banana plant fossils. 09 Banana plants usually don't fossilize in places where they grow naturally, so the high percentage of fossils strongly suggested that the trees had been intentionally planted. What's more is that with the benefit of advanced genetic comparison technology, researchers were able to claim that a type of banana had been introduced from New Guinea to Southeast Asia, not vice versa. This claim suggested that bananas grown in New Guinea were passed on to nearby regions in some way. Archaeologists also came upon grains of starch, from taro roots, dating back from up to 10,000 years ago. 10 This discovery of taro starch was significant because taro didn't grow naturally where it was found. It must have been brought from the lowlands and planted there.

Before we finish, I want to ask you all to think about something. When agriculture develops in an area, you expect social transformations to occur as well, right? 11 It seems natural that easier living conditions will lead to certain changes in society. For example, a surplus of resources often encourages population growth and a wider disparity between rich and poor and produce hierarchical structures. However, it is interesting to note that the social structures in New Guinea have remained egalitarian. Personally, I think this is a little odd. I mean, think about the birth of agriculture. When people learned how to grow food and started to exercise control over their environment, their culture developed and increased in complexity. What are your thoughts on the relationship between agriculture and society?

[**Vocabulary**] nomadic[noumǽdik] 유목의　crop rotation 윤작　terrain[təréin] 지형　deforestation[di:fɔ:ristéiʃən] 삼림 벌채　swamp[swamp] 늪　highland[háilənd] 고지대　succession[səkséʃən] 연쇄, 잇따름　scrutinize[skrú:tənàiz] 세심히 살피다, 면밀히 조사하다　pit[pit] 구덩이　pothole[páthòul] 포트홀(움푹 패인 곳)　ditch[ditʃ] 도랑　deduce[didjú:s] 추측하다　mound[maund] 흙더미, 언덕　compatible[kəmpǽtəbl] 호환이 되는, 화합하는　mushy[mʌ́ʃi] 곤죽 같은　soggy[sági] 눅눅한, 질척한　marsh[mɑːrʃ] 습지　microfossil[màikroufásl] 미세 화석　starch[stɑːrtʃ] 녹말 가루　taro[tɑ́ːrou] 타로토란　lowland[lóulənd] 저지대　hierarchical[hàiərɑ́ːrkikəl] 계급[계층]에 따른　egalitarian[igæ̀litέ(:)əriən] 평등한

06 Main Topic

What does the professor primarily discuss?

Ⓐ The expansion of agriculture from New Guinea to Southeast Asia
Ⓑ The widespread distribution of agricultural technology in New Guinea
Ⓒ The exceptional development of agriculture in New Guinea
Ⓓ The method of studying the development of agriculture in New Guinea

07 Detail

According to the lecture, why were researchers unable to find evidence for their theory in New Guinea during the 1960s and 70s?

Ⓐ Swamps were difficult to analyze without proper equipment.
Ⓑ Carbon-based materials readily decomposed in the wet area.
Ⓒ Crops raised in early New Guinea were already extinct.
Ⓓ Land is cleared not necessarily for growing produce.

08 Organization

Why does the professor mention successive layers of sediment?

Ⓐ To explain how people cultivated crops and trees in the area
Ⓑ To emphasize that they were related to the progress of agricultural technology
Ⓒ To explain the reason why agriculture in the region developed
Ⓓ To illustrate that they indicated the origin of agriculture in the region

09 Detail

What evidence did researchers find concerning the cultivation of bananas in New Guinea?
Choose 3 answers.

- [A] A phenomenon resulting from people's involvement was found.
- [B] Bananas were grown in New Guinea and exported to Southeast Asia through trade.
- [C] The land seemed to have been prepared for a certain purpose.
- [D] Genetic analysis made it possible to trace where the banana species was introduced.
- [E] Swampy areas like the Kuk were advantageous for the growth of bananas.

10 Detail

Why was the presence of taro starch in the highlands important?

- [A] Taro was not indigenous to the region.
- [B] Taro was a staple crop in New Guinea.
- [C] Taro was a difficult plant to cultivate.
- [D] Taro was a relatively old plant species.

11 Inference

What can be inferred about the impact of agriculture on New Guinea?

- [A] The advancement of agriculture was related to social changes.
- [B] The usual implication of agriculture did not apply to the society.
- [C] The development of agriculture generated an increase in population.
- [D] The development of agriculture led to egalitarianism.

TEST 8　Set 1 Lecture 2

Listen to part of a lecture in a biology class.

강의의 주제: 생체 모방 기술

P OK. Let's get started. As you all know, this is a lecture concerning biomimetics. The purpose of this lecture is to provide a brief introduction in order to clarify some questions regarding the topic. 12, 13 First, let me explain what the term means. Biomimetics or biomimicry, is the imitation of natural systems and elements for the purpose of solving complex human problems. As we know, living organisms have developed and evolved over geological-scale time periods through natural selection to help these organisms adapt well to their environments. Researchers want to borrow some of the adaptations and generate various engineering applications from them, including things such as self-healing and tolerance of and resistance to destructive environmental factors. Humans are attempting to solve problems and develop new technologies based on understanding of and inspiration by the functional principles that make nature tick. So, why don't we start off by exploring some of the possible applications?

도마뱀붙이의 붙는 능력

What do you think of small lizards? 13 For example, geckos and their sticky gecko feet? Technically speaking, the gecko feet cannot literally be termed sticky. When you touch the gecko feet, they are rather dry and smooth. They just seem like they would be sticky because geckos don't fall off when they are climbing up and down the trees or ceilings as if they were magically defying gravity. In fact, gecko feet easily adhere to other objects because of how their toe pads are designed. Their toe pads are comprised of millions of tiny filaments that resemble threadlike or hair-like structures. The little filaments interact with molecular systems of various surfaces. In physical chemistry, this phenomenon is called *"van der Waals forces", which is the sum of the attractive or repulsive forces between positive and negative molecules. 14 A great example of this can be commonly observed during the winter, as your hair sticks to your sweater as you take it off. A similar phenomenon can be said to occur to geckos. This interaction between a surface and the toe pad creates a force that pulls the gecko towards the surface. Imagine the possibilities if we take the same concept and create a machine that allows us to climb walls like these amazing creatures. Wouldn't that be something?

딱정벌레의 적외선 감지 능력

13 Let's look at another example. Beetles, which have the ability to precisely detect infrared radiation, can sense forest fires from hundreds of kilometers away. This ability allows beetles to lay their eggs in recently burned woods, thereby maintaining distance between offspring and the predators and other kinds of threats. In a forest fire, the predators would have already escaped to different parts of the woods. 15 Furthermore, live trees pose a great threat to beetle eggs as they might kill the eggs with their toxic chemicals or sticky resin. So, the main question is...whether we can take this mechanism and invent a small machine that has a long-distance-forest fire-sensing function that will allow us to respond to these forest fires immediately. As you can see, the most important purpose of biomimetics is to find a way to recreate these mechanisms found in nature in actual devices used by humans. Clearly, nature can sometimes produce a far more efficient and effective natural mechanism that surpasses human creations. Therefore, we analyze natural structures and imitate the functions of different natural mechanisms in order to gain more advanced technologies.

심해 해면의 광섬유

13 I want to mention another concrete example concerning this particular issue. You have probably been reading various articles about the deep-sea ecosystems that some of the most interesting creatures on Earth inhabit. Recently, maritime scientists discovered a deep-sea sponge that has fiber optics embedded into its biological structure. After much research, the function and purpose of these fibers turned out to be very similar to the artificial fiber optics that people use. 17 As you may know, optical fibers can have a variety of applications such as in cables, medical uses, decorations, you

name it. However, a great drawback of commercial fiber optics is that they can be very costly and they have to be made with expensive machines that produce an extreme amount of heat. However, deep-sea sponge fibers are naturally created in the sea, which could be very cost-effective. We could basically just collect these materials from the seabed. Moreover, the silica-based fibers of the deep-sea sponge provide great resilience to external damages. In fact, sponge fiber optics has better qualities than commercial fiber optics. But even if the deep-sea sponge is a promising source of technology, deep-sea conditions are hostile. Not only are the pressures in the area at least 200 times greater than the atmospheric pressure at sea level, but it is also a location of frequent volcanic activity. [16]So, we can reasonably assume that collecting the material from this deep-sea area for experiments will take a lot of time and effort. There is no doubt that we want to take advantage of this biological mechanism. Which is why mimicking this ability and research in this field is very promising. Discovering a way to produce more resilient optical fibers at less cost will most likely allow us to send information faster with more convenience.

되기 때문에 비용 효율이 높아요. 우리가 그냥 해저에서 이 물질을 수집할 수도 있다는 말이에요. 게다가 이산화 규소를 기반으로 하는 심해 해면 섬유는 외부의 손상에 대해 대단한 회복력을 갖고 있죠. 사실 해면의 광섬유는 상업적인 광섬유보다 품질이 더 좋아요. 하지만 심해 해면이 각광받는 기술의 원료라고 해도, 해저의 상태는 적대적이죠. 그 지역의 압력은 해수면보다 200배는 높을 뿐만 아니라, 화산 활동이 빈번하게 발생하는 곳이에요. [16]그래서 우리는 실험을 위해 심해에서 이 물질을 수집하기 위해 많은 시간과 노력이 필요하다는 것을 예상할 수 있죠. 의심할 여지 없이 우리는 이 생물학적 방법의 이점을 이용하기를 원해요. 그래서 이 능력을 모방하고 이 분야를 연구하는 것이 매우 유망한 이유예요. 회복력 있는 광섬유를 더 저렴하게 생산하는 방법을 발견하는 것은 우리가 좀 더 빠르고 편리하게 정보를 전송할 수 있게 할 것입니다.

[**Vocabulary**] biomimetics[bàioumimétiks] 생체 모방 기술   natural selection 자연 선택, 자연 도태   tolerance[tálərəns] 저항력   synthesize[sínθisàiz] 합성하다   gecko[gékou] 도마뱀붙이   filament[fíləmənt] 가는 실   threadlike[θrédlaik] 실같이 생긴   repulsive[ripʌ́lsiv] 밀어내는   infrared radiation 적외선   resin[rézin] 송진   maritime[mǽrətàim] 바다의, 해양의   fiber optics 광섬유 (내시경이나 광 통신에 쓰이는 실 같이 가는 섬유)   embed[imbéd] 끼워넣다   seabed[síːbèd] 해저   silica[síləkə] 실리카, 이산화규소   resilience[rizíljəns] 회복력, 복원력   hostile[hástl] 적대적인   mimicking[mímikiŋ] 모방하는 것

[각주]
* **van der Waals forces** 독일 과학자 Johannes Diderik van der Waals의 이름을 따서 만들어진 개념으로 각 분자나 원자가 적당한 거리에 위치하면 양극의 정전 작용으로 서로 끌어당기는 힘을 가리킨다. 대체적으로 이 힘은 미약하지만, 많은 분자들이 작용하면 힘은 커질 수 있다.

12 Main Topic

What does the professor mainly discuss?

Ⓐ The field of adopting designs from nature
Ⓑ Various adaptations of animals and insects
Ⓒ The research possibilities in the recently emerging study
Ⓓ The procedure of applying biomimetics to human technology

교수는 주로 무엇에 대해 논하고 있나?

Ⓐ 자연에서 유래한 설계를 이용하는 분야
Ⓑ 동물과 곤충들의 다양한 적응법들
Ⓒ 최근 생겨난 학문의 연구 가능성
Ⓓ 생체 모방 기술을 인간의 기술에 적용하는 과정

13 Organization

How does the professor organize the lecture?

Ⓐ He uses various examples to denounce a field of study.
Ⓑ He cites scientific articles and experiments to explain a certain concept.
Ⓒ He briefly describes a concept and lists examples to support it.
Ⓓ He briefly explains a concept and describes its actual applications.

교수는 강의를 어떻게 구성하나?

Ⓐ 연구 분야를 비난하기 위해 다양한 예시를 사용한다.
Ⓑ 특정 개념을 설명하기 위해 과학 기사들과 실험을 인용한다.
Ⓒ 개념을 간단하게 설명하고 그것을 지지하기 위해 다양한 예를 열거한다.
Ⓓ 개념을 간단하게 설명하고 그것의 실제 적용법을 설명한다.

14 Organization

Why does the professor mention a sweater?

Ⓐ To illustrate a particular kind of attractive force
Ⓑ To explain how a gecko can climb surfaces without falling
Ⓒ To give an example of another sticky material
Ⓓ To suggest that biomimetics can be applied to sweaters

교수는 왜 스웨터를 언급했나?

Ⓐ 특별한 인력에 대해 설명하기 위해
Ⓑ 도마뱀붙이가 떨어지지 않고 어떻게 표면을 오를 수 있는지 설명하기 위해
Ⓒ 끈적거리는 다른 물질의 예를 들기 위해
Ⓓ 생체 모방 기술이 스웨터에 적용될 수 있음을 제안하기 위해

15 Detail

According to the professor, how does a beetle benefit from its ability to detect forest fires?

Ⓐ It can hide in shelters before a forest fire occurs.
Ⓑ It can minimize the impact of harmful substances.
Ⓒ It can avoid competing with other insects over the resin from the tree.
Ⓓ It can ensure the stability of its temperatures.

교수에 따르면, 딱정벌레는 산불을 탐지하는 능력을 통해 어떤 이득을 얻는가?

Ⓐ 산불이 발생하기 전에 안식처에 숨을 수 있다.
Ⓑ 유해한 물질들의 영향을 최소화할 수 있다.
Ⓒ 나무의 송진을 두고 다른 곤충과의 경쟁을 피할 수 있다.
Ⓓ 체온을 유지할 수 있다.

16 Inference

What can be inferred about the silica-based fibers of the deep-sea sponge?

Ⓐ They are being refined for better qualities.
Ⓑ They are causing commercial optical fibers to become useless and obsolete.
Ⓒ They are too problematic for practical use.
Ⓓ They need to be researched further before being applied to daily life.

이산화규소를 기반으로 하는 심해 해면 섬유에 관해 추론할 수 있는 것은 무엇인가?

Ⓐ 더 나은 질을 위해 개선 중이다.
Ⓑ 상업적 광섬유를 쓸모 없게 만든다.
Ⓒ 실용하기에는 너무 문제가 많다.
Ⓓ 일상 생활에 적용되기 전에 더 많은 연구가 필요하다.

17 Inference

Listen again to part of the lecture. Then answer the question.

> P: As you may know, optical fibers can have a variety of applications such as in cables, medical uses, decorations, you name it.

Why does the professor say this:
P: ...you name it.

Ⓐ To suggest that the students come up with more uses for optical fibers
Ⓑ To imply that he won't list any more applications of optical fibers
Ⓒ To express that listing the uses of optical fibers is a waste of time
Ⓓ To encourage that the students do more research about optical fibers

강의의 일부를 다시 들으시오. 그러고 나서 질문에 답하시오.

> P: 알다시피, 광섬유는 케이블, 의학 용품, 장식 기타 등등에 다양하게 적용될 수 있죠.

교수는 왜 이 말을 했나?
P: ……기타 등등에.

Ⓐ 학생들이 광섬유의 더 많은 용도를 떠올리도록 제안하기 위해
Ⓑ 그가 더 많은 광섬유의 적용 사례들을 언급하지 않겠다는 것을 암시하기 위해
Ⓒ 광섬유의 사용을 열거하는 것은 시간 낭비라는 것을 표현하기 위해
Ⓓ 학생들이 광섬유에 대해 더 조사하도록 격려하기 위해

TEST 8　Set 2 Conversation

Listen to part of a conversation between students.

TA 직업 관련 상황

W　Hi, it's been a long time. How's everything? I heard that you were doing a TA in a biology department. Is it going well?

M　Right. I've been working in a bio lab for 3 years. It seemed to be going well, but yesterday, I've lost the lab key. I checked every place but I couldn't find it. So I'm afraid of telling the professor about this incident. He'll be very disappointed.

W　Have you ever lost it before?

M　No, it was my first time. 02 I'm really worried about the professor's reaction. What if I get fired?

W　Oh, there should be a reason why your professor has hired you as a TA for 3 years. He's probably well-aware of your responsibility and dedication. You don't have to worry too much about this happening. It was just the first time.

생물 발광에 대한 학생의 흥미

　　By the way, we are planning "Hawk Watching" this year. Do you want to join us?

M　My friend participated last year and he said it was very interesting and learned a lot about a hawk's habitat and migration. 03 I think that's because he wants to be an ornithologist. I'm thinking of majoring in a different field, so I'm not sure whether I want to take part in it or not.

W　Can I ask which major you are interested in?

M　01, 04 I read a book regarding bioluminescent fish in the deep sea a few days ago, which was so fascinating. I want to be a marine biologist.

W　I'm sorry, bioluminescent?

M　Yes, it is the production and emission of light by a living organism. It is also known as chemiluminescence. Certain types of chemicals generate light when mixed together, which causes the glow. If you've ever seen a firefly, you have encountered a bioluminescent organism. Even though it is actually very rare among terrestrial animals, it is not as rare as you might think in the ocean.

학생들 사이의 대화 중 일부를 들어 보시오.

W　안녕. 오랜만이다. 어떻게 지내? 생물학과에서 조교를 하는 중이라고 들었어. 잘되고 있어?

M　맞아. 생물학 실험실에서 3년째 일하고 있어. 잘되고 있는 것 같았는데, 어제 실험실 열쇠를 잃어버렸어. 모든 장소를 다 확인했는데, 찾을 수가 없었어. 그래서 이 일에 대해 교수님께 말하는 게 두려워. 굉장히 실망하실 거야.

W　전에 잃어버린 적 있어?

M　아니, 이번이 처음이야. 02 교수님 반응이 정말 걱정돼. 만약 해고되면 어떡하지?

W　교수님이 너를 3년 동안 조교로 고용한 데는 이유가 있을 거야. 교수님이 너의 책임감과 헌신을 잘 알고 있을 거야. 이 일에 대해 너무 많이 걱정할 필요는 없어. 처음이잖아.

　　그나저나 우리는 올해 "매 관찰"을 계획하고 있어. 참여할래?

M　내 친구가 작년에 참여했는데, 매우 흥미로웠고 매의 서식지나 이동에 대해 많은 것을 배웠다고 하더라. 03 내 생각에 걔가 조류학자가 되고 싶어서 그런 것 같아. 나는 다른 분야를 전공할까 생각 중이거든. 그래서 이번에 참여를 할지 안 할지 잘 모르겠어.

W　어떤 전공에 관심이 있는지 물어봐도 될까?

M　01, 04 내가 며칠 전에 생물 발광을 하는 심해 물고기에 대한 책을 읽었는데 매우 흥미로웠어. 나는 해양 생물학자가 되고 싶어.

W　미안한데, 생물 발광?

M　맞아. 생물체가 만들고 뿜어내는 빛이야. 또한 화학 발광으로 알려져 있기도 해. 특정 종류의 화학 물질이 서로 섞일 때 빛을 만들어 내는데, 그것이 그 반짝거림을 야기하지. 반딧불이를 본 적이 있다면, 생물 발광 생명체를 본 적이 있는 거야. 실제로 육상 동물 사이에서는 굉장히 희귀한데 바다에서는 생각하는 것만큼 희귀하지는 않아.

W　와우, 놀라운데. 바다에서 빛을 내뿜는 생명체라고? 이 기능을 왜 가지고 있는 거야?

W Wow, that's amazing. A living organism which gives off light in the ocean? Why do they have this function?

M Unfortunately some functions of bioluminescence are still unknown; we just speculate that it is used to warn off predators, to lure or attract prey and to communicate with each other.

생물 발광에 대한 프로젝트

I saw a post in our department website stating that Professor Hermann is looking for students who are willing to participate in a project related to the issue in California. 05 I'm planning to apply for it. Even though I'm only an undergraduate student, the professor couldn't ignore my passion and inspiration for the project. To meet the prerequisites, I will take 500 level courses with upper students next semester.

W But, as far as I know, to take advanced courses, you need special approval from a professor.

M Yes, I know. So I made an appointment with my academic advisor about this. I'm sure he'll give me permission if I tell him of my intentions.

W Yes, I guess so. Can you explain the project in more detail?

M He is doing his research on marine animals which live in the deep sea, near Santa Maria. He will especially focus on bioluminescent single cell plankton like diatoms and copepods. Copepods are sometimes called the insects of the sea because a tremendous number of them exist in the sea about 10,000 species. Even though the organism has been known for more than a 100 years, there is very limited information about its structure and evolutionary history especially regarding its bioluminescent trait. So, Professor Hermann made a huge aquarium to conduct an experiment regarding the organism.

W Wow, that sounds interesting to me. Oh, I have to hurry to my next class. It was nice talking to you.

M See you around.

M 안타깝게도 생물 발광의 기능은 아직 알려지지 않았어. 우리는 그냥 포식자들에게 경고를 하고, 먹이를 유혹하거나 끌어들이고, 서로 대화하기 위해 사용된다고 추측할 뿐이야.

우리 학과 웹 사이트에서 Hermann 교수님이 이 주제와 관련해서 캘리포니아에서 진행되는 프로젝트에 참여할 학생들을 찾고 있다는 것을 봤어. 05 나는 그 프로젝트에 지원할 계획이야. 아직 학부생이긴 하지만, 교수님은 그 프로젝트에 대한 나의 열정과 의욕을 무시할 수 없을 거야. 전제 조건을 맞추기 위해, 다음 학기에 상급자들과 함께 500 레벨의 수업을 들을 거야.

W 하지만 내가 알기로는 상급 수업을 듣기 위해서는 교수의 특별 허가가 필요해.

M 맞아. 알아. 그래서 그것과 관련해서 지도 교수님과 약속을 잡았어. 교수님께 내 의도를 말하면 허락해 줄 거라고 확신해.

W 맞아. 나도 그렇게 생각해. 그 프로젝트에 대해 더 자세히 설명해 줄래?

M 교수님께서는 산타마리아 근처 심해에 사는 해양 동물을 연구하실 거야. 특히 규조류와 요각류 같이 생물 발광하는 단세포 플랑크톤에 집중하실 거야. 요각류는 약 10,000종 정도로 엄청나게 많은 수가 바다에 존재하기 때문에 때때로 바다의 곤충이라고 불리기도 해. 이 생물이 알려진 지 100년이 넘었음에도 불구하고, 특히 생물 발광하는 특징과 관련된 구조와 진화 과정에 대해서는 매우 제한된 정보만 있어. 그래서 Hermann 교수님은 이 생물에 대한 실험을 진행하기 위해 거대한 수족관을 만들었어.

W 와우, 재미있겠다. 오, 나는 서둘러서 다음 수업에 가봐야겠어. 대화해서 즐거웠어.

M 다음에 봐.

[**Vocabulary**] bioluminescent[bàioulù:mənésnt] 생물 발광의, 생물 발광을 하는   chemiluminescence[kèmilù:mənésns] 화학 발광   terrestrial animal 육상 동물   prerequisite[prirekwəzət] 전제 조건   diatom[dáiətəm] 규조류   copepod[kóupəpàd] 요각류   organism[ɔ́:rgənìzm] 생물

01 Main Topic

What is the conversation mainly about?

Ⓐ Whether the student would be willing to participate in Hawk Watching
Ⓑ Requirements to apply for a project
Ⓒ The student's interest in a particular field of study
Ⓓ Reasons the student should change his major

대화는 주로 무엇에 관한 것인가?

Ⓐ 학생이 매 관찰에 참여하길 원하는지 여부
Ⓑ 프로젝트에 지원하기 위한 요구 조건들
Ⓒ 특정 학문 분야에 대한 학생의 흥미
Ⓓ 학생이 전공을 바꿔야 하는 이유들

02 Inference

Listen again to part of the conversation. Then answer the question.

> M: No, it was my first time. I'm really worried about the professor's reaction. What if I get fired?
> W: Oh, there should be a reason why your professor has hired you as a TA for 3 years.

Why does the student say this:
W: Oh, there should be a reason why your professor has hired you as a TA for 3 years.

Ⓐ To question the student's devotion to the biology department
Ⓑ To reassure the student about the expected reaction from the professor
Ⓒ To explain why a TA position is very competitive
Ⓓ To emphasize the student's responsibility as a TA

대화의 일부를 다시 들으시오. 그리고 나서 질문에 답하시오.

> M: 아니, 이번이 처음이야. 교수님 반응이 정말 걱정돼. 만약 해고되면 어떡하지?
> W: 교수님이 너를 3년 동안 조교로 고용한 데는 이유가 있을 거야.

학생은 왜 이 말을 했나?
W: 교수님이 너를 3년 동안 조교로 고용한 데는 이유가 있을 거야.

Ⓐ 생물학과에 대한 학생의 헌신에 의구심을 나타내기 위해
Ⓑ 예상되는 교수의 반응에 대해서 학생을 안심시키기 위해
Ⓒ 조교 자리가 굉장히 경쟁적인 이유를 설명하기 위해
Ⓓ 조교로서의 학생의 책임을 강조하기 위해

03 Detail

Why does the student hesitate to take part in Hawk Watching?

Ⓐ His friend was disappointed at it.
Ⓑ He already took part in it last year.
Ⓒ It is not his interest.
Ⓓ He has no time because of a project.

왜 학생은 매 관찰에 참여하는 것을 망설이나?

Ⓐ 그의 친구가 그것에 대해 실망했다.
Ⓑ 이미 작년에 참여했었다.
Ⓒ 그것은 그의 관심사가 아니다.
Ⓓ 프로젝트 때문에 시간이 없다.

04 Inference

Listen again to part of the conversation. Then answer the question.

> M: I read a book regarding bioluminescent fish in the deep sea a few days ago, which was so fascinating. I want to be a marine biologist.
> W: I'm sorry, bioluminescent?

Why does the student say this:
W: I'm sorry, bioluminescent?

Ⓐ To check if the student heard the term correctly
Ⓑ To remind that the student knew the meaning of the term
Ⓒ To get more information about the term
Ⓓ To correct the explanation about bioluminescence

대화의 일부를 다시 들으시오. 그러고 나서 질문에 답하시오.

> M: 내가 며칠 전에 생물 발광을 하는 심해 물고기에 대한 책을 읽었는데 매우 흥미로웠어. 나는 해양 생물학자가 되고 싶어.
> W: 미안한데, 생물 발광?

학생은 왜 이 말을 했나?
W: 미안한데, 생물 발광?

Ⓐ 학생이 용어를 올바르게 들었는지 확인하기 위해
Ⓑ 학생이 용어의 의미를 알고 있다는 것을 상기시키기 위해
Ⓒ 용어에 대한 더 많은 정보를 얻기 위해
Ⓓ 생물 발광에 대한 설명을 정정하기 위해

05 Detail

Which of the following statements is true about the project in California?

Ⓐ Applicants usually hold university degrees.
Ⓑ It mainly focuses on terrestrial animals.
Ⓒ Students who major in marine biology are eligible to apply for it.
Ⓓ The student is well-prepared for the project.

다음 중 캘리포니아에서 진행되는 프로젝트에 대해 사실인 것은?

Ⓐ 지원자들은 대게 학사 학위를 가지고 있다.
Ⓑ 주로 육상 동물에 초점을 맞춘다.
Ⓒ 해양 생물학 전공인 학생들은 지원할 자격이 있다.
Ⓓ 학생은 그 프로젝트에 대한 준비가 잘 되어 있다.

TEST 8 Set 2 Lecture 1

Listen to part of a lecture in a biology class.

P Various reactions take place in our body continuously through the action of enzymes. Enzymes are catalysts that start and accelerate chemical reactions. Our bodies require enzymes to metabolize food at a rate fast enough to sustain life. 07 Therefore, you might wonder what we would do without enzymes in our digestive systems. Enzymes are necessary to digest food and break down nutrients. Without enzymes, we would not be able to digest anything and our bodies would not function. For example, sucrose is primarily present in sugar, and if our bodies did not have sucrase, the digestive enzyme for sucrose, we would be unable to enjoy anything with sugar.

Enzymes are critical in biology, but are they only workhorses in our bodies? 06 Have you ever wondered why enzymes draw attention from the industry? When jeans first became popular, they were bright blue because they were dyed using natural indigo dye. As people wore and washed their jeans, they faded, which looked pretty good, so they began to wash the color out of their jeans intentionally. Clothing companies quickly recognized the market potential for faded jeans and began to sell prewashed jeans. These manufacturers tried several methods to make their faded jeans attractive.

Stone-washed jeans were introduced in the 1980's. During the manufacturing process, pumice stones, very light and permeable rocks that can float in water, were thrown into washing machines with jeans. The pumice stones acted like sandpapers and wore away the surface of the jeans, washing some of the dye particles from the fabric. 08 However, there were several problems with this process. First, the pumice stones caused the machines to break down quickly. Second, the process damaged the fabric and caused the rivets and buttons to lose their shine. Third, the quality of the abrasion process was difficult to control, so it was difficult to achieve the desired look. Finally, customers did not want their jeans to look so worn out. They were looking for faded jeans, not destroyed jeans.

표백제를 이용한 청바지 염색

Companies then tried a new method using bleach, a chemical substance that removes color and disinfects, and it is very acidic. For example, just spraying the bleach on a silk shirt can dissolve it. Therefore, handling strong, acidic bleach was very dangerous. In addition, bleach is toxic and can cause respiratory problems, like asthma. The factory workers were at risk during accidents with the dangerous chemical. 09 Bleach not only affects the people who handle it, but also the environment and the organisms that live in it. Therefore, using such a harmful chemical resulted in serious environmental issues. For example, the factories that used bleach spewed toxic wastewater. When the Environment Protection Agency learned about these harmful effects and the contamination of the water supply near these factories, these companies were heavily fined. Restoring the ecosystem and cleaning up the waste was costly. To recover from their massive financial losses, companies raised the price of their jeans. 09 Unfortunately, the bleached jeans were not attractive because the bleach was too strong and dissolved the fabric, ruining the shape of the jeans. Consumers were unwilling to buy over-priced, mushy jeans. Therefore, the jeans' companies sought a new, better solution.

바이오 스톤 표백제를 이용한 방법

10 In 1989, researchers in Europe invented the perfect solution, biostone bleach, which causes an enzyme reaction that only affects the color of the jeans. This method is by far the most cost-effective and environmentally friendly way to fade denim. Let me explain in more detail. Jeans are made from cotton, which is a plant by-product. Plants consist mainly of cellulose, which is the basic building block for paper and many textiles. Due to its resilience and flexibility, cellulose cotton fibers can be twisted into threads and woven into cloth. More importantly, because cellulose is a type of carbohydrate, it can be broken down using an enzyme called cellulase, which is a

기업들은 그래서 표백제를 사용하는 새로운 방법을 시도했는데, 표백제는 색을 제거하고 소독하는 화학 물질인데, 그것은 강한 산성이에요. 예를 들면, 표백제를 실크 셔츠 위에 뿌리기만 해도 표백제는 그것을 녹일 수 있어요. 그러므로 강한 산성 표백제를 다루는 것은 매우 위험했어요. 게다가, 표백제는 독성이 있어서 천식 같은 호흡기 질환을 야기시킬 수 있어요. 공장 근로자들은 위험한 화학 물질로 인해 사고를 당할 위험이 있었습니다. 09 표백제는 그것을 다루는 사람들에게 영향을 줄 뿐 아니라, 환경과 그 안에 사는 유기체에 영향을 줍니다. 그러므로 이러한 유해한 화학 물질을 사용하는 것은 심각한 환경 문제를 야기했어요. 예를 들어, 표백제를 사용한 공장들은 유독성 폐수를 방출했습니다. 환경 보호 단체가 이 해로운 영향과 이런 공장들을 근처에 있는 상수도를 오염시킨 것을 밝혀냈을 때, 기업들은 엄청난 벌금을 물었습니다. 생태계를 복구하고 오염 물질을 치우는 데 많은 비용이 필요했어요. 그들의 엄청난 경제적 손실을 만회하기 위해, 기업들은 그들의 청바지 가격을 올렸어요. 09 불행하게도, 표백제로 색을 바랜 청바지들은 매력적이지 않았는데, 표백제가 너무 강해서 섬유를 녹여, 청바지들의 모양을 훼손시켰기 때문이에요. 고객들은 비싸고 너덜거리는 청바지를 살 생각이 없었죠. 그러므로 청바지 회사들은 새롭고 더 나은 방법을 찾아야 했습니다.

10 1989년, 유럽의 연구원들은 완벽한 해결책인 바이오 스톤 표백제를 개발했는데, 그것은 색깔에만 영향을 주는 효소의 반응을 야기해요. 이 방법은 결단코 청바지들을 탈색하기 위해 가장 비용 효율이 높고 친환경적인 방법이에요. 더 자세한 내용을 보도록 합시다. 청바지는 면으로 만들어지는데, 그것은 식물의 부산물이에요. 식물은 대개 셀룰로오스로 구성돼 있는데, 그것은 종이나 여러 섬유들을 구성하는 기본 구성 요소예요. 그 탄성과 유연성 덕분에, 셀룰로오스 면 섬유는 실로 엮이고 짜여 천이 될 수 있어요. 더 중요하게 셀룰로오스는 탄수화물의 일종이기 때문에, 그것은 셀룰라아제라고 불리는 효소에 의해 분해될 수 있는데, 그것은 곰팡이, 박테리아, 그리고 원생 동물에 의해 생성되는 효소의 일종이에요. 그래서, 우리가 이 효소를 청

type of enzyme generated mainly by fungi, bacteria, and protozoans. Therefore, if we spray this enzyme onto jeans, the material will start to break down and we will achieve a beautiful faded look.

바이오 스톤 표백제의 장점

Unlike previous methods, cellulase created evenly faded jeans without harming the material. Moreover, it was cheap, allowing companies to lower the price of their jeans, which increased sales. In addition, workers did not have to worry about noxious chemicals. This method reduced pollution, waste, quality variability, and imperfections. The jeans I am wearing today are not faded because they are old. 11 Enzymes produced these nicely faded jeans while protecting people and the environment. The same process was used on most of your jeans as well. If people ask me why biology is beneficial, I can tell them about these jeans.

바지 위에 뿌리면, 물질이 분해되기 시작하고 우리는 색 바랜 아름다운 스타일을 얻을 수 있는 거예요.

이전 방법들과는 다르게, 셀룰라제는 직물을 손상시키지 않고 고르게 색 바랜 청바지를 만들었죠. 심지어 그것은 쌌고, 그래서 기업들이 청바지 가격을 낮추게 했는데, 그것은 판매를 촉진시켰어요. 게다가, 근로자들은 유독한 화학 물질에 대해 걱정을 할 필요가 없었어요. 이 방법은 오염 물질, 폐기물, 품질 변동성, 그리고 결함들을 줄였어요. 오늘 내가 입고 있는 청바지는 오래 돼서 색이 바랜 것이 아니죠. 사람들과 환경을 보호하면서 효소가 이렇게 멋지게 색이 바랜 청바지를 만들었죠. 같은 과정이 여러분이 가진 대부분의 청바지에도 사용됐어요. 11 효소는 사람들과 환경을 보호하면서 색이 잘 바랜 청바지를 만들어냈습니다. 만약 사람들이 왜 생물학이 이로운가를 묻는다면, 나는 이 청바지에 대해 말할 수 있어요.

[**Vocabulary**] enzyme[énzaim] 효소　catalyst[kǽtəlist] 촉매　accelerate[əksélərèit] 가속화하다　sucrase[sjúːkreis] 수크라아제　sucrose[súːkrous] (설탕) 수크로오스, 자당　workhorse[wɜːrkhɔːrs] 열심히 일하는 사람(기계)　pumice stone 부석　permeable[pə́ːrmiəbl] 투과성의　abrasion[əbréiʒən] 마모, 마열　rivet[rívit] 리벳(못)　disinfect[dìsinfékt] 소독하다　asthma[ǽzmə] 천식　spew[spjuː] 내보내다, 뿜어져 나오다　wastewater[wéistwɔ̀ːtər] 오수, 폐수　mushy[mʌ́ʃi] 곤죽 같은　cellulose[séljəlòus] 셀룰로오스, 섬유소　resilience[rizíljəns] 탄성, 내구성, 회복력　carbohydrate[kàːrbouháidreit] 탄수화물　cellulase[séljəlèiz] 셀룰라제　protozoans[pròutəzóuən] 원생동물　variability[vɛ̀əriəbíləti] 가변성　imperfection[ìmpərfékʃən] 결함

06 Main Topic

What is the lecture mainly about?

Ⓐ The use of biological catalysts in industry
Ⓑ The function of enzymes in various fields of industry
Ⓒ The important enzymatic activities that happen in the human body
Ⓓ Several methods used to fade jeans

강의는 주로 무엇에 대한 것인가?

Ⓐ 산업 분야에서 생물 촉매제의 사용
Ⓑ 산업의 다양한 분야에서 효소의 기능
Ⓒ 신체에서 일어나는 중요한 효소의 활동들
Ⓓ 청바지 색을 바래는 데 사용되는 몇몇의 방법들

오답 해설 Ⓓ 청바지 색을 바래는 여러 방법들을 소개한 것은 생물 촉매제인 효소가 제조업에서 왜 각광을 받게 되었는지를 설명하기 위함이다.

07 Organization

How does the professor introduce his discussion of enzyme?

Ⓐ By explaining the connection between industries and enzymes.
Ⓑ By introducing ways to cause physical changes to jeans
Ⓒ By illustrating the role of enzymes in the human body
Ⓓ By recalling their applications in various industries

교수는 효소에 대한 논의를 어떻게 시작했나?

Ⓐ 산업과 효소의 연관성을 설명하면서
Ⓑ 청바지에 물리적 변화를 야기시키는 방법들을 소개하면서
Ⓒ 신체에서 일어나는 효소의 역할을 예로 들어 주면서
Ⓓ 다양한 산업에서 효소의 적용을 상기시키면서

08 Organization

Why does the professor mention pumice stones?

Ⓐ To explain several disadvantages of using pumice stones
Ⓑ To imply that there is a limited number of ways to fade jeans
Ⓒ To highlight another practical way to fade jeans
Ⓓ To describe the process of fading jeans with pumice stones

교수는 왜 부석을 언급했나?

Ⓐ 부석 사용의 단점 몇 가지를 설명하기 위해
Ⓑ 청바지의 색을 바래는 방법이 제한적이라는 것을 암시하기 위해
Ⓒ 청바지의 색을 바래는 또 다른 실용적인 방법을 강조하기 위해
Ⓓ 부석으로 청바지 색을 바래는 과정을 묘사하기 위해

정답 해설 Ⓒ 교수는 부석이나 표백제의 부정적인 측면을 강조해 효소를 이용한 청바지색 바래기의 긍정적인 측면을 강조하고 있다. another practical way는 효소를 이용한 바이오 스톤 표백제를 의미한다.

09 Detail

Which of the following correctly describes a problem of using bleach?
Choose 2 answers.

- [A] Buttons and rivets were tarnished by the acid.
- [B] The procedure was lengthy and complicated.
- [C] Factories were expensive to build and maintain.
- [D] Chemicals were a threat to workers and the environment.
- [E] The texture of the jeans was overly softened.

다음 중 표백제 사용의 문제를 정확히 묘사한 것은 무엇인가?
2개의 답을 고르시오.

- [A] 단추와 리벳이 산 때문에 변색이 됐다.
- [B] 과정이 길고 복잡했다.
- [C] 공장을 짓고 유지하는 비용이 비쌌다.
- [D] 화학 물질은 근로자들과 환경을 위협하는 존재였다.
- [E] 청바지의 질감이 과하게 부드러워졌다.

정답 해설 [E] 표백제가 섬유를 녹이고 너덜거리게 만들었다고 한 것을 overly softened라고 표현했다.

10 Detail

Why is biostone bleach used to fade jeans?

- [A] Because customers care about the environment
- [B] Because cotton is susceptible to cellulose
- [C] Because enzymes selectively affect the fabric surface
- [D] Because jeans easily lose their color to bleach

청바지 색을 바래기 위해 왜 바이오 스톤 표백제가 사용됐나?

- [A] 고객들이 환경에 신경쓰기 때문에
- [B] 면이 셀룰로오스에 민감하기 때문에
- [C] 효소가 선택적으로 섬유 표면에 영향을 주기 때문에
- [D] 청바지가 표백제에 의해 쉽게 색을 잃기 때문에

11 Inference

Listen again to part of the conversation. Then answer the question.

> P: Enzymes produced these nicely faded jeans while protecting people and the environment. The same process was used on most of your jeans as well. If people ask me why biology is beneficial, I can tell them about these jeans.

Why does the professor say this:
P: If people ask me why biology is beneficial, I can tell them about these jeans.

- [A] To explain the application of enzymes for making jeans commercial
- [B] To ask the students to give their opinions about biology
- [C] To emphasize the importance of applying a scientific study
- [D] To encourage the students to learn and apply biology

강의의 일부를 다시 들으시오. 그리고 나서 질문에 답하시오.

> P: 효소는 사람들과 환경을 보호하면서 색이 잘 바랜 청바지를 만들어 냈어요. 만약 사람들이 왜 생물학이 이로운가를 묻는다면, 나는 이 청바지에 대해 말할 수 있어요.

교수가 이 말을 한 이유는 무엇인가?
P: 만약 사람들이 왜 생물학이 이로운가를 묻는다면, 나는 이 청바지에 대해 말할 수 있어요.

- [A] 청바지를 상업적으로 만들기 위한 효소의 적용을 설명하기 위해
- [B] 생물학에 대한 학생들의 의견을 묻기 위해
- [C] 과학적 연구를 적용하는 것의 중요성을 강조하기 위해
- [D] 학생들에게 생물학을 배우고 적용하도록 장려하기 위해

영단기 TOEFL

ACTUAL TEST

TEST 09

TEST 9 Set 1 Conversation

Listen to part of a conversation between a student and a professor.

S Hello, Professor Brown. Are you busy right now?
P Not at all. Come on in, Michelle. So what can I do for you today?
S **01** I was wondering if you could give me some help with the paper I'm working on. I need more specific guidelines to write a competitive one.
P The paper that's due next week? What about it?
S I'm writing it on the Greek mathematician and physicist, Archimedes, and his famous story.
P Could you give me more details? Or how about starting with that story first?
S OK, Hiero of Syracuse had given his goldsmith pure gold to make a gold crown. After receiving the crown, the king suspected the goldsmith had cheated him by eliminating the gold and combining the crown with the same weight of silver. So the king ordered Archimedes to solve the problem of whether the crown was pure or not. Contemplating for a few days, he had chance to go to the public bath. Stepping into a bath, he realized that the water level had increased. The more his body submerged into the water, the more water overflowed out of the bathtub. By noticing the change in the water volume, he thought the volume of water displaced must be equal to the volume of the submerged part of his body. **02** Since gold weighs more than silver, he reasoned that a crown mixed with silver would have to be larger to have the same weight as one consisting only of gold. He postulated one mixed with silver would displace more water than its pure gold counterpart when it was placed in the water. **03** After he did the experiment with the crown, he detected fraud in the manufacture of the golden crown. So I think you can bet how the king reacted to the goldsmith.

학생과 교수의 대화 중 일부를 들어 보시오.

S 안녕하세요. Brown 교수님. 지금 바쁘신가요?
P 전혀. 들어오렴. Michelle. 무엇을 도와줄까?
S **01** 제가 쓰고 있는 보고서와 관련해서 도움을 얻을 수 있을지 궁금해서요. 경쟁력 있는 보고서를 쓰기 위해 좀 더 구체적인 가이드라인이 필요해요.
P 다음 주까지 내야 하는 보고서? 무엇에 관한 것이니?
S 저는 그리스인 수학자이자 물리학자인 아르키메데스와 그의 유명한 이야기에 대해 쓰고 있어요.
P 좀 더 자세하게 말해 줄래? 아니면 우선 그 이야기로 시작하는 게 어때?
S 좋아요. 시라큐스의 히에론 왕은 금관을 만들기 위해 금세공인에게 순금을 주었어요. 왕관을 받은 후에, 왕은 금세공인이 금을 빼고 같은 무게의 은을 왕관에 섞어서 자신을 속이지 않았을까 의심했죠. 그래서 왕은 아르키메데스에게 이 왕관이 순금인지 아닌지에 대한 문제를 풀게 했어요. 며칠 동안 고심하던 중에 그는 공중목욕탕에 갈 기회가 있었어요. 욕조 안에 들어가면서 그는 물의 높이가 높아졌다는 사실을 깨달았어요. 그의 몸이 물에 더 많이 잠길수록, 더 많은 물이 욕조 밖으로 흘러나왔죠. 물의 부피 변화를 알아차리면서 그는 넘친 물의 부피가 잠긴 몸의 부피와 틀림없이 같을 것이라고 생각했어요. **02** 금이 은보다 무게가 더 나가기 때문에, 은과 섞인 왕관이 금으로만 구성된 것과 같은 무게를 갖기 위해서는 더 커야 할 것이라고 추론했어요. 그는 물에 넣었을 때 은이 섞인 왕관이 순금 왕관보다 더 많은 물을 넘치게 할 것이라고 추측했죠. **03** 왕관을 가지고 실험을 한 후에 금관을 만드는 과정에서 속임수가 있었다는 것을 알아냈어요. 그래서 왕이 금세공인에게 어떻게 했는지 짐작하시겠죠.

이야기는 사실이 아님	P	**04 That's a very good summary and an interesting story, indeed. But it's just a story itself.** First and foremost, Archimedes himself never wrote about this episode, although he spent plenty of time illustrating the laws of buoyancy and the lever. **05 So, without an official record of the story, it is hard to accept it as true. Also, since no sophisticated equipment existed back then, it would be impossible to measure the volume accurately.** Even when he tried to conduct the experiment regarding this idea, the volume change was not as considerable as could be measured, so they couldn't get a meaningful result.
	S	Wow, people actually accepted the story as the truth. I mean it is a very prevalent story. How come it's not based on reality? That's something I didn't take into account. Then I really lost the direction of my paper.
보고서에 대한 대안 제시	P	How about elaborating on this perspective? You know, like Newton's apple, which illustrates how Newton devised his theory of gravity after watching an apple falling from a tree in his mother's garden in Lincolnshire, although there is no solid evidence to suggest that the apple hit him on the head, as the story goes? It's not important whether these stories are true or not because these give people a moment of inspiration. I think you can present your idea on these powerful stories.
	S	Oh, that's a brilliant alternative. Thank you, professor.

[**Vocabulary**] mathematician [mæθəmətíʃən] 수학자　physicist [fízisist] 물리학자　goldsmith [góuldsmiθ] 금세공인　contemplate [kάntəmplèit] 숙고하다　postulate [pάstʃulèit] 상정하다　buoyancy [bɔ́iənsi] 부력　prevalent [prévələnt] 널리 퍼져 있는

01 Main Topic

Why does the student visit the professor's office?

Ⓐ To ask the professor if the story about Archimedes is true
Ⓑ To get feedback on a paper
Ⓒ To discuss stories which inspired people
Ⓓ To find out how to do research for a paper

학생은 왜 교수의 연구실을 방문했나?

Ⓐ 아르키메데스에 대한 이야기가 사실인지를 교수에게 물어보기 위해
Ⓑ 보고서에 대한 피드백을 얻기 위해
Ⓒ 사람들에게 영감을 준 이야기들에 대해 논의하기 위해
Ⓓ 보고서를 위한 조사 방법을 알아보기 위해

02 Detail

How did Archimedes find out the amount of silver mixed in the crown?

Ⓐ By adding water in the process of manufacturing a crown
Ⓑ By asking the goldsmith about the truth behind the manufacture of the crown
Ⓒ By displacing gold into silver
Ⓓ By realizing the difference in volume of each material

아르키메데스는 왕관에 섞인 은의 양을 어떻게 알아냈나?

Ⓐ 왕관을 제조하는 과정에서 물을 추가함으로써
Ⓑ 금세공인에게 왕관 제조에 대한 진실을 물어봄으로써
Ⓒ 금을 은으로 대체함으로써
Ⓓ 각 물질의 부피 차이를 깨달음으로써

03 Inference

What can be inferred about the goldsmith?

Ⓐ He would encounter an unfortunate situation.
Ⓑ The king would forgive him.
Ⓒ He completed his task faithfully.
Ⓓ He would gain huge profit by selling gold.

금세공인에 대해 추론할 수 있는 것은?

Ⓐ 그는 불행한 상황에 직면했을 것이다.
Ⓑ 왕은 그를 용서했을 것이다.
Ⓒ 그는 충성스럽게 그에게 맡겨진 일을 완성했다.
Ⓓ 그는 금을 팔아 많은 이익을 얻었을 것이다.

04 Inference

Listen again to part of the conversation. Then answer the question.

> P: That's a very good summary and an interesting story, indeed. But it's just a story itself.

Why does the professor say this:
P: ... But it's just a story itself.

A To imply that the student needs to do more research about the story
B To emphasize people's interest in the story
C To explain the inconsistency between the story and the truth
D To share the professor's opinion with the student

대화의 일부를 다시 들으시오. 그러고 나서 질문에 답하시오.

> P: 아주 좋은 요약이었고, 흥미로운 이야기였어. 하지만 이건 단지 이야기일 뿐이야.

교수는 왜 이 말을 했나?
P: … 하지만 이건 단지 이야기일 뿐이야.

A 학생이 그 이야기에 대해 더 많이 조사할 필요가 있다는 것을 암시하기 위해
B 이 이야기에 대한 사람들의 흥미를 강조하기 위해
C 이야기와 사실 사이의 불일치를 설명하기 위해
D 교수의 의견을 학생과 공유하기 위해

05 Detail

What are the reasons that the story about Archimedes is not true?
Choose 2 answers.

A Feasible technology did not exist back then.
B Water volume is not measurable.
C People doubted Archimedes' knowledge.
D There is no concrete evidence.
E It was recorded as a made-up story.

아르키메데스에 대한 이야기가 사실이 아닌 이유는?
2개의 답을 고르시오.

A 그 당시에 실현 가능한 기술이 존재하지 않았다.
B 물의 부피는 측정할 수 없다.
C 사람들은 아르키메데스의 지식을 의심했다.
D 구체적인 증거가 없다.
E 꾸며낸 이야기로 기록되어 있다.

TEST 9 Set 1 Lecture 1

Listen to part of a lecture in a geology class.

P Visually speaking, the Earth might seem static, but in reality, it is not. The surface of the Earth constantly changes by natural forces. A lot of these changes happen so gradually that it is very hard to witness the progress; of course, that doesn't mean that shifts on the Earth's surface are not happening. The Earth has undergone these gradual shifts for millions of years. 06 This phenomenon concerns a basic type of geological science called uniformitarianism. Uniformitarianism states that geological forces, such as erosion and uplifts shape the Earth in the past and today. Furthermore, uniformitarianism states that these forces are consistently modifying the Earth's shape slowly over a period. This idea was the most fundamental and ordinary basis of understanding the Earth's movement.

However, how would you feel if someone challenged this long-standing theory? One scientist asserted that the features of the Earth's surface changed through a single abrupt, and extremely intense catastrophic event. 07 One region geologists cannot explain using uniformitarianism is the Channeled Scablands. OK, let's take a look at the geological areas. Well, first of all, they are located in Washington State countryside. This picture will help you understand what I mean. Take a look at the steep ravines there. How do you think the place was formed?

S1 08 I think a river could have carved it out, like the Grand Canyon.

P That could have been the case, but the closest river is 90 kilometers east of around the Scablands' landscape. Although it does seem similar to the Grand Canyon, there was no significant source of water which is close enough to shape the land. Any other ideas?

S2 I think I heard that glaciers could expand, shrink, and shape this type of land. They would rip the ground

and leave a landscape just like the one in the picture.
P Good guess, but...again, no ice has been seen in the south region of Washington State since the Ice Age.

Bretz의 이론

S1 Then, how in the world did that land form?
P Many geologists had the same question. The formation of the land was a total mystery that took 50 years to solve. American geologist J. Harlen Bretz began studying the Scablands in 1922. He found that neither water erosion nor slow-moving glaciers made the Scablands. Instead, he hypothesized that a sudden, massive flood swept over the land at the end of the Ice Age. During that time, a giant glacier blocked the flow of water into the river. 09 This glacier served as an ice dam that shut off the flow of water in and out of the lake for a very long time. At the end of the Ice Age, the temperature of the Earth had increased. The pressure from the lake and the temperature caused the glacier to break and melt, and the lake made a massive flood in the northwestern part of the United States, which caused a sudden pressure imbalance that shaped the region into what we see today. When Bretz presented his hypothesis, other geologists criticized it. Most believed that geological formations occurred very slowly over thousands of years, so when Bretz claimed that the Scablands may have formed in a few hours, most geologists thought the theory was ridiculous.

Bretz 가설의 증거

After many years of research, Bretz found several pieces of evidence to prove his theory. For example, he discovered that Missoula Lake, which is located in Idaho, just east of the Scablands, may be the evidence of his theory. In addition, when he was flying over the area in an airplane, Bretz saw large ripples in Missoula Lake, which pointed to past water flow. He found that these ripples in the lake were extended all the way to the Scablands. During the Ice Age, a glacier probably filled in the lake. Then, when the Ice Age ended, the glacier burst and it released enormous amounts of water. It is possible that such a flood could shape the land in just a few hours. After the evidence proved Bretz's hypothesis, geologists began to consider this theory. In fact, Other theories only explained certain isolated features of the Scablands, **10** but Bretz's hypothesis explained all the features of the Scablands, which is the main reason other geologists were persuaded to adopt this theory.

Bretz의 이론과 동일 과정설 연계의 중요성

But that is not to say that we should disregard uniformitarianism. **06** I wanted to talk to you about Bretz's theory to let you know that we no longer strictly rely on the single theory, uniformitarianism. **11** We have now started to pay attention to new possibilities of catastrophic events within the boundary of uniformitarianism. I mean it's true that the land was formed within hours by flood, but the components of the flood, such as the water or the ice dam by a glacier, were the results of several millions of years.

할 수 있었지만, **10** Bretz의 이론은 수로 암반 용암 지대의 모든 특징을 설명할 수 있었고, 이것이 다른 지질학자들이 이 이론을 채택하게 설득한 주 요인이었습니다.

하지만 우리가 동일 과정설을 무시해야 한다고 말하는 것은 아닙니다. **06** 우리가 더 이상 하나의 이론인 동일 과정설에만 의지해서는 안 된다는 것을 알려 주기 위해 Bretz의 이론을 언급한 거예요. **11** 우리는 이제 동일 과정설의 영역 안에서 대변동의 새로운 가능성에 집중해야 합니다. 그러니까 이 지대가 홍수로 인해 몇 시간 내에 형성된 것은 맞지만, 홍수의 구성원인 물이나 빙하로 인한 얼음 댐은 몇 백만 년 전의 결과이기도 하다는 말이에요.

[**Vocabulary**] uniformitarianism[jùːnəfɔ̀ːrmitɛ́əriənìzm] 동일 과정설   erosion[iróuʒən] 부식   uplift[ʌ́plift] 융기
long-standing 오래된   catastrophic[kæ̀təstráfik] 대변동의, 파멸의   Channeled Scabland 수로 암반 용암 지대
ravine[rəvíːn] 산골짜기, 협곡   ripple[rípl] 잔물결   yield[iːld] 만들어 내다

06 Main Topic

What is the topic of the lecture?

(A) The formation of geologically interesting places
(B) The effect of glaciers on geological formations
(C) The importance of uniformitarianism regarding the creation of the Scablands
(D) The viewpoints concerning a geological phenomenon

강의의 주제는 무엇인가?

(A) 지질학적으로 흥미로운 장소들의 형성
(B) 빙하가 지질학적 형성에 준 영향
(C) 수로 암반 용암 지대의 형성에 관한 동일 과정설의 중요성
(D) 어떤 지질학적 현상에 관한 관점들

07 Detail

Which of the following correctly describes uniformitarianism?

(A) It is a theory that most accurately explains geological changes on Earth.
(B) It is a theory that fails to fully explain a certain geologic area.
(C) It is a theory with shortcomings and requires more research.
(D) It is a theory that arouses controversy among geologists.

다음 중 동일 과정설을 바르게 묘사한 것은 무엇인가?

(A) 지구의 지질학적 변화를 가장 정확하게 설명한다.
(B) 특정 지질학적 지역을 완전히 설명해 주지는 못한다.
(C) 단점이 있는 이론으로 더 많은 연구가 필요하다.
(D) 지질학자들 사이에 논쟁을 일으킨다.

오답 해설 (C) 동일 과정설이 특정 지질학적 현상을 설명하지 못한다는 언급은 있지만, 더 많은 연구가 요구된다고 하지는 않았다. 교수는 동일 과정설로 설명되지 않는 지역을 다른 이론으로 설명할 수 있다고 했다.

08 Inference

Listen again to part of the lecture. Then answer the question.

> S: I think a river could have carved it out, like the Grand Canyon.
> P: That could have been the case, but the closest river is 90 kilometers east of around the Scablands' landscape.

What does the professor imply when he says this:
P: That could have been the case...

(A) He provides a compliment because the student suggests a possible answer to the phenomenon.
(B) He implies there could be another explanation for the geological formation.
(C) He shows uncertainty about the student's answer.
(D) He does not think the student understands the question.

강의의 일부를 다시 들으시오. 그리고 나서 질문에 답하시오.

> S: 제 생각에는 Grand Canyon처럼 강이 그곳을 깎은 것 같아요.
> P: 그럴 수도 있겠지만 수로 암반 용암 지대 주변에서 가장 가까운 강은 동쪽으로 90km 떨어져 있어요.

교수가 이 말을 할 때 암시한 것은 무엇인가?
P: 그럴 수도 있겠군요……

(A) 학생이 현상에 대한 가능성 있는 답을 했기 때문에 칭찬하고 있다.
(B) 지질학적 형성에 대한 다른 설명이 있을 수 있음을 암시하고 있다.
(C) 학생의 답에 확신하지 못하고 있다.
(D) 학생이 질문을 이해했다고 생각하지 않는다.

09 Detail

According to Bretz's theory, what was the role of the glacier regarding the formation of the Scablands?

Ⓐ It broke off into huge chunks of ice and directly carved out the area.
Ⓑ It provided a sudden source of water, which shaped the geological features of the area.
Ⓒ It slowly melted and changed the geological area over hundreds of years.
Ⓓ It formed a dam that limited the flow of water and pressurized the region.

Bretz의 이론에 따르면, 수로 암반 용암 지대의 형성에 작용한 빙하의 역할은 무엇인가?

Ⓐ 큰 얼음 덩어리로 갈라져서 직접적으로 그 지역을 깎아냈다.
Ⓑ 갑작스런 물이 유입되는 원천을 제공하여 그 지역의 지질학적 형태를 만들었다.
Ⓒ 천천히 녹아서 수백 년 동안 지형을 변화시켰다.
Ⓓ 물의 흐름을 제한하고 그 지역에 압력을 가하는 댐을 만들었다.

10 Inference

Listen again to part of the lecture. Then answer the question.

> P: ...but Bretz's hypothesis explained all the features of the Scablands, which is the main reason other geologists were persuaded to adopt this theory. But that is not to say that we should disregard uniformitarianism.

What does the professor imply when he says this:
P: But that is not to say that we should disregard uniformitarianism

Ⓐ He is dissatisfied with the public's ignorance of uniformitarianism.
Ⓑ He thinks that uniformitarianism needs to be studied in the field of geology.
Ⓒ He believes that uniformitarianism can still be accepted.
Ⓓ He has a disdain for uniformitarianism and prefers a recent theory.

강의의 일부를 다시 들으시오. 그리고 나서 질문에 답하시오.

> P: Bretz의 이론은 수로 암반 용암 지대의 모든 특징을 설명할 수 있었고, 이것이 다른 지질학자들이 이 이론을 채택하게 설득한 주 요인이었습니다. 하지만 우리가 동일 과정설을 무시해야 한다고 말하는 것은 아닙니다.

교수가 이 말을 할 때 암시한 것은 무엇인가?
P: 하지만 우리가 동일 과정설을 무시해야 한다고 말하는 것은 아닙니다.

Ⓐ 그는 대중이 동일 과정설을 간과하는 것을 못마땅하게 여기고 있다.
Ⓑ 그는 지질학계에서 동일 과정설에 대한 연구가 필요하다고 생각한다.
Ⓒ 그는 동일 과정설이 여전히 받아들여질 수 있다고 믿는다.
Ⓓ 그는 동일 과정설을 경시하고 최근의 이론을 선호한다.

11 Inference

What does the professor imply about the formation of the Scablands?

Ⓐ It is still a mystery to the majority of geologists.
Ⓑ Bretz's theory is the only idea that defines it.
Ⓒ Both uniformitarianism and Bretz's theory are not enough to explain it.
Ⓓ Two geological theories have been applied to account for it.

교수가 수로 암반 용암 지대의 형성에 대해 암시한 것은 무엇인가?

Ⓐ 여전히 대부분의 지질학자들에게 수수께끼이다.
Ⓑ Bretz의 이론은 그것을 분명히 밝힌 유일한 이론이다.
Ⓒ 동일 과정설과 Bretz의 이론 모두 그것을 설명하기에 충분치 않다.
Ⓓ 두 개의 지질학적 이론들이 그것을 설명하는 데 적용되었다.

정답 해설 Ⓓ 홍수로 인해 빠른 시간 안에 지형이 만들어졌다는 Bretz의 이론도 맞지만, 물을 가두어 놓았던 얼음 댐은 오랜 시간에 걸쳐 만들어졌으므로 동일 과정설도 맞다. 교수는 두 이론을 이용해서 이 지역의 형성을 설명했다.

TEST 9 Set 2 Conversation

Listen to part of a conversation between a student and a university employee.

학생의 용건: 기숙사 재신청에 대한 정보 요청

S Hi, 01 I came here to ask about the housing application. I am a current resident of Charles hall, so I thought students who are currently residing in a dormitory don't have to apply for housing again. But I read the notice posted on the student service center homepage, and it said that current residents needed to reapply for a dormitory if they want to extend their stay. Did I miss the reapplication deadline?

E Right. To reserve a residence hall assignment for a new academic year, you will need to complete the application process. There are 3 stages of reapplication. One is coming up next month, but we still have time before the others.

기숙사 보증금에 대한 질문

S Then, I better get started. Could you explain each stage? I'm sorry. I'm only a freshman so the whole procedure is unfamiliar.

E OK, 05 so do you have a tenant account?

S I do. I created it when I applied last semester.

E That's good. That makes the process much easier. First, you should visit our homepage and check a pop-up regarding the announcement. If you click that pop-up, it will direct you to the housing reapplication page, where you fill it out a form. The application will allow students to select hall preferences and request specific room types. After your application has been submitted successfully, you will receive an automatic transmission confirmation. Oh, and there is the $1,000 non-refundable deposit.

S Really? 02 I mean $1,000 is not a big deal, but non-refundable... hmm... I mean I'm planning to go on an exchange program in Spain next semester. If I am accepted into the program.

E Oh, then you will go to Spain, and stay there for the whole semester.

S Yes, in that case, I'll probably lose my deposit, right?

학생과 대학교 직원의 대화 중 일부를 들어 보시오.

S 안녕하세요. 01 기숙사 신청에 대해서 물어보려고 왔어요. 제가 현재 찰스 홀에서 거주하고 있어서, 현재 기숙사에 거주하는 학생은 기숙사 신청을 다시 할 필요가 없다고 생각했어요. 그런데 학생 서비스 센터 홈페이지에 올려진 안내문을 읽었는데, 현재 거주자들도 이용 기간을 연장하고 싶다면 기숙사를 다시 신청해야 한다고 하더라고요. 제가 재신청 기한을 놓쳤나요?

E 맞아요. 새로운 학기에 기숙사를 배정받으려면 신청 과정을 마쳐야 해요. 재신청을 하기 위해서는 세 개의 단계가 있어요. 첫 번째는 다음 달로 곧 다가오는데, 나머지는 아직 시간이 있어요.

S 그러면 시작하는 게 좋겠네요. 각 단계를 설명해 주실 수 있나요? 죄송해요. 제가 신입생이어서 전체 과정이 낯서네요.

E 좋아요. 05 입주자 계정이 있나요?

S 있어요. 지난 학기에 신청할 때 만들었어요.

E 좋아요. 덕분에 과정이 훨씬 쉬워졌어요. 첫 번째로, 우리 홈페이지에 방문해서 공지와 관련된 팝업을 확인하세요. 그 팝업을 클릭하면, 기숙사 재신청 페이지로 연결될 것이고, 거기서 양식을 작성합니다. 학생은 선호하는 기숙사를 선택하고 특정 방 종류를 요청할 수 있어요. 신청서가 성공적으로 제출되면, 자동으로 전달되는 확인서를 받을 거예요. 오, 그리고 환불이 안 되는 보증금 1,000달러가 있어요.

S 정말로요? 02 제 말은 1,000달러가 크다는 것은 아니지만 환불이 안 된다는 게… 음… 제가 다음 학기에 스페인으로 교환 학생 프로그램을 갈 계획이거든요. 만약 그 프로그램이 된다면요.

E 오, 그러면 학생은 스페인으로 갈 것이고, 전체 학기를 거기서 보내겠네요.

S 네, 그럴 경우, 아마 제 보증금을 포기해야겠죠?

E ⁰³Not necessarily. The school is willing to make an exception for special circumstances like yours. As long as you submit a study-abroad notification, we will defer your deposit and you can use the deposit for a dorm when you come back to school. ⁰⁵If you decide to extend your program and not to come back to the states, it will be applied to your account to cover any unpaid balance or a refund will be issued.

S That's good. So, could you explain the other steps?
E Second, it's open housing day, when the school allows applicants to visit each dormitory to make a fully-informed decision. As you know, we are a city university and dormitories are located far away from each other, so each dorm has unique traits and neighbors. ⁰⁴We give students the opportunity to look around a room and choose the right place for their taste. For example, there is a farmer's market near Killington Hall, so students living there enjoy fresh food at cheap price. ⁰⁴Also, Coopers Hall is just 5 minutes away from the City Art Museum, so it was very popular among art major students.
S So, what's the last stage?
E Students will decide where they are going to stay and residence hall assignments will be sent via e-mail.

S Thank you for the kind explanation. Ah, one more thing! Is it possible to live with my friend?
E When you fill out the application form, you can choose friends to stay with you in the same room together. However, the University can't guarantee particular assignment requests because we have a limited number of staff. And just you know, the University reserves the right to reassign students to different residence halls if the need arises. For more information, you should visit our website.
S OK, I'll visit the website first. Thanks for your help.

[Vocabulary] dormitory[dɔ́ːrmətɔ̀ːri] 기숙사   a residence hall 기숙사   a non-refundable deposit 환불이 안 되는 보증금[계약금]   a big deal 대단한 것, 큰 것   make an exception 예외를 허락하다   circumstance[sə́ːrkəmstæns] 상황, 환경   trait[treit] 특성, 특징   guarantee[gærəntíː] 보장하다, 약속하다

01 Main Topic

What is the conversation mainly about?

Ⓐ Ways to choose a preferable room in a dormitory
Ⓑ Ways to make a request to extend a stay in a dormitory
Ⓒ Ways to find out the school's policy regarding room assignment
Ⓓ Ways to apply for a student exchange program

대화는 주로 무엇에 관한 것인가?

Ⓐ 기숙사에서 선호하는 방을 선택하는 방법들
Ⓑ 기숙사 이용 기간 연장을 신청하는 방법들
Ⓒ 방 배정에 대한 학교 정책을 알아보는 방법들
Ⓓ 교환 학생 프로그램에 지원하는 방법들

02 Inference

What can be inferred about the $1,000 non-refundable deposit?

Ⓐ It is more costly than the student expected.
Ⓑ The student has a situation to take into consideration.
Ⓒ It is difficult for the student to pay it on time.
Ⓓ A refund cannot be made under any circumstances.

환불이 안 되는 보증금 1,000달러에 대해 추론할 수 있는 것은?

Ⓐ 학생이 예상했던 것보다 비용이 더 나간다.
Ⓑ 학생이 고려해야 할 상황이 있다.
Ⓒ 학생은 제때 지불하기 어렵다.
Ⓓ 환불은 어떤 상황에서도 불가하다.

03 Organization

Why does the university employee mention study abroad notification?

Ⓐ To check if the student knows the school's policy
Ⓑ To explain how the deposit can be used
Ⓒ To confirm about the study abroad program
Ⓓ To explain the school's policy about a refund

대학교 직원은 왜 해외 유학 신고서를 언급했나?

Ⓐ 학생이 학교 정책을 아는지를 확인하기 위해
Ⓑ 보증금이 어떻게 사용될 수 있는지를 설명하기 위해
Ⓒ 해외 유학 프로그램에 대해 확인하기 위해
Ⓓ 환불에 대한 학교의 정책을 설명하기 위해

04 Organization

Why does the employee mention the City Art Museum?

Ⓐ To explain that there are various room types in a dormitory
Ⓑ To emphasize the advantage of a city university
Ⓒ To illustrate how a dormitory gives benefit to art-major students
Ⓓ To explain that the school endeavors to meet students' needs

직원은 왜 시립 미술관을 언급했나?

Ⓐ 기숙사에 다양한 종류의 방이 있다는 것을 설명하기 위해
Ⓑ 도시 대학의 장점을 강조하기 위해
Ⓒ 기숙사가 어떻게 예술 전공 학생들에게 혜택을 주는지를 설명하기 위해
Ⓓ 학교가 학생들의 요구를 만족시키기 위해 노력하는 것을 설명하기 위해

05 Detail

Which of the following statements are true about the dormitory application process?
Choose 2 answers.

Ⓐ The deposit can be used to settle outstanding balance.
Ⓑ The school is able to guarantee a particular room type as per the student's request.
Ⓒ It would be hard to apply for a residence hall without a tenant account.
Ⓓ The school does not allow students to choose roommates.
Ⓔ There is plenty of time to start the actual process.

다음 중 기숙사 신청 과정에 대해 사실인 것은?
2개의 답을 고르시오.

Ⓐ 보증금은 미납분을 정산하기 위해 사용될 수 있다.
Ⓑ 학교는 학생들의 요구에 따라 특정 방 종류를 보장할 수 있다.
Ⓒ 입주자 계정이 없으면 기숙사 신청이 힘들 것이다.
Ⓓ 학교는 학생이 룸메이트를 선택하는 것을 허락하지 않는다.
Ⓔ 실제 과정을 시작하기까지는 시간이 많다.

TEST 9 Set 2 Lecture 1

Listen to part of a lecture in an ecology class.

P   The voyages of Christopher Columbus and other European explorers stimulated the mass migration of a lot of people. Colonization became a battle between nations as these explorers continually discovered and claimed uncharted lands. They built settlements in the North and South Americas as pioneers of a new period in history. However, people were not the only thing that moved during this migration period. Many plant and animal species were transported for the first time between the new world and the old world. After Columbus' arrival in the Americas, the plants and animals along with the bacterial life of these two worlds began to mix. The contact made between these two parts of the globe caused the circulation of a variety of new plants, crops, and livestock, which supported an increase in population in both the old and new world.

06, 08 We call this circulation the Columbian Exchange. Although Columbus did not actually take part in most of these exchanges, the process was named the Columbian Exchange because it was initiated by his adventures. In fact, not all of these exchanges were intentional, which means that some of them happened unconsciously. One important component of the Columbian Exchange was the transfer of plants between the old and new world, both those grown for food and weeds. Root vegetables from the Americas were especially important in the development of agriculture in Europe, such as potatoes. But the Columbian Exchange also had a terrible result for Native Americans. They were susceptible to some of the bacteria and viruses that European explorers had become immune to. You can say that European explorers brought contagious diseases to the Americas and caused a lot of Native Americans to die.

But I'll save this part of the Columbian Exchange for another lecture and continue to focus on its agricultural significance. Weeds were also a part of this complicated exchange between nations. Let's begin by talking about the term "weed". For one thing, the word "weed" is not considered a proper scientific term. 07I mean sometimes people use the term "weed" to mean slightly different things based on the needs of specific situations. For our purposes, let's say that a weed is a type of plant that is not cultivated on purpose. 07Instead, it's a plant that can grow and spread on its own, enduring harsh conditions and easily colonizing damaged or harsh environments, for example, burnt forests or deserts. Usually, weeds compete for nourishment with crops, which is why people spend so much time killing weeds with pesticides or by other physical means. Crops are heavily influenced by external conditions, but weeds exhibit resilience and persistence. Farmers have to protect their fields from the destruction that weeds cause in order to prevent their crops from wilting and dying from malnourishment.

The curious part of the Columbian Exchange was that the introduction of weeds was largely a one-way deal, since it was European weeds and grasses that invaded the Americas, rather than vice versa. For example, only a few American weeds have managed to survive in Europe, and even those, not in great numbers. In contrast, many aggressive European weeds such as clover, *dandelion and *plantain intertwined rapidly with American ecosystems.

Now, consider why weeds went in a single direction. I mean there must have been opportunity for American plants to be introduced into Europe, whether on purpose or by accident. There were so many ways for agricultural exchanges to happen and in fact, different types of seeds from all kinds of plants were introduced from the Americas to Europe. However, while they flourished in the Americas, they never fully took in Europe. It most likely had something to do with the manner of the European settlement in the Americas. Let me explain more. There was the simultaneous introduction of livestock, which was another important component of the Columbian Exchange. The cattle and horses adapted very quickly to the New World grasslands and their population soon exploded. ⁰⁹Lots of weeds came over by riding on the hides and hair of these animals, which fed on native plants as they grazed, which removed competition and allowed weeds to adapt quickly and successfully. If native plants were not removed, then the weeds would have needed to compete for nutrients in the soil. ¹⁰However, since the livestock ate up the native plants, weeds could absorb the nutrients in abundance without the need for competition. Furthermore, at the beginning of the European settlement, a lot of forests were cut down or burnt to make room for the building of pioneers' settlements initially. However, due to the elimination of native plants by intentional fire, weeds found themselves in very favorable growing conditions, without competition.

잡초의 영향

What was it about weeds that made such a big impact? As weeds proliferated, they harmed the ecosystem in the Americas. In fact, weeds are still one of the greatest threats to the Americas' natural environment. Major weed intrusions alter the natural diversity and balance of ecological communities. These changes threaten the survival of many plant populations because weeds compete with native plants for space, nutrients and sunlight. Such unintentional exchanges of plant and animal species between countries are still ongoing. ¹¹Perhaps this situation must be accepted as an inevitable phenomenon that cannot be stopped by human endeavor.

[**Vocabulary**] uncharted[ʌntʃɑ́ːrtid] 미지의 pioneer[pàiəníər] 개척자 hemisphere[hémisfìər] 반구 susceptible[səséptəbl] 취약한 contagious[kəntéidʒəs] 전염성의 resilience[rizíljəns] 회복력 persistence[pərsístəns] 지속됨, 고집 wilt[wilt] 시들다 dandelion[dǽndəlàiən] 민들레 plantain[plǽntin] 질경이 hide[hid] (동물의) 가죽 proliferate[prəlífərèit] 급증하다

[각주]

* **dandelion** 프랑스어 dent de lion(사자의 이빨)에서 유래된 민들레는 잎의 모양이 톱니나 이빨과 닮아서 붙은 이름이다. 4~5월에 노란색으로 꽃이 핀다.
* **plantain** 꽃은 5~7월에 녹색으로 피고 어린잎은 데쳐서 나물로 먹는 질경이는 약재로도 쓰인다. 잎은 비뇨기관염, 화상, 벌에 쏘인데, 치질, 결합조직을 치료한다. 라틴아메리카에서는 민속 전통약으로 암을 치료하는 데 사용했고, 중국에서는 설사나 결핵 궤양을 치료하거나 해독차로 만들어 마셨다.

06 Main Topic

What is the lecture mainly about?

Ⓐ Issues and concerns associated with weeds
Ⓑ The competitive ability of foreign species against native plants
Ⓒ The explosive growth of plants during the Columbian Exchange
Ⓓ An unintentional natural phenomenon

강의의 주된 내용은 무엇인가?

Ⓐ 잡초와 관련된 문제와 우려
Ⓑ 토착 식물에 대항하는 외래 종의 생존 능력
Ⓒ 콜럼버스 교환 동안의 식물의 폭발적인 증가
Ⓓ 의도하지 않은 자연적인 현상

07 Detail

What can be inferred from the term "weed"?
Choose 2 answers.

Ⓐ The term itself is not very consistently defined by people.
Ⓑ The term refers to a resilient plant, not easily affected by the environment.
Ⓒ The term indicates that absorb nourishment more quickly than other plants.
Ⓓ The term refers to a plant that is prone to growing in exotic terrain.

'잡초'라는 용어에서 추론할 수 있는 것은 무엇인가?
2개의 답을 고르시오.

Ⓐ 사람들에 의해 일괄적으로 정의되지 않는다.
Ⓑ 환경에 쉽게 영향 받지 않는 회복력 있는 식물을 가리킨다.
Ⓒ 다른 식물들보다 더 빨리 영양분을 흡수하는 식물을 가리킨다.
Ⓓ 외국 지형에서 자라기 쉬운 식물을 가리킨다.

08 Detail

Why is the introduction of American and European plants and animal populations called the Columbian Exchange?

Ⓐ Columbus indirectly initiated the exchange through his explorations.
Ⓑ Columbus persuaded the Native Americans to engage in trade with the settlers.
Ⓒ Columbus carried weeds into the Americas by using livestock.
Ⓓ Columbus tried to institute an exchange system between Europe and the Americas.

미국과 유럽 식물의 도입과 동물 종의 소개가 왜 콜럼버스 교환이라고 불리나?

Ⓐ 콜럼버스가 그의 탐험을 통해 간접적으로 교환을 시작했다.
Ⓑ 콜럼버스가 아메리카 원주민들을 설득해 정착민들과 무역에 관여했다.
Ⓒ 콜럼버스가 가축을 사용하여 미주대륙으로 잡초를 가져왔다.
Ⓓ 콜럼버스가 유럽과 미주대륙 간 교환 시스템을 도입하려 했다.

09 Detail

How were the seeds of weeds introduced to the Americas?

(A) The Europeans furtively imported the weed seeds to the Americas.
(B) The cattle and horses' feces contained the weed seeds.
(C) The seeds were carried on the skins of animals.
(D) The weeds were planted intentionally by European settlers.

| 잡초의 씨앗은 어떻게 미주대륙에 소개되었나?

(A) 유럽인들이 몰래 잡초 씨앗을 미주대륙으로 수입했다.
(B) 소와 말의 배설물에 잡초의 씨앗이 있었다.
(C) 씨앗은 동물의 피부를 통해 옮겨졌다.
(D) 잡초는 유럽 정착민들에 의해 의도적으로 심어졌다.

10 Detail

What are two favorable conditions for the transplantation of weeds?
Choose 2 answers.

[A] The seeds of the weeds brought by the European settlements were very healthy and prolific.
[B] The temperate climate in the Americas helped the weeds to grow easily.
[C] The deforestation created the right environment for the weeds to grow easily.
[D] The weeds were placed in a favorable position for the intake of essential nutrients.

잡초의 적응에 좋은 두 가지 환경은 무엇인가?
2개의 답을 고르시오.

[A] 유럽 정착민들이 가져온 잡초의 씨앗은 매우 건강하고 열매를 많이 맺었다.
[B] 미주대륙의 온화한 기후는 잡초가 손쉽게 자라는 데 도움이 되었다.
[C] 삼림 벌채는 잡초가 쉽게 자랄 수 있는 적절한 환경을 만들었다.
[D] 잡초는 중요 영양분을 섭취하기 위해 유리한 위치에 놓여 있었다.

11 Inference

What can be inferred about the introduction of weeds during the Columbian Exchange?

(A) The growth of weeds should have been prevented for the protection of the ecosystem.
(B) The problems caused by weeds are being studied and need to be solved by scientists.
(C) The movement of biological species such as weeds between countries is beyond human control.
(D) The Columbian Exchange caused more damage than benefit to the ecosystem.

콜럼버스 교환 동안 잡초의 도입에 대해 추론할 수 있는 것은 무엇인가?

(A) 생태계 보호를 위해 잡초의 성장을 방지했어야 했다.
(B) 잡초에 의한 문제들은 과학자들에 의해 연구되는 중이고 해결되어야 한다.
(C) 잡초의 국가 이동과 같은 생물학적 종의 이동은 불가항력이다.
(D) 콜럼버스 교환은 생태계에 이점보다는 더 많은 해를 야기했다.

TEST 9 Set 2 Lecture 2

Listen to part of a lecture in an art history class.

P As we've learned, the primary colors, in theory, represent the most basic colors that can produce all other colors when mixed. However, you will realize that the three primary colors, red, blue, and yellow, do not yield the best secondary colors. For example, mixing red and blue won't necessarily give you the beautiful violet that you would expect. To get a vivid violet, a little white has to be added. A similar case would be when you try to make a nice cyan out of just green and blue. It would be better to just use a pure blue pigment. 12 Actuality, primary colors are not perfect colors, as stated by science. I mean that the idea behind primary colors may lack a scientific background.

In fact, this idea that red, blue, and yellow represent three primary colors did not exist until approximately 200 years ago. 13 Until this theory on primary colors was accepted, the most popular theory was proposed by Sir Isaac Newton, who gave a scientific explanation for colors. Newton was the first to understand the rainbow. He set up a prism near his window, and it dispersed light into a large array of colors on the color spectrum. Thus, he theorized that different wavelengths of light created the different colors of light. Interestingly, as the light wavelength increased, the light color changed from violet to blue to green to yellow to orange to red. This phenomenon can be observed in the visible light spectrum, which ranges from 400 to 700 nanometers in wavelength. Based on this experiment, he published *Optics* in 1704, and, of course, there was no mention of the concept of "primary colors" in this book.

Until *Johann Wolfgang von Goethe came along, no one had questioned the validity of Newton's ideas about light and color. He was the first one who introduced the concept of primary colors. Goethe claimed that color was not solely a physical phenomenon, existing only as a measurable property within the presence of light. Color was not a segment within light, but rather a product of a harmonious mixture of light and dark. This means Goethe thought color results from an interaction of both light and shadow.

괴테가 정의한 색깔과 감정 간의 상관관계

I wonder if his artistic opinion may seem odd to you. As you are aware, Goethe was, in fact, a literary figure. He was a famous writer who composed novels, poems, and plays. He was not a painter who worked with colors, but rather a writer who created literature with words. Then, how did he originate the theory of primary colors? Goethe was famous during the Romantic Movement of Western literature. You may be familiar with Goethe for his acclaimed work called *Faust*, which is noted for the author's insights into spirituality and philosophy. Another work by Goethe, *The Sorrows of Young Werther*, affected the public's emotion to such an extent that young men started to dress as the story's protagonist Werther. As a Romantic writer, Goethe was inspired by an emotional and spiritual understanding of the world, rather than an objective, scientific view. 14 The writer envisioned different colors as varying representations of the spectrum of human emotion, and even as a tool that stimulated different emotional responses in people.

색깔의 심리학적 의미

S Sounds a lot like psychology.
P You're right. The color is also used in psychology. You might be aware, by instinct or learning, that red symbolizes anger and blue represents sadness. 15 Likewise, color psychologists believe that the color green has a calming effect on people... Well, I don't want to get off track, so we should continue talking about Goethe for now.

괴테의 실험

14 To understand the relationship between color and feelings, Goethe conducted an experiment to identify which colors best corresponded to the stimulation of which emotions. In his experiment, Goethe failed to find a reliable answer to his curiosity, which is the relationship between colors and emotions. Nevertheless, this experiment yielded another unexpected result... the relationship between different

빛 안에서의 분류가 아니라, 오히려 빛과 어둠의 조화로운 혼합의 결과였죠. 즉, 괴테는 색깔은 빛과 그림자의 상호 작용에 의해 만들어진 결과라고 생각했습니다.

이런 그의 예술적인 주장이 이상하게 보일 수 있겠네요. 여러분이 알고 있듯이, 사실, 괴테는 문학적 인물이거든요. 그는 소설, 시, 그리고 희곡을 쓴 유명한 작가였어요. 그는 색을 가지고 작업을 하는 화가가 아니라, 말로 문예를 창작하는 작가였죠. 그렇다면, 어떻게 그가 원색에 관한 이론을 만들게 되었을까요? 괴테는 서양 문학의 낭만주의 시대에 유명했어요. 여러분들은 《파우스트》란 걸작으로 괴테에 대해 잘 알고 있을텐데, 정신과 철학에 대한 작가의 날카로운 통찰력으로 주목을 받았죠. 괴테의 또 다른 작품인 《젊은 베르테르의 슬픔》은 대중들의 감정에 큰 영향을 끼쳐서 젊은 청년들이 이야기의 주인공인 베르테르처럼 옷을 입기도 했어요. 낭만주의 작가인 괴테는 세상에 대한 객관적이고 과학적인 시각보다는 감성적이고 정신적으로 세상을 이해하는 방법으로 영감을 받았어요. 14그 작가는 광범위한 인간 감정의 다양한 표현수단으로, 심지어 사람들에게 다른 감정들을 자극하는 도구로서 갖가지 색을 마음 속에 그렸죠.

S 꼭 심리학처럼 들리네요.
P 맞아요. 색깔은 심리학에서도 사용되죠. 여러분들은 본능적으로 혹은 학습을 통해, 빨간색이 분노를 상징하고 파란색이 슬픔을 상징한다는 것을 알고 있을 거예요. 15이런 식으로, 색 심리학자들은 초록색이 사람들에게 진정 효과를 준다고 믿었어요…… 음, 논점에서 벗어나고 싶지 않으니, 지금은 괴테에 대한 이야기를 계속 이어나가도록 하죠.

14색깔과 감정에 대한 이러한 관계를 이해하기 위해서, 괴테는 어떤 색이 어떤 감정의 자극에 가장 잘 상응하는지 실험 하기로 했습니다. 그의 실험에서, 괴테는 그의 궁금증에 대한 믿을 만한 답을 찾는 데 실패했어요. 그럼에도 불구하고, 이 실험은 예상치 못한 결과를 가져왔는데…… 바로 다른 색깔들 간의 관계예요. 예를 들어, 괴테는 특정한 색이 다른 특정한 색 옆에 놓였을 때 어떻게 변하는지 연구했어요.

colors. For instance, Goethe studied the way a color changes when it is placed next to another color. In particular, he discovered that by applying different lights and shadows to certain colors, he could produce new colors. For example, colors that were exposed to the sun, which produces the most light, seemed clearer than they were originally. However, aside from this unexpected discovery, Goethe did not succeed in discovering the relationship between colors and emotions.

It was in 1806 before Goethe had a satisfactory discovery. At the time, a German painter named Philipp Otto Runge sent a letter to Goethe that outlined a new color theory that focused especially on the connection between colors and emotions. His ideas revolved around the general theme that nearly all human emotions are actually influenced by three colors, which are red, blue, and yellow. Runge rarely used a scientific or chromatic approach in his discovery of these symbolic colors. [16]Instead he chose the colors, red, blue, and yellow because he simply felt that in nature, the three colors each symbolize different parts of the day from morning to night and thus contributed to the emotional reactions occurring in people. I mean he chose these colors with his artistic intuition.

After four years, Goethe wrote the book called *Theory of Colours*. In the book, Goethe stated that the red, blue, and yellow are primary colors. Because Goethe was already an established author at the time, so he was able to popularize the idea. In other words, Goethe claimed that primary colors are the most basic colors that express human emotions and that they can affect each other when they are placed closely together. Therefore we can say that this concept of colors was established not by only one author.

S Then, what about Runge? Did Goethe share any credit with him?
P You see, in his book, Goeth did not directly mention that Runge or Runge's letter helped him establish the theory. In fact, Goethe added a disclaimer to his book

that Runge's hypothesis did not influence his discovery or the work. ¹⁷So, people thought Goethe was the only one who made a single contribution to the foundation of the theory. But, now we all know the truth, so eventually its history speaks for itself.

17 그래서 사람들은 이 이론을 정립한 유일한 사람이 괴테라고 생각했어요. 하지만 우리는 이제 진실을 알고 있고, 결국 역사가 모든 걸 말해주죠.

[**Vocabulary**] primary color 원색   yield [jiːld] 내다, 산출하다   secondary color (두 가지 원색을 등분 혼합한) 등화색   pigment [pígmənt] 염료, 안료   prism [prízəm] 분광기   array [əréi] 집합체, 정렬   wavelength [wéivlèŋθ] 파장   validity [vəlídəti] 타당성   acclaimed [əkléimd] 칭송 받은   spirituality [spìritʃuǽləti] 정신성   protagonist [proutǽgənist] 주인공   envision [invíʒən] 마음 속에 그리다   disclaimer [diskléimər] 부인, 권리 포기 각서   speak for itself 자명하다, (그 이상의) 설명이 필요없다

[각주]
* **Johann Wolfgang van Goethe** 독일의 시인, 극작가, 소설가이자 철학자로 대표작으로 《파우스트》와 《젊은 베르테르의 슬픔》이 있다. 독일 문학의 최고봉을 상징하는 괴테는 '거물'로 칭송 받고 있다.

12 Main Topic

What is the lecture mainly about?

Ⓐ The relationship between primary colors and emotions
Ⓑ An overview of an concept about colors
Ⓒ The recent development of the idea of primary colors
Ⓓ A summary of Goethe's influence in an art history

강의는 주로 무엇에 대한 것인가?

Ⓐ 원색과 감정 간의 관계
Ⓑ 색깔에 대한 개념의 개요
Ⓒ 원색의 개념에 대한 최근의 전개
Ⓓ 미술사에서 괴테의 영향력에 대한 개요

13 Organization

Why does the professor mention Isaac Newton?

Ⓐ To emphasize Goethe's contribution in the field of science
Ⓑ To present how he came up with the primary color theory
Ⓒ To demonstrate how his theory of colors affected Goethe's theory of primary colors
Ⓓ To show the foundation of the theory related to color

교수는 왜 아이작 뉴턴을 언급했나?

Ⓐ 과학 분야에서 괴테의 기여를 강조하기 위해
Ⓑ 그가 어떻게 원색 이론을 만들어냈는지 보여 주기 위해
Ⓒ 색깔에 대한 그의 이론이 어떻게 괴테의 원색 이론에 영향을 주었는지 보여 주기 위해
Ⓓ 색깔과 관련된 이론의 설립을 보여 주기 위해

14 Detail

Why did Goethe decide to study and research colors?

Ⓐ To come up with a theory of colors by using the light spectrum
Ⓑ To explain how to apply suitable colors according to situations
Ⓒ To study the relationship between perception and colors
Ⓓ To describe colors that affected emotions in his literary works

괴테는 왜 색깔을 연구하고 조사하기로 결정했나?

Ⓐ 빛의 스펙트럼을 이용해 색깔 이론을 만들어내기 위해
Ⓑ 상황에 따라 적합한 색깔을 적용하는 법을 설명하기 위해
Ⓒ 인식과 색깔의 관계를 연구하기 위해
Ⓓ 그의 작품에서 감정에 영향을 주는 색깔을 묘사하기 위해

15 Inference

Listen again to part of the lecture. Then answer the question.

> P: Likewise, color psychologists believe that the color green has a calming effect on people... Well, I don't want to get off track, so we should continue talking about Goethe for now.

Why does the professor say this:
P: Well, I don't want to get off track.

Ⓐ To remind the students to do research on psychological aspects of colors
Ⓑ To continue with what he was talking about
Ⓒ To express uncertainty about the information he mentioned
Ⓓ To indicate that previous discussion was unimportant

강의의 일부를 다시 들으시오. 그러고 나서 질문에 답하시오.

> P: 이런 식으로, 색 심리학자들은 초록색이 사람들에게 진정 효과를 준다고 믿었어요…… 음, 논점에서 벗어나고 싶지 않으니, 지금은 괴테에 대해 이야기를 계속 이어나가도록 하죠.

교수가 이 말을 한 이유는 무엇인가?
P: 음, 논점에서 벗어나고 싶지 않으니.

Ⓐ 학생들이 색의 심리학적 측면에 대한 연구를 하도록 상기시키기 위해
Ⓑ 원래 말하던 주제를 이어가기 위해
Ⓒ 그가 언급한 정보의 불확실성을 표현하기 위해
Ⓓ 앞선 논의가 중요하지 않다는 것을 표현하기 위해

16 Detail

Why did Runge believe that red, blue, and yellow affected human emotions?

Ⓐ They produced a variety of mixed colors.
Ⓑ The combination of the three colors was attractive to human.
Ⓒ They synchronized different parts of the day.
Ⓓ Their effect was proven by scientific experiments.

룽게는 왜 빨강, 파랑, 그리고 노랑이 사람의 감정에 영향을 준다고 믿었나?

Ⓐ 그것들은 다양한 혼합된 색을 만든다.
Ⓑ 이 세 가지 색의 혼합은 사람들에게 매력적이다.
Ⓒ 그것들은 하루의 일상의 부분들과 들어맞는다.
Ⓓ 그것의 영향력은 과학적 실험으로 증명되었다.

17 Inference

What can be inferred about the concept of primary colors?

Ⓐ It was originated from light wavelengths.
Ⓑ It was established by one person's contribution.
Ⓒ It produces the best secondary colors when mixed together in certain proportions.
Ⓓ It resulted from the combination of various fields.

원색의 개념에 대해 추론할 수 있는 것은 무엇인가?

Ⓐ 빛의 파장에서 비롯되었다.
Ⓑ 한 사람의 기여로 정립되었다.
Ⓒ 그것들은 특정 비율로 혼합하면 최고의 등화색을 만든다.
Ⓓ 그것은 다양한 분야의 조합으로 만들어 졌다.

정답 해설 Ⓓ 과학자인 뉴턴이 제시한 색 이론에 대한 반발로, 소설가이자 철학가인 괴테가 원색의 개념을 떠올렸고, 미술 분야의 룽게가 감정에 영향을 주는 세 가지 색을 제시하면서 완성된 개념이다.

영단기 TOEFL

ACTUAL TEST
무료 해설 강의

한정 혜택

최신 출제 경향 반영 & 비교할 수 없는 압도적 강의력,
지금 '영단기 토플'에서 무료 해설 강의로 확인하세요.

ACTUAL TEST READING
01. 초빈출 600단어 이용 Voca 문제 만점 공략 학습법
02. 단숨에 정답을 골라내는 '3초 오답 소거법'으로 고효율 Reading 전략
03. 고난도 문항의 전형적인 오답 유형 분석 및 대응 학습법 제시

ACTUAL TEST LISTENING
01. ETS가 실제 출제하는 유형만 집중 공략! 문제 유형 딱 4개로 파악되는 출제 포인트
02. 전 토플러에게 꼭 필요한 리스닝 오답 논리 패턴 완벽 학습
03. Academic Conversation 유형 등 신경향 완벽 대비 해설 강의

ACTUAL TEST SPEAKING
01. 고득점 대비 Speaking 전달력 훈련으로 1점 더 챙기는 파이널 전략
02. 고득점 표현 반복 말하기 연습으로 채점자 설득 전략
03. 고득점용 Note-taking 전략으로 통합형 완벽 대응

ACTUAL TEST WRITING
01. '만능 에세이 템플릿'으로 독립형 문항을 빠르고 쉽게 접근하여 검토 시간 5분 버는 실전 전략
02. Writing 만점을 위한 유용한 표현 완벽 정리
03. 초빈출 통합형 주제 학습으로 최신 경향 및 실전 완벽 대비 해설 강의

ACTUAL TEST Reading
해설 강의 샘플 수강권
No. SXO4-YDYO-V2G2-YGP9

ACTUAL TEST Listening
해설 강의 샘플 수강권
No. SXO4-ZFG8-2PFP-6ZOZ

ACTUAL TEST Speaking
해설 강의 샘플 수강권
No. SXO5-16HL-87Z4-1S9O

ACTUAL TEST Writing
해설 강의 샘플 수강권
No. SXO5-1U7C-J4T5-EZW2

- 쿠폰 번호 입력 시 등록되며 등록된 강의는 30일 동안 수강 가능합니다.
- 영단기 로그인→ 내 회원 정보→ 쿠폰 등록 후 내 강의실에서 등록된 강좌를 확인하실 수 있습니다
- 무료 해설 강의 제공은 당사의 사정에 따라 예고 없이 중단될 수 있으며, 관련 문의는 영단기 홈페이지(eng.conects.com)에서 문의 가능합니다.

영단기 TOEFL
ACTUAL TEST
LISTENING

영단기 연구소

직접 시험 보고 연구한 저자의 REAL 콘텐츠

문제집

eng.conects.com

커넥츠 영단기

영단기 TOEFL
ACTUAL TEST
LISTENING

직접 시험 보고 연구한 저자의 REAL 콘텐츠

문제집

TOEFL iBT
LISTENING

영단기 TOEFL

ACTUAL TEST

TEST 01

Listening Section Directions

This section tests your understanding of conversations and lectures. This test includes two conversations and three lectures. You will hear each conversation or lecture only once. Your answers should be based on what is stated or implied in the conversations and lectures. You may take notes as you listen, and you may use these notes to help you answer the questions.

Set 1 Conversation

Questions 01 ~ 03 of 11

01 Why does the student visit the professor?

- Ⓐ To get some advice on citing the sources for a paper
- Ⓑ To get some information about a paper outline
- Ⓒ To ask about how to lay out a paper
- Ⓓ To ask how to find sources for research

02 Why does the professor recommend writing an outline?

- Ⓐ To see the development while writing the student's paper
- Ⓑ To assure the topic of the student's paper is appropriate
- Ⓒ To remember all information included in the student's paper
- Ⓓ To change the student's paper format easily

03 What information will the student include in the paper?
Choose 2 answers.

- A The change in the roles of castles
- B The strength of castles when used for military purposes
- C The walls that lords built around castles
- D The law applied to privileged people

Questions 04 ~ 05 of 11

Listen again to part of the conversation. Then answer the question.

04 What does the professor imply when she says this:
   (A) She thinks that more information should be included in the student's paper.
   (B) She expresses approval of the topic of the student's paper.
   (C) She believes that the student needs help to finish in the paper.
   (D) She pays a compliment about the student.

05 Why does the professor suggest going to the weekly workshop?
   (A) She cannot provide details about the student's request.
   (B) She thinks that the student will find the workshop very interesting.
   (C) She knows that the student is busy writing a paper.
   (D) She wants the student to participate in school services.

Set 1 Lecture 1

Questions 06 ~ 08 of 11

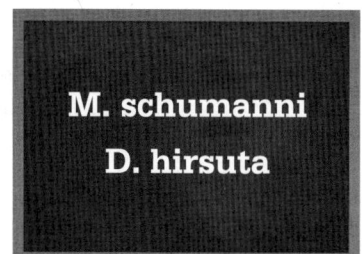

M. schumanni
D. hirsuta

06 What is the lecture mainly about?

- (A) The cooperative relationship shared among living organisms
- (B) The contentious methods employed by M. schumanni ants for D. hirsuta trees
- (C) The mutually advantageous relationship between the leafcutter ants and the fungus
- (D) The efforts to prevent the destruction of the environmental balance in nature

07 What does the professor say about the relationship between M. schumanni ants and D. hirsuta trees?

Choose 2 answers.

- [A] The ants impede the expansion of the trees by secreting a toxic herbicide.
- [B] The trees provide a shelter for the ants.
- [C] The ants stimulate the trees to absorb nutrients from the ground.
- [D] The ants weed away the surrounding area for the trees.

Listen again to part of the lecture. Then answer the question.

08 Why does the professor say this:

- (A) To gradually transit into a different topic
- (B) To remind the students of the characteristics of various ants
- (C) To continue discussing another type of ant
- (D) To emphasize the difficulty of understanding ants

Questions 09 ~ 11 of 11

09 Why does the professor mention a queen leafcutter ant?

　Ⓐ To describe the procedure for the formation of her colony
　Ⓑ To emphasize the important role a fungus plays in the survival of leafcutter ants
　Ⓒ To elaborate on the biological hierarchy that characterizes the social structure of ants
　Ⓓ To emphasize the biological benefit to ants through chemical secretions

10 What is the function of the fungus regarding its relationship with the leafcutter ants?

　Ⓐ It provides the ants with nourishment by preparing leaves appropriate for ingestion.
　Ⓑ It speeds up the digestive system of the ants.
　Ⓒ It provides shelter for the ants from harsh climates and predators.
　Ⓓ It forms a chemical concoction that improves the development and growth of ants.

11 What does the professor imply about leafcutter ants?

　Ⓐ The ants are destructive yet highly discerning, only attacking plants that threaten the environmental balance.
　Ⓑ The ants adjust their levels of consumption temporally, hereby keeping the stability of the environment.
　Ⓒ The aggressiveness of ants actually benefits the environment by getting rid of weeds.
　Ⓓ The ants present a research opportunity since they secrete a special chemical.

Set 2 Conversation

Questions 01 ~ 03 of 17

01 Why does the student go to see the professor?

    Ⓐ To discuss an interesting aspect of history class he took last semester

    Ⓑ To talk about why he lost his interest in economics

    Ⓒ To figure out how to choose a double major

    Ⓓ To discuss which major he should choose

02 What is the "bottom-up" approach in history?

    Ⓐ It is the idea that a few powerful people dominate history.

    Ⓑ It is the idea that various aspects of history are fundamental facts to understand our future.

    Ⓒ It is the idea that interesting events have happened throughout history.

    Ⓓ It is the idea that ordinary people played more important roles than influential people in history.

03 Why is the student worried about double majoring?

    Ⓐ He thinks that the amount of work might be more than he can stand.

    Ⓑ He doesn't have enough time to complete two majors.

    Ⓒ He wants to graduate as soon as possible.

    Ⓓ He thinks he cannot decide the thesis topic on time.

Questions 04 ~ 05 of 17

04 What does the professor say about writing a thesis for a double major?

Ⓐ The paper is judged by a higher standard than single major submissions.
Ⓑ The student is required to prepare a lengthy paper to cover both majors.
Ⓒ The student needs to speak to heads of department to choose the right topic.
Ⓓ It is possible that the student's proposal won't be approved due to the difficulty of choosing various topics.

Listen again to part of the conversation. Then answer the question.

05 What does the professor mean when she says this:

Ⓐ She implies it is the first time to suggest a double major to students.
Ⓑ She thinks the student has a high chance to complete a double major program successfully.
Ⓒ She implies that doing a double major could be challenging to the student.
Ⓓ She thinks the student doesn't have to get help about doing a double major.

Set 2 Lecture 1

Questions 06 ~ 08 of 17

06 What is the lecture mainly about?

    Ⓐ Planets located outside the habitable zone
    Ⓑ Technology used to observe exoplanets
    Ⓒ Planets that can substitute Earth in the future
    Ⓓ Recent postulations concerning celestial bodies

07 According to the lecture, what are the two conditions for planetary habitability?
Choose 2 answers.

    A A host star with a mass equal to or larger than that of the sun
    B Sufficient pressure to maintain liquid water on the surface of the planet
    C Terrestrial composition of solid materials
    D A warm and constant temperature similar to that of Earth

08 Why does the professor mention the mass and radius of Gliese 581d?

    Ⓐ To emphasize that a planet with high density is capable of maintaining its atmosphere
    Ⓑ To explain that a massive planet has more surface area to carry living organisms
    Ⓒ To illustrate a big planet has a wide orbit and keeps its distance from the host star
    Ⓓ To emphasize a planet with intense gravity is likely to contain water in a solid form

09 In the lecture, the professor describes the characteristics of Gliese 581d.
Indicate whether each of the following is the characteristic.
Put a check(✓) in the correct boxes.

	Yes	No
It yields results that do not comply with the initial assumption.		
It has enough natural force that attracts matter to itself.		
It is unlikely to contain water according to computer simulations.		
It is in a short orbital radius around the host star.		
It is difficult to observe the planet using current technology.		

10 What can be inferred about the length of the orbit?

Ⓐ It is directly proportional to the mass of a planet.
Ⓑ It is directly proportional to the temperature of a planet.
Ⓒ It is inversely proportional to the mass of a planet.
Ⓓ It is inversely proportional to the temperature of a planet.

11 What can be inferred about technology regarding astronomy?

Ⓐ Advanced technology increases the likelihood of the existence of extraterrestrial life.
Ⓑ Advanced technology aids scientists with their research.
Ⓒ Astronomy is flawed because of technological limitations.
Ⓓ Astronomers should study planets by using technology rather than just make conjectures.

Set 2 Lecture 2

Questions 12 ~ 14 of 17

12 What is the lecture mainly about?

Ⓐ An experiment that deals with two types of decision-making
Ⓑ Variables that people should consider in different decision-making situations
Ⓒ A tendency that people show when making a difficult decision
Ⓓ Comparison between an easy decision and a difficult decision

13 Why does the professor mention deciding which company to apply for?

Ⓐ To criticize numbers of people who make decisions with their unconscious minds
Ⓑ To provide an example of an important decision with a few variables
Ⓒ To explain the way to achieve a better decision
Ⓓ To illustrate complex variables involved in decision-making

14 Why did the researchers make half of the group watch a movie in the decision-making experiment?

Ⓐ To pose constraints on making decisions consciously
Ⓑ To improve their ability to make the right decisions
Ⓒ To allow them to concentrate on their decision making
Ⓓ To prove that watching a movie helps the decision-making process

Questions 15 ~ 17 of 17

Listen again to part of the lecture. Then answer the question.

15 Why does the professor say this: 🎧
- Ⓐ To indicate disagreement with the outcome of the experiment
- Ⓑ To indicate that the result might be unexpected
- Ⓒ To express uncertainty about the outcome
- Ⓓ To remind the students of the result

16 What are two characteristics of conscious and unconscious minds?
Choose 2 answers.
- Ⓐ The unconscious mind is more efficient at sorting many variables.
- Ⓑ The conscious mind puts more emphasis on unimportant factors.
- Ⓒ People find it convenient to make decisions with their unconscious minds.
- Ⓓ The conscious mind has an uncomplicated processing system.

17 Which of the following describes the professor's attitude toward the conclusion of the study?
- Ⓐ He thinks that the result of the study can be interpreted differently.
- Ⓑ He shows an inclination to choose a conscious mind over an unconscious mind.
- Ⓒ He criticizes that employers are fond of particular business tactics.
- Ⓓ He doesn't think that the result of the experiment is applicable to all situations.

영단기 TOEFL

ACTUAL TEST

TEST **02**

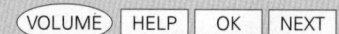

Listening Section Directions

This section tests your understanding of conversations and lectures. This test includes two conversations and three lectures. You will hear each conversation or lecture only once. Your answers should be based on what is stated or implied in the conversations and lectures. You may take notes as you listen, and you may use these notes to help you answer the questions.

Set 1 Conversation

Questions 01 ~ 03 of 17

01 Why does the student go to see the professor?

    Ⓐ To ask if the date of the quiz can be moved back

    Ⓑ To complain that there are no Francis Bacon articles in the library

    Ⓒ To request for extra copies of Francis Bacon articles

    Ⓓ To ask questions about Francis Bacon and his scientific methods

02 What is the student's problem?

    Ⓐ The student thinks the article is difficult to understand.

    Ⓑ The student cannot get the material that the professor assigned to read.

    Ⓒ The student cannot understand why the article is so important.

    Ⓓ The student does not know about the electronic version of the article.

03 What does the professor say about Francis Bacon?
Choose 2 answers.

    A He built the foundation of western philosophy.

    B He did not choose the traditional approach to science.

    C His approach was very similar to Aristotle's.

    D He had to undergo various scientific and political adversities.

    E His deductive reasoning is adequate for preserving data and acknowledging patterns.

Questions 04 ~ 05 of 17

04 Why does the professor mention the electronic version of the article on Francis Bacon?
  (A) To let her know that preparing the quiz requires a lot of time
  (B) To emphasize the convenience of reading the article in its electronic version
  (C) To suggest another way to prepare the student's upcoming task
  (D) To explain to her how to access the article online

Listen again to part of the conversation. Then answer the question.

05 What does the student imply when she says this: 🎧
  (A) She does not want to waste her time talking with the professor.
  (B) She feels the quiz will be very hard with all the information from the reading.
  (C) She thinks she needs to start reading the article as soon as possible.
  (D) She tries to get some extra time to finish the reading for the quiz.

Set 1 Lecture 1

Questions 06 ~ 08 of 17

06 What is the lecture mainly about?

- Ⓐ A procedure of the establishment of the capital city in the United States
- Ⓑ The importance of Philadelphia as the capital city of the United States
- Ⓒ The reasons that the North was considered as a better place for the capital city than the South
- Ⓓ The relationship between the North and South in the United States

07 Why was the central government so weak?

- Ⓐ Because it lacked funds to gain the support of each state
- Ⓑ Because the British government opposed to its establishment
- Ⓒ Because each state was controlled by different entities
- Ⓓ Because the American Revolutionary War divided the country into the North and South

08 What did the United States Funding Act of 1790 aim to do?

- Ⓐ To treat the issue of outstanding payment as a national concern
- Ⓑ To pacify the frustration of the Southern states
- Ⓒ To unite various states into one strong nation
- Ⓓ To stimulate the national economy

Questions 09 ~ 11 of 17

Listen again to part of the lecture. Then answer the question.

09 What does the professor mean when she says this:
- Ⓐ She thinks the students have frequently heard about the Southerners' situation.
- Ⓑ She wants to find out whether the students would like her to review the Southerners' reaction.
- Ⓒ She thinks the students can likely deduce the Southerners' response.
- Ⓓ She wants the students to explain what they know about the Southerners.

10 Why was The Compromise of 1790 deemed necessary?
- Ⓐ Because the South was more populous and economically wealthy than the North
- Ⓑ Because the South had gained a foothold in the North during the Revolutionary War
- Ⓒ Because the South was at a disadvantage regarding the payment of the national debt
- Ⓓ Because the South wanted to purchase actively large tracks of land for the new capital

11 According to the professor, how was the capital relocated from Philadelphia?
- Ⓐ The North and South chose a location where both sides were satisfied.
- Ⓑ The central government supported the South with funds and legislations.
- Ⓒ The South made other provisions for the new capital city.
- Ⓓ The North relinquished Philadelphia as the capital city in consideration of the situation of the South.

Set 1 Lecture 2

Questions 12 ~ 14 of 17

12 What does the professor mainly discuss?

- Ⓐ The recent developments in infrared radiation imaging
- Ⓑ The reasons neurological research is important
- Ⓒ The relationship between personal traits and inner areas of the brain
- Ⓓ The equipment used to detect activities that take place in the brain

13 What is the function of NIRS in neuroscience research?

- Ⓐ It shows a three-dimensional view of the brain.
- Ⓑ It produces full-color images.
- Ⓒ It provides information about brain responses.
- Ⓓ It accurately reflects internal brain structures.

14 Why are computers used together with NIRS?

- Ⓐ To solve problems associated with NIRS
- Ⓑ To convert the collected data into a diagram
- Ⓒ To connect to the brain through wires
- Ⓓ To quantify brain stimulation

Questions 15 ~ 17 of 17

15 Why does the professor mention a study involving the frontal lobe?
- Ⓐ To illustrate the reason that NIRS became an effective method in psychology fields
- Ⓑ To suggest that human personality is relatively constant
- Ⓒ To emphasize an instrumental method used in psychology studies
- Ⓓ To explain that the frontal lobe controls emotions

16 According to the lecture, what is the similarity between brain maps and geographical maps?
- Ⓐ They explain phenomena that cannot be directly observed.
- Ⓑ They are often complemented by other methods.
- Ⓒ They may be flawed by including outdated information.
- Ⓓ They are utilized to locate a certain spatial region.

17 What can be inferred about NIRS?
- Ⓐ Studies are being conducted to obtain accurate information using NIRS.
- Ⓑ A lot of time is needed before NIRS can yield better results.
- Ⓒ There is a limit to the information provided by NIRS.
- Ⓓ It is too problematic to apply NIRS to the examination of brains.

Set 2 Conversation

Questions 01 ~ 03 of 11

01   Why does the student go to the office?

　　Ⓐ To organize a hiking club in the school
　　Ⓑ To plan to set up club booths
　　Ⓒ To try to advertise the club he joined
　　Ⓓ To complain that there are no hiking clubs on campus

Listen again to part of the conversation. Then answer the question.

02   What does the staff imply when she says this: ⌒

　　Ⓐ She doesn't have any idea why the student came to the office.
　　Ⓑ She thinks that she is not a suitable person to help the student.
　　Ⓒ She doesn't intend to provide the information the student requested.
　　Ⓓ She doesn't know how to help the student.

03   What can be inferred about the staff's attitude towards the student?

　　Ⓐ She tries to empathize with the student.
　　Ⓑ She thinks that the student is overly demanding.
　　Ⓒ She is annoyed by the student's lack of information.
　　Ⓓ She is not satisfied with the print center's service.

Questions 04 ~ 05 of 11

04 What are the requirements to set up a booth on campus?
Choose 2 answers.
- [A] To enroll as an official club
- [B] To gather enough members to register
- [C] To visit the student services office to pay the service fee for setting up a booth
- [D] To visit the place providing student services

Listen again to part of the conversation. Then answer the question.

05 What does the staff mean when she says this: 🎧
- [A] She is not sure she understands the student's question.
- [B] She thinks that the rate of discount is sufficient for the student.
- [C] She implies that the information is incorrect.
- [D] She is uncertain about the discount rate offered by the printing service.

Set 2 Lecture 1

Questions 06 ~ 08 of 11

06 What is the main purpose of the lecture?

  Ⓐ To examine the steps of metamorphosis by following the life of a butterfly
  Ⓑ To discuss the advantages of complete metamorphosis over incomplete metamorphosis
  Ⓒ To explain the significance of metamorphosis in the life cycles of various species
  Ⓓ To describe a biological process by which insects develop and change their body structure

Listen again to part of the lecture. Then answer the question.

07 What does the professor mean when he says this: ⌒

  Ⓐ He thinks that discussing other species is not worth the time.
  Ⓑ He intends to return to what he was discussing.
  Ⓒ He plans to explain the lecture at a slow pace.
  Ⓓ He believes that the students need time to understand.

08 Why does the professor mention grasshoppers and dragonflies?

  Ⓐ To imply that they are the best-known examples of metamorphosis
  Ⓑ To emphasize that how they develop their reproductive ability
  Ⓒ To illustrate that they evolve to stop competing for the same food and habitat
  Ⓓ To explain that variations exist in incomplete metamorphosis

Questions 09 ~ 11 of 11

09 Which of the following is a crucial difference between complete metamorphosis and incomplete metamorphosis?

- Ⓐ The number of life cycle stages
- Ⓑ A change in mouth structure
- Ⓒ The ability to mate
- Ⓓ A susceptibility to weather

10 What is the critical function of a larva stage?

- Ⓐ To feed and prepare for its growth
- Ⓑ To form a strong structure called the cocoon
- Ⓒ To develop preliminary wings
- Ⓓ To protect against predators

11 According to the professor, which of the following are biological benefits for insects that undergo metamorphosis?

Choose 2 answers.

- ☐ A It allows for insects to commit themselves to their aims.
- ☐ B It allows larvae to live underwater or underground to protect themselves from predators.
- ☐ C It makes mating and reproduction easier for adult insects because they live in different habitats from their larvae.
- ☐ D It establishes less competition between adult insects and their larvae.

영단기 TOEFL

ACTUAL TEST

TEST **03**

TOEFL Listening

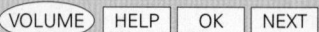

Listening Section Directions

This section tests your understanding of conversations and lectures. This test includes two conversations and three lectures. You will hear each conversation or lecture only once. Your answers should be based on what is stated or implied in the conversations and lectures. You may take notes as you listen, and you may use these notes to help you answer the questions.

Set 1 Conversation

Questions 01 ~ 03 of 11

01 Why does the student go to the bookstore?

  (A) To buy a textbook for his psychology class
  (B) To receive a refund for an unused book
  (C) To inquire about the store's return policy
  (D) To sell his textbook to a book distributor

02 Why does the student go to return the book two weeks after the class started?

  (A) He needed to make sure that he could receive credits without taking the class.
  (B) He was delayed because of returning from France following his student exchange program.
  (C) He realized that the book was not one of the required materials for the class.
  (D) He discussed his situation with a professor who taught a similar class.

03 Why did the school implement the one-week return policy?

  (A) To accommodate the schedules of busy students
  (B) To discourage students from practicing dishonesty
  (C) To stop students from getting refunds for their books
  (D) To retail new books instead of used ones

Questions 04 ~ 05 of 11

Listen again to part of the conversation. Then answer the question.

04 What does the student imply when he says this:
- Ⓐ He does not want to settle for anything less than a full refund.
- Ⓑ He feels that the amount is a small fraction of the original price.
- Ⓒ He thinks that the commission for the distributor is too much.
- Ⓓ He wants to ensure how much he could receive a refund.

05 What can be inferred about the student?
- Ⓐ He decides to concede to his present situation concerning the textbook.
- Ⓑ He is glad about the fact that he can sell his book at a buyback price.
- Ⓒ He continues to feel uncertain because he is unsatisfied with the woman's advice.
- Ⓓ He is upset at the school because the psychology class is not offered next year.

Set 1 Lecture 1

06 What does the professor primarily discuss?

 Ⓐ The historical value of a warship called the San Jose
 Ⓑ Archaeological aspects of a sunken ship
 Ⓒ The method used for restoring a ship
 Ⓓ The importance of excavating shipwrecks

07 What can be inferred about shipwrecks?

 Ⓐ They are the main concern for archaeologists.
 Ⓑ They are well-preserved because of underwater conditions.
 Ⓒ They are connected to historical events.
 Ⓓ Their discovery is more profitable than searching for artifacts on dry land.

08 Why were the artifact findings on the San Jose important?

 Ⓐ Because the artifacts provided information on how people spent their ordinary lives at the time
 Ⓑ Because archaeologists learned a new wartime technology through the weapons found on the ship
 Ⓒ Because archaeologists were able to make huge economic gain by selling the artifacts that were discovered on the ship
 Ⓓ Because the artifacts helped archaeologists determine about how the ship sank in 1628

Questions 09 ~ 11 of 11

09 According to the lecture, what was the actual reason for the sinking of the San Jose?
- Ⓐ The cannons were not tied tightly to the deck, thereby rolling around and throwing the ship off-balance.
- Ⓑ The ship cargo, such as sculptures and tools, was too heavy for the ship to handle.
- Ⓒ It failed to contain the weight sufficiently to maintain its balance.
- Ⓓ Cold sea water damaged the ship because it froze the wooden structures.

10 In the lecture, the professor describes the benefits of hydrophobic coating.
Indicate whether each of the following is an advantage.
Put a check(✓) in the correct boxes.

	Yes	No
Comparatively inexpensive to use		
Immediately responsive		
Environmentally friendly		
Relatively easy to apply		
Continuously renewable		

Listen again to part of the lecture. Then answer the question.

11 What does the professor imply when she says this:
- Ⓐ The method was not accepted because of its limitations.
- Ⓑ The method was not completely satisfactory.
- Ⓒ Other methods were adopted to restore the ship.
- Ⓓ Archaeologists expected the method to yield different results.

Set 2 Conversation

Questions 01 ~ 03 of 17

01 Why does the student go to see the professor?

  Ⓐ To get some help with her paper on philosophy
  Ⓑ To check if there are any chances to get hired
  Ⓒ To convince the professor that she is qualified as a TA
  Ⓓ To decide which major she should choose

02 What can be inferred about how the student's paper will turn out to be?

  Ⓐ It will primarily concern the biography of John Locke.
  Ⓑ It will elaborate on how John Locke interacted with other influential thinkers of modern politics.
  Ⓒ It will describe how the Declaration of Independence affected the John Locke's philosophy.
  Ⓓ It will focus on the John Locke's philosophy such as principles of humanism and individual freedom.

Listen again to part of the conversation. Then answer the question.

03 Why does the professor say this:

  Ⓐ To imply that the student is not qualified to be a teaching assistant
  Ⓑ To disparage the student's lack of academic experience
  Ⓒ To ask the student which grade she is currently in
  Ⓓ To show his disappointment at not being able to hire the student

Questions 04 ~ 05 of 17

04 What is the student's assumption about the TA position in the philosophy department?

Ⓐ It is suitable only for the graduate students with a major in Philosophy.
Ⓑ It has a similar hiring policy to other departments.
Ⓒ It is only for those students who have taken the advanced courses in the major.
Ⓓ Graduate experience is required to teach the basic courses.

05 For what purpose does the professor mention Jeremy Bentham?

Ⓐ To discuss his moral philosophy
Ⓑ To check the student's knowledge and understanding of the philosopher
Ⓒ To ask the student's opinion of the philosopher
Ⓓ To remind the student that the philosopher was discussed in the Introductory Philosophy 101

Set 2 Lecture 1

Questions 06 ~ 08 of 17

06 What does the professor mainly discuss?

    Ⓐ The possibility of opting for biofuel instead of fossil fuel
    Ⓑ The sources for the production of biofuel
    Ⓒ The advantage of biofuel as an energy source
    Ⓓ The environmental importance of using biofuel

Listen again to part of the lecture. Then answer the question.

07 Why does the professor say this:

    Ⓐ To express strong agreement on the use of ethanol
    Ⓑ To show doubt about the application of ethanol
    Ⓒ To remind the students of the positive aspects of ethanol
    Ⓓ To express reservations about the disadvantages of using ethanol

08 Why is ethanol insufficient to replace gasoline?

    Ⓐ Ethanol is extracted from a restricted range of staple crops like sugar cane and corn.
    Ⓑ Ethanol is required in greater quantities than traditional fuels, in order to produce the same energy output.
    Ⓒ Ethanol increases people's dependence on fossil fuels.
    Ⓓ Ethanol is not a stable source of energy because its use as a fuel is still at an experimental stage.

09 Why is rapeseed the leading source of biodiesel?

Ⓐ Rapeseed has a high percentage of oil in its weight.
Ⓑ Rapeseed is the most plentiful plant in the U.S.
Ⓒ Rapeseed cannot be consumed by humans or livestock.
Ⓓ Rapeseed is not difficult to cultivate.

10 According to the lecture, why are algae useful as a fuel source?
Choose 2 answers.

A They contain a high oil proportion.
B They multiply quickly.
C They are technologically feasible.
D They can be harvested from nature.
E They are rapidly converted into oil.

11 What is the professor's attitude towards biodiesel?

Ⓐ He believes that biodiesel cannot replace fossil fuels.
Ⓑ He thinks people should concentrate more on various problems concerning biodiesel.
Ⓒ He is skeptical about the production of biodiesel because of its high maintenance cost.
Ⓓ He thinks biodiesel would eventually become an alternative source of traditional fuels.

Set 2 Lecture 2

Questions 12 ~ 14 of 17

12 What is the lecture mainly about?

Ⓐ The evolution of living organisms into various distinct species

Ⓑ The requisites for the occurrence of species allocation

Ⓒ The effect of waterways in the Amazon Basin on living organisms

Ⓓ The explanation behind speciation in the Amazon Rainforest

13 What is the outcome of speciation?

Ⓐ A particular species gets divided into several groups.

Ⓑ Species are located far away from each other.

Ⓒ The divided groups of species are unable to reproduce with one another.

Ⓓ The evolution of species is confronted by geographical barriers.

14 What are the two requisites for species allocation?
Choose 2 answers.

A Frequent contact among species

B The separation of species for an extended period of time

C High mountains and large oceans

D The presence of geographic barriers

Questions 15 ~ 17 of 17

15 Why did speciation seem to be a mystery in the Amazon Rainforest?

Ⓐ Because the Amazon Rainforest is oversized
Ⓑ Because typical geographic barriers are not found in this area
Ⓒ Because the Caribbean Sea is too large for speciation
Ⓓ Because thin strip of land is appropriate for speciation

16 Why does the professor mention the Isthmus of Panama?

Ⓐ To explain the long, thin strip of land divides the Caribbean Sea and the Pacific Ocean
Ⓑ To give an example of a natural formation that segregates an area
Ⓒ To emphasize the importance of various types of geographic barriers
Ⓓ To indicate that the Isthmus of Panama is an area with repeated speciation

Listen again to part of the lecture. Then answer the question.

17 What can be inferred about the professor when he says this?

Ⓐ He wants to prove that Alfred Wallace's accomplishments were mocked by the scientific community.
Ⓑ He shows respect for Alfred Wallace's efforts in solving the curiosity about speciation.
Ⓒ He criticizes the scientific community for ignoring Alfred Wallace's studies.
Ⓓ He emphasizes the need for further scientific research regarding speciation in the Amazon.

영단기 TOEFL

ACTUAL TEST

TEST 04

Listening Section Directions

This section tests your understanding of conversations and lectures. This test includes two conversations and three lectures. You will hear each conversation or lecture only once. Your answers should be based on what is stated or implied in the conversations and lectures. You may take notes as you listen, and you may use these notes to help you answer the questions.

Set 1 Conversation

Questions 01 ~ 03 of 17

01 What is the goal of the woman's experiment?
- Ⓐ To demonstrate the characteristics of ammonia gas
- Ⓑ To prove that a litmus paper reacts with ammonia gas
- Ⓒ To show the formation of a particular gas
- Ⓓ To determine a mistake in the experiment

02 What does the man suggest to the woman?
- Ⓐ She should watch him repeating the experiment.
- Ⓑ She should receive an explanation of the experiment.
- Ⓒ She would be better off getting information about hydrogen gas.
- Ⓓ She can redo her task under his observation.

Listen again to part of a conversation. Then answer the question.

03 Why does the man say this: ⌒
- Ⓐ To indicate that the woman needs to be more precise
- Ⓑ To imply that the woman should use a different acid
- Ⓒ To suggest a different experiment for the woman
- Ⓓ To discourage the woman from becoming a scientist

Questions 04 ~ 05 of 17

04 What mistake does the woman make during her experiment?
- Ⓐ A characteristic concerning a gas was overlooked.
- Ⓑ Test tubes were confused and mixed up.
- Ⓒ Materials used in the experiment were contaminated.
- Ⓓ Nitric acid mixture with sodium carbonate failed to react.

05 What will the woman do next?
- Ⓐ She will clean the lab apparatus she used.
- Ⓑ She will review her notes on ammonia gas.
- Ⓒ She will write an official record for the experiment.
- Ⓓ She will conduct another chemistry experiment.

Set 1 Lecture 1

Questions 06 ~ 08 of 17

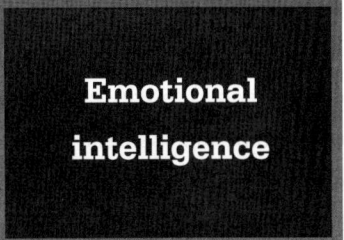

06 What is the main purpose of this lecture?

(A) To inform about emotional intelligence's history and development
(B) To explain how to evaluate emotional intelligence through various tests
(C) To discuss the necessity of emotional intelligence in the field of psychology
(D) To discuss reactions to emotional intelligence in the society

07 Why did early psychologists reject emotional intelligence?

(A) They believed that emotion and intelligence were separated from one concept.
(B) They believed that emotion and intelligence were at variance with each other.
(C) They believed that neither emotion nor intelligence could be evaluated by a simple test.
(D) They believed that emotion and intelligence required another condition if they were to work together.

08 Why does the professor mention Daniel Goleman?

(A) To show that he was the first to discuss emotional intelligence, and how the study of it developed through history
(B) To explain how emotional intelligence has been widely accepted by the public
(C) To demonstrate how his work was largely mocked
(D) To emphasize that his book is an important work in the development of study of emotional intelligence

Questions 09 ~ 11 of 17

09 According to the professor, what are the advantages of using the Self-Report Assessment? Choose 2 answers.

Ⓐ It is the most accurate way of measuring emotional intelligence.
Ⓑ People can calculate their score on emotional intelligence.
Ⓒ People like taking it because they enjoy learning about themselves.
Ⓓ Researchers can easily evaluate many participants with simple answers.

10 Why does the professor mention an image of someone smiling?

Ⓐ To show the importance of understanding others' feelings
Ⓑ To suggest another method to measure emotional intelligence
Ⓒ To explain the difficulty of perceiving what emotion is being portrayed in the pictures
Ⓓ To emphasize how recently emotional intelligence has been developed

11 What can be inferred about the lecture?

Ⓐ The study of emotional intelligence has been accepted and established for a long time.
Ⓑ Psychologists have yet to fully develop assessment systems of emotional intelligence.
Ⓒ People like to learn more about themselves by judging various images shown by psychologists.
Ⓓ Society values emotional intelligence over IQ.

Set 1 Lecture 2

 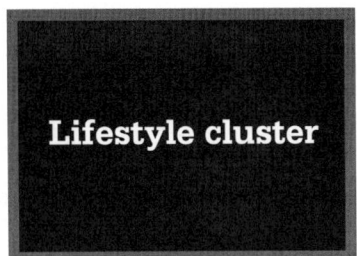

12 What is the lecture mainly about?

    Ⓐ The factors involved in identifying specific marketing groups
    Ⓑ The reason corporations are interested in the development of marketing campaigns
    Ⓒ The reason lifestyle clusters can be useful in marketing a company's products
    Ⓓ The methods used when setting up a market strategy to promote sales

13 Why does the professor mention cultivators?

    Ⓐ To make sure that students understand cultivators can be used on farms
    Ⓑ To support the idea that companies use the demographic information to sell their products
    Ⓒ To demonstrate the different criteria that can be included in demographics
    Ⓓ To illustrate how ZIP codes categorize regions easily

Listen again to part of the lecture. Then answer the question.

14 What does the professor imply when he says this: 🎧

    Ⓐ He thinks students learn more about demographics in political science.
    Ⓑ He thinks that the political examples he mentioned are not relevant.
    Ⓒ He wants to focus on the commercial situation related to the topic.
    Ⓓ He wants students to cover political information in another class.

Questions 15 ~ 17 of 17

15 What is the main advantage of using the Internet to analyze target markets?

   Ⓐ It increases the chance for politicians to be elected.
   Ⓑ It provides large amounts of data for companies to market their goods.
   Ⓒ Companies can advertise their products to large regions.
   Ⓓ Companies can make their products effectively using "lifestyle clusters" with the help of the Internet.

16 According to the lecture, what is "lifestyle cluster"?

   Ⓐ It means people with shared backgrounds reside in similar areas.
   Ⓑ It means that the population can be segmented by several factors.
   Ⓒ It means that computers can be used to analyze buying patterns.
   Ⓓ It means that a college town is segmented by many factors.

17 Why does the professor mention a university town?

   Ⓐ To analyze the buying pattern of customers in a university town
   Ⓑ To demonstrate how difficult demographics can be applied to marketing
   Ⓒ To explain market segmentation for promoting sales
   Ⓓ To question that every region has its own lifestyle cluster

Set 2 Conversation

Questions 01 ~ 03 of 11

01 Why does the student visit the professor?

Ⓐ To discuss how important primary sources are
Ⓑ To get some help in doing research for a paper
Ⓒ To learn how to use sources to complete a paper
Ⓓ To get approval for the topic for a paper

02 What does the student think about the craft union?

Ⓐ It played a decisive role in protecting skilled workers.
Ⓑ It was unable to empower craftsmen.
Ⓒ It discriminated against skilled workers.
Ⓓ It had a paradoxical policy.

03 Why does the professor mention *The Diary of Anne Frank*?

Ⓐ To explain how the student could find valuable information
Ⓑ To provide an example of a primary source
Ⓒ To emphasize how important sources are when writing a paper
Ⓓ To compare the book with the student's paper

Questions 04 ~ 05 of 11

04 What does the professor suggest the student to do?
Choose 2 answers.

- [A] To keep from using tertiary sources for academic research
- [B] To get help to access to a place academic materials are located
- [C] To talk to the library staff to find the right website
- [D] To search for various kinds of information related to the topic

Listen again to part of the conversation. Then answer the question.

05 Why does the professor say this:

- Ⓐ To commend the student on bringing up a good idea
- Ⓑ To indicate that the student needs to be concerned with other aspects
- Ⓒ To emphasize that using the Internet is an easy way to find sources
- Ⓓ To advise the student not to find sources on the Internet

Set 2 Lecture 1

Questions 06 ~ 08 of 11

06 What is the lecture mainly about?

   Ⓐ A comparison between kelp forests and other marine ecosystems
   Ⓑ The several biological species that inhabit kelp forests
   Ⓒ The characteristics of different layers of kelp forests
   Ⓓ The role and condition of kelp forests

07 According to the professor, what are the similarities between tropical rainforests and kelp forests?
Choose 2 answers.

   Ⓐ Both provide distinctive layers because of their environmental traits.
   Ⓑ Both provide protection and shelter from harsh surroundings.
   Ⓒ Both foster the variety and variability of life in their ecosystems.
   Ⓓ Both consist of the largest plants in their areas.
   Ⓔ Both are affected by natural disasters.

08 Why does the professor mention Charles Darwin?

   Ⓐ To describe what Charles Darwin found while researching kelp forests
   Ⓑ To sympathize with Charles Darwin's concern for the consequence of dying kelp forests
   Ⓒ To illustrate the beneficial relationship between kelp forests and the species in the marine ecosystem
   Ⓓ To emphasize the biological complexity and ecological importance of kelp forests

Questions 09 ~ 11 of 11

Listen again to part of the lecture. Then answer the question.

09 Why does the professor say this:
- (A) To check if students actually understand the meaning of El Niño
- (B) To introduce the Spanish meaning of the term
- (C) To get help with the Spanish meaning of El Niño
- (D) To inform where El Niño originated

10 According to the professor, what impact does El Niño have on kelp forests?
- (A) It causes sudden flood, which eradicates habitats of marine species.
- (B) It destroys the food web existing in kelp forests.
- (C) It thins out some nutrients in a certain area of the ocean.
- (D) It raises the water level and impedes kelp forests from reaching sunlight.

11 Why does the professor mention sea otters?
- (A) To specify one of the many animal species that inhabits kelp forests
- (B) To elaborate on the environmental significance of sea otters in kelp forests
- (C) To highlight the damage caused by human intervention in kelp forests
- (D) To explain the relationship between people and the animals

영단기 TOEFL

ACTUAL TEST

TEST 05

Listening Section Directions

This section tests your understanding of conversations and lectures. This test includes two conversations and three lectures. You will hear each conversation or lecture only once. Your answers should be based on what is stated or implied in the conversations and lectures. You may take notes as you listen, and you may use these notes to help you answer the questions.

Set 1 Conversation

Questions 01 ~ 03 of 11

01   What is the conversation mainly about?

  (A) A film about Thomas Jefferson
  (B) Various places to find resources for a paper
  (C) A student's concern about finding reliable online sources
  (D) Questions about the Lewis and Clark expedition

02   According to the professor, what are two achievements of the Lewis and Clark expedition? Choose 2 answers.

  [A] Spreading Thomas Jefferson's policy throughout the western United States
  [B] Finding out the undiscovered regions of the country
  [C] Studying the daily lives and culture of Native Americans
  [D] Discovering new animal species

03   Why did the student choose to write about the Lewis and Clark expedition?

  (A) The student wants to learn more than is covered in class.
  (B) The student considers it more interesting than the Jeffersonian philosophies.
  (C) The student has written about it in the botany class.
  (D) The student found its various aspects in the botany class.

Questions 04 ~ 05 of 11

Listen again to part of the conversation. Then answer the question.

04   What does the professor imply when he says this:
   Ⓐ The professor can easily deduce the problem which is related to the Internet.
   Ⓑ The professor feels that the Internet contains unsurprising information.
   Ⓒ The professor seems indifferent about the student's comment.
   Ⓓ The student should have been aware of the fact that the Internet is not reliable.

05   What does the professor suggest the student to do?
   Choose 2 answers.
   Ⓐ To refrain from using the Internet sources
   Ⓑ To refer to government websites for checking reliability of information
   Ⓒ To verify the qualification of the creator of the website
   Ⓓ To take into account that various kinds of information exist

Set 1 Lecture 1

Questions 06 ~ 08 of 11

06 What is the main topic of the lecture?

- Ⓐ The circumstances that led to banking panic
- Ⓑ The strategies that were used to end banking panic
- Ⓒ The effect of banking panic on the Great Depression
- Ⓓ An economic disaster in American history

07 According to the lecture, why does a banking panic begin?

- Ⓐ Because people demand liquidation of assets
- Ⓑ Because people suddenly try to convert their deposits into cash
- Ⓒ Because people refrain from using cash
- Ⓓ Because people sell their stocks until the market crashes

08 What does the professor state about Black Thursday?

- Ⓐ It directly caused the series of banking panics.
- Ⓑ It was one of the reasons for the Great Depression, but not the only one.
- Ⓒ It was induced by sudden stock-market investments.
- Ⓓ It led to a lack of cash in the banks.

Listen again to part of the lecture. Then answer the question.

09 Why does the professor say this: 🎧
- Ⓐ To imply that the Emergency Banking Act permanently affected the economy
- Ⓑ To emphasize that the Emergency Banking Act was not as successful as it seemed
- Ⓒ To illustrate the importance of the Emergency Banking Act on recuperating the American economy
- Ⓓ To note that the Emergency Banking Act was a helpful but short-term solution

10 Which of the following is the function carried out by the FDIC?
- Ⓐ It stops existing banking panics from escalating.
- Ⓑ It guarantees bank users a portion of their savings.
- Ⓒ It separates commercial banks from investment banks.
- Ⓓ It gives an incentive to bank users in the form of cash.

11 What can be inferred about Roosevelt's economic solutions?
- Ⓐ They were not as primary as the New Deal programs.
- Ⓑ They backfired on the fiscal problem.
- Ⓒ They turned banks into powerful institutions in the U.S.
- Ⓓ They paved the way for a sound economy.

Set 2 Conversation

Questions 01 ~ 03 of 17

01 Why does the student go to see the professor?

　Ⓐ The student is struggling to come up with a topic for the essay.
　Ⓑ The student was summoned by the professor.
　Ⓒ The student needs to change certain words in the essay.
　Ⓓ The student wants to improve the essay.

02 Why does the professor mention the play *The Importance of Being Earnest*?

　Ⓐ To suggest seeing the complete play for writing an essay
　Ⓑ To provide a creative and accurate summary of the play
　Ⓒ To imply that the student should recognize the importance of honesty
　Ⓓ To discuss a part of the student's essay that describes the play

Listen again to part of the conversation. Then answer the question.

03 What does the professor imply when she says this: ⋂

　Ⓐ She is accusing the student openly.
　Ⓑ She is subtly expressing skepticism.
　Ⓒ She is expressing surprise at the student's talent.
　Ⓓ She is asking a simple question.

Questions 04 ~ 05 of 17

04 What was the problem with the student's essay?
- Ⓐ It included false information about Wilde's play.
- Ⓑ The student failed to cite its sources properly.
- Ⓒ The student used confusing words and phrases.
- Ⓓ It was turned in after the due date.

05 Which of the following lessons does the professor primarily emphasize?
- Ⓐ Students need to read their books meticulously before writing essays.
- Ⓑ Students should avoid making careless mistakes by keeping records of information.
- Ⓒ Students should never turn in their tasks after the due date.
- Ⓓ Students need to practice creativity when writing literary essays.

Set 2 Lecture 1

Questions 06 ~ 08 of 17

06 What is the lecture mainly about?

    Ⓐ Discussing various physical characteristics of crocodiles

    Ⓑ Describing crocodiles' various survival techniques

    Ⓒ Emphasizing the importance of crocodiles' sound signals in their survival

    Ⓓ Analyzing an interactive method used by crocodiles

07 What is a common misconception about crocodiles?

    Ⓐ Crocodiles do not make cries to signal different situations and conditions.

    Ⓑ Crocodiles behave individually and do not interact with each other.

    Ⓒ Only a few species of crocodiles are capable of making sound signals.

    Ⓓ Crocodiles are very interactive animals that live others of their species.

08 According to the lecture, what are two functions of American Alligator's signal calls during the mating season?

Choose 2 answers.

    A Preventing competition from other male alligators

    B Attracting female alligators with a cry

    C Calling for help from nearby alligators

    D Protecting newborn babies from predators

Questions 09 ~ 11 of 17

09 What can be inferred about the television program on crocodiles?
 Ⓐ Its credibility has to be checked by experts.
 Ⓑ It contains crocodile contents programmed with the help of reptile experts.
 Ⓒ It sometimes contains unreliable information.
 Ⓓ It should be analyzed critically and developed by students.

Listen again to part of the lecture. Then answer the question.

10 Why does the professor say this:
 Ⓐ To emphasize how brave it is to challenge a fully matured female crocodile
 Ⓑ To discuss how mother crocodiles are capable of protecting their young
 Ⓒ To ask the students about the problems faced by a mother crocodile
 Ⓓ To indicate disagreement with the previous argument about the function of crocodiles' calls

11 Why does the professor mention dogs?
 Ⓐ To emphasize crocodiles share similar organ structures that resemble other mammals
 Ⓑ To explain crocodiles have the most diverse set of signals and calls among reptiles
 Ⓒ To emphasize the interactive strategy that crocodiles have developed
 Ⓓ To show crocodiles are similar to dogs regarding level of biological sophistication

Set 2 Lecture 2

Questions 12 ~ 14 of 17

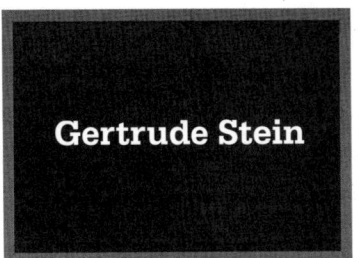

12 What is the lecture mainly about?

  Ⓐ The influence of renowned artists on Gertrude Stein
  Ⓑ The distinct writing style of a well-known author
  Ⓒ An artistic figure who later became a writer
  Ⓓ The application of Cubism to a literary work

13 Why did Gertrude Stein become famous?

  Ⓐ Because of her vague use of language
  Ⓑ Because of her humorous writings
  Ⓒ Because of incorporating Cubism in her poems
  Ⓓ Because of her unique literary style

Listen again to part of the lecture. Then answer the question.

14 Why does the professor say this: ∩

  Ⓐ To show the agreement with the student's opinion
  Ⓑ To imply that the student's opinion needs to be revised
  Ⓒ To emphasize the professor doesn't understand the student's opinion
  Ⓓ To indicate the professor needs to debate with the student

Questions 15 ~ 17 of 17

15 What can be inferred about Stein's *Three Lives*?

Ⓐ It was a creative literary work that brought popularity to Stein.
Ⓑ It was an example that clearly showed Stein's artistic ability.
Ⓒ It was met with different reactions from its primary and later audiences.
Ⓓ It was repeatedly exposed to the public.

16 Why does the professor mention Ernest Hemingway?

Ⓐ To elaborate on his works that incorporated Cubism into literature
Ⓑ To highlight how influential a literary figure was
Ⓒ To emphasize that Cubism had influence on Stein's writings
Ⓓ To explain some authors who made social contact with Gertrude Stein

17 What will the professor discuss in the following class?

Ⓐ Another work of literature by Gertrude Stein
Ⓑ A literary work by an author who was influenced by Gertrude Stein
Ⓒ Another type of writing style distinguished from Stein's one
Ⓓ A particular type of literary work with a complicated plot

영단기 TOEFL

ACTUAL TEST

TEST 06

Listening Section Directions

This section tests your understanding of conversations and lectures. This test includes two conversations and three lectures. You will hear each conversation or lecture only once. Your answers should be based on what is stated or implied in the conversations and lectures. You may take notes as you listen, and you may use these notes to help you answer the questions.

Set 1 Conversation

Questions 01 ~ 03 of 17

01 Why does the student visit the librarian?

- Ⓐ To get information about a play
- Ⓑ To find ways of completing a task
- Ⓒ To discuss reactions to a play
- Ⓓ To hear about the experience of watching a play

02 Why does the librarian think that the critics' reaction to the play is exceptional?

- Ⓐ Because critics don't like plays with a tragic theme
- Ⓑ Because critics are generally skeptical about conventional themes
- Ⓒ Because critics make disparaging remarks about plays
- Ⓓ Because critics are usually objective when writing reviews about plays

03 Why does the student mention the Internet?

- Ⓐ To emphasize the difficulty of finding resources
- Ⓑ To show the reason why he chose to check out other resource materials
- Ⓒ To explain how he looked up the newspaper resources
- Ⓓ To emphasize how the Internet is different from a newspaper

Questions 04 ~ 05 of 17

04　What does the librarian advise the student to do?
　　　Choose 2 answers.
　　　- [A] To read one of the positive reviews of the play
　　　- [B] To access to a private network as an alternative way
　　　- [C] To attend one of the school's plays that are currently being performed
　　　- [D] To see video footage of the play
　　　- [E] To check out various periodicals about the play

Listen again to part of the conversation. Then answer the question.

05　What does the student imply when he says this: 🎧
　　　- [A] The student thinks that there is a profound intention behind the assignment.
　　　- [B] The student wants to find a positive review of the play among many negative ones.
　　　- [C] The student thinks that watching plays is important to gain understanding the director's intentions.
　　　- [D] The student believes that the play seems to be attractive to people.

Set 1 Lecture 1

Questions 06 ~ 08 of 17

06 What is the main topic of the lecture?

  Ⓐ The advantage that arises from the gradual change of genetic traits
  Ⓑ The biological factors that influence mutation
  Ⓒ The bone structure of birds compared to that of dinosaurs
  Ⓓ The evolutionary mechanism behind the physical features of birds

07 Which of the following correctly describes genetic mutation?

  Ⓐ All random genetic changes that occur naturally in the DNA of living organisms
  Ⓑ Unnoticeable copy errors that occur when genes are passed onto the next generation
  Ⓒ The accumulated output that increases an organism's chances of survival
  Ⓓ A scientific jargon that describes behavioral adaptation to a given environment

08 Why does the professor mention monkeys and artwork?

  Ⓐ To elaborate on the intelligence of monkeys that sets them apart from other animals
  Ⓑ To explain how monkeys can learn to produce artworks through training
  Ⓒ To provide an example of natural selection that occurred a long time ago
  Ⓓ To illustrate the process of natural selection through an analogy

Questions 09 ~ 11 of 17

09 According to the professor, why is the body structure of birds thought to have been developed from that of theropods?
Choose 2 answers.

- [A] Both had bones that consisted of an elastic substance.
- [B] Both had a light body with a small number of bones.
- [C] Both had feathers that are made up of similar material.
- [D] Both showed similar movement patterns.
- [E] Both had durable and sturdy bones.

Listen again to part of the lecture. Then answer the question.

10 Why does the student say this:

- (A) To indicate that he is astounded by the unexpected evolutionary relationship between bird bones and dinosaur bones
- (B) To point out that the professor's explanation seems to be insufficient
- (C) To emphasize his belief that the evolution of dinosaur bones into bird bones is an unlikely event
- (D) To show that he did not understand the professor's explanation about the concept of the evolution

11 What can be inferred about birds?

- (A) Birds would find it easier to maintain their populations if their wings were made up of other material.
- (B) Birds' wings have increased in hardness and strength.
- (C) Birds chose not to develop feathers from scales as they evolved.
- (D) Birds' feathers would have evolved from scales, had there been enough scales.

Set 1 Lecture 2

Questions 12 ~ 14 of 17

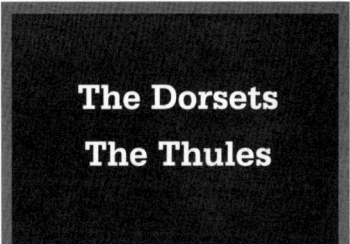

12 What is the main idea of the lecture?

   Ⓐ The Thule's migration to the Dorset territory
   Ⓑ The reason that the two peoples competed each other
   Ⓒ The comparison between two ancient civilizations
   Ⓓ The ways two civilizations used to survive

13 What can be inferred about the Dorset's shelters?

   Ⓐ Snow houses provided effective protection against the cold weather of the Arctic.
   Ⓑ Their shelters were easier to build out of materials other than snow.
   Ⓒ Their shelters were built using a unique method that they developed.
   Ⓓ The Dorset generally lived in structures that were not composed of snow.

14 Which of the following functions did iron meteorites serve for the Dorset?

   Ⓐ They were used to smelt strong weapons to prepare for wars.
   Ⓑ They were turned into durable devices for everyday activities such as farming.
   Ⓒ They were fashioned into implements that facilitated food provision.
   Ⓓ They were used to build houses in order to resist the cold.

Questions 15 ~ 17 of 17

15 According to the professor, which activities were practiced by the Thule but not by the Dorset?
Choose 2 answers.
- [A] Building snow houses
- [B] Making iron tools
- [C] Hunting whales
- [D] Using equipment with a special function

16 What can be inferred about the migration of the Thule into northeastern Canada and Greenland?
- [A] They migrated to find a better and warmer environment.
- [B] They were short on food and had to find a new territory for food.
- [C] They tried to conquer the Dorset's territory.
- [D] They followed their sustenance.

Listen again to part of the lecture. Then answer the question.

17 Why does the professor say this:
- [A] To explain how one of the people had an effect on the other
- [B] To assert that the mystery about the Dorset's decline must be solved
- [C] To introduce another reason for the Dorset's disappearance
- [D] To express uncertainty about the Thule's involvement in a phenomenon

Set 2 Conversation

Questions 01 ~ 03 of 11

01 Why does the student visit the professor's office?

    Ⓐ To find an appropriate topic for a senior thesis
    Ⓑ To receive help about planning tutoring schedules
    Ⓒ To get information about the chosen senior thesis topic
    Ⓓ To get advice regarding a senior thesis

02 What can be inferred about the tutoring position at Belgrade High School?

    Ⓐ The student applied for the position because of his senior thesis.
    Ⓑ The student is able to earn credits by joining the position.
    Ⓒ The student considers getting the placement as a stroke of luck.
    Ⓓ The student will need to spend more time working compared to other tutoring jobs.

03 Why is the student worried about writing a thesis during the first semester of his senior year?

    Ⓐ The student might be swamped with heavy workload.
    Ⓑ A professor would show unwillingness to help the student.
    Ⓒ The student has to gain teaching experience to prepare for writing a thesis.
    Ⓓ It takes time to prepare a topic for the senior thesis.

Questions 04 ~ 05 of 11

Listen again to part of the conversation. Then answer the question.

04 Why does the professor say this:
- Ⓐ To imply that the student doesn't have to worry about writing a thesis
- Ⓑ To assure that the student will meet the thesis deadline
- Ⓒ To emphasize that the topic of his thesis is appropriate
- Ⓓ To express that writing a paper helps some tutoring experience

05 What does the professor suggest the student do?
- Ⓐ To take a course directly related to the chosen thesis topic
- Ⓑ To apply for various internship positions
- Ⓒ To change the thesis topic to match the student's situation
- Ⓓ To consult with a leading expert on the thesis topic

Set 2 Lecture 1

Questions 06 ~ 08 of 11

06 What is the main purpose of the lecture?

Ⓐ To explain the factors that affect the amount of carbon dioxide in the ocean
Ⓑ To identify the relationship between the ocean and climate change
Ⓒ To explain how human activities cause global warming
Ⓓ To discuss the effects of climate change on the ocean, and how they can be mitigated

07 What can be inferred about the fact that water molecules are dipolar?

Ⓐ It can explain the importance of how electrical properties work in molecules.
Ⓑ It shows how closely the water molecules are connected to each other at an atomic level.
Ⓒ It proves the reason the water absorbs carbon dioxide, which subsequently causes environmental destruction.
Ⓓ It can be used to understand the concept of the molecular structure of the water.

08 What does the professor say about the difference in temperatures in the ocean and land?

Ⓐ It explains the reason organisms become more sensitive to their environment.
Ⓑ The temperature in the ocean is limited because more energy is required to alter it.
Ⓒ The vast difference in temperatures on land signifies that it is more easily affected by global warming.
Ⓓ This fact is proof that the ocean has a greater capability to deter global warming.

Questions 09 ~ 11 of 11

Listen again to part of the lecture. Then answer the question.

09 Why does the professor say this:
- Ⓐ To imply that the increase of a particular material might cause an adverse consequence to nature
- Ⓑ To emphasize there are many challenges the clam chowder industry faces
- Ⓒ To encourage students to look for ways to recover the environmental balance
- Ⓓ To explain how a species of shellfish affects the environment

10 What is the result of carbonic acid?
- Ⓐ The amount of carbon dioxide in the environment is decreased.
- Ⓑ It deters the creation of the material that comprises a sea animal.
- Ⓒ Water takes in and consumes carbon dioxide.
- Ⓓ Water molecules are more closely compressed.

11 Why does the professor mention 3,200 jobs?
- Ⓐ To emphasize how many people lost jobs in the U.S.
- Ⓑ To show that people should repair the damage they have been doing to environment
- Ⓒ To explain the number of people is needed to cultivate shellfishes
- Ⓓ To arouse attention to an aftermath of grave damage to environment

영단기 TOEFL

ACTUAL TEST

TEST 07

Listening Section Directions

This section tests your understanding of conversations and lectures. This test includes two conversations and three lectures. You will hear each conversation or lecture only once. Your answers should be based on what is stated or implied in the conversations and lectures. You may take notes as you listen, and you may use these notes to help you answer the questions.

Set 1 Conversation

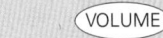

Questions 01 ~ 03 of 11

01   What is the conversation mainly about?

   Ⓐ Transportation arrangements for a school trip
   Ⓑ The exhibition at an art gallery
   Ⓒ Fundraising activities for the school
   Ⓓ Details of a student activity

02   What does the student say about the Student Activity Center?

   Ⓐ It manages fundraising activities for field trips.
   Ⓑ It introduces students to various job opportunities.
   Ⓒ It supports students starting their careers after school.
   Ⓓ It is known for organizing school activities for students.

03   What two features does the student mention about the High Line?
Choose 2 answers.

   ☐ A Its function has been changed.
   ☐ B It shouldn't be used to transport passengers.
   ☐ C It was transformed into a park by public demand.
   ☐ D It was not always in active use.

Questions 04 ~ 05 of 11

04 Why does the director emphasize the information in the poster?

Ⓐ Because the poster needs to be updated to attract more students
Ⓑ Because the poster should present the plan for the entire tour
Ⓒ Because the poster includes a name of the person in charge of the activity
Ⓓ Because the poster indicates that a bus is available for transportation

Listen again to part of the conversation. Then answer the question.

05 Why does she say this: 🎧

Ⓐ To inform the student that she had graduated from a school in New York
Ⓑ To indicate that she is aware of the city
Ⓒ To suggest that she can be of some help to the student
Ⓓ To emphasize that she knows people living in New York

Set 1 Lecture 1

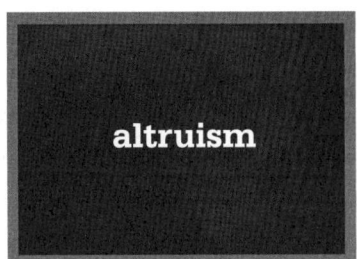

06 What is the lecture mainly about?

Ⓐ The intellectual ability and social behavior of primates
Ⓑ A psychological concept illustrated through experiments involving primates
Ⓒ Levels of altruistic behavior difference depending on environmental conditions
Ⓓ The reasons behind altruistic behaviors of primates

07 How does the professor introduce the lecture?

Ⓐ By explaining that the term altruism originally stems from a Latin term
Ⓑ By suggesting that altruism is universally observed, even in animals
Ⓒ By discussing widespread misconceptions about animals
Ⓓ By coming up with a relatable, but imaginary example

08 According to the professor, what is altruism?

Ⓐ Sacrificing one person in order to save more than one person
Ⓑ Offering beneficence when being observed by others
Ⓒ Weighing the advantages of a situation and taking the best action
Ⓓ Being considerate about the needs of another person

09 Why did the researchers give two types of tools, a stick and a ball, to the second chimpanzee?

Ⓐ To confirm that chimpanzees selected tools with specific intent
Ⓑ To test the intellectual capacity of chimpanzees
Ⓒ To observe the use of different tools by chimpanzees
Ⓓ To make sure that chimpanzees were willing to hand over tools

10 Which of the following can be inferred from the chimpanzee experiment?
Choose 2 answers.

A Chimpanzees are more likely to respond to a help request if they know what is happening.
B Chimpanzees tend to actively overcome barriers in order to assist others more effectively.
C Chimpanzees exhibit different levels of altruism depending on given conditions.
D Chimpanzees show a strong willingness to sacrifice themselves for the betterment of their species.

11 What does the professor probably believe about altruism in animals and humans?

Ⓐ Animal altruism has evolved by imitating human altruism.
Ⓑ Animals are more active in expressing their altruism than humans are.
Ⓒ Animals and humans act similarly with an unselfish regard for others.
Ⓓ Human altruism depends a lot on situations compared to animal altruism.

Set 2 Conversation

Questions 01 ~ 03 of 17

01 What is the main topic of this conversation?

    Ⓐ Looking for methods to deal with financial problems

    Ⓑ Planning a career after graduation

    Ⓒ Applying for a work-study program

    Ⓓ Earning money by working part-time

02 What is the officer's opinion about a work-study program?

    Ⓐ It does not seem attractive to the student.

    Ⓑ Students rarely apply for it.

    Ⓒ The student may not qualify for it.

    Ⓓ It is not helpful towards the student's studies.

03 What is the benefit of off-campus jobs for the student?

    Ⓐ A wide selection of job types and locations

    Ⓑ A high possibility of getting a job

    Ⓒ Competitive wages

    Ⓓ A variety of methods of salary payment

Listen again to part of the conversation. Then answer the question.

04 Why does the officer say this:
- Ⓐ To encourage the student to change the major
- Ⓑ To inform that the student's major makes it difficult to get a scholarship
- Ⓒ To ask which major the student is currently interested in
- Ⓓ To come up with an alternative way

05 What are two suggestions the officer gives to the student?
Choose 2 answers.
- ☐ A Search for a suitable work-study program for the student
- ☐ B Request an application form from the accounting firm
- ☐ C Look for entities related to a prospective career
- ☐ D Visit a place where the student can find the information

Set 2 Lecture 1

Questions 06 ~ 08 of 17

06 What does the professor mainly discuss?

 Ⓐ The activation of visual regions, caused by music
 Ⓑ The development of music in society
 Ⓒ Various reactions provoked by music
 Ⓓ The effect music has on people

07 Why does the visual cortex become active when people listen to music?

 Ⓐ Because the brain is divided into left and right hemispheres
 Ⓑ Because people enjoy writing and playing music
 Ⓒ Because people come up with perceptions corresponding to music
 Ⓓ Because the outer layer of the cerebral cortex is stimulated

08 What function does the limbic system carry out in the human brain?

 Ⓐ It causes people to have different tastes in music.
 Ⓑ It is associated with stored information and feelings.
 Ⓒ It helps people to produce music from individual memories.
 Ⓓ It controls motor movement of the eye.

09 Why does the professor mention the bone pipe?
  Ⓐ To highlight the technical ability and the hard work of ancient people
  Ⓑ To suggest that music swayed people emotionally even during ancient times
  Ⓒ To discuss the history behind the creation of musical instruments
  Ⓓ To give an example of the musical accomplishments of ancient people

Listen again to part of the lecture. Then answer the question.

10 Why does the professor say this:
  Ⓐ To accentuate the value of an activity's influence on ancient people
  Ⓑ To gauge the time and energy required for the production of the instrument
  Ⓒ To describe the various materials used to make the pipe
  Ⓓ To encourage students to share their opinions about the ancient instrument

11 According to the professor, why did ancient people use music?
  Ⓐ To increase productivity when farming
  Ⓑ To intimidate the animals they hunted
  Ⓒ To increase their aggression
  Ⓓ To induce collaborative relationships

Set 2 Lecture 2

 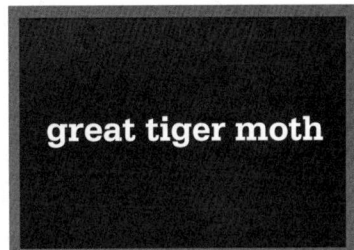

12 What is the professor mainly discussing?

- Ⓐ The reason that great tiger moths consume a particular plant
- Ⓑ The adaptation that allows great tiger moths to evade a predator
- Ⓒ Different strategies used by various moths to survive
- Ⓓ Physical traits of great tiger moths to increase their ability to survive

Listen again to part of the lecture. Then answer the question.

13 Why does the professor say this: 🎧

- Ⓐ To solve the curiosity of the students about other organisms
- Ⓑ To express that the students would not believe the statement
- Ⓒ To indicate that the following statement is unimportant
- Ⓓ To imply that the students don't understand the lecture

14 Why does the professor mention the way normal moths react when caught in spider webs?

- Ⓐ To demonstrate how moths use their scales to escape from spider webs
- Ⓑ To emphasize how great tiger moths are different from other moths
- Ⓒ To discuss how moths evolved into having scaled wings
- Ⓓ To show the difference between moths and butterflies

Questions 15 ~ 17 of 17

15 According to the professor, what are the two unique characteristics of the great tiger moth?
Choose 2 answers.
- [A] Accumulation of poison in its wings
- [B] A foul odor that signals predators to flee
- [C] Wings that feature conspicuous hues
- [D] The ability to blind its predators by spraying powder

16 What did the experiment mentioned in the lecture try to prove?
- [A] The toxin in the wings of great tiger moths is caused by their larvae diet.
- [B] The oleander plants are not harmful to moths.
- [C] The oleander plants are poisonous to spiders and should be removed.
- [D] Great tiger moth larvae like oleander plant leaves more than other plant leaves.

17 What can be inferred about great tiger moths?
- [A] They are hard to find around oleander plants.
- [B] They would not need oleander plants if they didn't have their natural enemies.
- [C] They need to be eliminated because they kill off oleander plants.
- [D] They intelligently choose oleander plants leaves over other plant leaves as their diet.

영단기 TOEFL
ACTUAL TEST

TEST 08

Listening Section Directions

This section tests your understanding of conversations and lectures. This test includes two conversations and three lectures. You will hear each conversation or lecture only once. Your answers should be based on what is stated or implied in the conversations and lectures. You may take notes as you listen, and you may use these notes to help you answer the questions.

Set 1 Conversation

Questions 01 ~ 03 of 17

01 What is the conversation mainly about?

- Ⓐ An assignment that the professor mistakenly lost
- Ⓑ A student's plan after graduation
- Ⓒ An internship opportunity the student should take part in
- Ⓓ A teaching approach the student learned

02 Which of the following are included in the consensus method?
Choose 2 answers.

- A Choosing resources for discussion
- B Writing down students' thoughts if they don't reach a consensus
- C Asking an instructor to take active participation in a discussion
- D Using examples to support students' own ideas
- E Following the majority's opinion

03 Why does the professor mention a fire alarm?

- Ⓐ To explain an instructor's role
- Ⓑ To warn about a situation which can happen while teaching students
- Ⓒ To emphasize the importance of a teacher's duty
- Ⓓ To see if the student recognizes a teacher's responsibility

Questions 04 ~ 05 of 17

04 Which of the following is true about the fellowship opportunity?
   Ⓐ It is designed for students who apply for a graduate school.
   Ⓑ It will focus on a process by which individuals develop an ability for learning.
   Ⓒ It includes leading a group discussion and guiding students.
   Ⓓ Only outstanding students are allowed to participate in it.

Listen again to part of the conversation. Then answer the question.

05 Why does the student say this:
   Ⓐ To explain why the student decided not to go to a graduate school
   Ⓑ To show the student's uncertainty about an academic career
   Ⓒ To emphasize the student's interest in the internship
   Ⓓ To emphasize how hard it is to apply for a graduate school

Set 1 Lecture 1

Questions 06 ~ 08 of 17

06 What does the professor primarily discuss?

Ⓐ The expansion of agriculture from New Guinea to Southeast Asia
Ⓑ The widespread distribution of agricultural technology in New Guinea
Ⓒ The exceptional development of agriculture in New Guinea
Ⓓ The method of studying the development of agriculture in New Guinea

07 According to the lecture, why were researchers unable to find evidence for their theory in New Guinea during the 1960s and 70s?

Ⓐ Swamps were difficult to analyze without proper equipment.
Ⓑ Carbon-based materials readily decomposed in the wet area.
Ⓒ Crops raised in early New Guinea were already extinct.
Ⓓ Land is cleared not necessarily for growing produce.

08 Why does the professor mention successive layers of sediment?

Ⓐ To explain how people cultivated crops and trees in the area
Ⓑ To emphasize that they were related to the progress of agricultural technology
Ⓒ To explain the reason why agriculture in the region developed
Ⓓ To illustrate that they indicated the origin of agriculture in the region

Questions 09 ~ 11 of 17

09 What evidence did researchers find concerning the cultivation of bananas in New Guinea? Choose 3 answers.

- [A] A phenomenon resulting from people's involvement was found.
- [B] Bananas were grown in New Guinea and exported to Southeast Asia through trade.
- [C] The land seemed to have been prepared for a certain purpose.
- [D] Genetic analysis made it possible to trace where the banana species was introduced.
- [E] Swampy areas like the Kuk were advantageous for the growth of bananas.

10 Why was the presence of taro starch in the highlands important?

- (A) Taro was not indigenous to the region.
- (B) Taro was a staple crop in New Guinea.
- (C) Taro was a difficult plant to cultivate.
- (D) Taro was a relatively old plant species.

11 What can be inferred about the impact of agriculture on New Guinea?

- (A) The advancement of agriculture was related to social changes.
- (B) The usual implication of agriculture did not apply to the society.
- (C) The development of agriculture generated an increase in population.
- (D) The development of agriculture led to egalitarianism.

Set 1 Lecture 2

Questions 12 ~ 14 of 17

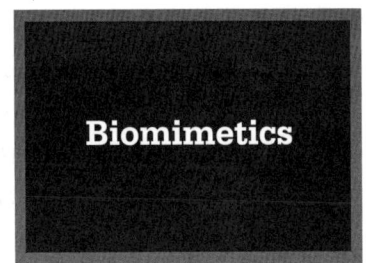

12 What does the professor mainly discuss?

   Ⓐ The field of adopting designs from nature
   Ⓑ Various adaptations of animals and insects
   Ⓒ The research possibilities in the recently emerging study
   Ⓓ The procedure of applying biomimetics to human technology

13 How does the professor organize the lecture?

   Ⓐ He uses various examples to denounce a field of study.
   Ⓑ He cites scientific articles and experiments to explain a certain concept.
   Ⓒ He briefly describes a concept and lists examples to support it.
   Ⓓ He briefly explains a concept and describes its actual applications.

14 Why does the professor mention a sweater?

   Ⓐ To illustrate a particular kind of attractive force
   Ⓑ To explain how a gecko can climb surfaces without falling
   Ⓒ To give an example of another sticky material
   Ⓓ To suggest that biomimetics can be applied to sweaters

15 According to the professor, how does a beetle benefit from its ability to detect forest fires?

Ⓐ It can hide in shelters before a forest fire occurs.
Ⓑ It can minimize the impact of harmful substances.
Ⓒ It can avoid competing with other insects over the resin from the tree.
Ⓓ It can ensure the stability of its temperatures.

16 What can be inferred about the silica-based fibers of the deep-sea sponge?

Ⓐ They are being refined for better qualities.
Ⓑ They are causing commercial optical fibers to become useless and obsolete.
Ⓒ They are too problematic for practical use.
Ⓓ They need to be researched further before being applied to daily life.

Listen again to part of the lecture. Then answer the question.

17 Why does the professor say this: ∩

Ⓐ To suggest that the students come up with more uses for optical fibers
Ⓑ To imply that he won't list any more applications of optical fibers
Ⓒ To express that listing the uses of optical fibers is a waste of time
Ⓓ To encourage that the students do more research about optical fibers

Set 2 Conversation

Questions 01 ~ 03 of 11

01 What is the conversation mainly about?

  Ⓐ Whether the student would be willing to participate in Hawk Watching
  Ⓑ Requirements to apply for a project
  Ⓒ The student's interest in a particular field of study
  Ⓓ Reasons the student should change his major

Listen again to part of the conversation. Then answer the question.

02 Why does the student say this: ◯

  Ⓐ To question the student's devotion to the biology department
  Ⓑ To reassure the student about the expected reaction from the professor
  Ⓒ To explain why a TA position is very competitive
  Ⓓ To emphasize the student's responsibility as a TA

03 Why does the student hesitate to take part in Hawk Watching?

  Ⓐ His friend was disappointed at it.
  Ⓑ He already took part in it last year.
  Ⓒ It is not his interest.
  Ⓓ He has no time because of a project.

Questions 04 ~ 05 of 11

Listen again to part of the conversation. Then answer the question.

04 Why does the student say this:
   Ⓐ To check if the student heard the term correctly
   Ⓑ To remind that the student knew the meaning of the term
   Ⓒ To get more information about the term
   Ⓓ To correct the explanation about bioluminescence

05 Which of the following statements is true about the project in California?
   Ⓐ Applicants usually hold university degrees.
   Ⓑ It mainly focuses on terrestrial animals.
   Ⓒ Students who major in marine biology are eligible to apply for it.
   Ⓓ The student is well-prepared for the project.

Set 2 Lecture 1

Questions 06 ~ 08 of 11

06 What is the lecture mainly about?

    Ⓐ The use of biological catalysts in industry

    Ⓑ The function of enzymes in various fields of industry

    Ⓒ The important enzymatic activities that happen in the human body

    Ⓓ Several methods used to fade jeans

07 How does the professor introduce his discussion of enzyme?

    Ⓐ By explaining the connection between industries and enzymes.

    Ⓑ By introducing ways to cause physical changes to jeans

    Ⓒ By illustrating the role of enzymes in the human body

    Ⓓ By recalling their applications in various industries

08 Why does the professor mention pumice stones?

    Ⓐ To explain several disadvantages of using pumice stones

    Ⓑ To imply that there is a limited number of ways to fade jeans

    Ⓒ To highlight another practical way to fade jeans

    Ⓓ To describe the process of fading jeans with pumice stones

09 Which of the following correctly describes a problem of using bleach?
Choose 2 answers.

- [A] Buttons and rivets were tarnished by the acid.
- [B] The procedure was lengthy and complicated.
- [C] Factories were expensive to build and maintain.
- [D] Chemicals were a threat to workers and the environment.
- [E] The texture of the jeans was overly softened.

10 Why is biostone bleach used to fade jeans?

- (A) Because customers care about the environment
- (B) Because cotton is susceptible to cellulose
- (C) Because enzymes selectively affect the fabric surface
- (D) Because jeans easily lose their color to bleach

Listen again to part of the conversation. Then answer the question.

11 Why does the professor say this:

- (A) To explain the application of enzymes for making jeans commercial
- (B) To ask the students to give their opinions about biology
- (C) To emphasize the importance of applying a scientific study
- (D) To encourage the students to learn and apply biology

영단기 TOEFL

ACTUAL TEST

TEST 09

Listening Section Directions

This section tests your understanding of conversations and lectures. This test includes two conversations and three lectures. You will hear each conversation or lecture only once. Your answers should be based on what is stated or implied in the conversations and lectures. You may take notes as you listen, and you may use these notes to help you answer the questions.

Set 1 Conversation

Questions 01 ~ 03 of 11

01 Why does the student visit the professor's office?

- Ⓐ To ask the professor if the story about Archimedes is true
- Ⓑ To get feedback on a paper
- Ⓒ To discuss stories which inspired people
- Ⓓ To find out how to do research for a paper

02 How did Archimedes find out the amount of silver mixed in the crown?

- Ⓐ By adding water in the process of manufacturing a crown
- Ⓑ By asking the goldsmith about the truth behind the manufacture of the crown
- Ⓒ By displacing gold into silver
- Ⓓ By realizing the difference in volume of each material

03 What can be inferred about the goldsmith?

- Ⓐ He would encounter an unfortunate situation.
- Ⓑ The king would forgive him.
- Ⓒ He completed his task faithfully.
- Ⓓ He would gain huge profit by selling gold.

Listen again to part of the conversation. Then answer the question.

04 Why does the professor say this: ∩
- Ⓐ To imply that the student needs to do more research about the story
- Ⓑ To emphasize people's interest in the story
- Ⓒ To explain the inconsistency between the story and the truth
- Ⓓ To share the professor's opinion with the student

05 What are the reasons that the story about Archimedes is not true?
Choose 2 answers.
- [A] Feasible technology did not exist back then.
- [B] Water volume is not measurable.
- [C] People doubted Archimedes' knowledge.
- [D] There is no concrete evidence.
- [E] It was recorded as a made-up story.

Set 1 Lecture 1

Questions 06 ~ 08 of 11

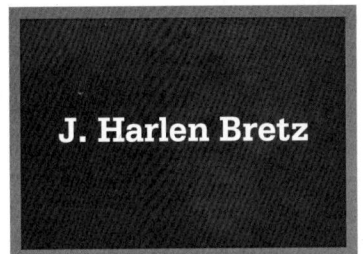

06 What is the topic of the lecture?

- Ⓐ The formation of geologically interesting places
- Ⓑ The effect of glaciers on geological formations
- Ⓒ The importance of uniformitarianism regarding the creation of the Scablands
- Ⓓ The viewpoints concerning a geological phenomenon

07 Which of the following correctly describes uniformitarianism?

- Ⓐ It is a theory that most accurately explains geological changes on Earth.
- Ⓑ It is a theory that fails to fully explain a certain geologic area.
- Ⓒ It is a theory with shortcomings and requires more research.
- Ⓓ It is a theory that arouses controversy among geologists.

Listen again to part of the lecture. Then answer the question.

08 What does the professor imply when he says this: ⌒

- Ⓐ He provides a compliment because the student suggests a possible answer to the phenomenon.
- Ⓑ He implies there could be another explanation for the geological formation.
- Ⓒ He shows uncertainty about the student's answer.
- Ⓓ He does not think the student understands the question.

09 According to Bretz's theory, what was the role of the glacier regarding the formation of the Scablands?

  Ⓐ It broke off into huge chunks of ice and directly carved out the area.

  Ⓑ It provided a sudden source of water, which shaped the geological features of the area.

  Ⓒ It slowly melted and changed the geological area over hundreds of years.

  Ⓓ It formed a dam that limited the flow of water and pressurized the region.

Listen again to part of the lecture. Then answer the question.

10 What does the professor imply when he says this: ⌒

  Ⓐ He is dissatisfied with the public's ignorance of uniformitarianism.

  Ⓑ He thinks that uniformitarianism needs to be studied in the field of geology.

  Ⓒ He believes that uniformitarianism can still be accepted.

  Ⓓ He has a disdain for uniformitarianism and prefers a recent theory.

11 What does the professor imply about the formation of the Scablands?

  Ⓐ It is still a mystery to the majority of geologists.

  Ⓑ Bretz's theory is the only idea that defines it.

  Ⓒ Both uniformitarianism and Bretz's theory are not enough to explain it.

  Ⓓ Two geological theories have been applied to account for it.

Set 2 Conversation

Questions 01 ~ 03 of 17

01 What is the conversation mainly about?

(A) Ways to choose a preferable room in a dormitory

(B) Ways to make a request to extend a stay in a dormitory

(C) Ways to find out the school's policy regarding room assignment

(D) Ways to apply for a student exchange program

02 What can be inferred about the $1,000 non-refundable deposit?

(A) It is more costly than the student expected.

(B) The student has a situation to take into consideration.

(C) It is difficult for the student to pay it on time.

(D) A refund cannot be made under any circumstances.

03 Why does the university employee mention study abroad notification?

(A) To check if the student knows the school's policy

(B) To explain how the deposit can be used

(C) To confirm about the study abroad program

(D) To explain the school's policy about a refund

Questions 04 ~ 05 of 17

04 Why does the employee mention the City Art Museum?
- Ⓐ To explain that there are various room types in a dormitory
- Ⓑ To emphasize the advantage of a city university
- Ⓒ To illustrate how a dormitory gives benefit to art-major students
- Ⓓ To explain that the school endeavors to meet students' needs

05 Which of the following statements are true about the dormitory application process?
Choose 2 answers.
- A The deposit can be used to settle outstanding balance.
- B The school is able to guarantee a particular room type as per the student's request.
- C It would be hard to apply for a residence hall without a tenant account.
- D The school does not allow students to choose roommates.
- E There is plenty of time to start the actual process.

Set 2 Lecture 1

Questions 06 ~ 08 of 17

06 What is the lecture mainly about?

Ⓐ Issues and concerns associated with weeds
Ⓑ The competitive ability of foreign species against native plants
Ⓒ The explosive growth of plants during the Columbian Exchange
Ⓓ An unintentional natural phenomenon

07 What can be inferred from the term "weed"?
Choose 2 answers.

A The term itself is not very consistently defined by people.
B The term refers to a resilient plant, not easily affected by the environment.
C The term indicates that absorb nourishment more quickly than other plants.
D The term refers to a plant that is prone to growing in exotic terrain.

08 Why is the introduction of American and European plants and animal populations called the Columbian Exchange?

Ⓐ Columbus indirectly initiated the exchange through his explorations.
Ⓑ Columbus persuaded the Native Americans to engage in trade with the settlers.
Ⓒ Columbus carried weeds into the Americas by using livestock.
Ⓓ Columbus tried to institute an exchange system between Europe and the Americas.

Questions 09 ~ 11 of 17

09 How were the seeds of weeds introduced to the Americas?

Ⓐ The Europeans furtively imported the weed seeds to the Americas.
Ⓑ The cattle and horses' feces contained the weed seeds.
Ⓒ The seeds were carried on the skins of animals.
Ⓓ The weeds were planted intentionally by European settlers.

10 What are two favorable conditions for the transplantation of weeds?
Choose 2 answers.

[A] The seeds of the weeds brought by the European settlements were very healthy and prolific.
[B] The temperate climate in the Americas helped the weeds to grow easily.
[C] The deforestation created the right environment for the weeds to grow easily.
[D] The weeds were placed in a favorable position for the intake of essential nutrients.

11 What can be inferred about the introduction of weeds during the Columbian Exchange?

Ⓐ The growth of weeds should have been prevented for the protection of the ecosystem.
Ⓑ The problems caused by weeds are being studied and need to be solved by scientists.
Ⓒ The movement of biological species such as weeds between countries is beyond human control.
Ⓓ The Columbian Exchange caused more damage than benefit to the ecosystem.

Set 2 Lecture 2

Questions 12 ~ 14 of 17

  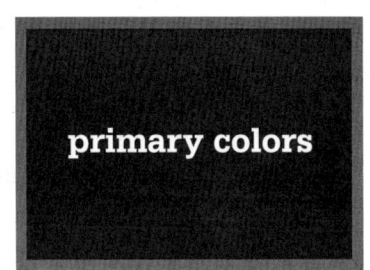

12 What is the lecture mainly about?

 Ⓐ The relationship between primary colors and emotions
 Ⓑ An overview of an concept about colors
 Ⓒ The recent development of the idea of primary colors
 Ⓓ A summary of Goethe's influence in an art history

13 Why does the professor mention Isaac Newton?

 Ⓐ To emphasize Goethe's contribution in the field of science
 Ⓑ To present how he came up with the primary color theory
 Ⓒ To demonstrate how his theory of colors affected Goethe's theory of primary colors
 Ⓓ To show the foundation of the theory related to color

14 Why did Goethe decide to study and research colors?

 Ⓐ To come up with a theory of colors by using the light spectrum
 Ⓑ To explain how to apply suitable colors according to situations
 Ⓒ To study the relationship between perception and colors
 Ⓓ To describe colors that affected emotions in his literary works

Questions 15 ~ 17 of 17

Listen again to part of the lecture. Then answer the question.

15 Why does the professor say this:

- Ⓐ To remind the students to do research on psychological aspects of colors
- Ⓑ To continue with what he was talking about
- Ⓒ To express uncertainty about the information he mentioned
- Ⓓ To indicate that previous discussion was unimportant

16 Why did Runge believe that red, blue, and yellow affected human emotions?

- Ⓐ They produced a variety of mixed colors.
- Ⓑ The combination of the three colors was attractive to human.
- Ⓒ They synchronized different parts of the day.
- Ⓓ Their effect was proven by scientific experiments.

17 What can be inferred about the concept of primary colors?

- Ⓐ It was originated from light wavelengths.
- Ⓑ It was established by one person's contribution.
- Ⓒ It produces the best secondary colors when mixed together in certain proportions.
- Ⓓ It resulted from the combination of various fields.

영단기 TOEFL
ACTUAL TEST
LISTENING

직접 시험 보고 연구한 저자의 REAL 콘텐츠

시험 직전 단기 마무리
· 문제 유형별 고득점 풀이 전략 제시
· 빈출 주제와 최신 경향 완벽 반영

영단기 TOEFL ACTUAL TEST LISTENING의 전략
· 최고난도의 지문과 문제로 구성된 9회분의 모의고사로 실전 대비를 최종 마무리한다.
· 출제 포인트를 단숨에 파악할 수 있는 LISTENING STRATEGIES를 제시하여 실전 시험을 준비한다.
· 정답 및 오답 포인트를 짚어주는 날카로운 해설로 고득점 달성에 필수적인 논리적 문제 해결 능력을 키운다.

영단기가 함께한
토플 단기 고득점 STORY

'두 달 만에 102 달성!' — 102점 달성
문제유형부터 단어, 문제 풀이 노하우 등 처음 토플을 공부하는 저도 잘 이해할 수 있도록 선생님들께서 잘 지도해주셨어요.

민ㅇ연 수강생 | 신은미, 마크 김, 수리, 민상홍 선생님

'단기 고득점, 저도 가능하더라구요!' — 93점 달성
잘못된 문법과 논리구조들을 첨삭을 통해서 교정한 것이 단기간 실력향상에 큰 도움이 됐어요!

정ㅇ연 수강생 | 영단기 토플

'직장인도 시간 낭비말고 영단기 토플에서 시작하세요!' — 93점 달성
영단기 토플의 실제 강의와 동일한 인강 시스템은 저처럼 지방에 거주하는 직장인에게 안성맞춤인 강의였어요.

전ㅇ진 수강생 | 박세연, 크리스틴 한, 빅토리아 신, 최종훈 선생님

'첫 토플 108점 달성!' — 108점 달성
영단기 토플이 특별했던 건 선생님께서 1:1로 제가 부족한 부분을 꼼꼼하게 체크해주신다는 거였어요!

김ㅇ영 수강생 | 영단기 토플

'MBA 진학 도전도 이제 자신 있어요!' — 95점 달성
특강 예상문제가 실제 시험에 출제되어 놀라움과 감사함을 동시에 느꼈어요!

문ㅇ수 수강생 | 영단기 토플

'선생님만 믿고 따라갔더니!' — 101점 달성
매주 주말마다 실전 시험과 구성도 똑같고 성적도 잘 분석해주는 영단기 ETS 모의고사를 풀면서 실전 시험에 대비했어요.

김ㅇ규 수강생 | 영단기 토플

**더 이상 남들의 이야기가 아닙니다.
영단기와 함께라면 당신도 단기 고득점의 주인공이 될 수 있습니다.**

영단기 토플이 추천하는 유형별 단기 고득점 방법

1. 저렴한 가격으로 토플 공부하고 싶은 합리적인 토플러?!

 **9,900원 패스**

- ✓ 월 9,900원으로 토플 포함 전 과목 무제한 수강
- ✓ 토플 고득점 선배의 꿀팁 비밀자료 무제한 열람
- ✓ 전 세계 10개국 이상의 교환학생 성공기 제공

2. 당장 내일이 시험이라 시간이 없는 토플러?!

- ✓ 영단기 선생님이 직접하는 약점보완형 첨삭
- ✓ 24시간 내에 Speaking/Writing 첨삭 완료

3. 약점을 보완하고 싶은 토플러?!

 **TOEFL 실전모의고사**

- ✓ 공식 토플 주관사가 엄선한 100% 토플 기출문제 수록
- ✓ 2019년 개정 뉴토플 문항 완벽 반영
- ✓ 실제 시험과 동일한 기준으로 ETS가 제공하는 성적표 확인 가능

영단기 토플 eng.conects.com